WILDLIFE OF THE AUSTRALIAN RAINFORESTS

A STATE-BY-STATE GUIDE

First published in the United Kingdom and Australia in 2021 by
John Beaufoy Publishing Ltd
11 Blenheim Court, 316 Woodstock Road, Oxford OX2 7NS, England
www.johnbeaufoy.com

Photo Credits
Front cover Barred Cuckoo-shrike *Coracina lineata,* © Peter Rowland/kapeimages.com
Back cover *top to bottom:* Cairns Birdwing Butterfly *Ornithoptera euphorion* © Angus
McNab, Green Tree Frog *Litoria caerulea* © Angus McNab, Torresian Striped Possum
Dactylopsila trivirgata © Angus McNab, Green Python *Morelia viridis* © Angus McNab
Spine White-eared Monarch *Carterornis leucotis* © Michael Schmid
Title page Estuarine Crocodile *Crocodylus porosus* © Peter Rowland/kapeimages.com
Throughout As credited

A number of the images displayed in this book have been used under one or more
creative commons licences. These have been indicated by a 'CC' after the photographer's
name. A link to the various creative commons licences can be found at https://
creativecommons.org/licenses.

ISBN 978-1-913679-03-3

Editor and indexer: Krystyna Mayer

Project Manager: Rossemary Wilkinson

Designed by Gulmohur Press, New Delhi

Printed and bound in Malaysia by Times Offset (M) Sdn. Bhd.

WILDLIFE OF THE AUSTRALIAN RAINFORESTS
A STATE-BY-STATE GUIDE

Peter Rowland, Angus McNab & John Harris

Peter Rowland
New South Wales & Northern Territory

Angus McNab
Queensland, Tasmania & Christmas Island

John Harris
Victoria & Western Australia

JOHN BEAUFOY PUBLISHING

CONTENTS

Introduction

This book describes Australia's various rainforest types, some of the typical flora associated with them and the fauna that depends on rainforests for survival, or utilizes them regularly or infrequently to forage or seek shelter. It is divided into bioregions according to the Interim Biogeographic Regionalisation Assessment (IBRA). The IBRA was developed in 1993–1994 as a key tool for identifying land for conservation and establishing a national system of reserves under Australia's Strategy for the National Reserve System 2009–2030. It is endorsed by all levels of Australia's government. At the time of writing, the current version is IBRA7.

Under IBRA7, Australia's landscapes are classified into 89 large geographically distinct bioregions based on common climate, geology, landform, native vegetation and species information. The bioregions are further refined to form 419 subregions that are more localized, and homogenous geomorphological units within each bioregion.

Under the IBRA7 revision, four new oceanic bioregions were added to the previous IBRA version (6.1): Indian Tropical Islands, Pacific Subtropical Islands, Subantarctic Islands and Coral Sea. These allowed for the inclusion of Australia's island territories, including Christmas Island, Coral Sea Islands, Lord Howe Island, Macquarie Island and Norfolk Island.

Each of the IBRA bioregions described includes a detailed overview of the bioregion, a list of the key fauna that can be found there and images of the region. For each bioregion one or more representative sites have been described that contain rainforests (including vine thickets). These sites are generally open to the public, although some may require permits or permissions for access. Site descriptions contain location descriptions, GPS coordinates, travel options and distances, information on relevant fees and permits, an overview of some of the main tracks and trails, and photographic images. Detailed accounts of some of the key vertebrates and, to a lesser extent, invertebrates that can be found in the rainforests are provided to enable a deeper understanding of their habits and biology. For ease of references, the species are arranged alphabetically within their groups, under their common names.

The book is divided into states but some bioregions overlap states. In this case we have placed the bioregion in the state where its northernmost border is.

The authors all have a broad knowledge and experience of Australia, and the writing of the individual sections was divided up among them to utilize each of their strengths. Peter has been a resident of New South Wales for more than 35 years and has worked extensively throughout the state. He has undertaken four research trips to the Northern Territory, the most recent in 2018. Angus has lived and worked in both Queensland (10 years) and Tasmania (two years), and spent a month studying the movements of Common Wolf Snakes on Christmas Island. John lives in Victoria working as an ecological consultant; he also runs flora and fauna tours to Western Australia, and has worked and volunteered in the state's north. John is a past president of the Field Naturalists Club of Victoria.

The taxonomy used in the book largely follows the IOC World Bird List (10.2) (birds); Jackson & Groves (2015) (mammals); Wilson & Swan (6th edn, 2021) (reptiles); Eipper & Rowland (2019) (amphibians); Australian Faunal Database (5/5/2020) (invertebrates); and Flora of Australia (5/5/2020) (plants).

Glossary

abdomen Rear segment of body, behind thorax.

adult Animal that has attained full maturity and is capable of reproduction.

antenna(e) Pair of sensory organs on an invertebrate's head.

aquatic Refers to habitat in or near water.

arboreal Tree dwelling.

arthropod Invertebrate with jointed exoskeleton; includes spiders, crustaceans and insects.

banyan The process that fig trees *Ficus* spp. use to drop aerial roots from their branches down to the ground.

bill/beak Elongated front portion of head or jaw of birds and other animals (including cetaceans).

buttresses Flanges or bracket-like structures at bases of certain rainforest trees.

camps (colonies) Refers to large groups (particularly of bats).

canthal stripe A stripe that runs from snout to eye in frogs.

carapace Hard shell covering head and body (cephalothorax), as in crayfish.

carrion Flesh of dead animals.

casque Armoured part of head.

CBD Central Business District.

cere Fleshy covering around nostrils at base of upper mandible.

chelipeds Claws of crayfish.

cloaca Shared passageway for faeces, urine and reproduction.

clutch Refers to eggs laid in single reproductive event.

closed forest A forest that is dominated by trees whose crowns touch or overlap.

colour morph Refers to aberrant colouration that varies from standard colour and pattern.

compound leaf A leaf consisting of multiple distinct parts that join to single stem.

congener Animal or plant of the same genus as another.

conspecific Belonging to same species.

constriction Act of coiling tightly around an animal, causing suffocation.

crepuscular Active at dawn and/or dusk.

crest Long feathers or spines usually attached to head.

cryptic Camouflaged by body colour and/or shape.

deciduous Refers to seasonal loss of leaves or other parts of a plant.

digit(s) Toe or finger.

dimorphism Distinct physical differences between sexes.

distal Section of limb or attachment furthest from body.

diurnal Active during the day.

dorsal Upper surface, or back.

dorsolateral Upper part of side of animal.

echolocation Refers to using sound emitted and analysing returning echo, to determine location of prey or surroundings.

ecotone Transitional zone between two different plant communities (for example rainforest and dry forest).

ectothermic Refers to body temperature moderated by temperature of an animal's surroundings.

electrosensor(s)/electroreceptor(s) Sensor that detects electric field emitted by other living animals.

endemic Native to a region.

epiphyte Plant that grows on surface of another without deriving nutrition from that plant (like an orchid).

extant Still in existence (not destroyed or extinct).

exudate Liquid emerging from plant or invertebrate.

family Taxonomic category above genus and below order.

feral Refers to introduced animal that has become established in the wild.

forbs Herbaceous flowering plant (not including grasses, sedges or rushes).

fossorial Capable of burrowing.

frugivore Fruit eater.

genus (genera) Taxonomic category above species and below family.

glean Gather or collect.

harp trap Harp-like trap used for catching microbats.

herbivore Plant eater.

hibernation Period of inactivity (normally during winter).

honeydew Sugar-rich liquid produced by sap-sucking insects.

incisors Chisel-shaped front teeth used for biting or gnawing.

insectivorous Feeding on insects.

invertebrate Animal without a backbone.

iris Coloured part of eye surrounding pupil.

keels Ridges on scales of some reptiles.

lappet Small piece of flesh extending from body.

larva(e) Newly hatched, invertebrate life stage.

lores Parts of a bird's face between base of bill and front of eyes.

macropods Group of herbivorous marsupials that includes kangaroos, wallabies and pademelons.

mandible Jaw-like mouthparts used for grasping and cutting.

mechanoreceptor(s) Sensory cell that detects mechanical pressure or distortion.

membrane Thin layer of tissue.

metamorphosis Act in which an animal changes physical state (as from tadpole to frog).

midlateral Middle part of side of animal.

migrant/migratory Undertaking regular geographical movements (for example from wintering grounds to breeding grounds).

monsoon forest Closed forest growing in regions with long dry season. Typically contains large number of deciduous tree species.

nocturnal Active at night.

nomadic Of erratic and changeable movements.

noseleaf Naked plate around nostrils of bats, used in echolocation.

nuchal Area where head and neck join.

occipital-carapace length (OCL) Measurement of size of crayfish from rear of eye socket to posterior edge of carapace.

omnivorous Feeding on both animal and plant matter.

onomatopoea Formation of a word based on sound it mimics (for example 'boom').

ovipositor Special organ in some female insects, used for depositing eggs.

parasitic/parasitism Refers to (symbiotic) relationship between species, where one benefits at detriment of the other.

plumage Layer of feathers or down on body (in birds).

posterior Rear of body.

prehensile (tail) Adapted to grasp or attach to objects.

pronotum Prominent plate-like covering over all or part of dorsal thorax.

pteropodid Bat in Pteropodidae (megabat) family.

Ramsar Site Wetland site designated as of international importance for conservation and sustainable use, especially for waterfowl.

reticulated Forming net-like pattern or reticulum.

riffle Refers to rippled or broken water, typically associated with fast-flowing water cascading over rocks or logs.

riparian Found on banks of rivers, streams, creeks and other waterways.

roost Perching place for observation, resting or sleeping.

rostrum Extension of carapace between eyes of crayfish, ending in spine at apex.

rudimentary Poorly developed and non-functional.

scat(s) Animal droppings.

sclerophyll Refers to stiff-leaved plants (especially forest types).

sedentary Spending entire life in relatively restricted region.

semi-aquatic Living on land but spending amounts of time in water.

semelparous Refers to reproductive strategy characterized by death after single reproductive season.

setae Tiny, hair-like projections on toe-pads of some geckos.

simple leaf Single undivided leaf attached to twig by its stem.

sloughing (or ecdysis) Process of shedding skin.

spawn Term used to describe clutch of frog eggs. Act of spawning occurs when female releases her eggs into the water as male sprays sperm over them, allowing them to be fertilized.

species Category into which a genus is divided. For example, *Homo* (genus) *sapiens* (species) are modern humans.

subapical Area of a structure just below its apex.

subcostal Area of wing just inside from the leading edge or front margin.

submarginal Part of wing just inside the wing edges or margin.

subspecies Level of taxonomic division below species.

substrate Underlying layer or material on which an organism lives.

taxonomy Classification of living things based on shared characteristics.

teat Nipple from mammary gland.

terrestrial Living on or spending time on the ground.

territory Area defended by individual animal or group of animals.

thorax Middle section of body of an insect, between head and abdomen.

tornus Inner rear corner of (insect) wings.

tubercle Raised projection.

tympanum Membrane covering entrance to ear of frog.

understorey Lower level of vegetation in a forest.

vent Exterior opening of anus or cloaca.

ventral Undersurface or belly of animal.

vertebral Along line of spine (vertebrae).

vertebrate Animal with backbone or notochord.

zoospore Spore of an alga or fungus capable of sustained movement using its flagellum.

Origins of Australia's Rainforests

Australia's rainforests are considered to be some of the most ancient of all rainforests remaining on Earth. The World Heritage listed Wet Tropics in north-eastern Queensland contain rainforest elements that are believed to be more than 110 million years old. The world's highest concentrations of remnant flowering plants (angiosperms), which emerged during the Cretaceous period, are also found here.

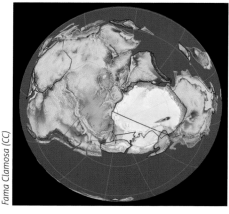

Gondwana at 420 million years ago (view centred on the South Pole)

Fama Clamosa (CC)

About 180 millon years ago (mya), during the Jurassic period, the ancient supercontinent of Pangea broke up to form the two land masses of Gondwana and Laurasia. Gondwana contained the land areas that would eventually form the continents of the southern hemisphere, while Laurasia contained those that were destined for the northern hemisphere. During the Jurassic period, the conifer families Podocarpaceae and Araucariaceae became established, and forests containing these ancient elements of modern Australian rainforests covered much of Australia throughout the Cretaceous period (145–66 mya). By 50 mya, paleo-Antarctic rainforest lineages were widespread throughout Gondwana, but most likely more concentrated on what would become Australia and Antarctica. These continents were the last to separate from Gondwana (about 33 mya), breaking apart and allowing the Southern Ocean to form between the two, and as a consequence reducing the cooling effects the previous ocean currents had on northern Australia.

Due to the increased humidity and rainfall, Australia's paleo-Antarctic rainforest became widespread throughout much of the continent. As the continent continued to travel north, the drying climate forced the retreat of Australia's rainforest to the wetter areas, resulting in the patchy distributions we see today. Remaining strongholds occur along the coast of eastern Australia, and west through the continent's tropical north to the Kimberley region in Western Australia. Dry rainforest and vine thickets are scattered in pockets further inland.

A detailed geological timeline and the significant processes that occurred during each geological period are shown in Appendix 1 (p. 363).

Chris mcc64 (CC)

Bunya Pine *Araucaria bidwillii*

Cultural Significance of Australia's Rainforests

For millennia, rainforests across Australia have held cultural significance for Aboriginal peoples. Archaeological evidence suggests that Aboriginal people inhabited the Wet Tropics rainforests of northern Queensland for at least 40,000 years before the arrival of Europeans. As the Wet Tropics rainforests were rich in resources (food, shelter, materials), they were permanently inhabited and believed to have had the highest population density in the country. They were the 'supermarkets, pharmacies and hardware stores' for Aboriginal people. Some traditional owners actively protected their rainforests from fires in adjacent vegetation communities in an effort to protect the resources that the rainforests offered.

The rainforests are also important areas for customs, and provide Aboriginal people with identity. The Southern Cassowary is an important cultural asset to many of the traditional owners in the Wet Tropics, while some rainforests in the Northern Kimberley are culturally important sites and feature in cultural stories such as those linked to the Gwion (Bradshaw) rock art. Due to their resources, rainforests were important places for tribes to gather. The Bunya Mountains in south-east Queensland was one such place where tribes travelled for hundreds of kilometres to meet and celebrate the Bunya Pine *Araucaria bidwillii* nut harvest. This was also an opportunity to trade goods, share stories, pass on knowledge and even wed.

Today, Aboriginals are actively involved in managing their country in many parts of Australia, and their traditional ecological knowledge is being combined with science to create positive outcomes for all those involved, not least the environment.

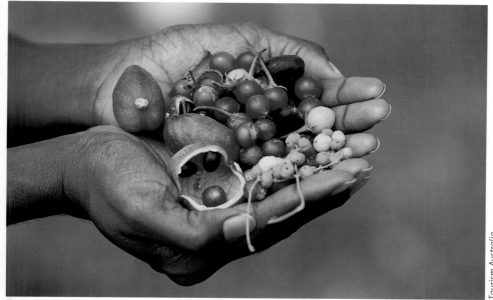

Australian 'bush tucker' fruits

Tourism Australia

Modern Australian Rainforests

Less than 3 per cent (about 3,600,000ha) of Australia's total forest area is rainforest. It occurs in the Northern Territory and every state except South Australia. Queensland is home to the largest extent of rainforests, almost 2,000,000ha (55 per cent), Tasmania is second with about 700,000ha (about 20 per cent of the state's total forested area). New South Wales has just under 600,000ha, the Northern Territory around 287,000ha, Victoria 20,000ha and Western Australia only 7,000ha.

According to the Australian Department of Agriculture and Water Resources, Australia's rainforest types are categorized into two distinct classes: open forest, which has 50–80 per cent crown cover, and closed forest, with more than 80 per cent crown cover. About 2,590,000ha of the rainforests are closed forests, constituting the largest component (about 71 per cent) of all closed forest ecosystems in Australia. The remaining rainforests are open forests, accounting for about 3 per cent of Australia's total open forested area. Australia's rainforest types can be further categorized as low (up to 10m in height), medium (>10–30m) and tall (>30m). About 176,000ha of open rainforest and 595,000ha of closed rainforest is low, 824,000ha of open rainforest and almost 1,800,000ha of closed rainforest is medium, and 7,000ha of open rainforest and 211,000ha of closed rainforest is tall.

Australian rainforests are broadly classed as macrophyll (or mesophyll), notophyll, microphyll and nanophyll, according to the general size and structure of the leaves of the dominant canopy plants. Macrophyll rainforests are found in wetter lowland areas and the dominant canopy plants have large leaves (>127mm), notophyll rainforest canopy plants have leaves 76–127mm long, microphyll rainforest canopy plants have leaves of 25–76mm in length, while the dominant canopy plants of nanophyll rainforest have leaves shorter than 25mm. Leaf size typically decreases as both latitude and elevation increase, and is closely linked to rainfall, temperature and soil fertility.

The classification of rainforest types in Australia is a very difficult task, given the huge range of taxonomic diversity and structural complexity. However, they have been divided into the following five subgroups: tropical and subtropical rainforests, dry rainforests and vine thickets, monsoon vine forests, warm temperate rainforests and cool temperate rainforests. These five subgroups are outlined in further detail below and are referred to throughout this book.

Tropical & Subtropical Rainforests

The rainforest types in this subgroup contain a complex assemblage of species. The multi-layered canopy normally exceeds 30m in height, typically with numerous emergent species, and is dominated by notophylls and macrophylls. The canopy consists primarily of evergreen species, although some deciduous species are also present. Many of the larger trees have buttresses, and there are species with both compound and simple leaves. The understorey typically contains free-standing palms and climbing rattans (more so in the tropics), and both lianas and epiphytes are generally abundant.

Common emergents, canopy-forming and subcanopy trees include the

Bangalow Palm *Archontophoenix cunninghamiana*, Black Bean *Castanospermum australe*, Black Booyong *Heritiera actinophylla*, Blue Quandong *Elaeocarpus grandis*, Brush Bloodwood *Baloghia inophylla*, Brushbox *Lophostemon confertus*, Crow's Ash *Flindersia australis*, Hoop Pine *Araucaria cunninghamii*, Illawarra Flame Tree *Brachychiton acerifolius*, Lilly Pilly/Cherry *Syzygium* spp., Moreton Bay Fig *Ficus macrophylla*, Pepperberry *Cryptocarya obovata*, Pigeonberry Ash *Cryptocarya erythroxylon*, Prickly Ash *Orites excelsa*, Red Apple *Syzygium ingens*, Red Cedar *Toona ciliata*, Rosewood *Dysoxylum fraserianum*, Sandpaper Fig *Ficus coronata*, Soft Corkwood *Caldcluvia paniculosa*, Giant Stinging Tree *Dendrocnide excelsa*, Turnipwood *Akania lucens*, White Beech *Gmelina leichhardtii*, White Booyong *Heritiera trifoliata* and Yellow Carabeen *Sloanea woollsii*.

Strangler Fig, Daintree Rainforest, Queensland

Kathryn Himbeck

Understorey shrubs can include the Featherwood *Polyosma cunninghamii*, Narrow-leaved Palm Lily *Cordyline stricta*, Orange Thorn *Citriobatus pauciflorus*, Steelwood *Sarcopteryx stipata*, Walking-stick Palm *Linospadix monostachya* and White Bolly Gum *Neolitsea dealbata*.

Climbing vines and scramblers include the Burny Vine *Trophis scandens*, Giant Pepper Vine *Piper novaehollandiae*, Lawyer Vine *Calamus muelleri*, Prickly Supplejack *Ripogonum discolor* and Water Vine *Cissus antarctica*.

Epiphytes, ferns and other forbs can include the Bird's Nest Fern *Asplenium australascium*, Cunjevoi/Native Lily *Alocasia brisbanensis*, Elkhorn *Platycerium bifurcatum*, Giant Maidenhair *Adiantum formosum*, Horseshoe Felt Vine *Pyrrosia confluens*, Native Yam *Dioscoea transversa*, Orange Lomandra *Lomandra spicata*, Pastel Flower *Pseuderanthemum variabile*, Prickly Tree Fern *Cyathea leichardtiana*, rat's tail orchids *Dendrobium* spp., Settlers Flax *Gymnostachys anceps* and Strap Water Fern *Blechnum patersonii*.

Tropical Rainforests occur northwards from Mackay, predominantly in the Cape York Peninsula and Wet Tropics bioregions. They are complex closed forests with the most diverse assemblage of tree species of any Australian forest type. More than 2,750 plant species have been recorded in tropical rainforests (over 10 per cent of all Australian flora).

Subtropical rainforests are typically a feature of regions with fertile substrates that receive in excess of 1,300mm of rainfall a year. They tend to be most extensive in sheltered gullies up to around 900m above sea level, and are patchily distributed between Rockhampton, Queensland, and Narooma, New South Wales. Subtropical rainforests are similarly complex closed forests with a diverse assemblage of tree species, second only in species diversity to tropical rainforests. The canopy is dense and multilayered, standing at 20–40m in height.

Antarctic Beech Trees

Alan Wiggington (CC)

Dry Rainforests & Vine Thickets

Angus McNab

Dry rainforest on Queensland's Fraser Island

Dry rainforests are closed forests with a varying canopy height, reaching up to 25m in some places and as low as 10m in others. They grow mainly on rocky substrates, in regions where the average annual rainfall is 600–1,100mm. Buttressed trees are rare and the understorey typically lacks palm species. The canopy contains evergreen and deciduous trees and, to a lesser extent, some semi-deciduous trees. Dry rainforests are patchily distributed in lower rainfall areas between Chillagoe, Queensland, and the Mitchell River Gorge, Victoria. Vine thickets occur in the drier extremes, with pronounced seasonal droughts.

Littoral rainforests and coastal vine thickets are a specific type of dry rainforest that occur in coastal areas, mainly within 2km of the ocean. Their range extends from Princess Charlotte Bay, Queensland, to around Lakes Entrance, Victoria. They can grow on headlands, cliffs and sand dunes, and vary in height depending on their exposure to strong winds. Sheltered areas are typically home to taller forests and thickets, while those exposed to strong winds can be short and more thicket-like.

Peter Rowland

Giant Stinging Tree *Dendrocnide excelsa*

Common emergents, canopy-forming and subcanopy trees of dry rainforests include the Black Bean *Castanospermum australe*, Brush Bloodwood *Baloghia inophylla*, Crow's Ash *Flindersia australis*, Deciduous Fig *Ficus superba*, Guioa/Wild Quince *Guioa semiglauca*, Hoop Pine *Araucaria cunninghamii*, Plum Pine *Podocarpus elatus*, Port Jackson Fig *Ficus rubiginosa*, Python Tree *Gossia bidwillii*, Shatterwood *Backhousia sciadophora*, Silky Oak *Grevillea robusta*, Giant Stinging Tree *Dendrocnide excelsa*, Wild Quince *Alectryon subcinereus*, Whalebone *Streblus brunonianus* and Yellow Tulip *Drypetes australasica*.

Understorey shrubs can include the Brittlewood *Claoxylon australie*, Orange Thorn *Citriobatus pauciflorus*, Red Kamala *Mallotus philippensis*, Red Olive Berry *Cassine australe* and Silver Croton *Croton insularis*.

Climbers include the Blood Vine *Austrosteenisia blackii*, Gum Vine *Aphanopetalum resinosum*, Scrambling Jasmine *Jasminum volubile*, Staff Climber *Celastrus australis*, Sweet Morinda *Morinda jasminoides* and Three-leaved Water Vine *Tetrastigma nitens*.

Epiphytes may be present but are not typical and can include the Cucumber Orchid *Dendrobium cucumerinum* and Tongue Orchid *D. linguiforme*.

Monsoon Vine Forests

K. M. Rawlings

Rainforest on Christmas Island

This subgroup contains dry rainforests that occur in regions with distinct wet and dry seasons. The canopy is dense (>70 per cent foliage cover) with heights that vary depending on seasonal rainfall and access to permanent water. The vegetation is dominated by notophylls; buttressed trees are absent and both palms and epiphytes are very few in number.

Monsoon vine forests in wetter areas, or areas with access to permanent waterbodies, are dominated by evergreen trees, and have some palms, but fewer vines. The canopy height is up to 30m and the understorey is a dense assemblage of smaller trees, ground ferns and sedges.

Monsoon vine forests in drier areas, without access to permanent water (areas that are seasonally dry), are strongly associated with rocky escarpments, protected rocky gorges and the leeward sides of beach dunes. They have a lower canopy height (5–10m), and are dominated by lianas, creeping vines and scramblers. These are also known as monsoon vine thickets.

In the Northern Territory and northern Western Australia, monsoon vine forests occur in small, discrete patches that are relatively widespread. They are more abundant in the Northern Territory, with about 15,000 patches (1–4,000ha, average 3.6ha) covering around 0.2 per cent of the Territory (total 270,0000ha). Despite their small overall size, the monsoon vine forests contain about 13 per cent of the described flora in the Northern Territory. Monsoon vine forests in Western Australia are even more restricted, with approximately 1,500 known patches, totalling 7,000ha, ranging from a few canopy trees to patches several hundred hectares in size.

Trees here can include: Australian Ebony *Diospyros ferrea*, Banyan Fig *Ficus virens*, Birimbiri or Ebony Wood *Diospyros humilis*, Bitangoor *Calophyllum soulattri*, Black Olive Plum *Elaeodendron melanocarpa*, Black Plum *Vitex acuminata*, Boab *Adansonia gregorii*, Broad-leaved Paperbark *Melaleuca viridiflora*, Cajuput *Melaleuca cajuputi*, Coffee or Coffee Bush *Breynia cernua*,

15

Corkwood *Euodia elleryana*, Currant or Coffee Fruit *Grewia breviflora*, Freshwater Mangrove *Carallia brachiata*, Goonj *Celtis philippensis*, Gubinge *Terminalia ferdinandiana*, Jarnba or Mistletoe Tree *Exocarpos latifolius*, Jigal or Bauhinia *Bauhinia cunninghamii*, Karnbor *Melaleuca dealbata*, Lime Berry *Micromelum minutum*, Mangarr *Sersalisia sericea*, Mango Bark *Canarium australianum*, Marool Plum or Blackberry Tree *Terminalia petiolaris*, Mirda or Helicopter Tree *Gyrocarpus americanus*, Native Witch-hazel *Turraea pubescens*, Red Coondoo *Mimusops elengi*, Sandpaper Fig *Ficus scobina*, Scaly Ash *Ganophyllum falcatum*, Soft Bollygum *Litsea glutinosa*, Tim Tim *Timonius timon*, Tuckeroo *Cupaniopsis anacardioides*, Wild Apple *Syzygium eucalyptoides*, Wild Prune *Sersalisia sericea* and Yarrabah Satinash *Syzygium angophoroides*.

Tall shrubs can include: Blue Tongue or Native Lassiandra *Melastoma affine*, Broad-winged Hop Bush *Dodonea platyptera*, Ceylon Leadwort *Plumbago zeylanica*, Common Screwpine *Pandanus spiralis*, Flowers of Magic *Clerodendrum costatum*, Gooralgar or Snowball Bush *Flueggea virosa* and Northern Sandalwood *Santalum lanceolatum*.

Common climbers can include: Austral Sarsaparilla *Smilax australis*, Fragrant Opilia *Opilia amentacea*, Goolyi Bush *Caesalpinia major*, Jinjalgurany or Crab's Eye Bean *Abrus precatorius*, Native Jasmine *Jasminum didymium*, Ngoorla or Bush Caper *Capparis lasiantha*, Oyster-catcher Bill *Tylophora cinerascens*, Snake Vine *Tinaspora smilacina* and Supplejack *Flagellaria indica*.

Ferns and herbs can include: Climbing Fern *Stenochlaena palustris*, Coleus *Plectranthus scutellarioides*, Giant Sword Fern *Nephrolepis biserrata*, Hard Fern *Blechnum orientale*, Maidenhair Creeper *Lygodium flexuosum*, Necklace Fern *Lindsaea ensifolia*, Nutrush *Scleria ciliaris*, Oakleaf Fern *Drynaria quercifolia*, Old World Forked Fern *Dicranopteris linearis*, Polynesian Arrowroot *Tacca leontopetaloides*, Tropical Panicgrass *Panicum trichoides* and White Butterfly Orchid *Dendrobium affine*.

Warm Temperate Rainforests

These complex, closed forests typically have a multi-layered canopy, dominated by evergreen microphyll and notophyll tree species. They have simpler structures and species composition than subtropical rainforests, and tree diversity decreases in a southerly direction as well as at higher elevations. Buttressed trees are rare and palms are uncommon, as are lianas and epiphytes. Stands of trees grow on rocky substrates with moderately fertile soils, mainly in sheltered areas such as gullies and slopes, especially in hilly regions.

Northern Warm Temperate Rainforests occur mainly from the Lamington Plateau, Queensland, south to Batemans Bay, New South Wales, and overlap with the southern warm temperate rainforests south of the Shoalhaven River, New South Wales.

Common canopy-forming tree species include the Coachwood *Ceratopetalum apetalum*, Lilly Pilly *Syzygium smithii* and Sassafras *Doryphora sassafras*. Other common tree species include the Hard Corkwood *Endiandra sieberi*, Possumwood *Quintinia sieberi*, Prickly Ash *Orites excelsa*, Soft Corkwood *Caldcluvia paniculosa* and Sweet Pittosporum *Pittosporum undulatum*. Tall shrubs include the Brush Muttonwood *Myrsine howittiana*, Brush Pepperbush *Tasmannia insipida*,

Callicoma *Callicoma serratifolia*, Narrow-leaved Palm Lily *Cordyline stricta* and Orange Thorn *Citriobatus pauciflorus*.

Vines and scramblers include the Black Silkpod *Parsonsia purpurascens*, Climbing Panax *Cephalaralia cephalobotrys*, Common Milk Vine *Marsdenia rostrata*, Austral Sarsaparilla *Smilax australis*, Prickly Supplejack *Ripogonum discolor* and Wonga Vine *Pandorea pandorana*.

Ferns and other forbs include the Bat's Wing Fern *Histiopteris incisa*, Bird's Nest Fern *Asplenium australasicum*, Blue Flax Lily *Dianella caerulea* var. *producta*, Common Ground Fern *Calochlaena dubia*, Gristle Fern *Blechnum cartilagineum*, Rough Tree Fern *Cyathea australis* and Trim Shield Fern *Lastreopsis decomposita*.

Dorrigo National Park, New South Wales

Southern Warm Temperate Rainforests have a patchy distribution in deep, moist gullies of the coastal ranges and foothills, up to 800m above sea level. They occur from the Shoalhaven River, New South Wales, to the Gippsland coastal foothills, Victoria, with the most southerly patches being in Wilsons Promontory National Park. The warm temperate rainforest patches are typically less than 100ha in size and are usually bordered by wet sclerophyll forests. Stands of trees grow on moderately fertile soils in regions that receive about 900–1,300mm of annual rainfall.

The canopy is relatively uniform, up to 20m in height, and is dominated by the Australian Blackwood *Acacia melanoxylon*, Lilly Pilly *Syzygium smithii*, Sassafras *Doryphora sassafras* and Sweet Pittosporum *Pittosporum undulatum*. Other trees and tall shrubs include the Blanket-leaf *Bedfordia arborescens*, Hazel Pomaderris *Pomaderris aspera*, Kanooka *Tristaniopsis laurina* and Brush Muttonwood *Myrsine howittiana*. The understorey is dominated by ferns, and some of the many smaller shrubs that also contribute to the understorey include the Large Mock-olive *Notelea venosa*, Prickly Currant-bush *Coprosma quadrifida* and Victorian Christmas-bush *Prostanthera lasianthos*.

Woody vines or lianas that can be found in this community include the Forest Clematis *Clematis glycinoides*, Jungle Grape *Cissus hypoglauca*, Common Milk Vine *Marsdenia rostrata*, Mountain Clematis *Clematis aristata*, Austral Sarsaparilla *Smilax australis*, Wombat Berry *Eustrephus latifolius* and Wonga Vine *Pandorea pandorana*.

Ferns include the Common Finger Fern *Grammitis billardierei*, Fishbone Water Fern *Blechnum nudum*, Kangaroo Fern *Microsorum pustulatum*, Mother Shield Fern *Polystichum proliferum*, Rough Tree Fern *Cyathea australis* and Soft Tree Fern *Dicksonia antarctica*.

17

Cool Temperate Rainforests

Cool temperate rainforest stands are generally smaller than 100ha and are patchily distributed along the misty summits and plateaus, including the upper slopes and gullies of the Great Dividing Range, typically above 900m. In southern Queensland (the northern part of their range) rainfall exceeds 1,750mm per year, but can be around 1,000mm in southern Tasmania. The Otway Ranges in south-west Victoria are an anomaly, being generally below 500m and having upwards of 2,000mm of rain per year.

Cool temperate rainforests are usually associated with more fertile soils than warm temperate rainforests, situated on a substrate of granite, basalt and siltstone. Their structure is relatively simple, more so in the north, with only one or two nanophyll and microphyll evergreen species dominating the canopy. The canopy is predominantly below 30m in height, but can reach 40m. Epiphytes and lianas may be present but are not typical, and palms are absent, with the exception of Lord Howe Island. The understorey is dominated by ferns, including tree ferns and a high diversity of mosses and lichens. This rainforest type is most diverse in the higher rainfall regions of Tasmania.

Melba Gully, Great Otway National Park, Victoria

Cool temperate rainforest shrubs include the Austral Mulberry *Hedycarya angustifolia*, Banyalla *Pittosporum bicolor*, Gippsland Waratah *Telopea oreades*, Mountain Pepper *Tasmannia lanceolata*, Musk Daisy-bush *Olearia argophylla*, Prickly Currant-bush *Coprosma quadrifida* and Victorian Christmas-bush *Prostanthera lasianthos*. Climbers or lianas include the Mountain Clematis *Clematis aristata* and Twining Silkpod *Parsonsia brownii*. Ferns are abundant, including the Hard Water Fern *Blechnum wattsii*, Kangaroo Fern *Microsorum pustulatum*, Mother Shield Fern *Polystichum proliferum*, Rough Tree Fern *Cyathea australis* and Soft Tree Fern *Dicksonia antarctica*.

Northern Cool Temperate Rainforests occur northwards of the Barrington Tops Plateau and the canopy is dominated by the Antarctic Beech *Nothofagus moorei*, Mountain Laurel *Kalmia latifolia* and Possumwood *Quintinia sieberi*.

Southern Cool Temperate Rainforests occur south of the Barrington Tops Plateau and the canopy is dominated by the Black Oliveberry *Elaeocarpus holopetalus*, Australian Blackwood *Acacia melanoxylon*, Celery-top Pine *Phyllocladus asplenifolius*, Deciduous Beech *Nothofagus gunnii*, Leatherwood *Eucryphia lucida*, Myrtle Beech *Nothofagus cunninghamii*, Pinkwood *Eucryphia moorei*, Sassafras *Doryphora sassafras* and Southern Sassafras *Atherosperma moschatum*.

Conservation & Threats

Australia is one of 17 countries described as 'megadiverse'. These nations combined support more than 70 per cent of the Earth's total biological diversity. Remarkably, 45 per cent of Australia's birds, 83 per cent of mammals, 93 per cent of reptiles, 94 per cent of amphibians and 84 per cent of plants are endemic. Australia has the highest percentage of endemic vertebrate species (excluding fish) of all countries.

About 15 per cent of Australia's forest-dependent vertebrate species reside in rainforests, including 11 per cent of birds, 17 per cent of mammals and reptiles, 23 per cent of amphibians and 12 per cent of fish. Additionally, around 20 per cent of Australia's vascular plants are rainforest dwellers. About 3,581,000ha of Australia's remaining rainforests are located in IUCN protected areas, about 63 per cent of the total rainforest area. Australia, Burundi, Singapore and Sri Lanka are the only countries to have more than 50 per cent of their remaining forests protected.

Australia has an obligation to identify places for, plus protect and conserve places on, the UNESCO World Heritage List. A number of Australia's rainforest areas have already been listed. These are places that have natural and/or cultural values of outstanding global significance. World Heritage Sites include the Tasmanian Wilderness, Greater Blue Mountains Area (New South Wales), Gondwanan Rainforests of southern Queensland and southern New South Wales, Queensland's Wet Tropics, Fraser Island (Queensland) and Kakadu National Park (Northern Territory).

Under the Convention of Biological Diversity, the Australian government committed to a target of protecting 17 per cent of the continent within the National Reserve System (NRS) by 2020. Figures released in 2018 showed that close to 20 per cent was held in the NRS. Another key aim was to give priority to bioregions with less than 10 per cent of their remaining area protected in reserves. Currently, all of the 89 bioregions listed under IBRA7 have some representation in the NRS, although 28 of these have less than 10 per cent of their remaining area protected.

The Convention of Biological Diversity also aims to protect key habitats, including those identified as significant for threatened species. Other targets are wetlands listed under the Ramsar Convention and areas that are an integral component of larger national or international conservation goals.

Logging

Since the arrival of Europeans in Australia, widespread clearance of rainforest has taken place and ecosystems that remain today are mostly fragmented and patchily distributed. In the Wet Tropics region of north-east Queensland, before its inclusion on the UNESCO World Heritage List in 1988, about 20 per cent of rainforests had been selectively logged. Further logging was banned in 1988.

During this same period, Australia has recorded the largest documented number of vertebrate extinctions of any continent. More than 50 species of Australian animal have been declared extinct, including 27 mammals, 23 birds and four frogs, with others assumed to be extinct. A similar number of Australian plants is also classed as extinct, and a number of Australia's rainforest

John Harris

Old stump, showing axemen step cuts - Triplet Falls, Great Otway National Park, Victoria

floral communities are now critically endangered, including the littoral rainforest and coastal vine thickets of eastern Australia, and the lowland rainforest of subtropical Australia.

Australia is the only nation in the developed world to make the World Wildlife Fund's (WWF) global list of deforestation hotspots, alongside undeveloped countries such as Borneo, Brazil, Congo Basin, Kenya, Malawi, Mozambique, Papua New Guinea, Sumatra, Tanzania, Zambia and Zimbabwe. Although the clearing of Australia's rainforests has greatly reduced in recent times, the fragmentation that past logging activities caused is a major threat to the continued viability of many fauna and flora populations that have become isolated. Australia's iconic Koala is a notable inclusion on the list of animals affected by deforestation. Although it is not a rainforest-dependent species, its numbers are declining along the country's east coast at a rate of 21 per cent per decade.

More than 75 per cent of Australia's threatened terrestrial fauna species and two-thirds of its threatened plants species have deforestation or habitat fragmentation listed as a key threatening process. Deforested areas are particularly prone to soil erosion, salinity and drought.

Globally, the primary cause of deforestation is the acquirement of more land for agricultural purposes. Mining and infrastructure are also significant drivers of deforestation. Australia is no exception. Historically, the demand for pasture for livestock was the main driver. During the 1990s and early 2000s there were large-scale bans on excessive tree clearing in Queensland and New South Wales, and Queensland banned the logging of rainforests on public land in 1994. Logging of old-growth forests and rainforests still continues in other states.

Climate Change

Climate change is a term used to describe the fluctuating climate of the Earth throughout geological history. The pattern has been cyclical over the last

650,000 years, with seven documented cycles of glacial advance and retreat. The last of these ended about 11,700 years ago – the end of the last ice age – and marked the beginning of our modern climate era. Scientists attribute most of these climate change cycles to tiny variations in the Earth's orbit, which affect the amount of solar energy reaching the planet's surface.

The rapid warming trend that we are currently witnessing in this cycle (Figure 1, p. 22) is almost certainly due to human influence. One of the main causes is the amount of carbon dioxide (CO_2) and other greenhouse gases in the Earth's atmosphere. At the time of writing, the current CO_2 level measured in the Earth's atmosphere (June 2020) is 416 parts per million (ppm). When humans first appeared on Earth this figure was 180 ppm (Appendix 1, p. 363).

While air and ocean temperatures and glacial ice and snowfall trends in polar regions and other areas around the globe show that global mean temperatures are rising, a range of technology is being used by scientists to record and measure climate change trends (current and historic). These include measuring the amount of CO_2 in glacial ice cores and deep-ocean sediments, studying the colour and width of tree rings, monitoring the health and changes in coral reefs (such as severe bleaching events) and measuring the amount of carbon in layers of sedimentary rocks. Studies of each of these show that the current warming trend is occurring about ten times faster than the rate seen in the period that followed the last ice age.

Anthropogenic climate change from human activity since the mid-twentieth century is a significant threat to the world's biodiversity. In addition to its direct impacts, climate change can increase the severity of other threatening processes, including the ability of invasive animals and plants to populate an area, the frequency of intensity of droughts, rainfall patterns and fire regimes.

Increased temperatures not only affect the availability and evaporation rates of surface water and ground moisture, but are also altering the chemical balance of available groundwater. This includes altering the pH, changing levels of pollutants and increasing the prevalence of disease and disease-bearing organisms such as the Chytrid Fungus *Batrachochytrium dendrobatidis*, which are becoming more widespread.

Evidence is growing about the impacts that climate change is expected to have on the abundance and distribution of species. Of particular concern are the associated effects on interactions between organisms, such as pollination of plants by insects, ocean acidification and ocean temperature changes, which will result in significant changes to ecosystem composition, structure and function.

A growing body of evidence indicates that certain plant and animal species are moving to higher elevations and towards the Earth's poles in response to increasing temperatures. Occupation of these cooler elevations or latitudes can be restricted by rainfall, soil composition and topography, however, when a species or community occurs in a location where southwards or northwards movement is not possible (as in southern Tasmania). Then the only potential option is to move to higher, cooler elevations in order to offset rising temperatures. Those species that are already found in these areas are most at risk of extirpation (localized extinction) or total extinction. Additionally, the floral communities at these higher elevations are changing as new species are able to invade areas that were previously too cool for them to survive in.

Australia's total CO_2 emissions from all measured sources for the 12-month period up to June 2019 was 532 million tonnes. During the unprecedented bushfires of the 2019–2020 Australian summer, it was estimated that 400–700 million tonnes of CO_2 were released into the atmosphere. Between 90 and 95 per cent of the CO_2 emissions from these bushfires are forecast to be reabsorbed by the process of vegetation regrowth over the next 10 years, which leaves potential net CO_2 emissions of 20–70 million tonnes. Using the price of carbon credits under the Australian federal government's Emissions Reduction Fund (currently $15 per tonne), the estimated cost of the 2019–2020 bushfires in regard to CO_2 emissions alone is AUD $300million to AUD $1.05 billion.

In addition to the intensive bushfires, 2019 was Australia's hottest year on record, with mean recorded temperatures 1.52 °C above the 1961–1990 average. It was also the driest year on record, with mean rainfall of just 277.6mm. The previous lowest was in 1902, recording 314.5mm. This trend was observed in every state and territory. The hottest days in Australia's recorded history were 17 and 18 December 2019, with an average recorded temperature across the nation of 41.9 °C.

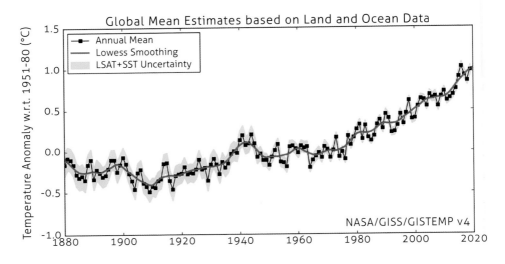

Figure 1 Land-ocean temperature index, 1880 to present, with base period 1951–1980. The solid black line is the global annual mean temperature and the solid red line is the five-year Lowess smoothing. The gray shading represents the total land surface air temperature (LSAT) and sea-surface temperature (SST) annual uncertainty at a 95 per cent confidence interval.
(Source: Nasa, https://data.giss.nasa.gov/gistemp/graphs, accessed 14/4/2020.)

Bushfires

Australia has had bushfires for more than 60 million years, and they have been one of the most significant driving forces in Australia's environment. Fire is an integral shaper of Australia's biodiversity. Many plants have considerable resistance to fires. Some, like banksias, eucalypts and wattles, have fire-triggered seeds or possess epicormic shoots or lignotubers that sprout only after a fire has passed. Animals are dependent on the resilience of plants like these for food and shelter.

Although low-intensity fires and some fire regimes are beneficial, the

Queensland's McKenzie River rainforest after fire

increased (about 40 per cent) frequency and intensity of bushfires in recent decades has been devastating. But the indiscriminate, untargeted nature of managed fires or the exclusion of fire from an area altogether can also be very damaging. Indeed, inappropriate fire management is the second biggest threat to birds and other animals after habitat clearance and fragmentation.

In Australia's past, rainforests were typically too wet to burn, except during periods of prolonged drought and when subjected to exceptional drying. Frequent fires in adjacent sclerophyll vegetation since the late Miocene epoch, however, have modified the ecotone between the two and have gradually eroded the fringes of rainforests. The increasing drying effects of climate change are resulting in larger areas of rainforest being destroyed by more frequent, higher intensity bushfires (in addition to fire, rainfall and soil fertility play a

Smoke pouring from numerous fires in New South Wales on January 3, 2020

role in shaping the distribution and extent of Australia's rainforests).

Following the 'Black Saturday' bushfires of 2009, a major study of Australia's weather patterns from 1973 was conducted. A long-term upwards trend in 'fire' weather was identified. The findings of this study were a significant step towards improving the seasonal forecasting of high-risk bushfire weather patterns, enabling policy makers to make longer term decisions around bushfire management.

Some of Australia's most significant fires since European settlement (1788) are detailed in Appendix 2 (p. 366).

Cyclones

In addition to rising temperatures, climate change has resulted in more frequent high-intensity storms, including cyclones and floods. In recent years, tropical northern Australia has seen a number of category 3 or higher cyclones. (Note: category 3 cyclones have winds of 165–224km/h; category 4 cyclones winds of 225–279km/h; and category 5 cyclones winds in excess of 280km/h).

The most famous cyclone in Australian history is undoubtedly Cyclone Tracy – not necessarily for its intensity, although the category 3 cyclone reached wind gusts of 217km/h, but for the fact that it killed 71 people and destroyed about 70 per cent of buildings in the Northern Territory's capital, Darwin. The natural disaster took place between Christmas Eve and Boxing Day, 1974.

NASA (CC)

Australia's north was battered by Cyclone Trevor (east) and Cyclone Veronica (west) in March 2019

The real impact of a cyclone, however, depends on a number of factors: its intensity and size, the speed at which it travels, the storm tides it generates and the region it hits. Of course, the more populated the region, the more potential there is for human casualties, injuries and damage to property and infrastructure. There is also the devastating environmental damage, including damage to reefs, beach erosion, uprooting and defoliation of trees, as well as flooding.

While it may be possible to place a monetary value on the damage that cyclones have on the economy (for example, AUD $2.2 billion for Cyclone Debbie in 2017), the true extent of the impacts they can have on the environment is immeasurable. The rainforest in Kutini-Payamu (Iron Range) National Park was so battered by Cyclone Trevor over a 10-hour period in 2019 that it could take the rainforest decades to recover. Ancient trees were lost, most of the rainforest canopy was defoliated, thousands of animals and plants died, the rainforest floor was left exposed to the heat of the sun, and the ancient rainforest is now at risk of being lost forever if an intense bushfire strikes. If this was to occur to the already severely damaged area, many unique animal, plant and fungi species could become extinct.

The cyclones that have had the most impact on the Australian mainland in the last 20 years are detailed in Appendix 3 (p. 368).

Invasive Species

A large number of invasive fauna and flora species have been introduced into Australia since European settlement. Today, Australia has 32 species of introduced mammal alone, which predate on native fauna, compete for food and shelter, or have negative impacts on the structure and composition of the natural environment that natives depend upon for survival. There are also a number of introduced birds (15), reptiles (four), amphibians (one) and invertebrates (no

Around 4 million feral cats occur within Australia, with each cat killing up to 30 animals every day

Angus McNab

figure available). Some of the major invasive animals, plants and fungi species recorded are outlined in Appendix 4 (p. 370).

Introduced predators, primarily the Domestic Cat and European Red Fox, have had an enormous impact on native animals, with an estimated 400 different vertebrate species being hunted as part of their collective diets. The number of feral cats in Australia alone has been conservatively estimated at around 4 million, with each cat killing up to 30 animals every day. They have become established in every habitat on the continent. Another major animal pest is the Cane Toad, which has spread throughout much of northern and eastern Australia. It has powerful toxins that can kill almost any animal that consumes it, or its eggs or tadpoles.

In addition to introduced pest animals, a range of invasive plants and fungi has been recorded in Australia. Many of these impact rainforest ecosystems to varying degrees. Introduced plants can invade the margins of rainforest and inhibit conservation measures, particularly in more fragmented environments.

Of the major environmental fungi pests in Australia, perhaps the most significant is the Chytrid Fungus. Chytridiomycete fungi are a diverse group, occurring in the soil and water of most environments. They are important for the health and function of the environment and are responsible for the biodegradation of materials such as cellulose, chitin and pollen. The Chytrid Fungus, however, causes mass mortalities in frog populations. The infection is spread through waterborne zoospores that infect the skin of its host, causing erosion, ulceration and sloughing, so that the host can become terminally ill after just 10 days of exposure. Chytridiomycosis has devastated the world's frog populations, including those already under threat from other environmental and anthropogenic pressures.

The threats posed by invasive animals, plants, fungi and their associated

Scott Eipper

The Baw Baw Frog has suffered massive declines, largely due to Chytrid Fungus

diseases present real danger to the integrity of the biodiversity of Australia's rainforests. The costs and resources demanded in mitigating the risks these pose and managing their spread is considerable, and more research is needed to identify the most effective and economical ways of doing so. Combined with the current and predicted effects of climate change, the finely balanced rainforests, reliant on a narrow band of ecological and climatic conditions, are severely threatened.

Safety Information

Australia is a beautiful and rugged country where you may encounter potentially dangerous wildlife, stinging plants, expansive remote areas and temperatures that can cause major health issues. While the majority of sites described here are managed by local or regional authorities, there are several ways in which you can ensure your safety while visiting Australia's rainforests.

Make sure someone knows where you have gone. The itinerary of a trip to the more remote areas should be lodged with the appropriate authorities, but family or friends should be notified before regular trips (particularly if travelling alone), with departure and expected arrival/return dates and times in case of any travelling issues.

Ensure your vehicle is roadworthy and suitable for the terrain and region you are visiting, including spare tyre(s) and a spare set of keys. If venturing to more remote areas, take a tool kit, shovel, essential spare parts, additional food and water and a first aid kit in case things do not go to plan. You should always ensure that you take adequate clothing, allowing sufficient extra clothing for changeable weather.

If travelling on forest tracks, be alert for possible heavy machinery (such as logging vehicles) and other road users or pedestrians. It is recommended that you carry a good quality UHF radio, either installed in your vehicle or hand held, when travelling on forest tracks. In areas where logging, mining or infrastructure operations occur, vehicles have designated UHF channels to communicate with the ground crews and drivers. It is very handy to know if there is a vehicle coming your way before you meet it head on. You can also let them know of your position by announcing your location (like the track you are on) and which direction you are travelling.

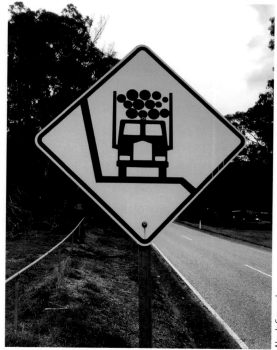

Akash Samuel

Logging sign along secondary road

There are many areas in Australia where there may be no services, including fuel stops and mobile phone coverage, for hundreds of kilometres. Personal Locator Beacons (PLBs) and Emergency Position-Indicating Radio Beacons (EPIRBs), are distress beacons that operate on the 406 MHz range and can be bought or hired in Australia for land, maritime and air usage. PLBs are smaller and more easily transported, so are recommended for land-based travel. They are designed to be carried by individuals, and the emitted signal operates continuously for a minimum of 24 hours once activated. EPIRBs are larger and are required by boats travelling more than 2km from shore. Once activated, they emit a signal for a minimum of 48 hours. The signal of both is detected by satellites, although models with an inbuilt Global Positioning System (GPS) allow for greater accuracy and faster detection of location. These devices can save your life if you are not able to contact emergency services by phone or radio (see www.beacons.amsa.gov.au/index.asp for more information).

When walking, a hat is essential for keeping the sun off your head and face, and good walking shoes are a must. Wear sunscreen, even on overcast days, and use insect repellent (biting insects, especially mosquitoes, have the potential to spread disease). Ensure that you carry adequate drinking water and drink frequently.

Carry an up-to-date first aid kit, including at least two pressure immobilization bandages, and make yourself aware of first aid practices. There are many

Peter Rowland

Typical first aid kit with personal locator beacon

venomous creatures throughout Australia, including snakes, spiders and marine animals. Never place your hands and feet where you cannot see them, never walk around at night without a torch, and always wear shoes and long trousers in locations where these creatures are likely to be present. Estuarine Crocodiles are the top predator in many of the waterways (both fresh and saltwater) of northern Australia. Do not walk near the edge of or swim in water that may contain crocodiles (often indicated by signs, but not always, so check with local authorities). Do not camp next to a waterway, and be aware that crocodiles can be present on land and in the ocean too. They are very fast moving and often underestimated.

While encounters with potentially dangerous animals are relatively uncommon in Australia (especially in wilderness areas), it is very unusual for an encounter to result in serious injury and fatalities are very rare. Advances in medical research have provided us with the first aid measures, antivenoms and other medical treatments to reduce the severity of animal-related injuries and disease. It is also wise to familiarize yourself with first aid treatments for venomous animals before travelling to an area.

In the event of an emergency in Australia, the triple zero (000) service provides the quickest way to receive help:

- Dial Triple Zero '000'.
- Stay calm.
- Request Police, Fire or Ambulance when asked which service you require.
- Provide your location (try and give as much detail as possible).
- If you are travelling, give the direction and destination of travel and the most recent landmark or intersection you passed.
- Stay on the line for further instructions.

Note: other emergency numbers for mobile devices are 112 and 106 (911 is diverted to 112 by some mobile operators). You can also download the Emergency + Smartphone app to your phone or device.

Icons and Measurements

Icons are provided to show the fauna groups that the species described belongs to:

 Birds

 Mammals

 Reptiles

 Amphibians

 Invertebrates

Abbreviations and measurements used within text:

asl above sea level
mm millimetres
cm centimetres
m metres
km² square kilometres
°C degrees centigrade

QUEENSLAND

1. Cape York Peninsula 2. Wet Tropics 3. Central Mackay Coast
4. South-east Queensland

State Overview

Queensland is Australia's second largest state or territory, covering an area of just under 1.75 million km² (22.5 per cent of the country's land mass), and contains 20,000km² of rainforest (55 per cent of Australia's total). Divided between four major rainforest regions, tropical rainforest (Cape York Peninsula and the Wet Tropics), subtropical rainforest (Eungella) and cool-temperate rainforest (South East Queensland), Queensland is home to some of the world's oldest rainforests. The majority of Queensland's (70 per cent) rainforests occur in the north of the state in the Wet Tropics bioregion.

Wooroonooran National Park

As a large state, Queensland has an extensive fauna list containing about 600 birds, 160 mammals, 500 reptiles and 130 frogs. This diversity stems from the range of habitat types – wet, dry, rocky, arid evergreen, deciduous to the misty cloud covered tropical rainforests in the north. Further, these ecosystems contain a vast diversity of plants that influence temperature and provide the diversity of niches that has, in part, allowed for the diversification of fauna. Throughout each level of the rainforest, from the fertile soil and leaf litter-covered floor, to the dense understorey, up the moss and lichen-covered buttresses, tree trunks and saplings, and into the high-sitting epiphytes and lianas that stretch into the dense canopy of strangler figs and rainforest trees, wildlife has been able to flourish.

Rainfall also plays a significant role in rainforest function, providing the water that allows for the flow of waterfalls, streams, rivers and soaks supplying the moisture that creates the high humidity levels. Similarly, elevation plays a critical role in both isolated rainforest patches such as those at Mt Elliot or Cape Melville, while also allowing for an increase in the diversity and endemicity of flora and fauna as temperature and rainfall vary. The significance of these factors, together with the ecological diversity and unique values of Queensland's rainforests, has been recognized by UNESCO, and Queensland's World Heritage List sites include the Wet Tropics of Queensland World Heritage Area, Gondwana Rainforests of Australia World Heritage Area and Fraser Island World Heritage Area, making the state's rainforest an essential place to visit for any wildlife enthusiast. Although granted many protections, Queensland's rainforests are still recovering from the impacts of logging and are threatened by many factors, including weeds, fire, feral animals, cyclones (in tropical regions) and fragmentation.

Fraser Island

Cape York Peninsula

1. Kutini-Payamu (Iron Range) National Park 2. Kulla National Park 3. Cape Melville

For wildlife enthusiasts the first thing that comes to mind when the Cape York Peninsula is mentioned is Kutini-Payamu (Iron Range) National Park and the incredible diversity of rainforest species that inhabit what is actually a very small area (346km^2). The Cape York Peninsula covers an area of 121,100km^2, which is predominantly eucalyptus and melaleuca woodlands dominated by the Darwin Stringybark *Eucalyptus tetrodonta*. Very little of Cape York contains rainforest; this is restricted to isolated patches along the east coast. With at least 430 birds, 100 mammals, 200 reptiles and 50 amphibians, it is easy to understand why wildlife enthusiasts want to visit Cape York. High on most people's rainforest wish list are the Palm Cockatoo, Eclectus Parrot and Green Python.

Peach Creek, McIlwraith Range

Anders Zimny

Key Species

BIRDS

Black-eared Catbird, Black-winged Monarch, Chestnut-breasted Cuckoo, Eclectus Parrot, Fairy Gerygone, Frill-necked Monarch, Green-backed Honeyeater, Lemon-bellied Flycatcher, Magnificent Riflebird, Northern Scrub-robin, Palm Cockatoo, Papuan Pitta, Red-cheeked Parrot, Red Goshawk, Tropical Scrubwren, Trumpet Manucode, White-faced Robin, Yellow-billed Kingfisher, Yellow-legged Flycatcher.

MAMMALS

Australian Spotted Cuscus, Bare-backed Fruit-bat, Bare-rumped Sheathtail Bat, Cape York Melomys, Cape York Pipistrelle, Cape York Rat, Cinnamon Antechinus, Eastern Dusky Leaf-nosed Bat, Fawn Leaf-nosed Bat, Giant White-tailed Rat, Greater Large-eared Horseshoe Bat, Long-nosed Echymipera, Papuan Sheathtail Bat, Southern Common Cuscus, Tree Mouse.

REPTILES

Black-tailed Bar-lipped Skink, Blue-tailed Monitor, Brown-headed Snake, Canopy Goanna, Cape Melville Bar-lipped Skink, Cape Melville Leaf-tailed Gecko, Cape Melville Rainbow-skink, Cape Melville Shadeskink, Coastal Eastern Cape Litter-skink, Giant Tree Gecko, Green Python, Lined Rainbow-skink, Mangrove Skink, McIlwraith Bar-lipped Skink, McIlwraith Leaf-tailed Gecko, McIlwraith Ring-tailed Gecko, Long-tailed Skink, Translucent Litter-skink.

AMPHIBIANS

Cape Melville Boulder Frog, Cape Melville Tree Frog, Cape York Graceful Tree Frog, Cape York Nursery Frog, Fringed Tree Frog, Kutini Boulder Frog, Long-snouted Tree Frog, Northern Nursery Frog, Rattling Nursery Frog, Shrill Whistlefrog, Slender Whistling Frog, Zweifel's Boulder Frog.

INVERTEBRATES

Giant Rainforest Mantid, Hercules Moth, Monteith's Leaf Insect, Priam Birdwing, Spiny Rainforest Katydid.

Roughly half of Cape York is used for pastoralism, and the coastal areas contain some of Australia's most famous fishing sites. Access is generally limited to the dry season, particularly for vehicles, which are predominantly restricted to the Peninsula Development Road that runs 571km from Lakeland to Weipa. Several small townships can be visited in Cape York, including Coen, Cooktown, Aurukun, Lockhart River and Bamaga. Many stations can also be visited. Flights to Cape York run from Cairns year round.

The climate is largely hot and humid (relative to much of Australia), averaging 20–31 °C, and more than 1,000mm (up to 1,600mm) of rain per year. However, this can vary dramatically, particularly when cyclones occur. The wet and dry seasons run during November–April and May–October respectively, and play a role in fire management when the Cape is burnt. Cape York is subjected to numerous fire-management plans and implementations depending on land ownership, so large areas are burnt every year. Bushfires, cyclones and invasive species are the primary factors that threaten the bioregion's biodiversity.

Angus McNab

Ulysses Swallowtail (underwing)

Eclectus Parrot *Eclectus roratus*

Cuatrok77 (CC)

Large and vibrantly coloured, the Eclectus Parrot is a beautiful, unmistakable bird that has obvious sexual dimorphism. Males are bright green with red flanks, an orange bill, and red underwings with dark blue flight feathers. Females are bright red with a blue breast, black bill and blue underwings, with darker blue flight feathers. Living in rainforest and nearby eucalypt forest between the Iron and McIlwraith Ranges, these birds build nests high up in tree hollows, reducing predation risk. However, this was not enough to stop collectors from climbing trees to poach both birds and eggs. The Smuggler Fig was the most famous tree exploited by collectors for Eclectus Parrot nests. The fallen tree may still have some of the old pegs that were used for climbing by collectors embedded in what is left of it.

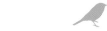

Frill-necked Monarch *Arses lorealis*

Mark Sanders

This is a lovely black and white bird of the northern rainforests. The sexes look alike except for the small black chin-patch and black lores of the male, while the female has a white chin and pale lores. Both sexes have white underparts, a black head, black wings and a white rump and collar (which can be raised). A pale blue eye-wattle contrasts with the black and white head. Although very light coloured (mainly white), it can be difficult to spot in the dark rainforest. Relatively loud for a smallish bird, it can be seen hunting along branches and tree trunks, picking at small invertebrates that it will chase if the prey manages to evade it.

Papuan Pitta *Erythropitta macklotii*

A seasonal visitor that migrates from Papua New Guinea to Cape York during the wet season (November–April), this bird is highly prized by avid birdwatchers. There are many challenges to spotting it as it bounces across the rainforest floor or calls from high in the canopy. Fortunately, being brightly coloured does make the species relatively easy to spot. The red nape, blue breast-band and red underparts make it unlike any other bird inhabiting the northern Australian rainforests. The call is a deep, mournful, pigeon-like whistle, resembling the words *kwoor-kwoor*. A shorter, single-note version of this call may be heard. Previously known as the Red-bellied Pitta, this species was recently split into multiple species and subspecies, with *E. m. digglesi* occurring in Australia.

Jason Thompson

White-faced Robin *Tregellasia leucops*

This small, yellow-breasted robin has a black head, olive-green upperparts and white facial markings, which contrast with the whiskers at the base of the black bill. It is a common sight in the understorey, and like other 'yellow robins' has a tendency to perch on vertical stems, tree trunks and hanging vines. One of the more inquisitive birds in the

Angus McNab

rainforest, this species will approach the patient observer. It is not uncommon for it to feed on the small invertebrates that are disturbed as you walk through the rainforest. Usually alone outside the breeding season, multiple birds may inhabit a relatively small area without directly cohabiting.

Australian Spotted Cuscus *Spilocuscus nudicaudatus*

Angus McNab

More commonly thought of as a Papua New Guinean mammal, this is one of two cuscus species that inhabit the northern rainforests of Cape York Peninsula. Superficially 'possum'-like in appearance and behaviour, it is an arboreal mammal with a predominantly naked, prehensile tail. The bare, pointed face has notably forwards-facing, reddish eyes and small ears that can be hard to discern due to the thick fur. Colour patterns vary between individuals, but most are shades of greyish-white with varying amounts of mottling (more pronounced in males than females). Some individuals may be completely white, yet somehow still blend into their environment. Although nocturnal, it is common to see the species during the early morning.

Bare-backed Fruit-bat *Dobsonia magna*

Angus McNab

Very similar to the better-known flying-foxes of northern and eastern Australia, the Bare-backed Fruit-bat is a large, fruit-eating bat, named for the lack of fur on its back. Unlike the flying-foxes it does not roost in large camps but tends to roost in small numbers. Rather than being furred, the skin has the same leathery texture as the wings. The head and underparts are furred, darker black on the head and browner on the underparts. Like the flying-foxes, this species plays an important role in spreading seeds throughout the forest and tropical woodland. It is the only fruit-bat known to inhabit caves, though it may roost in a variety of habitats including car ports and balconies.

Cape York Melomys *Melomys capensis*

A common inhabitant of rainforest and surrounding sclerophyll forest, this species replaces the Fawn-footed Melomys (p. 57), which occurs down most of the east Australian coast into New South Wales. Its buff-orange-brown upperparts meet sharply with clean white underparts; the feet are also white. Melomys species can be

Angus McNab

difficult to distinguish from other rodents, but have a distinctly 'roman nose' and mosaic-scaled tail that is not seen in co-occurring rodents. Agile climbers, melomys can be seen from ground level up into the canopy as they search for seeds and fruits during the night. Nests are grass lined and usually in a tree hollow, and juveniles are carried around by the mother. As the juveniles age, they cling to her back, before eventually being forced to live on their own.

Giant White-tailed Rat *Uromys caudimaculatus*

One of Australia's largest and most formidable rats, you could confuse this species for a possum when it sits up in a tree. Weighing almost 1kg, it is capable of eating through tin cans and can bite straight to the bone. Therefore, it is best to not get too close to it; its hissing should be an obvious deterrent. Uniformly grey above, the underparts are white and the large, clawed feet are pale pinkish. The long tail varies in colour and is typically darker at the base, with varying amounts of white towards the tip. The diet is varied but contains fruits, invertebrates and larger seeds that other rodents lack the strength to crack open.

Angus McNab

Long-nosed Echymipera *Echymipera rufescens*

Angus McNab

Known by multiple names, the Long-nosed Echymipera, Spiny-cheeked Bandicoot or Rufous Spiny Bandicoot is one of the least-seen bandicoots in the tropical rainforest and grassland of Cape York. This moderately sized bandicoot is dark-furred overall, with both paler and darker hairs throughout the upper coat. The cheeks and feet are pale and the snout is long with little hairs at the tip. Unlike other bandicoots, it only has four pairs of upper incisors (not that you can see them). Little is known about its behaviour, although like all bandicoots it is omnivorous. Throughout the night it searches the forest floor for invertebrates such as centipedes and fallen fruits, or digs for tubers and roots.

Brown-headed Snake *Glyphodon tristis*

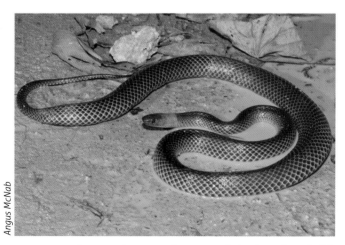

Angus McNab

A robust snake with a pugnacious reputation, this species is commonly seen crossing roads and tracks throughout the rainforest at night. The glossy-brown dorsal scales shine reflectively and have a slim pale edging that gives a reticulated look, which differs from the pale ventral scales. The broad nape-band is varying shades of yellowish-orange and extends on to the rear of the head and sides of the face, and at times around the small eyes. Growing to 1m in length, its diet is predominantly forest floor-dwelling skinks. It can inflict a medically significant dangerous bite and most individuals are quick to defend themselves. VENOMOUS

Cape Melville Bar-lipped Skink
Glaphyromorphus othelarrni

Long, elongate, yet robust skinks, the bar-lipped skinks are leaf-litter specialists. Like other members of the group, this species spends much of its time under logs and leaf litter. It is restricted to Cape Melville, and has been recorded at elevations from 110m to the top of the plateau. A glossy skink, the back is a rich brown that becomes silvery-grey on the flanks. Black bars run across the dorsal surface from the nape to the mid-back, where they fade to small, faint rows of spots. These bars form jagged rows on the flanks, which again fade from the mid-flank towards the tail. Bar-lipped skinks are most often seen at dusk.

Conrad Hoskin

Cape Melville Rainbow-skink *Carlia wundalthini*

Restricted to boulder fields covered with rainforest and vine thickets above 400m on the Cape Melville Range, this species was described in 2014. Like most rainbow-skinks, males change colour from their usual non-breeding brown to have an impressive orange flush to the neck, throat and flanks during the breeding season. Females, although more drab, are quite pretty, with a broken line of small, paler tan-brown dots along the flanks. Separating this skink from others in Cape Melville's rainforest can be done by counting the number of fingers, as it only has four, while most skinks have five. By day it can be seen basking in small patches of sunlight, or foraging through the leaf litter in search of small invertebrates.

Conrad Hoskin

Giant Tree Gecko *Pseudothecadactylus australis*

Angus McNab

Aptly named, this species is one of Australia's largest geckoes. That said, it is still able to squeeze itself into tiny tree hollows to avoid predators. Well camouflaged against a tree, this grey-brown lizard has pale bars or blotches down the back and on to the nape, and a notably white chin and throat. A nocturnal species, it is often seen with little more than its head poking out of a tree hollow, a position it may sit in for hours before coming out to hunt. Having large, sticky toe-pads allows it to move high into the canopy to find food and retreat sites, and it is therefore rarely seen on the ground.

Green Python *Morelia viridis*

Angus McNab

The jewel of the Cape York Peninsula, the Green Python is a small, slender, vibrant emerald-green python renowned for its beauty worldwide. Born electric-yellow with small brown markings, individuals turn green as they age, with some acquiring white flecks that may form a vertebral stripe down the back. The species is most commonly seen in one of two positions, either resting in a tight coil during the day up a tree, or in an ambush position low to the ground at night. As ambush predators, these pythons sit low over small mammal trails waiting for potential prey such as the Cape York Melomys (p. 37) to run past. Within Australia the around 1.5m Green Python is restricted to the rainforest of the Iron and McIlwraith Ranges.

McIlwraith Leaf-tailed Gecko *Orraya occultus*

Anders Zimny

Almost invisible on the moss-covered granite boulders along the creeks of the McIlwraith Range, this large, flat gecko sits and waits for prey. During the night, it moves slowly from its diurnal retreat in cracks and crevices between the rocks to a hunting position. It is mottled grey-brown with rows of small tubercles down the back and flanks, and stands on long, spindly legs with its body raised just slightly from the rock's surface. If it was not for the bright eyeshine that individuals give off under light, you might never see it. The teardrop-shaped, lightly banded tail has spiked edges that further break up the outline.

Cape Melville Tree Frog *Litoria andiirrmalin*

Angus McNab

This tree frog is varying shades of mottled brown on the dorsum, with a greyish-white ventral surface. The back and head may have sporadically dispersed, faint yellow blotches. Not only is it restricted to Cape Melville, it is also limited to the boulder fields surrounding a very small number of streams that flow from below the boulder field. This potentially makes it one of Australia's most range-restricted frogs, as individuals rarely move from stream-side vine thickets. The young are darker than the adults, with small black blotches along the flanks, and a sharp colour delineation between the brown back and paler flanks.

41

Cape York Graceful Tree Frog *Litoria bella*

A bright green and yellow frog, this species spends much of its time high in the canopy during the dry season, sitting in a water-conserving position. During the wet season and after rain events, it climbs down to creeks, streams and ephemeral pools to breed. It is during this time of year that you can properly appreciate the beauty of this frog, with its finely granular green dorsum, yellow belly, yellow eyes, bright bluish-purple thighs and vibrant orange feet with large toe-pads. Similarities may be noted with the Graceful Tree Frog, from which it was taxonomically split in 2016, which occurs commonly down the east coast of Australia to the central coast of New South Wales.

Angus McNab

Fringed Tree Frog *Litoria eucnemis*

This species is the most northerly occurring and isolated member of the Green-eyed Tree Frog complex. It inhabits rainforest streams and creeks of the Iron, McIlwraith and Huon Ranges. Males come down to the water's edge to call from ferns and other low-hanging vegetation during the wet season. During the dry season, individuals may move a considerable distance from streams and waterbodies to sit high in the canopy. The colour and pattern varies considerably between individuals – some have spots, blotches or mossy patterns, while colours vary between yellows, browns and greens, but all have a green upper margin to the golden iris, fringed toes and a pointed lappet on each heel.

Angus McNab

Long-snouted Frog *Litoria longirostris*

Restricted to the creeks and rainforest streams of the McIlwraith Range, this is a small, pale grey-brown to dark brown frog that is covered in small tubercles. In addition to the tubercles across the body, there is a notable tubercle situated above each eye. Named for its elongated snout, which is obvious and triangular in profile, it has one other unique feature not seen in any other Australian frog. Rather than laying its eggs in the water, the eggs are deposited on vegetation or rocks that overhang the water. As the tadpoles hatch they drop into the water from their raised position.

Anders Zimny

Rattling Nursery Frog *Cophixalus crepitans*

At less than 15mm in size this species is little more than a camouflaged speck among the leaf litter. The body is reddish-brown with fine black markings on the legs and a dark, loosely 'W'-shaped mark between the shoulders. The mouth tends to be darker than the rest of the body and there is a black spot behind the eye. In wet conditions males elevate themselves into shrubs and call from raised positions. The buzzing, rattling call they give is almost insect-like. As in some other species of *Cophixalus*, reproduction in this species is not fully understood, but is assumed to involve direct development.

Anders Zimny

Kutini-Payamu (Iron Range) National Park

Kutini-Payamu (Iron Range) National Park and the surrounding area is home to 15 endemic bird species, out of almost 240 in total. The national park was gazetted in 1981 and contains the largest area of lowland rainforest in Australia, covering 346km² (expanded from 330km² in 2011). It is bordered by mangroves and beaches to the east and the heathland of the Tozer Range to the west. Lockhart River is the northernmost town on the east coast of Australia and is a remote, coastal indigenous community home to a mix of Aboriginals and Torres Strait Islanders. In 1987 the community was given a trust title of the lands and administration of the lands. The traditional name of Iron Range is Kutini-Payamu, which means Cassowary (Kutini) and Rainbow Serpent (Payamu).

At the beginning of the Second World War an American air base (predominantly for bombers) was set up at Lockhart River, and the dense rainforests were used to train troops in jungle warfare before they were sent to south-east Asia.

Although wildlife is abundant here year round, the best time of year to visit is during the wet season (when

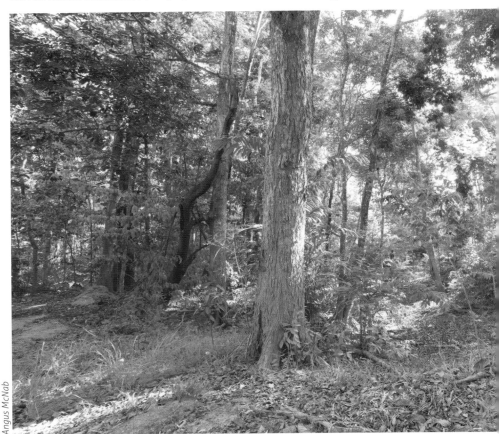

Angus McNab

Kutini-Payamu National Park is a popular birding destination, with almost 240 species recorded here

seasonal migrants have arrived), although this may mean that you have to fly in. It is important to familiarize yourself with the local bird and frog calls, because you will probably hear the animals before you see them. Similarly, the many skinks and small reptiles are often given away by the rustling of the leaf litter as they search for prey. Unfortunately, many of the species that occur here are very difficult to find and photograph, particularly species like the Trumpet Manucode.

GPS Coordinates
-12.77971, 143.29889 (Ranger station)

Getting There
By road from Cairns, take Highway 1 to Mareeba (65km), then follow route

81 north for 595km before turning right on to Portland Road for the final 105km to Lockhart River and Chilli Beach, 20km further. Lockhart Airport is serviced by Skytrans out of Cairns Airport. There are no passenger services by water, but vehicles can be freighted by barge between Cairns and Lockhart River (see www.seaswift.com.au), which takes three days.

Tracks & Trails
The Chilli Beach Walking Track (720m, return) runs between Chilli Beach and the camp grounds to the north, and is an excellent spot for many good species. Searching around any of the three camp grounds, Gordon Creek, Rainforest or Cook's Hut should provide access to all the rainforest species in the park. Until recently the Old Coen Road Walking Track has provided a fantastic walk through the rainforest, across rainforest streams, and has been the only access into the rainforest off the main road; however, Cyclone Trevor, which caused devastating damage to the park, has affected the track.

Fees & Permits
Fees are not payable for day trips but are payable for camping in Queensland national parks and reserves.

Facilities
Twenty-four-hour public toilets are located on Portland Road and at the Cook's Hut camping area.

Services Nearby
Lockhart River (<10km) has a hospital, police station, fuel, groceries, postal service, EFTPOS, airport, car hire, four-wheel-drive taxi, fishing charters and a sea barge service to Cairns. Archer River Roadhouse (140km) has fuel, accommodation and food.

KULLA (McIlwraith Range) National Park

The KULLA (McIlwraith Range) National Park is the second jointly managed national park in Queensland, named as an acronym of local clan groups, Kaanju, Umpila, Lama Lama and Ayapathu. Jointly managed by the KULLA Land Trust and Queensland Government, the park covers 1,587.9km² of rugged terrain along the Great Dividing Range. The majority of the McIlwraith Range is inaccessible due to the escarpments, granite gorges, waterfalls, rainforest and mountains throughout the area, which peak at 824m above sea level.

The park contains more than 260 bird species, 60 mammals, 80 reptiles, 20 frogs and what is considered the largest undisturbed tropical rainforest area in Australia. There is a huge diversity of significant plants, many of which are endemic. There are, of course, also numerous endemic animals, such as the McIlwraith Leaf-tailed Gecko and Long-snouted Frog, and isolated populations of species

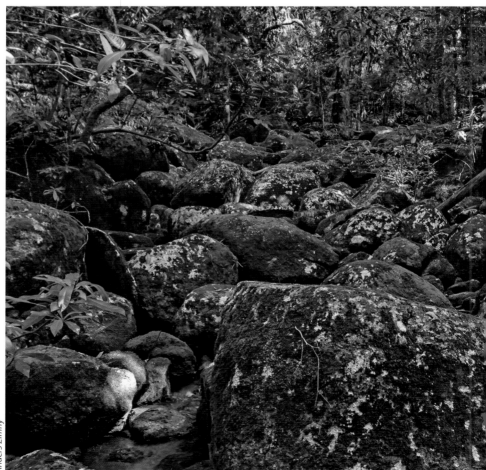

Anders Zimny

Mountain stream on western side of range

such as the Southern Cassowary. This is the southernmost point at which the majority of fauna that overlaps between Australia and New Guinea occurs, species like the Southern Common Cuscus, Green Python, Palm Cockatoo and Magnificent Riflebird. The high rainfall, approximately 1,500mm per year, is of benefit not only to the rainforest species but also to those of the wet sclerophyll forest and other vegetation communities on the surrounding plains, where the water runs from the west side of the range and out to the Gulf, through the Archer River. There is no public access to the park. To enter it you are required to have permits from both the Queensland Government and the KULLA Land Trust.

GPS Coordinates
-13.87736, 143.33212

Getting There
From Cairns, take Highway 1 to Mareeba (65km), then follow route 81 north for 511km to Coen. Access to the park requires Queensland Government and KULLA Land Trust permits.

Tracks & Trails
Currently there is no public access to the park.

Fees & Permits
Fees are not payable for day trips but are payable for camping in Queensland national parks and reserves.

Facilities
There are no facilities within the park.

Services Nearby
The town of Coen is just outside the park entrance and has mobile reception and a small number of shops, including a mechanic, pub and general store.

Red Goshawk

Cape Melville National Park

Remote, isolated and challenging to access, Cape Melville is not somewhere that often comes to mind when people think of Cape York rainforests. In part, this is because very few people visit Cape Melville and significantly fewer visit its rainforest. Isolated on top of a 600m granite boulder mountain that comprises the Melville Range, the rainforest is inaccessible and there is no way through the boulder fields to the Hoop Pine *Araucaria cunninghamii* covered plateau. Jointly managed by the Cape Melville, Flinders and Howick Islands Aboriginal Corporation and the Queensland Government, the park was originally gazetted in 1973 and extended in 1996 and 2005.

Although the 1,370km² national park is home to more than 190 bird species, 15 mammals, 40 reptiles and 159 frogs, there are very few rainforest-reliant species and the majority of these animals occur in the hot, dry savannah that surrounds the Melville Range. The isolated rainforest is important for a number of species, particularly birds that can retreat to the shade and cooler temperatures that are difficult to avoid on the hot dry savannah.

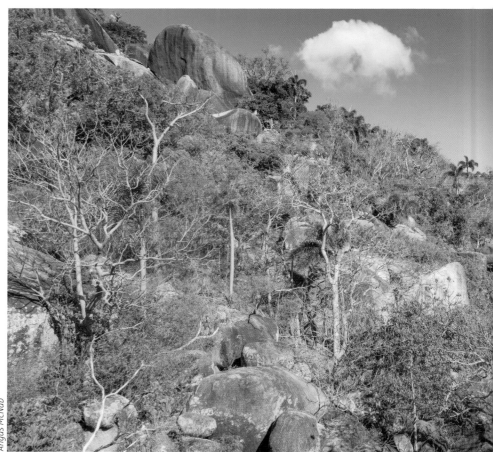

Angus McNab

Cape Melville National Park's rainforest is located at the top of a 600m granite boulder mountain range

There are five endemic reptiles and three endemic frogs, all of which occur in the rainforest and surrounding boulder fields. The latter also have numerous endemic plants, most famously the Foxtail Palm *Wodyetia bifurcata*, which was once restricted to the Melville Range but is now cultivated in gardens around the world.

GPS Coordinates
-14.43005, 144.56565

Getting There
From Cairns, take Highway 1 to Mareeba (65km), then follow route 81 north for 247km to Laura, turn right on to Endeavour Battlecamp Road, and continue for 217km to Cape Melville, via Kalpowar Crossing. From Cooktown it can take up to 12 hours, driving 180km via Wakooka outstation. Four-wheel-drive vehicles are required as there are large sections of soft sand along Endeavour Battlecamp Road.

Tracks & Trails
While extensive areas of the park are accessible and you can walk and fish on the beautiful beaches or birdwatch in the savannah woodland, there is very little access to the rainforest. The Nookai day-use area provides access to a beautiful small freshwater creek that flows from deep within the boulder field. This area is the only accessible patch of rainforest in the park.

Fees & Permits
There are no access fees, but fees are payable for camping in Queensland national parks and reserves.

Facilities
There are no facilities in the Cape Melville National Park. All visitors must be self-sufficient and prepared for the remote area. Camping is available on the eastern side of Bathurst Bay near Cape Melville (Crocodile, Wongai, Oystercatcher and Granite camping areas) and at Ninian Bay, and must be booked in advance online. Cape Melville National Park (Cape York Peninsula Aboriginal Land/CYPAL) is closed throughout the wet season every year from 1 December to 31 July (inclusive). These dates may vary depending on weather and road conditions.

Services Nearby
There are no services in proximity to Cape Melville National Park. The closest towns are Cooktown (180km) and Laura (217km).

Wet Tropics

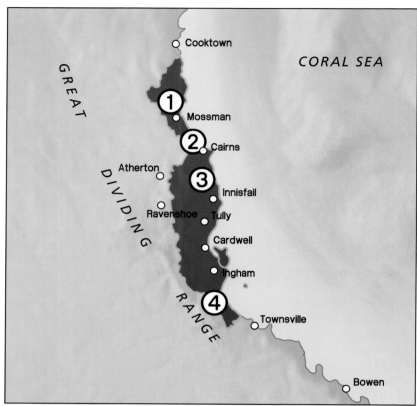

1. Daintree National Park 2. Kuranda National Park 3. Wooroonooran National Park
4. Paluma Range National Park

The Wet Tropics bioregion covers an area of 19,929km² between
Cooktown and Townsville, and contains the largest area of rainforest
in Australia. The rainforest that remains is just a portion of what
once covered the broader area. Being rich in large trees, the area was
heavily logged for the Kauri Pine *Agathis robusta,* Red Cedar *Toona
ciliata,* Silky Oak *Grevillea robusta,* and walnut and ash species, which
caused significant fragmentation of the rainforest landscape. Add
to this mining, agriculture, horticulture and dairy farming, and the
rainforest has changed significantly since European arrival. However,
these practices founded or increased the size of a number of towns,
including Atherton, Cairns, Cardwell, Ingham, Innisfail, Mossman, the
Palm Islands, Ravenshoe, Townsville and Tully, which now provide
access to the World Heritage Wet Tropics of Queensland sites.

Angus McNab

Rainforest near Kuranda

A large proportion (8,944km²) of the bioregion is protected by World Heritage status, and includes 57 national parks, one marine park, 26 conservation parks, 19 state forests, 21 forest reserves and 94 nature refuges. Contained within these are more than 4,508 bird species, 130 mammals, 170 reptiles, 60 frogs, 230 butterflies, 4,600 plants and 900 fungi, many of which are endemic and threatened.

Rainforest makes up 34 per cent of the bioregion and extends from sea level to the top of Queensland's tallest mountains (Bartle Frere at 1,622m and Bellenden Ker at 1,593m). While hot and humid year round at sea level, temperatures can drop to freezing on the Atherton Tablelands. Rainfall is seasonal, yet Australia's wettest place, Bellenden Ker, receives an average of 8,140mm rain per year. The lowland areas receive an average of more than 4,000mm per year. The highest rainfall events coincide with cyclones, which over the past years have included category 5 cyclones such as Larry and Yasi.

Key Species

BIRDS
Atherton Scrubwren, Barred Cuckoo-shrike, Black Butcherbird, Blue-faced Parrot-finch, Bower's Shrikethrush, Bridled Honeyeater, Buff-breasted Paradise Kingfisher, Chowchilla, Dusky Myzomela, Golden Bowerbird, Green Oriole, Grey-headed Robin, Lesser Sooty Owl, Lovely Fairy-wren, Macleay's Honeyeater, Pale-yellow Robin, Papuan Frogmouth, Pied Monarch, Southern Cassowary, Tooth-billed Bowerbird, Victoria's Riflebird, Wompoo Fruit-dove, Yellow-breasted Boatbill, Yellow-spotted Honeyeater.

MAMMALS
Atherton Antechinus, Bennett's Tree Kangaroo, Daintree River Ring-tailed Possum, Diadem Leaf-nosed Bat, Eastern Blossom-bat, Fawn-footed Melomys, Giant White-tailed Rat, Green Ring-tailed Possum, Herbert River Ring-tailed Possum, Least Blossom-bat, Lemuroid Ring-tailed Possum, Long-tailed Pygmy-possum, Lumholtz's Tree Kangaroo, Musky Rat-kangaroo, Spectacled Flying-fox, Torresian Striped Possum.

REPTILES
Amethystine Python, Atherton Tableland Mulch-skink, Boyd's Forest Dragon, Chameleon Gecko, Estuarine Crocodile, Four-fingered Shadeskink, Limbless Snake-tooth Skink, Northern Bar-sided Skink, Northern Crowned Snake, Northern Leaf-tailed Gecko, Pale-lipped Shadeskink, Prickly Forest Skink, Red-throated Rainbow-skink, Slaty-grey Snake, Yellow-blotched Forest Skink.

AMPHIBIANS
Australian Lace-lid, Australian Woodfrog, Beautiful Nursery Frog, Buzzing Nursery Frog, Common Mist Frog, Green-eyed Tree Frog, Kuranda Tree Frog, Mottled Barred Frog, Northern Barred Frog, Orange-thighed Tree Frog, Rain Frog, Robust Whistlefrog, Southern Ornate Nursery Frog, Tapping Nursery Frog, Waterfall Frog, White-browed Whistlefrog.

INVERTEBRATES
Cairns Birdwing, Golden Orb-weaving Spider, Hercules Moth, Ulysses Swallowtail, velvet worm.

Peter Rowland

Spotted Catbird

Buff-breasted Paradise Kingfisher *Tanysiptera sylvia*

Angus McNab

Arguably the prettiest Australian kingfisher, this species migrates between Australia and Papua New Guinea each year, spending the summer months (wet season – November–April) in northern Australia's rainforest and vine thickets. Individuals are deep blue with a bright orange breast and partial collar, thick red bill, black eye-stripe, white back and long white tail streamers (which are shorter in females than in males). Migrating to Australia to breed, it finds a suitable termite mound in which to build its nest. Spending much of its time below the canopy, it can be difficult to detect despite its vibrant colouration. Fortunately it is relatively vocal, giving away its location. Kingfisher Park (Julatten) has long been a favoured breeding site for the species and remains one of the best locations to see this bird.

Chowchilla *Orthonyx spaldingii*

Mark Sanders

The northern replacement of the Australian Logrunner (p. 89), this sexually dimorphic species inhabits the rainforest floor. Both males and females have a dark head, neck, back and wings, with white underparts and a blue eye-ring. The male has completely white underparts, while the female has a buff-orange throat and breast. Juveniles are brownish-orange and finely streaked or barred. Highly vocal, the birds can regularly be heard calling to their partner or other members of their covey, which are rarely far away. The onomatopoeic call gives rise to the species' name. You can often sit and watch as individuals scratch their way along track edges in search of invertebrates. Although capable of flight, Chowchillas are most commonly seen walking, with flight used to cross open areas and escape threats.

Golden Bowerbird *Prionodura newtoniana*

Camouflage is obviously not important to the male of this species, which is bright golden yellow, with pale brown upperparts and face. The female is comparatively drab, being shades of pale grey and brown and much harder to spot in the rainforest. The male spends much of his time around a tall, elongated bower that is constructed from sticks between two saplings, with a small, well-defined display perch surrounded by moss and lichens. The call of this species is unlike that of any other Australian bird, an electronic buzz that must be heard to be believed, as you would not initially think it came from a bird. Far from abundant, this species is widely dispersed throughout higher elevation rainforests. One of the best-known, reused and photographed bowers is along the Birthday Creek Falls trail in Paluma.

Angus McNab

Grey-headed Robin *Heteromyias cinereifrons*

A subtly beautiful robin endemic to the rainforest of north Queensland, this is one of five robins in the Wet Tropics bioregion. The shadows from the canopy often mute the colours of this small bird, which has a grey head and breast that contrast with the brown ear-coverts, brown back, rufous flanks and pink legs. As it flies between perches, the black-edged white wing-bar flashes brightly. Juveniles are mostly unstreaked orangish across most of the body. Hopping across the forest floor, the birds are often seen flicking at leaves on the ground in search of prey, or looking at the ground from an elevated position on either a thin branch or tree trunk.

Angus McNab

Macleay's Honeyeater *Xanthotis macleayanus*

Angus McNab

This medium-sized honeyeater is relatively common throughout the Wet Tropics rainforest. Endemic to the Wet Tropics bioregion, it is a multitude of colours. The plumage is predominantly shades of brown with a greyish-white streaked throat, white-edged feathers in the upperwings, and a yellow shoulder-patch that extends on to the breast. A dark cap contrasts with the orange skin around the eye, which encompasses the thin white eye-stripe that extends from the black bill. Multiple individuals may be seen together in loose flocks foraging in both the mid-storey and upper canopies. Breeding occurs before the wet season and eggs are laid in a small, bowl-shaped nest.

Pale-yellow Robin *Tregellasia capito*

Angus McNab

The Wet Tropics equivalent of the White-faced Robin (p. 35), this small robin has a pale yellow belly, that is not as brightly coloured as in the other 'yellow robins'. Similarly, the pale greyish head, white lores, white throat, olive-green mantle and olive-grey wings are more subtle than in other robins. The legs are pinkish. Individuals regularly perch themselves on both broad and narrow vertical trunks. The young are a mottled orange-yellow-brown and do not take long to attain adult colouration. Breeding occurs during the summer months and young individuals can be prolific at times. Voracious hunters, the birds regularly grab small invertebrates from the ground and fly back to a perch to consume them.

Southern Cassowary *Casuarius casuarius*

Not the tallest, but Australia's heaviest native bird, the Southern Cassowary is a rainforest specialist that has had over 240 plant species recorded in its diet. It is well known to eat fruits and seeds, which are evident in the scats that are commonly seen along walking trails. Large and black with a vibrantly coloured head, neck and wattles, a large head casque and prehistoric dinosaur-looking feet, this

Anders Zimny

species is unique among Australia's birds; furthermore it is flightless. However, it is adept at moving through the dense undergrowth of the rainforest in silence. Usually solitary, young are raised by the male. Chicks, which are rarely far from the father, are small with brown and white stripes that run the length of the body. Adults can be dangerous if approached while with their young.

Tooth-billed Bowerbird *Scenopoeetes dentirostris*

Unlike other bowerbirds, the Tooth-billed Bowerbird male does not construct a 'bower', but rather meticulously cleans a space on the rainforest floor and strategically places leaves pale side up across his 'display platform'. This can be a large area up to 3m wide and usually around the base of a small tree or sapling. A perch from which the male can call is situated above or close to the display area. The leaves used for display are selectively chewed from their tree by the bowerbird. Both the male and female have dark brown upperparts with a heavily streaked breast. The throat and breast are darker brown, fading to white in the underparts. This species does not occur throughout the tropical rainforests, but is confined to higher elevation rainforests above 500m.

Angus McNab

55

Victoria's Riflebird *Ptiloris victoriae*

Angus McNab

A member of the bird-of-paradise family (Paradisaeidae), Victoria's Riflebird is one of three riflebird species in Australia. The glossy black males are well known for the incredible performance that they put on to impress females from their display posts. During the display the wings are raised over the head, showing the glossy blue-black throat-shield and making the olive-green underparts more visible. This is done while calling and showing the bright yellow mouthparts. The females, although not as showy, are still fantastic-looking birds. They have brown upperparts and heavily patterned underparts with rows of brown chevrons that change from whitish under the throat and breast to buff-orange on the belly. Both sexes have a long, slightly curved bill.

Diadem Leaf-nosed Bat *Hipposideros diadema*

Angus McNab

Unlike most of the leaf-nosed bats that hunt small invertebrates, the Diadem Leaf-nosed Bat is also a predator of small vertebrates. Invertebrates are a major part of its diet, but prey items also include small birds, frogs, reptiles and potentially other bats. The larger size of this bat and its strong jaws make it a formidable hunter. The fur is predominantly tan-brown with large off-white patches down the back that vary in size and shape on each individual. The ears are large and rounded with pointed tips, and the noseleaf is quite broad, while the eyes are very small. Roosting bats are seen in caves, mine shafts and culverts that retain high humidity levels. Only a single young is born each year.

Fawn-footed Melomys *Melomys cervinipes*

This melomys is highly variable in appearance, but generally dull reddish to orange-brown, with a greyish face and a thin, scaly, grey-brown to blackish, sparsely furred tail (similar in length to head–body). The underparts, including the feet, are white to creamish-fawn. This is an arboreal species that feeds at night on leaves and fruits, and shelters during the day in a spherical nest of leaves and grasses in a tree. Females have four teats and normally 2–3 young in a litter, which are weaned at three weeks of age. Several litters may be raised during the long breeding season. Monogamous breeding pairs, with established territories, may be formed. Not rainforest restricted, the species can be found in a number of forested habitats.

Angus McNab

Green Ring-tailed Possum *Pseudochirops archeri*

Greenish, olive-green or lichen-green are good colour descriptions of this possum; it is notably different in colour from any of the other eight possums that inhabit the Wet Tropics rainforest. Although a nocturnal species, during the morning it can be seen moving through the canopy in search of a place to sleep. It does not build a drey but curls into a ball on an exposed branch using its back feet to hold on, while the prehensile white-tipped tail curls next to the head. Eating leaves, fruits and seeds, this is one of the few species that can eat the Stinging Tree *Dendrocnide moroides,* which causes extreme discomfort to any person who even brushes up against the plant.

Aniket Sardana

Lumholtz's Tree Kangaroo *Dendrolagus lumholtzi*

Angus McNab

One of two species of Australian tree kangaroo, both of which are restricted to the Wet Tropics bioregion, this one is the smaller, more commonly seen one. The body is pale to dark brown with darker to black extremities (feet, hands and tail-tip). The face is dark grey-black with small ears. Although the thought of a kangaroo in a tree is hard to comprehend, it is an extremely agile, excellent climber and can move through the canopy with ease while foraging for leaves from a range of rainforest trees. It can scale a tree in seconds and is quick across flat ground, where it is at most risk of predation. When concealed within the tree foliage it is difficult to spot. Unfortunately, habitat loss has decimated the potential distribution of the species and it no longer occurs in lowland regions (<800m).

Musky Rat-kangaroo *Hypsiprymnodon moschatus*

Michael Schmid

The small size, rat-kangaroo name and odd rat-like appearance may cause some confusion, but this is Australia's smallest macropod (270mm tall), not a rodent. Spending most of the day in the dense undergrowth, this grey-faced, rufous-reddish-brown mammal searches for seeds, fruits, fungi and invertebrates in the leaf litter. Although individuals do move into open patches of forest, this very wary animal is quick to move to cover once disturbed. The dark hands, feet and tail are similar to those of a bandicoot (but darker) and used for locomotion, using all four legs to move across the forest floor rather than jumping on the rear legs like a typical kangaroo. It inhabits rainforests from sea level to high-elevation areas, and can be commonly seen around Lake Barrine.

Spectacled Flying-fox *Pteropus conspicillatus*

Angus McNab

A large flying-fox, this species is readily identifiable by the tan brown 'spectacles' that surround the eyes and extend on to the muzzle. The nape matches the spectacles, while the rest of the fur and wings are dark brown-black. The species plays an important role in the distribution of rainforest trees. Roosting in large colonies, it moves through the rainforest during the night in search of fruits. Habitat loss is a significant threatening process for this species, as much of the Wet Tropics rainforest has been cleared for agriculture. As a result, its native food sources are in short supply and it is known to raid orchards, causing tension with local fruit growers. Camps are now regularly disturbed and moved along to appease fruit growers, councils and locals who dislike the noise and smell of the flying-fox camps.

Torresian Striped Possum *Dactylopsila trivirgata*

Angus McNab

This is Australia's only black and white possum. A moderately sized possum, it has white underparts and white back stripes that contrast with a black back. The dark face has a white 'Y'-shaped mark that extends between the ears to join the back stripes. The fluffy tail is black with a white tip. A highly active, arboreal possum, it is often heard before it is seen as it moves loudly through the canopy. Feeding on nectar, fruits and invertebrates, it is something of a generalist, but has a specialist fourth toe that can be used to extract grubs from wood, in a similar fashion to the Aye-aye *Daubentonia madagascariensis* of Madagascar.

Amethystine Python *Simalia amethistina*

Angus McNab

The Amethystine Python is Australia's largest snake, growing to a length of almost 6m. Being a python, it does not kill prey with venom, but by constriction. It is capable of killing a human and should be considered dangerous. Although much smaller than the larger pythons overseas, it has more than enough strength to constrict an adult human. Prey usually consists of smaller animals such as possums, the Australian Brush Turkey (p. 88), cuscus and macropods. Patterning varies throughout the range, but throughout the Wet Tropics individuals are usually dark backed with a series of jagged tan-brown bars across the dorsal surface from neck to tail, with a pale stripe that runs mid-dorsally along the length of the body. The head has enlarged scales, which distinguishes it from other rainforest pythons.

Boyd's Forest Dragon *Lophosaurus boydii*

Angus McNab

Arguably Australia's most stunning lizard, this dragon relies on its ability to remain still to avoid detection. Perching on vertical trunks along path edges, it is often fully exposed but remains difficult to detect. The body and long tail are shades of green with black barring across the back, and a vertebral crest runs the length of the body and on to the tail. The large, multicoloured, triangular head has a distinguished head-crest and rows of small white throat-spikes down the length of the gular pouch. Unlike most reptiles this species is poikilothermic rather than homeothermic, meaning that it does not bask in the sun but rather regulates its body temperature according to changes in the ambient air temperature. During the breeding season, eggs are laid in a small hole dug into the rainforest floor.

Chameleon Gecko *Carphodactylus laevis*

Uniquely shaped among Australia's geckoes, the Chameleon Gecko is tan-brown with small black and white spots across the back. It has a black and white banded, carrot-shaped tail and a large head with dark patches in front of each eye. Moving slowly across the forest floor on thin legs in search of prey, it is most commonly spotted sitting about 100mm above the ground in a head-down position waiting to ambush prey. As in all geckoes, the tail can be dropped and regenerated, but when a Chameleon Gecko drops its tail, it not only wriggles but can produce a sound to further distract any would-be predators.

Estuarine Crocodile *Crocodylus porosus*

This is the largest of Australia's reptiles and one of the most dangerous of predators. Growing up to 6m in length, and with the strength to take down and carry a full-grown cow, this is a species to be cautious of in all waterways of northern Australia. It is highly mobile and can cross long distances (8km plus) without water. Extremely stealthy and patient hunters, crocodiles are capable of quickly recognizing patterns in behaviour and learn the habits of their prey. Males are notably larger than females and will fight for territories during the breeding season. The eggs are laid during the wet season in a mound of vegetation constructed and cared for by the female. Females are particularly dangerous when guarding their nest. Some parental care is shown by female crocodiles, a trait not seen in many reptile species.

Angus McNab

John Harris

Northern Crown Snake *Cacophis churchilli*

Ground-dwelling and utilizing a range of shelter types, this is a small, secretive snake that is rarely seen. Spending its day under rocks, logs and debris, it comes out at night to hunt sleeping skinks. The skin is glossy and uniformly reddish-brown to grey-brown. A small, golden nape-band crosses from one side of the nape to the other. The crown is darker brown and surrounded by pale facial markings and flecking that extend from the rostral scale through the eyes to join the nape-band. The ventral surfaces are dark grey. Although not considered to be a dangerous snake, it is a member of the elapid family; the effects of a bite vary between people and can cause considerable discomfort. VENOMOUS

Angus McNab

Pale-lipped Shadeskink *Saproscincus basiliscus*

This common rainforest skink is a quick and agile species. It spends its nights sleeping on exposed branches, ferns and other vegetation, often overhanging or close to streams. A thin-bodied skink with a pointed face, the body is light brown, occasionally with a reddish flush and both dark and pale flecking along the length of the body and tail. The throat and lower lip are paler, often yellow with brown flecking. A dark stripe runs from behind the eye to just beyond the armpit, where it dissipates. Like in many shadeskinks, the body is iridescent rather than glossy – a characteristic that can be seen as it moves into sunny patches to bask. An active hunter, it can often be seen chasing flies and other small flying invertebrates, particularly along the water's edge.

Angus McNab

Red-throated Rainbow skink *Carlia rubrigularis*

This is a beautiful small brown rainforest skink. Its upperparts are relatively uniform brown with a pale dorsolateral stripe and darker flanks, both of which vary in intensity. The throat and lower portion of the face are usually a shade of reddish-orange that becomes significantly more pronounced on males that are ready to breed. The upperparts are relatively uniform brown with a pale dorsolateral stripe and darker flanks, both of which vary in intensity. A midlateral stripe may be present on some individuals, but absent in others. This skink, like other *Carlia* species, spends its time on the rainforest floor. Abundant in good habitat, competition is regularly seen as individuals wave their tails at each other, signalling for territories or trying to get the attention of the opposite sex. Fights are common as individuals chase each other across logs and through the leaf litter.

Angus McNab

Slaty-grey Snake *Stegonotus australis*

Thin for its length and with a broad head relative to its neck, the Slaty-grey Snake has a reputation for being quick to strike and is always ready to defend itself. A member of the colubrid family, it is venomous and bites tend to bleed more than would be expected, given the small fangs. This suggests that it secretes compounds in its saliva that act as anticoagulants in bite victims. The glossy skin can be variable shades of browns, greys or blacks, always with paler ventral scales that have a beautiful rainbow iridescent sheen. The scales may be darker edged, giving a reticulated pattern, but this is not always visible. VENOMOUS

Angus McNab

Australian Lace-lid *Litoria dayi*

Anders Zimny

This beautiful moderately sized frog is named for its fantastically laced eyelids. Ranging in colour from tan-browns to pale reds and faint yellows, the skin is granular, more so on the flanks. Individuals vary in pattern, with some having numerous white or yellow, flower-shaped blotches across the back. A red tinge may appear in the thighs, but this also varies between individuals. Living in close association with rainforest streams, particularly around riffle zones, many individuals may be found sitting in close proximity on rocks at the water's edge. Unfortunately, this species has suffered significant decline from the Chytrid Fungus and has not appeared to show signs of recovery at higher elevations above 400m above sea level, like some other chytrid-susceptible rainforest frogs.

Australian Woodfrog *Papurana daemeli*

Angus McNab

Uniquely shaped among Australian frogs, this large frog is the only member of its genus in Australia. Shades of brown cover this pointy-snouted frog, with the back being uniformly brown with some dark flecking. The back legs are solidly barred with darker brown, while the front legs have some barring. Two enlarged skin folds run dorsolaterally from behind the eye. The flanks are covered in small tubercles and the underparts are pale. Easily spotted by its large eyeshine, the species can be present in large numbers sitting on low rocks and stream edges. The call is somewhat comical, almost like laughter.

Common Mist Frog *Litoria rheocola*

A relatively drab little frog, this species is unlike the other torrent frogs in size or shape (with the exception of the Nyakala Frog *Litoria nyakalensis*, which is presumed to be extinct). Inhabiting flowing streams, male Common Mist Frogs rarely move far from riffle zones, where they perch at night and call from rocks and low vegetation year round. Females move considerable distances from streams, probably to avoid males returning to streams to breed. After suffering significant declines due to the Chytrid Fungus, there is some evidence that the species is making a recovery, having returned to some areas from which it was expatriated during the initial declines, and once again occurring at elevations greater than 800m above sea level.

Angus McNab

Kuranda Tree Frog *Litoria myola*

This species has one of the smallest distributions of any frog in Australia, living only in a small number of rainforest streams in and around Myola. Unlike most frogs, it cannot be separated morphologically from its closest relative, the Green-eyed Tree Frog *L. serrata*, with which it overlaps in habitat and distribution. Although statistically smaller, to identify this species you must hear it call, which also means you can only accurately identify males. Appearing like moss on a branch, the mottling and shading of each Kuranda Tree Frog is different. There are varying shades of green, brown and yellow on the tubercle-covered upper surfaces, while the smooth underparts are pale whitish-yellow. Each leg has a slightly fringed outer edge and the heel has a small lappet.

Angus McNab

Northern Barred Frog *Mixophyes schevelli*

Anders Zimny

A large, well-patterned frog, this species occurs in varying shades of brown, with some individuals showing reds and yellows. The back is smooth, with an irregular dorsal stripe that runs the length of the back. Patterns to the sides of the back stripe vary between individuals, and the flanks may be blotched. Both the arms and legs are heavily barred. A narrow dark band runs from the snout, through the eye, to just beyond the tympanum. Ground dwelling, its deep call can be heard from leaf litter close to streams. Barred frogs will call from underground. They bury themselves by day and through the winter periods, but start calling as conditions improve before they have even come to the surface.

Orange-thighed Tree Frog *Litoria xanthomera*

Angus McNab

A brightly coloured tropical tree frog, this species is a beautiful sight to behold when perched in a tree. It has vibrant orange-yellow underparts, bright green upperparts and a red-orange iris surrounding the black pupil of the eye. Relatively large and very vocal after rain, individuals can be seen climbing down from the canopy to find pools and rock crevices in which to lay their eggs. In the right conditions this frog can be abundant, but as the environment dries individuals move back into the canopy and you can go months without seeing them. As you wander creeks and streams you may notice that many individuals are being fed on by *Uranotaenia* mosquitoes, which often sit on the heads and rear legs of these frogs.

Rain Frog *Austrochaperina pluvialis*

Angus McNab

This beautiful little frog has a smooth body, with heavy mottling of dark brown on a light brown base across all the upper surfaces. A light brown stripe runs above the reddish eye, and there is a dark brown stripe from the snout to just beyond the armpit. The underparts are pale grey. Everyone believes that frogs are more vocal and seem happier in wet conditions, but this frog does not call in just a light drizzle, but needs significant rain to get the males calling. The high-pitched call is very insect-like, similar to the sounds of many katydids, and is made from the rainforest floor during heavy rain. Although very loud, the species can be hard to spot as it calls from within the leaf litter or even curled up leaves.

Southern Ornate Nursery Frog *Cophixalus australis*

Angus McNab

The majority of *Cophixalus* species are very small and the Southern Ornate Nursery Frog is no exception. It is a light greyish-brown frog with numerous tubercles and ridges down the dorsum, head and rear legs. The back and head have varying dark markings and flecks, in addition to a thin dark eye-stripe that runs above the tympanum. Telling *Cophixalus* apart can be difficult and they are best separated by call. Unfortunately, the Northern Ornate Nursery Frog *C. ornatus* is essentially indistinguishable where the two species overlap. Highly vocal in wet conditions, detecting this species can also be difficult as it often calls from dense vegetation or leaf litter; pinpointing where the high-pitched call is coming from can be a challenge.

Cairns Birdwing Butterfly *Ornithoptera euphorion*

Angus McNab

Males black; forewing upperside with iridescent green subcostal and tornal bands, and underside with submarginal bands of iridescent green. Hindwing upperside iridescent green with submarginal black spots, and underside iridescent green with submarginal gold-edged black spots. Females larger, black with discal and submarginal pale spots on forewing and submarginal rows of white, black and yellow spots on hindwing. Endemic to wet tropical rainforests in coastal and montane areas, from Cooktown south to Mackay and Eungella. Both sexes fly during the cooler parts of the morning and evening, often well into twilight. During these times they can be easily observed feeding at flowers within a few metres of the ground.

Golden Orb-weaving Spider *Nephila pilipes*

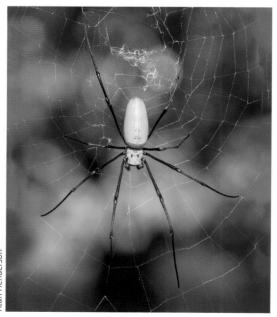

Alan Henderson

A large-bodied, long-legged spider, this species makes large, strong webs that have a golden hue in the sunlight. It is the female that comes to mind when people think of it, as the male is small and rarely seen. Many times larger than the male, the female has a large yellow abdomen and black legs, and sits pride of place in the large web that is strung across tracks and in the eaves of houses. The male usually remains out of sight, in fear of the female, which would happily consume him should he approach too closely at the wrong time. Although appearing dangerous, this species' bite is not toxic to humans.

Ulysses Swallowtail *Papilio ulysses*

Upperside iridescent blue with a black border; females usually with a lesser amount of iridescent blue scaling. The hindwing of both sexes with a large spathulate tail. Underside brown, the forewing with a broad submarginal band and a discal spot grey. Hindwing with a row of submarginal orange-brown spots edged in black, and a medial band of grey scales. Endemic to the Torres Strait Islands and coastal areas of Cape York and the Wet Tropics, south to near Mackay, where it occurs in wet tropical rainforest. It is usually associated with smaller freshwater waterways, but is also present in suburban areas if the host plants, such as Pink Euodia *Melicope elleryana,* are present. Both sexes are fast and frantic in flight, appearing as a series of blue flashes. At rest, the cryptic underside helps to conceal it.

Alan Henderson

Velvet worm *Onychophora* sp.

This worm is named for its velvet texture and worm-like appearance. However, unlike most worms, it has 14–16 clawed legs and appears more like a caterpillar. Only growing to 40–50mm long, this small creature occurs in a range of colours and is often beautifully patterned. Living in, on or under rotting logs, this small peripatid is very cryptic and rarely seen. However, it comes out at night to hunt. Appearing innocent, it predates on small invertebrates, covering them in a digestive slime. There are numerous species of *Onychophora* and the group remains poorly studied but is known to have existed for more than 500 million years.

Stephen Zozaya

Daintree National Park

Split into two sections, Mossman Gorge and Daintree, including Cape Tribulation, Daintree National Park covers an area of 1,162km² and is considered one of the most wonderful parts of the world by Sir David Attenborough. World Heritage listed in 1988 due to its exceptional biodiversity, the park supports more than 60 mammal species, 430 birds, 70 reptiles and 40 amphibians.

Daintree is a small town on the southern side of the Daintree River, nestled between the foothills of the MacDonnell Range to the west and the Coral Sea (including the Great Barrier Reef) to the east.

The Mossman Gorge section is predominantly inaccessible, but the areas that can be reached contain beautiful swimming holes and some fantastic wildlife-filled walks. The Daintree region supports a range of important wildlife habitats, including tropical rainforest, littoral rainforest, mangrove and marine.

The region has great spiritual and cultural significance to the indigenous Eastern Kuku Yalanji people, who lived on the land for tens of thousands of years before European settlement in the area in the late 1870s. The name 'Daintree' was given to the river by explorer George Dalrymple, who named

Dubuji Boardwalk, Cape Tribulation

it after geologist Richard Daintree, whose work ultimately led to the gold rush of 1877 – although he never actually visited the region himself.

Several riverboat charter cruises can be taken along the Daintree River and a vehicle ferry crosses the river at Lower Daintree, allowing access to Cape Tribulation and the ancient Daintree Rainforest.

GPS Coordinates
-16.473690, 145.348134 (Mossman Gorge)
-16.248651, 145.319432 (Daintree Village)

Getting There
By road, follow the Captain Cook Highway (Route 44) and Mossman-

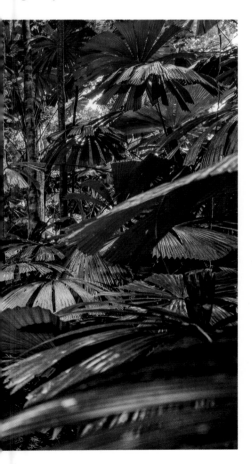

Daintree Road north from Cairns, 80km to Mossman Gorge or 112km to Daintree Village. Private charter boats operate on the river and a vehicle ferry operates across the river at Lower Daintree, giving access to Cape Tribulation (6 a.m.–midnight).

Tracks & Trails
Walking around the Daintree Village can produce a diversity of wildlife within the rainforest, grassland, river and gardens, by both day and night. Stewart Creek Road starts in Daintree Village and walking this section can yield many birds within the dense vegetation on either side of the road – this is perhaps one of the best areas for birdwatching. There are numerous walking trails, including *Baral Marrjanga Track* (270m) at Mossman Gorge (which is wheelchair accessible), *Marrdja Botanical Boardwalk* (1.2km), or, for the serious adventurer, the 7km *Mount Sorrow Track* will put you well into the rainforest. No matter where you walk in the Daintree, be aware of crocodiles, cassowaries, wait-a-while, stinging trees, and marine stingers (jellyfish) if swimming.

Fees & Permits
Fees are payable for camping in Queensland national parks and reserves.

Facilities
Daintree has restaurants, cafes, bars, a postal service, souvenir shops, an information centre and tourism operators. Noah's Beach camp ground provides the opportunity to stay between two World Heritage Sites.

Services Nearby
Most major services (fuel, mechanical repairs, banks, post office, supermarkets, restaurants, chemists, hospital and dental clinics) are located in Mossman, 36km south of the Daintree.

Kuranda National Park

Another part of the Wet Tropics World Heritage Area, the Kuranda National Park encompasses 274.1km² extending from around Palm Cove to the Mowbray River. It is best accessed from Kuranda along Black Mountain Road. The area is an important wildlife corridor linking the northern and southern sections of the Wet Tropics rainforest, which were separated during the last glacial maximum. A tropical climate dominates here year round, with summer being hotter and more humid (27–33 °C) with an average monthly rainfall of more than 375mm in January–March, while winters are drier and slightly cooler, averaging about 26 °C with a rainfall over less than 50mm per month during June–October.

A mountainous region, much of which is not accessible, the park provides habitat for more than 70 mammals, 340 birds, 75 reptiles and 40 amphibians, including the Southern Cassowary, Lumholtz's Tree Kangaroo, Boyd's Forest Dragon and a large number of endangered frog species.

Access to the park is limited during the summer months due to heavy rain.

Tourism Australia

Kuranda Skyrail is a great way to travel from Cairns to Kuranda

The township of Kuranda is at the southern end of the park and there are numerous wildlife-watching opportunities in the town itself.

Kuranda provides many opportunities to learn about the native fauna of the area through the Barron River Cruise, Australian Butterfly Sanctuary, Birdworld, Koala Garden, Kuranda Scenic Railway, the Skyrail, or through any of the amazing rainforest walks from town.

It is important to know that Myrtle Rust *Austropuccinia psidii* has been detected in the area and all efforts to reduce the spread of this disease should be made.

GPS Coordinates
-16.81992, 145.63589

Getting There
The village of Kuranda is a short drive (32km) from Cairns via National Route 1. Kuranda can also be accessed by the Skyrail Rainforest Cableway (departing from Smithfield), or by the Kuranda Scenic Rail (departing from Freshwater Station).

Tracks & Trails
Kuranda National Park is accessed via the Black Mountain Road, of which only the first 18km is accessible to two-wheel-drive vehicles; four-wheel-drive vehicles are required to continue beyond the bitumen. There is only one long walk through the park, the 18km (each way) *Twin Bridges Track* (also used for mountain biking). Mountain bikes, motorbikes and four-wheel drives can be used on the Black Mountain Road, which is four-wheel-drive only accessible for 20km of its 43km length. Around Kuranda there is a network of shorter walks that can be accessed from town, including the *Village Walk* (500m), *Jumrum Creek Conservation Park* (1.4km), the *Jungle Walk* (900m) and the *River* and *Esplanade Walk* (1.5km).

Facilities
Kuranda has all required services, accommodation and phone/internet reception. There are no camping facilities at Kuranda or in the national park. The closest camping is at Speewah Conservation Park.

Services Nearby
Most major services (fuel, mechanical repairs, banks, post office, supermarkets, restaurants, chemists and hospital) are located in Kuranda township and all are available in Cairns (27.2km).

Wooroonooran National Park

A large park in the centre of the Wet Tropics bioregion, Wooroonooran National Park is very diverse, with more than 60 mammal species, 290 birds, 60 reptiles and 30 amphibians.

Covering an area of 1,150km², this large rainforest patch contains Queensland's tallest mountains (Mt Bartle Frere, 1,622m and Mt Bellenden Ker, 1,593m) and is the wettest place in Australia. It contains numerous rivers, including the Johnstone River, creeks and magnificent waterfalls such as Josephine Falls, Nandroya Falls, Tchupala Falls, Kearneys Falls, White's Falls and Silver Creek Falls, some

of which flow through river-formed gorges. To access these water systems, there is an extensive network of walking trails. These also ensure that whether you undertake a short walk, or climb Walsh's Pyramid (922m), or to the top of Mt Bartle Frere, there will be plenty to see by both day and night.

A huge number of endemic species keep avid wildlife watchers on their toes, as tiny *Cophixalus* hop through the leaf litter, Southern Cassowaries roam the rainforest and Lumholtz's Tree Kangaroos bound through the trees. A night walk is highly recommended and reveals a

Angus McNab

Wooroonooran National Park contains an extensive network of walking trails through its tropical rainforest

completely different rainforest from that seen during the day.

Remember to stay vigilant around waterbodies, streams and rivers, as Estuarine Crocodiles occur in the area and are likely to see you before you see them. Divided into two sections, Palmerston and Josephine, this World Heritage Site has much to offer.

GPS Coordinates
-17.59333, 145.74004 (Palmerston)
-17.43231, 145.85951 (Josephine Falls)

Getting There
The north of the park is a 33km drive south of Cairns via the A1 (Bruce Highway), although the park has

many entrance points and is only minutes from Milla Milla, Babinda, Goldsborough and Malanda.

Tracks & Trails
This is a very large park and as such has multiple overnight hikes, a range of short hikes and numerous camp grounds. The longer walks include the *Goldfield Trail* (19km), the *Bartle Frere Trail* (15km) that makes its way to the top of Mt Bartle Frere (1,622m) from either the east or western side of the range, *Koolmoon Creek Track* (35.5km), *Cannabullen Creek Track* (13km), *Cardwell Range Track* (6.6km) and *Gorrell Track* (25.7km), which can also be accessed by bicycle. These are challenging walks and require walkers to be prepared for wet weather (year round) and leeches, and to be completely self-sufficient. There are numerous short walks throughout the park, many of which visit waterfalls, such as *Nandroya Falls Circuit* (2.5km). Camp grounds are scattered around the park, many of which are only accessible to hikers who are able to carry all their own gear.

Fees & Permits
Fees are payable for camping on Queensland national parks and reserves.

Facilities
Facilities vary throughout the park, but there are toilets, picnic areas, barbecues, hiking, walking, mountain bike trails, swimming, fishing and lookouts.

Services Nearby
Most major services (fuel, mechanical repairs, banks, post office, supermarkets, restaurants, chemists and hospital) are located in Innisfail (28km), Atherton (55km) and Cairns (33km).

Paluma Range National Park

Located at the southern end of the Wet Tropics bioregion, Paluma Range National Park is regularly shrouded in mist. Arriving from the hot, humid lowlands, a stop at the bottom of the range allows time for a swim with the freshwater turtles at Big Crystal Creek, which is highly recommended. Halfway up the range, stop at Little Crystal Creek to cool off as you play in the rockslides among the hoop pine before heading into the tropical rainforest.

Covering an area of 793km², three-quarters of the park is within the Wet Tropics World Heritage Area and the park exemplifies why the area was listed, showing exceptional natural beauty and biological diversity.

Once logged for both soft and hard timbers, remnants of old trees show the size that these giants once attained. Large trees still occur, dotted through the rainforest, showing the potential of the smaller trees that stand today.

The park has two sections, Jourama Falls and Mount Spec. Birdwatching is fantastic throughout the Paluma township, and a short walk down to Birthday Creek Falls may reveal the brightly coloured Golden Bowerbird. If not, there are still honeyeaters, parrots, thornbills and fernwrens.

Found after dark, several possum species, Northern Leaf-tailed Gecko

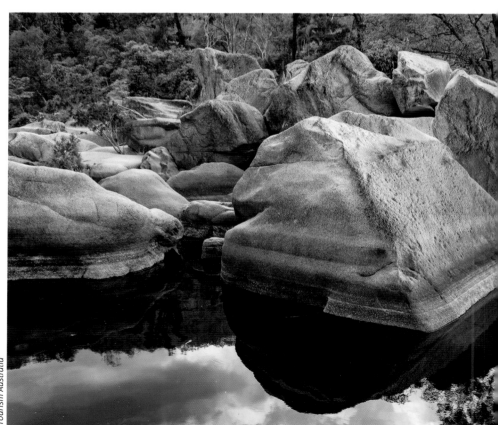

Tourism Australia

Jourama Falls

Saltuarius cornutus, Giant White-tailed Rat and a huge diversity of bats and snakes make their way out of their diurnal retreats. Unfortunately, many frogs have disappeared from Paluma, due to Chytrid Fungus. Although holding on in streams at lower elevations, they have not yet returned to the streams around the township. Behind Paluma as you head towards Mt Spec you may be lucky enough to spot a Platypus in the Running River.

GPS Coordinates
-18.86791, 146.12439 (Jourama Falls)
-19.008653, 146.192237 (Paluma)

Getting There
A drive through the expanding suburbs of Townsville to the Bruce Highway/A1 will take you through the cane fields

before you head into the mountains of the Paluma Range (88km). From Cairns it is a longer drive south via the Bruce Highway/A1 before heading up the Range (302km).

Tracks & Trails
Walking the main road through Paluma can be equally as fantastic for wildlife as any of the walking trails and just as picturesque, but to move into quieter sections of the rainforest, walking to *McClelland's Lookout,* the *'H' Track, Paluma Rainforest Walk, Cloudy Creek Track* and *Witt's Lookout Track* will provide excellent wildlife viewing opportunities. The *Birthday Creek Falls Track* is an easy walk and home to a well-used Golden Bowerbird bower that is regularly attended by a displaying male. Swimming is best at Big and Little Crystal Creek, rockslides at Big Crystal Creek can be walked to, and there is kayaking on Lake Paluma.

Fees & Permits
Fees are payable for camping in Queensland national parks.

Facilities
Throughout the township of Paluma there are toilets, picnic tables, barbecues and lookouts, and from here you can hike and mountain bike. At Lake Paluma there is camping, fishing, kayaking and swimming. There are some small shops in the township, but opening hours vary seasonally and depend on the store.

Services Nearby
All major services (fuel, mechanical repairs, banks, post office, supermarkets, restaurants, chemists, hospital and dental clinics) are located in Townsville (88km) and most facilities are available in Ingham (68km).

Central Mackay Coast

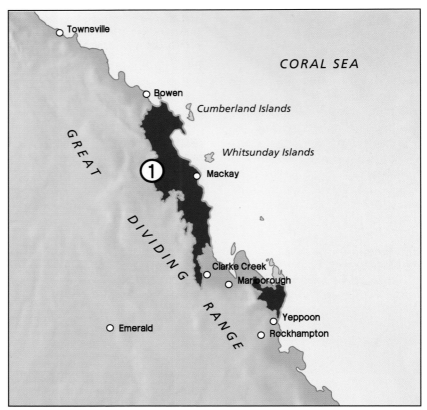

1. Eungella National Park

The Central Mackay Coast bioregion occurs in the tropical and subtropical climatic zone and covers 0.8 per cent of Queensland, an area of 14,640km². Centralized around the city of Mackay, the bioregion extends from just south of Bowen to around Clarke Creek, with an isolated section of the bioregion on the coast north of Yeppoon and east of Marlborough. The bioregion also encompasses numerous islands off the coast, including the Whitsundays and Airlie Beach regions. Within the bioregion there is one World Heritage Area, the Great Barrier Reef (which is partially protected within the Great Barrier Reef Coast Marine Park), 31 national parks, 13 conservation parks, 25 state forests and five forest reserves.

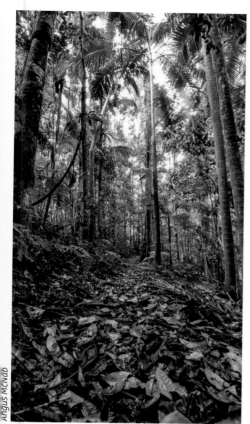

Angus McNab

Eungella National Park

The range of habitat types, from the islands, to the coast, to the high-elevation rainforest and everything in between, is reliant on the seasonal shifts in environmental conditions, which vary with the distinct wet and dry seasons. The variation in habitat types is further influenced by elevational change across the Great Dividing Range, with wetter conditions on its eastern slopes and distinctly drier conditions on the western slopes and into the Brigalow Belt North bioregion. The bioregion hosts over 700 vertebrate species, many of which are endemic both to the bioregion and its small isolated rainforest patches, or along the Clarke Range. The faunal diversity and endemism is strongly associated with the high diversity (thousands) of flora species that occur.

Key Species

BIRDS

Australasian Figbird, Australian King Parrot, Australian Swiftlet, Black-faced Monarch, Brown Cuckoo-dove, Brown Goshawk, Crimson Rosella, Dusky Myzomela, Eastern Yellow Robin, Eungella Honeyeater, Fan-tailed Cuckoo, Glossy Black Cockatoo, Greater Sooty Owl, Large-tailed Nightjar, Little Shrikethrush, Regent Bowerbird, Rufous Fantail, Russet-tailed Thrush, Superb Fruit-dove, Topknot Pigeon, White-headed Pigeon, Wompoo Fruit-dove, Wonga Pigeon.

MAMMALS

Buff-footed Antechinus, Eastern Horseshoe-bat, Fawn-footed Melomys, Gould's Long-eared Bat, Eastern Tube-nosed Bat, Large-footed Myotis, Long-nosed Bandicoot, Northern Brown Bandicoot, Platypus, Red-legged Pademelon, Yellow-footed Antechinus.

REPTILES

Bandy-bandy, Blue-throated Rainbow-skink, Cone-eared Calyptotis, Diamond-shielded Sunskink, Dwarf Crowned Snake, Eungella Shadeskink, Eungella Water-skink, Golden Crowned Snake, Hannah's Shadeskink, Lace Monitor, Major Skink, Mt Ossa Leaf-tailed Gecko, Orange-speckled Forest Skink, Peppered-belly Broad-tailed Gecko, Pink-tongued Lizard, White-crowned Snake.

AMPHIBIANS

Eastern Stony Creek Frog, Eungella Dayfrog, Eungella Tinkerfrog, Great Barred Frog, Liem's Tinkerfrog, Orange-eyed Tree Frog, Tusked Frog, White-lipped Tree Frog, Whirring Tree Frog.

INVERTEBRATES

Blue Tiger, Common Crow, Green Triangle, Orange Bush-brown, Red-banded Jezebel.

Peter Rowland

Regent Bowerbird (female)

Eungella Honeyeater *Bolemoreus hindwoodi*

Central Queensland's only endemic bird, this species is the main reason why most birdwatchers visit the Eungella region. This high-elevation endemic is not common in the rainforest of Eungella, but is restricted to plateau rainforest of the Clarke Range. It is a plain brown honeyeater with a paler, lightly streaked breast, blue-grey eyes and white stripe running from the bill below and behind the eye, essentially joining the ear-covert. Like most honeyeaters, it is relatively vocal and easy to detect if you are familiar with its call. Enthusiasts may try their luck searching along Dalrymple Road, particularly towards the end of the road, for this small, nondescript honeyeater.

Angus McNab

Wompoo Fruit-dove *Ptilinopus magnificus*

One of the largest and most brightly coloured of Australia's doves, the Wompoo Fruit-dove is named for its distinctive *wom-poo* call that is commonly heard in tropical and subtropical rainforests. It is brilliantly green backed, with a pale white head and bright red eyes. The breast is vibrantly purple, the wings have yellow wing-bars and the vent is yellow. Although obvious when seen, the bright colour combination provides excellent camouflage. Usually sitting high in the canopy, it can be difficult to spot, despite calling regularly. As is the case with most pigeons and doves, its nest is made of a small pile of twigs perched precariously on a branch.

Peter Rowland

Eastern Horseshoe-bat *Rhinolophus megaphyllus*

Angus McNab

One of the east coast's most common rainforest bats, this species spends its days roosting in caves or mine shafts that retain suitable humidity to prevent its wings from drying out. Although considered ugly by many, the face of the bats is highly specialized and aids in echolocation, improving its ability to detect prey and make its way through cluttered environments. The ears are very large, which helps with detecting prey – while roosting the ears can be seen to be rotating and picking up sound. The bats' colour varies depending on roosting habitat; although predominantly dark brown some individuals that roost in mine shafts can be bright orange. Eastern Horseshoe-bats hang individually from the roofs of roosting sites and do not cling to walls; they also do not cluster.

Eastern Tube-nosed Bat *Nyctimene robinsoni*

Anders Zimny

Hanging from a branch among the dead leaves, it can be hard to spot this bat sleeping during the day. The brown colouration of the wings wrapped around the body provides excellent camouflage. If you are fortunate enough to spot one, you will notice some differences from the other pteropodids, such as bright white-yellow spots on the wings, nostrils and ears, the patterning of which varies between individuals. The nose is also unusual in that the nostrils are tubular and extend from the face. Although rarely visible, the short tail is free. A relatively small pteropodid, this species is larger than most microbats but smaller than a flying-fox, and is often seen flying along creeklines at night. Listen for a distinctive call that is made as the bats fly through the forest.

Eungella Shadeskink *Saproscincus eungellensis*

Angus McNab

This is one of two shadeskinks that inhabit the Eungella region. It is a small rainforest skink that lives in rainforest stream and creek edges above 700m in the Clarke Range. A beautifully well-patterned skink with a notably long tail, it shows some sexual dimorphism, which is unusual in small Australian skinks. Males are more vibrantly patterned than females, with paler scales distributed across the back and extending on to the well-marked tail. Females are duller, with a browner overall colouration and less patterning. This species overlaps in distribution with the Diamond-shielded Sunskink *Lampropholis adonis*, which is very common and regularly seen in patches of sunlight (where the shadeskinks tend to remain in the shade).

Orange-speckled Forest Skink *Magmellia luteilateralis*

Angus McNab

Morphologically similar to the water skinks of the genera *Eulamprus* and *Concinnia*, this Eungella endemic was split from *Concinnia* and is now monotypic. It is brown dorsally, with small black flecks along its length. The vibrantly orange flanks stand out against the small black mark above the forearm and the white of the throat and neck-sides. Common along streams, it can be found in very large numbers in the higher elevation rainforest. Patches of sunlight that pierce through the canopy provide heavily utilized basking sites that are often visited by these robust skinks. When the sun is not shining, they are not commonly seen, as they move down under debris and rotten logs, and into leaf litter, waiting for the sunlight to return.

Liem's Tinker Frog *Taudactylus liemi*

Angus McNab

One of two tinker frogs in the Eungella region, Liem's Tinker Frog is a small, orange-brown, reddish to grey frog, mottled with darker markings and, in some individuals, with a dark X- shaped mark between the shoulders. The back is relatively smooth, with few scattered tubercles. The flanks can be the same colour as the back, or sharply delineated dark grey-charcoal. The underparts are yellow to white, occasionally with flecking. Unfortunately, this species has suffered declines from Chytrid Fungus. It is found along rainforest soaks and seeps that drain into streams, where it feeds on invertebrates. The male's call consists of 4 to 8 short metallic tinks, given from crevices and beneath rocks. Females lay about 45 eggs beneath rocks.

White-lipped Tree Frog *Litoria infrafrenata*

Angus McNab

This very large, bright emerald-green tree frog has a notable bright white stripe on the lower lip that extends to the shoulder. The upperparts are bright green and smooth, the flanks more of a yellow-green and granular, while the belly is white and very granular. The large feet and hands have pale greyish webbing, more so on the feet, while the thighs are pinkish. Some of the frogs are not bright green, with brown and grey individuals occurring. They are solitary animals – it is uncommon to see more than one or two individuals in close proximity to each other. There may, however, be more individuals together in people's gardens where they live in close proximity to the forest.

Eungella National Park

Extending from the lowlands to more than 1,200m up into the cloud-covered hills of the Eungella Plateau and the Clarke Range, Eungella National Park contains the longest continuous stretch of subtropical rainforest in Australia. Declared in 1941, the park has since expanded and is one of the best-known locations to watch Platypus in Australia. The park covers a large number of habitat types, and many of the longer walks provide the opportunity to explore them all, particularly the Mackay Highlands Great Walk. The region is very biodiverse, with more than 40 mammal species, 250 birds, 50 reptiles, 15 amphibians and 860 plants.

The area is warm and humid in summer, 20–30 °C, but daytime temperatures can drop to the 10–20 °C range during winter. Be aware that night temperatures can drop well into single figures. Rainfall is seasonal and peaks during the wet season (November–April), with monthly average rainfall being more than 170mm in December–March.

Being an isolated patch of rainforest 400km south of the Wet Tropics and 1,200km north of south-east Queensland's rainforests, there are many endemic species. They include the Eungella Honeyeater, which was first described in 1983 from a specimen collected from this

Tourism Australia

Araluen Falls in Finch Hatton Gorge

location. There are also the Eungella Spiny Crayfish, Orange-speckled Forest Skink, Peppered-belly Broad-tailed Gecko and two endemic frogs, the Eungella Dayfrog and Liem's Tinkerfrog. Unfortunately, a third endemic frog species, the Northern Gastric Brood Frog has not been seen since 1985, one year after being described.

GPS Coordinates
-21.13054, 148.49053

Getting There
A short drive west of Mackay (83km) via the Mackay-Eungella Road and State Route 64 takes you up into the Clarke Range for magnificent views and a notable drop in temperature and humidity. From Townsville, a long drive (407km) south via Bruce Highway/A1 will get you to Eungella, while it is a 409km drive north from Rockhampton.

Tracks & Trails
Much of the park is only accessible by foot, and there is a considerable number of trails in both the Clarke Range-Broken River area and Finch Hatton Gorge area. Walk along the *Broken River* and *Wishing Pool Circuit* in search of the Platypus, in the rainforest, surrounded by skinks, and in the eucalypt woodland. The trails cater to all fitness levels, from the short and flat *Sky Window Circuit* to the long and rugged *Mackay Highlands Great Walk,* 56km. At Finch Hatton Gorge, the *Wheel of Fire* passes pools and rivers with large trees towering above. With more than 20km of walking trails, there is something for everyone.

Fees & Permits
Fees are payable for camping in Queensland national parks.

Facilities
Both Eungella and Finch Hatton Gorge offer day-use areas, toilets, picnic tables, camping and mountain biking. It is important to note that phone reception is very limited throughout the park. There are also numerous forest drives that will provide the opportunity to see different sections of the park, but some of these tracks are for four-wheel-drive vehicles only.

Services Nearby
All major services (fuel, mechanical repairs, banks, post office, supermarkets, restaurants, chemists, hospital and dental clinics) are located in Mackay (82km).

South East Queensland

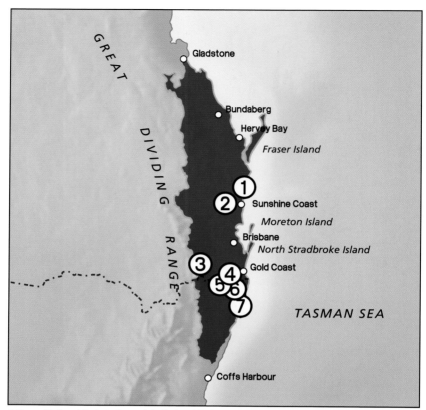

1. Noosa National Park 2. Conondale National Park 3. Main Range National Park
4. Lamington National Park 5. Border Ranges National Park (NSW) 6. Wollumbin National Park (NSW)
7. Nightcap National Park (NSW)

The South East Queensland bioregion lies within the tropical, subtropical and temperate climatic zones and covers 3.6 per cent of Queensland, an area of 62,484km². Within the region there are three World Heritage Sites: Fraser Island, the Gondwana Rainforests of Australia and the Great Barrier Reef. Two marine parks are situated along the coast, with 100 national parks, 133 conservation parks, 143 state forests, seven forest reserves and two Ramsar internationally important wetlands within the bioregion. However, this is all on the Queensland side of the border. 16,553.17km² of northern New South Wales is also within the South East Queensland bioregion and has a further 108 protected areas (2,247.57km²). From the ancient rainforests restricted to the high-elevation mountain tops, to the lowland coastal rainforest and the unique rainforests of the Fraser Island sand dunes, each rainforest patch is unique.

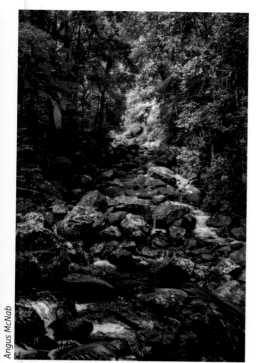

Main Range National Park

Angus McNab

Key Species

BIRDS

Albert's Lyrebird, Australian Brush Turkey, Australian Logrunner, Barred Cuckoo-shrike, Bassian Thrush, Channel-billed Cuckoo, Common Cicadabird, Green Catbird, Marbled Frogmouth, Pacific Emerald Dove, Paradise Riflebird, Regent Bowerbird, Satin Bowerbird, Spectacled Monarch, White-eared Monarch, White-headed Pigeon, White-throated Nightjar, Wonga Pigeon, Yellow-throated Scrubwren.

MAMMALS

Black Flying-fox, Black-striped Wallaby, Black-tailed Antechinus, Bush Rat, Eastern Long-eared Bat, Eastern Ring-tailed Possum, Eastern Tube-nosed Bat, Golden-tipped Bat, Large-footed Myotis, Little Bent-wing Bat, Northern Brown Bandicoot, Northern Free-tailed Bat, Red-legged Pademelon, Red-necked Pademelon, South-eastern Broad-nosed Bat, Southern Long-nosed Bandicoot, Subtropical Antechinus.

REPTILES

Blackish Blind Snake, Common Tree Snake, Land Mullet, Major Skink, Murray's Skink, Pink-tongued Lizard, Plain-backed Sunskink, Rainforest Cool-skink, Rose's Shadeskink, Rough-scaled Snake, Short-limbed Snake-skink, Southern Angle-headed Dragon, Southern Leaf-tailed Gecko, Stephens' Banded Snake, Swamp Snake, Three-toed Snake-tooth Skink, Tryon's Skink.

AMPHIBIANS

Cane Toad, Cascade Tree Frog, Dainty Tree Frog, Fleay's Barred Frog, Graceful Tree Frog, Hip Pocket Frog, Loveridge's Frog, Red and Yellow Mountain Frog, Red-eyed Tree Frog, Richmond Range Mountain Frog, Tusked Frog, Wilcox's Frog.

INVERTEBRATES

Australian Land Leech, Lamington Spiny Crayfish, Macleay's Swordtail, Richmond Birdwing, Southern Pink Underwing Moth.

There is a diversity of other habitat types in the area that are also well worth visiting and exploring for wildlife, as the bioregion is home to more than 1,000 vertebrate species. Its coastal scrubs, vine thickets, open woodland, dry sclerophyll forest and many other habitats, both natural and modified, are filled with all kinds of fauna. Unfortunately, expansion and growth has negatively impacted on many species in the bioregion, and local Koala populations are at significant risk of extinction. There are many locations to access the South East Queensland bioregion and its wildlife-filled rainforest as it extends along the coast from Coffs Harbour, New South Wales, north past the cities of Gold Coast, Brisbane, Sunshine Coast, Bundaberg and Gladstone, to the dry coastal corridor south of Rockhampton. A number of the bioregion's rainforests are classed as Threatened Ecological Communities.

Peter Rowland

Australian Logrunner (male)

Albert's Lyrebird *Menura alberti*

Tom Tarrant

Considerably more restricted in range than the better known Superb Lyrebird (p. 289), Albert's Lyrebird is limited to the rainforest of southeastern Queensland and northern New South Wales. A large, long-legged bird with plumage of varying shades of warm brown, it is the range of vocalizations that this species is most famous for. An incredible mimic, it can replicate the songs of other birds and probably any sounds that it hears, including machinery, tools, cameras and any number of other human-produced sounds. Males use these sounds and their own calls as they 'dance' on display platforms in the forest to impress females. The long, filamentous tail is positioned above the head as they display. The birds spend much of the day scratching at leaf litter, and it is easy to tell when they are present in the local area.

Australian Brush Turkey *Alectura lathami*

Angus McNab

Although a relatively large bird, this species is considerably smaller than a Southern Cassowary (p. 55), with which it has been confused on more than one occasion. Completely black bodied with a bright red head and yellow neck wattle, it is a mound builder. The male spends considerable amounts of time during the nesting season building a huge mound for the female to incubate her eggs in. Males 'rake' leaves from large distances, which can be irritating to people that have the birds living in or around their properties. Vegetation is added and removed to maintain the temperature of the eggs at around 34 °C until they hatch. The mounds retain warmth and are constantly visited by adult birds; they can also be inhabited by large pythons.

Australian Logrunner *Orthonyx temmincki*

The plumage of this ground-dwelling bird is mottled rufous-brown and olive-grey, and streaked with black on the wings, back and throat-sides. The face and breast-sides are grey and the belly is white. The female is distinguished from the male by the cinnamon, rather than white, throat and upper breast. The birds forage by raking through leaf litter on the forest floor, while supporting themselves on their spiny-tipped tails. The common call is a repeated piercing *weet*. The logrunner is found in temperate and subtropical rainforests and can be confiding while searching for food. Moving slowly and allowing the birds to move towards you can result in magnificent views of the species.

Angus McNab

Barred Cuckoo-shrike *Coracina lineata*

This striking and conspicuous bird is boldy barred grey and white on the breast, belly and undertail-coverts. The remaining plumage is grey with some black on the wings. There is a black facial patch from the base of the black bill to the bright yellow eye. The sexes are similar. The loud, chattering *aw-loo-ack-aw-loo-ack* call draws attention to its presence, particularly as groups travel from tree to tree. The species resides in rainforest and adjacent eucalypt forest, where it feeds predominantly on fruits and a small number of insects. It occurs in eastern Australia, from northern New South Wales to Cape York, as well as in Papua New Guinea and the Solomon Islands.

Peter Rowland

Bassian Thrush *Zoothera lunulata*

Angus McNab

This is a heavily mottled, ground-dwelling thrush with a clean, round white belly. The white eye-ring contrasts with the robust dark bill, while the legs are pinkish-brown. The upperparts are varying shades of brown with black scallops, and the throat, breast and flanks are white with dark brown-black scalloping. These colours and patterns provide excellent camouflage for this undergrowth specialist. Commonly seen along paths, individuals or pairs tend to bound away from observers, taking flight only if startled. Flight is low and direct, usually over a short distance. Foraging is often done on the edges of clearings and tracks, where individuals noisily flip leaves and scratch at the leaf litter in search of invertebrates.

Black-faced Monarch *Monarcha melanopsis*

Angus McNab

This beautiful bird has a blue-grey head, throat and upperparts, black face and russet underparts. It is perhaps the most familiar of the monarchs. It is similar in colouration to both the Spectacled Monarch (p. 95) and Black-winged Monarch *M. frater*. Its call is a distinctive *why-you-which-yew*. It is found along the eastern coast from Cape York to Melbourne, Victoria, further south than other monarch species, and inhabits rainforests and wet forests. It is a highly migratory species; most birds winter in north Queensland and Papua New Guinea, and return to the southern breeding areas in August/September. Some individuals remain in the same area for the entire year.

Brown Cuckoo-dove *Macropygia phasianella*

This large and common dove of the tropical rainforests has a subtle beauty compared with the more flamboyantly coloured fruit-doves. Appearing dull brown from a distance, on closer examination the numerous shades of warm and rich browns, with rufous-orange in the vent, rump and flanks, can be seen. Pale skin surrounds the strikingly blue eye, which can also be overlooked at a distance. Seen individually, in pairs, and in large numbers, individuals will flock to fruiting rainforest trees. These flocks can become very loud as the birds *coo* at each other. It is not only fruits that are eaten; seeds are also taken from a variety of rainforest trees and shrubs, then dispersed by this important rainforest species.

Angus McNab

Cicadabird *Coracina tenuirostris*

Males of this species are blue-grey with some black on the flight feathers. The eyes, bill and legs are dark. Females are greyish-brown above and whitish below, with blackish barring. Females resemble female White-winged Trillers *Lalage tricolor,* but are significantly larger, with a darker bill, grey crown and rufous wash on the flight feathers. The white tip on the underside of the tail also rules out any confusion with the Barred Cuckoo-shrike (p. 89) when viewed from below. The Cicadabird occurs in northern and eastern Australia, from central Victoria to the Kimberley, Western Australia. It is quiet and unobtrusive, and is typically seen singly or in pairs, foraging for insect prey and fruits in the canopy area of wetter forests. Its call is a cicada-like buzzing, given in bursts of 4–5 notes.

Michael Schmid

Green Catbird *Ailuroedus crassirostris*

Peter Rowland

Blending into the green of the canopy, the Green Catbird, named for its green colouration and the cat-like call that it screeches throughout the day, searches for fruits. It is darker emerald-green above with thin white wing-bars and black wing-tips. The underparts are paler green on the breast, becoming greenish-yellow on the belly; both are finely streaked with white. The bill is a pale cream colour and, along with the red eye, contrasts against the predominantly green head. A member of the bowerbird family, this species, along with the other two Australian catbird species, does not construct a bower. Males impress females in other ways.

Marbled Frogmouth *Podargus ocellatus*

Angus McNab

Confined to rainforests in central eastern Australia and the far north of Queensland, this frogmouth is mottled brown with orange-yellow eyes. It is difficult to distinguish from the Tawny Frogmouth *P. strigoides,* with which it overlaps in both parts of its range. The Tawny Frogmouth has yellow eyes. The Papuan Frogmouth *P. papuensis* is also found on Cape York Peninsula, Queensland, but its larger size, orange-red eyes and more heavily blotched wings distinguish it. All three species have the characteristic large, wide bill. The Marbled Frogmouth can be further identified by the prominent buff-barred plumes above its bill and its soft *koor-loo* call, which it utters repeatedly. All species feed largely on insects, which are captured by being pounced on from an elevated perch.

Pacific Emerald Dove *Chalcophaps longirostris*

Angus McNab

This beautiful stocky, ground-dwelling dove is distinguished by its emerald-green wings and dull purplish-brown head, neck and underparts. Young birds start darker brown with heavy blackish barring on the head, neck and underparts. The species mainly occurs in dense forests, thickets and mangroves, and is distributed in a broad coastal band through northern and eastern Australia, including offshore islands. Although primarily seen foraging on the forest floor for fallen fruits, it often perches on thicker tree branches to feed. It is typically solitary, but can form small groups or flocks. The common call is a low-pitched *coo*, often repeated several times in succession and rising slightly in pitch.

Paradise Riflebird *Lophorina paradisea*

Arthur Carew

Riflebirds are unlike any other Australian bird. Both sexes have long, slender, decurved bills and short tails. The adult male is velvet black above the oily-green below; the crown, throat, breast and central tail feathers are iridescent. The female is brown and lacks iridescence, but the white eyebrow, reddish wings and arrow-like scalloping on the underparts are distinctive. A loud, explosive *yaaas*, sometimes given twice, is a characteristic sound in the bird's rainforest habitat. In flight, the male's wings sound like rustling silk. Three species occur in Australia, but they do not overlap in range. The Paradise Riflebird occurs in southeastern Queensland and northeastern New South Wales, Victoria's Riflebird (p. 56) in Queensland's Wet Tropics, and the Magnificent Riflebird in northern Cape York Peninsula.

93

Regent Bowerbird *Sericulus chrysocephalus*

Peter Rowland

This is a relatively small, slender bowerbird. It has a long, straight, thin bill, which is yellow in adult males and dark brown in females. Both sexes are generally inconspicuous, which is surprising given the male's striking plumage. The majority of the male's body is deep velvety-black, with rich golden-yellow plumage on the head, nape and wings. The young male's eye is initially brown, but turns to bright yellow in its second year. The female's plumage is generally brown-black, with light brown scallops on the upper back and underparts. There is a sooty-black patch on the hindcrown and occasionally a second band on the nape, and the eyes are yellowish-brown. Males are most noticeable during the breeding season when they are displaying, but are otherwise quiet and secretive.

Satin Bowerbird *Ptilonorhynchus violaceus*

Angus McNab

The male Satin Bowerbird is perhaps the best-known of Australia's bowerbirds. It is found in the rainforests, woodland and adjacent areas of the country's eastern states. Mature males have deep glossy blue-black plumage, violet-blue irises and a contrasting white bill, while females and younger males (<7 years old) are generally olive-green and brown. The male builds an 'avenue'-type bower that consists of two parallel walls of sticks, placed on the ground and variably decorated with bright blue and violet-coloured objects to attract potential female mates. Decorations can be naturally occurring items, such as parrot feathers, flowers and berries, or manufactured objects, including blue pegs, bottle tops and straws. The walls of the bower are painted with mashed up vegetable matter and saliva, applied by the male with its bill.

Spectacled Monarch *Symposiachrus trivirgatus*

This slender, active flycatcher is almost fantail-like as it searches for insects among the outer foliage of trees in rainforests and dense riverine vegetation. It also enters wet sclerophyll forests in the south. It occurs in far eastern Australia, from Cape York Peninsula, Queensland, to southern New South Wales. Birds from the south migrate northwards in April–December each year.

Peter Rowland

The species is blue-grey above and orange-buff on the neck, breast and flanks, with a prominent black facial mask that extends beyond the eye. The remaining underparts are white, becoming more extensive in the Cape York Peninsula subspecies *albiventris*. Similarly coloured monarchs in Australia include the Black-winged Monarch *Monarcha frater* and Black-faced Monarch (p. 90).

White-eared Monarch *Carterornis leucotis*

The White-eared Monarch is endemic to Australia. It is often seen feeding in the upper rainforest canopy area in association with other monarch species, including the Spectacled Monarch (above) and Black-winged Monarch *Monarcha frater*. The bird is predominantly black and white above and greyish below, and can be distinguished by the three white patches surrounding the eye, the patch in front of the eye being smaller than the others. It may be confused with the similarly sized Grey Fantail (p. 288). It actively gleans insects and other invertebrates from foliage or seizes them in mid-air. Its main song is a whistled *you get away*, which is given in four notes, with the emphasis on the second.

Michael Schmid

White-throated Nightjar *Eurostopodus mystacalis*

Angus McNab

If it was not for this bird's boomingly loud call and bright eyeshine it would be hard to detect, due to its very good camouflage. While sitting on the ground or on a nest, it is nearly impossible to detect until it is too late and it flushes. Its brown, black, grey and white plumage and ability to stay still are fantastic features for this bird to have when roosting and nesting on the ground. During the night, when active, it calls from exposed branches, treetops and exposed rock faces. Its flight appears erratic, and when the wings are spread it lacks the white outer wing-patches that occur in other similar nightjar species.

Black Flying-fox *Pteropus alecto*

Angus McNab

Predominantly black, individuals of this mammal species may have white flecks on the belly fur and reddish-brown fur on the rear of the nape. The eyes are reddish, with faint reddish-brown eye-rings visible in some individuals. It is widely distributed through northern Australia from around Carnarvon, Western Australia, through the Top End, and northern and eastern Queensland, to around Sydney, New South Wales. It occurs in a variety of wooded habitats, including rainforests, open forests, paperbark woodland, mangroves and bamboo thickets, and feeds at night on eucalypt blossoms, fleshy fruits and occasionally leaves and tree sap. It roosts during the day, often in the company of other fruit-bat species. Individuals can travel up to 50km between roost sites and feeding grounds each night.

Black-striped Wallaby *Notamacropus dorsalis*

Angus McNab

This medium-sized wallaby is grey-brown above with a rufous-brown upper back and neck, and paler sides. It has a black stripe from the top of the head to the rump along the centre of the back, and a white stripe on the thigh. The face has white cheek-stripes, and the nose, forepaws and toes are black. This species is similar to the slightly larger Red-necked Wallaby, which lacks the black dorsal stripe. It is distributed in coastal and inland eastern Australia, from southern Cape York Peninsula, Queensland, to New England and Far North Coast regions, New South Wales. It lives in rainforests and woodland with a dense understorey, where it can be seen in groups, resting by day in dense vegetation and feeding during the night in open areas.

Black-tailed Antechinus *Antechinus arktos*

Angus McNab

One of the most recently described mammals in Australia, the Black-tailed Antechinus is significantly threatened with extinction. Museum records show that the species once had a much larger distribution. It is unclear why it has declined, given that the majority of its habitat is protected within national parks. Now known from very few sites in far south-east Queensland, the species is poorly understood and much more difficult to detect than co-occurring antechinus species. Notably larger than other antechinus in its range, this large, dark-furred animal is very robust and, as its name suggests, has a black tail. The larger size allows for an increased diversity of prey items that could potentially include small birds.

Bush Rat *Rattus fuscipes*

Although rarely seen, the Bush Rat is ever present and living in the undergrowth. It is fairly typically shaped and sized for a *Rattus* species. The fur can be dark-brown, grey, or reddish-brown above and fades into pale grey on the underparts. The pinkish-grey tail is naked, ringed with scales and approximately the same length as the body (an important feature in small mammal identification). The nose is slightly rounded and the ears and eyes are large. Like most rodents, this species is nocturnal and spends its nights foraging for a range of plant and invertebrate species. However, it must be aware of predators, as it is commonly preyed on, being eaten by snakes, owls, lizards and introduced predators such as cats and foxes.

Angus McNab

Eastern Long-eared Bat *Nyctophilus bifax*

The fur of this small to medium-sized bat is orange-brown above, and typically paler below. The head is blunt, with a shallow, centrally depressed ridge across the snout. The ears are long and ribbed, and meet on top of the head. It is found along eastern Australia and adjacent islands, from northern Cape York Peninsula, Queensland, to northeastern New South Wales. Within this range it inhabits rainforests and riverine forests, and less commonly open forests and woodland. It roosts either singly or in small groups in tree hollows, under loose bark, in dense foliage and occasionally in buildings. It forages at night, mainly for moths, by perching in foliage and waiting to detect prey close by before seizing it in short flights.

Angus McNab

Eastern Ring-tailed Possum *Pseudocheirus peregrinus*

Peter Rowland

This possum ranges from reddish-brown (most common) to grey and almost black on the back, with white patches behind the eyes and ears, and under the neck. The belly is white with orange to brown tinges on the limbs and tail. It has a long, prehensile tail, which is one-third white on its tip and used like a fifth limb to climb from branch to branch in the forest. It is widely distributed in eastern Australia, from Cape York Peninsula, Queensland, through eastern New South Wales and Victoria, to southeastern South Australia (including Kangaroo Island), and Tasmania (including islands of Bass Strait). The species inhabits rainforest, sclerophyll forests, woodland and scrub. It is predominantly arboreal and feeds at night on leaves, flowers and fruits, sheltering by day in nests constructed of sticks or grass in tree hollows, tree forks or dense vegetation.

Golden-tipped Bat *Phoniscus papuensis*

Bruce Thomson

On close inspection this bat can be seen to be a unique colour among Australia's microbats. Its fur is long and curly, dark brown to blackish and tipped with golden-yellow, which gives a golden-peppered appearance. The golden fur extends on to the forearms, legs, long tail and tail membrane. It roosts by day in disused dome-shaped birds' nests, dense vegetation or tree hollows. The species hunts in a different way from most bats. Rather than catching prey on the wing or gleaning it from the ground or off a tree, it specializes in taking spiders out of their webs. Due to this unique hunting technique, Golden-tipped Bats were once very difficult to detect, as they do not typically fly into mist nets, so it was not until the invention of the harp trap that the species was able to be studied.

Large-footed Myotis *Myotis macropus*

Angus McNab

Often referred to as 'fishing bats' the *Myotis* group is widespread globally. This species is not restricted to the rainforest, but frequents rainforest streams, using them as flyways to traverse through the dense environment. Flying low and fast over water, it is able to capture invertebrates that utilize waterways. One characteristic that can identify the species in flight is its habit of dragging its long toes across the surface as it flies close to the water. It can occasionally take small fish as prey, although this is thought to be very uncommon. As it frequents waterways, it can often be found roosting in small groups in bridges and culverts.

Little Bent-winged Bat *Miniopterus australis*

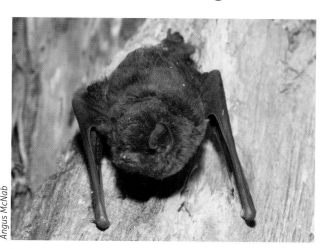

Angus McNab

Little Bent-winged Bats are dark brown above and paler below. The tip of the wing has a long joint of the third finger, which folds back and is bent under the wing while the bat is sleeping. The fur is quite long and thick on the crown and neck. The muzzle is short and the ears are triangular in shape. The species is distinguished from the Common Bent-winged Bat *M. schreibersii* by its smaller size. It occurs in rainforest, sclerophyll forests, paperbark swamps, banksia scrub and dense coastal forests, between Cape York Peninsula, Queensland, and Wollongong, New South Wales. It forages for insects below the forest canopy and in very densely vegetated habitats. The species roosts in large numbers in tunnels, caves, culverts, tree hollows, stormwater drains, mines, buildings and under bridges by day, often with other bat species.

Northern Brown Bandicoot *Isoodon macrourus*

The largest of Australia's bandicoots, this species occurs throughout northern and eastern Australia, north of Sydney, New South Wales. The brown coat is interspersed with black hairs and becomes paler on the flanks, merging into the whitish-grey underparts. The nose is long and pointed, the eyes large and the ears small. The presence of this species is often detected through the diggings that it leaves as it searches for invertebrates, tubers and other edible vegetation. These are narrow and conical, the same shape as the snout, which is used to pull out prey items. It is very common to find the diggings in residential gardens, but the introduction of cats, dogs and foxes has reduced the abundance of the species throughout its distribution.

Angus McNab

Northern Free-tailed Bat *Ozimops lumsdenae*

The fur of this species is brown to orange-brown above, tinged with yellow on the neck-sides, and is only slightly paler on the underparts. The skin on the wings, ears and muzzle is blackish-brown. It is similar to the Cape York Free-tailed Bat, but the forearm length is larger. The species occurs in coastal and inland areas of northern Australia, from Pilbara, Western Australia, through the Northern Territory, to southern Queensland and northern New South Wales. It is found in a variety of habitats, including rainforests, shrubland and grassland. It roosts by day in tree hollows, under loose bark, or in roof spaces and other cavities within buildings, emerging at night to forage on insects. Its flight is fast, with rapid wingbeats.

Ryan Francis

Red-necked Pademelon *Thylogale thetis*

Peter Rowland

This marsupial is generally brownish above, with a rufous forehead, neck and shoulders, and a grey-flecked back, thighs and tail. The belly is off white, becoming whiter on the chest and throat. The tail is short, around 45 per cent of the length of the head and body. It inhabits rainforest fringes and wet sclerophyll forests, where it occupies dense vegetation by day and feeds on grasses and leaves in adjacent open areas between dusk and dawn. More elusive than other macropods with which it co-occurs, it often lives in the same areas as the Red-legged Pademelon (p. 154), which tends to be even more elusive, crepuscular and less likely to come out into open areas. Females give birth to a single young at any time of the year.

Southern Long-nosed Bandicoot *Perameles nasuta*

Ethan Mann

This ground-dwelling mammal is greyish-brown above (faintly streaked with paler brown) and cream-white below, with a short, sparsely furred tail, long, pointed snout and moderately long, pointed ears. The upper surfaces of the feet are cream, and the claws are long and powerful for digging. This species can be distinguished from the smaller Southern Brown Bandicoot *Isoodon obesulus* by its paler tail, and longer ears and snout. It occurs along the coast of eastern Australia, from Mackay, Queensland, through eastern New South Wales, to southern Victoria. It is found in wet forests, rainforests, damp grassland and suburban gardens, where it feeds through the night on invertebrates and underground tubers, which it finds by digging through the topsoil. It shelters by day in a shallow burrow lined with leaves.

Barred-sided Skink *Concinnia tenuis*

This smooth-scaled lizard has long, slender limbs with five digits; the fourth toe of the hindlimbs is longer than the rest. It is pale brown to silvery-brown above, with black blotches along the length of the body and tail. The upper parts of the flanks are dark brown, with an uneven lower edge where they meet the paler creamish lower flanks, and numerous black blotches along the rear portion. The species is found along the coast and ranges of eastern Australia, from central Queensland to southern New South Wales, occurring on rocky slopes in rainforests and open forests, and in dense gardens in the northern part of its range and woodland in the south. It is active in trees and rock crevices and is diurnal, but can be active at night, foraging for invertebrates, including spiders, ants, insect larvae and some berries.

Angus McNab

Blackish Blind Snake *Anilios nigrescens*

Most members of the blind snake family may be confused with worms, although there are some notable differences. Like all snakes, the Blackish Blind Snake is covered in scales, has a forked tongue, and although not functioning to the same level as in most snakes, two visible eyes. The functionality of the eyes is thought to be limited to little more than light receptors, and it is thought that blind snakes cannot 'see'. Most commonly found on rainy nights, this species spends much of its time underground, under leaf litter or rotting logs. Its colour can vary from pinkish to black, and is often pinkish-black with a cream to white belly. Essentially incapable of biting a person, this snake eats the eggs of ants and termites.

Angus McNab

Common Tree Snake *Dendrelaphis punctulatus*

Angus McNab

This is a highly variable snake with colouration based on location. It is olive-green or blue-grey above in south-east New South Wales, black further north-east, and yellow with a blue-grey or brown head across northern Australia. All have pale blue skin, which appears as flecks between the body scales and is visible during defensive displays. The species typically has a bright yellow throat and paler yellow underparts, but can also be greenish, bluish or white. It is distributed through coastal and subcoastal northern and eastern Australia, from the Kimberley, Western Australia, through the Northern Territory, and northern and eastern Queensland, to Batemans Bay, New South Wales. It occurs in a wide range of vegetated habitats, including open forests, rainforests, mangroves and suburban gardens. It is diurnal and arboreal, but also forages on the ground, sheltering during the night in tree hollows and rock crevices, and feeding mainly on frogs, reptiles and birds, but also small mammals.

Land Mullet *Bellatorias major*

Anders Zimny

One of Australia's largest skinks, this species is robust and glossy bodied with a broad head, medium-length tail and low-keeled scales. It is blackish-brown to black above, and whitish with yellowish-orange underparts. Juveniles are bluish, with small, scattered white spots on the flanks. It is found in coastal and near-coastal southeastern Queensland and northeastern New South Wales, occurring in coastal rainforest margins and wet forests, and typically being seen basking in patches of sunlight. It quickly retreats to a burrow if disturbed, but will return to basking as soon as it thinks it is safe to come back out. It often inhabits disturbed areas with weeds and well-vegetated suburban gardens, and is primarily a frugivore, eating fallen fruits and berries, but also leaves and flowers.

Major Skink *Bellatorias frerei*

A large and robust skink, this species is very quick moving for its size. It is rarely far from cover and can slip through the leaf litter into cracks, crevices or other hiding places just as you spot it basking in the sun. It is variable in colour and pattern throughout its range, tending to have a brown back, with small black markings in each scale that give a striped appearance. The flanks are darker reddish-brown to black and dotted with pale cream spots. The underparts are shades of white, cream or yellow. Juveniles are more vividly marked than adults, but do not have the bright eye-ring of adults. The species is omnivorous, and its large size provides it with the opportunity to eat a larger range of food items than most skinks.

Pink-tongued Skink *Cyclodomorphus gerrardii*

Regularly confused with the well-known Eastern Blue-tongued Skink *Tiliqua scincoides* and often for a snake, the Pink-tongued Skink is large and robust for a skink, but slender compared with typical blue-tongued skinks. The long body and tail combined with the short legs do not give the appearance of a well-adapted climber – however, these skinks spend a lot of time in trees. The tail is semi-prehensile and the claws, although small, are sharp, providing enough grip to climb trees. Typically very pale brown all over, the body is covered in bands of varying thickness and colouration. Most individuals have dark bands down the length of the body, while some lack bands entirely. The head is large, with strong jaws for crushing snails and other prey.

Rainforest Cool-skink *Harrisoniascincus zia*

Angus McNab

This is a small, short-limbed skink with five digits on each limb and movable lower eyelids containing a small transparent disc. It is brown to blackish-brown above, with numerous blackish and pale brown flecks on the nape, back and tail. It has a faint dorsolateral stripe from head to tail. The upper flanks are blackish-brown and the lower flanks are brown flecked with paler brown. The underparts are white or yellow, with black flecks on the throat. It is found in upland rainforests and cool wet forests, and is highly secretive and fossorial, foraging in loose soil and leaf litter for small invertebrates. Females lay an average of five eggs per clutch. It is very similar to members of the *Lampropholis* genus, with which it can easily be confused.

Rough-scaled Snake *Tropidechis carinatus*

Angus McNab

This species has a strong keel on each midbody scale, giving it an uneven texture. Growing to 1.2m in length, this moderately sized snake is very easily confused with the Keelback *Tropidonophis mairii*, which is roughly the same size, shape and colour, as well as having keeled scales and utilizing the same habitats. However, the Rough-scaled Snake is venomous, while the Keelback is harmless. The presence or absence of a loreal scale, which differentiates these species, can be hard to discern so both species are best left alone. Light to tan brown, the body has black bands or rows of spots that fade along its length and are not always obvious. The snake is usually solitary, but multiple individuals can be found hunting frogs in the right conditions. VENOMOUS

Southern Leaf-tailed Gecko *Saltuarius swaini*

This species is as varied in colour as the mosses and lichens it sits on. Greens, greys, browns and blacks are all present, and vary with intensity during different times of the day. By day the colours appear faded and become dull as individuals press their bodies into the cracks, crevices and hollows of trees. At night the colours are much more vibrant, with pale patches on the back appearing more prominent against the streaked and blotched darker background. The eye colour is as varied as the body colours, and is usually pale with streaks of brown around the vertical pupil. The edges of the body and tail are frilled and spiked to break up the outline of this large gecko.

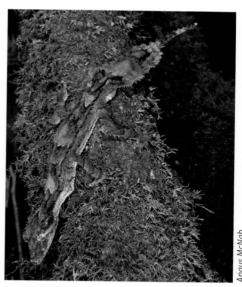

Angus McNab

Stephens' Banded Snake *Hoplocephalus stephensii*

This species is brown, grey or blackish, usually with brown or cream cross-bands, but on occasion individuals are unbanded. The head is broad and dark, blotched with cream and black-and-white barring on the lips. The underparts are cream to grey, with each ventral scale keeled. Unbanded individuals resemble the Pale-headed Snake *H. bitorquatus*. The species

Angus McNab

is found along the coast and ranges of southern Queensland and northern New South Wales, occuring in wetter forests, rainforests and vine thickets. It is largely arboreal and nocturnal, using hollows in large trees for shelter during the day. It predominantly feeds on frogs, reptiles and small mammals. It gives birth to up to nine young in a litter, generally in December–February. VENOMOUS

Three-toed Snake-tooth Skink
Coeranoscincus reticulatus

Angus McNab

This lizard could be confused with a snake. It is very elongated and has small, reduced limbs that are difficult to see and are not always used in locomotion. Although the legs can be utilized for movement, much of the propulsion is provided by ventral muscles pushing against the ground, as the legs are too small to lift the body. Spending much of its time under leaf litter, logs, rocks and other ground debris, individuals will come out to bask in exposed locations. Quick to retreat to shelter, it is often only the long tail that is seen as an individual slides silently under cover. The teeth are recurved, possibly to aid with holding on to earthworms and other soft-bodied prey such as beetle larvae.

Tryon's Skink *Karma tryoni*

Angus McNab

This skink is brown above with numerous irregular darker brown to blackish bands and a bold black shoulder-patch. The lips and cheeks are blackish with paler spots or stripes, and the sides of the neck and body have purplish-black patches. The underside is paler, white to bright yellow on the belly and with a yellow wash from the forelimb to the tail. The species is similar in appearance to Murray's Skink (p. 158). It has been recorded in upland rainforests (800–1,100m) in the McPherson and Border Ranges region on the New South Wales–Queensland border. Its prey consists of a variety of insects and other invertebrates, but frogs' eggs have been found in the gut of some individuals. Adult females give birth to live young.

Cane Toad *Rhinella marina*

Angus McNab

This introduced species has had devastating effects on Australian ecosystems due to its toxicity, although recent evidence shows that some of its predators are beginning to develop resistance, or strategies that allow them to eat Cane Toads. Adults are yellow to brown or greyish above with dark spotting, while younger individuals can have red-orange spots. Juveniles are grey to black, often flecked with orange and brown. The belly is pale brown to grey, with white or cream marbling. Not rainforest restricted, these toads live in a wide variety of habitats, thriving in agricultural and urban areas. The species is nocturnal, although juveniles and metamorphs are often seen around waterbodies by day. Females lay up to 35,000 black eggs in long strands, and tadpoles start to hatch after about five weeks.

Cascade Tree Frog *Litoria pearsoniana*

Angus McNab

This tree frog is bright green or mottled above with a dark-edged gold or yellow stripe extending from the nostril over the eye and broadening over the flanks. The back is smooth, without bumps or protrusions, and the underside is white. It is found from near Gympie, Queensland, south to the Hastings River region, New South Wales, where it feeds on arthropods around creeks and streams in rainforests and wet sclerophyll forests. It breeds in pools beside creeks and streams, and in slower sections of larger waterways. The male's call is given in two parts – the first a *wrekik-wrekik* and the second a loud *eeep* (not always repeated) – made from vegetation or branches overhanging the water. The eggs are laid in loose clusters attached to sticks or plant material, with about 450 in a clutch.

Dainty Green Tree Frog *Litoria gracilenta*

Angus McNab

The colouration of this tree frog varies from light to dark green. A yellow stripe extends along the head from the nostril, over the eye and on to the body. The back is slightly rough, made up of granular, tiny warty bumps or protrusions. The back of the thigh is usually blue or maroon, and the underparts are yellow to orange. The species is found through northeastern Australia from mid-New South Wales to southern Cape York Peninsula, Queensland. It occurs in small waterbodies, both natural and artificial, where it feeds on invertebrates. The males call from trees and shrubs surrounding the water, particularly after rain, in spring to early autumn. The call is a drawn-out *wahh* that lasts about a second and is repeated for extended periods.

Fleay's Barred Frog *Mixophyes fleayi*

Angus McNab

This frog is tan to dark brown on the smooth back, and has black bands on the legs and white underparts. Juveniles look similar to adults, but have bright red or orange eyes that fade to brown as they mature. The upper iris is metallic green-blue. The species lives around watercourses and leaf litter, where it feeds nocturnally on invertebrates and small vertebrates. The male's call is a single *wharrrup,* repeated frequently from the edge of a waterbody, or from burrows or beneath the leaf litter. Breeding occurs in shallow sections of permanent streams. About 900 eggs are laid in the water, usually in a constructed depression among gravel, and tadpoles start to develop after 30 weeks.

Hip Pocket Frog *Assa darlingtoni*

This species is grey to brown or blackish above, sometimes mottled or flecked, and some individuals have a 'V'-shaped mark over the shoulders and hips. The underside is white with brown markings. It occurs in eastern Australia, from the Sunshine Coast, Queensland, to Coffs Harbour, New South Wales, where it inhabits rainforests

Angus McNab

and wet forests and feeds nocturnally on invertebrates. The male's call is a series of 4–14 fast-paced *wruc*, produced from beneath leaf litter on the forest floor. Females lay about 15 eggs, and after hatching the tadpoles are collected by the male, who uses two hip pouches to rear them through metamorphosis. The fully formed young emerge from the pouch after a tadpole stage of 60–81 days.

Loveridge's Frog *Philoria loveridgei*

This endangered frog is brown to dark brown or yellowish above, typically with a dark stripe from the snout, through the eye to above the shoulder, often with a white upper edge. The body is smooth, and cream to dirty yellow below with darker flecking. It is found in a few upland locations on the south-east Queensland and New South Wales

Angus McNab

border, where it feeds by day and night on invertebrates. It lives in seepages in rainforests, where the male's call, a guttural *wrocc*, is made from within a chamber of mud, usually beneath rocks and leaf litter. About 100 eggs are laid in a foam nest, and tadpoles start to develop into frogs after seven weeks.

Red and Yellow Mountain Frog *Philoria kundagungan*

Angus McNab

This frog is reddish-orange to dark brown, yellow or black above, usually with a dark stripe from the rear of the eye to above the shoulder. The body is smooth, and the underside is bright yellow, occasionally with bright red markings. The species is found in a few upland locations on the south-east Queensland and New South Wales border, living in seepages in rainforests, and feeding on invertebrates. The male's call, a deep though soft *wrocc* that is repeated at longer intervals than in most frogs, is made from within a chamber of mud, usually beneath rocks and leaf litter. Little is known about the reproductive behaviour.

Red-eyed Tree Frog *Litoria chloris*

Angus McNab

The colouration of this tree frog varies from light to dark green, occasionally with yellow spots on the back. The eyes are bright red to orange, hence the species' common name. The backs of the thighs are bright blue. The back is almost smooth, with granular tiny warty bumps or protrusions. Males call from vegetation and the ground surrounding waterbodies between spring and early autumn. The call, made just before or after rain, is given in two parts. Individuals seek out small waterbodies both natural and artificial, including roadside ditches, dams and ephemeral pools beside rivers, streams and creeks. Spawn is produced in a single sheet or broad clusters of up to 1,350 eggs laid near the edge of the water, often attached to emergent vegetation.

Richmond Range Mountain Frog
Philoria richmondensis

Angus McNab

This endangered frog is reddish-brown to dark brown or yellow above, with a distinct pale-edged, dark stripe from the snout to above the shoulder. The body is smooth. The underside is bright yellow to grey with indistinct markings. This habitat specialist is found in seepages and gutters of mountain streams in rainforests and wet sclerophyll forests in a few upland locations (>550m) on the Richmond Range, New South Wales. It feeds by both day and night on invertebrates. The male's call, a guttural *wrocc,* is made from within a chamber of mud, usually beneath rocks and leaf litter. The eggs are laid in a foam nest and, once hatched, tadpoles metamorph after 10 weeks.

Tusked Frog *Adelotus brevis*

Angus McNab

This frog's upperparts are grey to brown or blackish, mottled with darker spots and flecks and low, rounded tubercles. The underside is black to grey with white markings. Bright red with darker banding occurs in the groin and armpit, extending on to the flanks and belly. Inside the jaws of males there are two prominent 'tusks' that are modified teeth; these are used in male combat. The species is found from Eungella, Queensland, to Ourimbah, New South Wales, inhabiting rainforests and wet forests near still pools, foraging at night for arthropods. The male's call is a chicken-like *chuck* and is uttered from beneath low vegetation at the water's edge. Females lay about 340 eggs that grow as tadpoles for about seven weeks before becoming frogs.

Wilcox's Frog *Litoria wilcoxii*

Angus McNab

This frog is dark brown above, with a dark stripe that extends from the snout, through the eye and along the flanks. The backs of the thighs are spotted with light yellow. Males exhibit a distinct colour change from tan-brown to bright yellow during the breeding season. The back is smooth, without bumps or protrusions. The species is found in northeastern Australia from Goulburn, New South Wales, to Mareeba, Queensland, where it occurs around creeks and streams in forests, feeding on invertebrates. It breeds in pools beside creeks and streams and in slower parts of main waterways. The call is a soft, purring *bobble*, repeated reasonably often. About 3,000 eggs are laid in a mass, loosely attached to the rocky base of a stream or to plant material, and tadpoles start to develop into frogs about eight weeks after hatching.

Lamington Spiny Crayfish *Euastacus sulcatus*

Ian Bool

Inhabiting rainforest streams above 300m elevation, this large crayfish is blue and white in the northern part of its range and red and white in the south of its range. It utilizes creek lines to move through the forest, and after rain events can be found walking across the rainforest floor, regularly utilizing walking tracks for easy movement. Quick to defend itself, a defensive pose is assumed with the pincers raised high above the head when threatened. This posture is often associated with a hiss to further intimidate would-be predators. Sensitive to changes in water temperatures, climate change is a factor that may impact the distribution and occurrence of this species.

Richmond Birdwing *Ornithoptera richmondia*

Males of this butterfly have forewing upperside black with iridescent green subcostal and submarginal areas, and underside with submarginal bands of green-blue. Hindwing upperside iridescent green with submarginal black and, at times, semitranslucent gold spots. Female larger and predominantly black with discal and submarginal pale spots on forewing, and submarginal white, black and yellow spots on hindwing. It is found in coastal south-eastern Queensland and northern New South Wales, along the foothills of the Great Dividing Range, where it is endemic to rainforests and, occasionally, sandy coastal forests. Both sexes are most easily observed during the cooler parts of the morning and afternoon when they descend to feed at flowers within a few metres of the ground. Host plants are the Richmond Birdwing vines *Pararistolochia pravenosa* and *P. laheyana*.

Mark Gillow

Southern Pink Underwing Moth *Phyllodes imperialis*

Adult moths have grey-brown forewings with white markings, and black hindwings with a pink patch on each and white spots along the rear edge. The body is grey-brown. Caterpillars start dull brown and develop two large white 'eye-spot' markings and a number of smaller white spots and markings on the upper surface as they mature. The southern subspecies *P. i. smithersi* is considered to occur in a region bounded by Kin Kin Creek, near Gympie, Queensland, to the north and Bellinger Island, New South Wales, to the south, while the northern subspecies *P. i. meyricki* occurs in northeastern Queensland. The species inhabits undisturbed lowland subtropical rainforest below 600m, where the host vine, Southern Carronia *Carroniaww multisepalea*, grows in a shrub-like manner.

Alan Henderson

Noosa National Park

Situated on the coast of south-east Queensland, established in 1939, this small national park covers 28.9km² and is best known for providing great opportunities to see Koalas, which are commonly seen in the car park. It is one of the most visited parks in Queensland – if not the most visited – and although it is in a heavily suburbanized area, it is home to more than 60 mammal species, 340 birds, 70 reptiles and 20 amphibians.

The park is one of the best places in which to see the Black-breasted Button-quail. With only small pockets of rainforest in the park, this rainforest/vine thicket-dwelling species has a patchy distribution with a restricted range in coastal and near-coastal southeastern Queensland. Other fantastic birds such as the Eastern Ground Parrot retain their last real stronghold in Queensland (predominantly in the Great Sandy National Park, but they also occur in some sections of Noosa National Park).

The park contains a diversity of habitats including melaleuca wetlands, eucalypt forest, wallum heathland and woodland in the four sections Noosa Headland, Emu Mountain, Peregian and East Weyba. While rainforest in the park is restricted, there are many species that rely on or utilize

Tourism Australia

Noosa Everglades

rainforest patches. The proximity to the coast means that the species in these small rainforest patches can vary dramatically from those in the nearby Sunshine Coast hinterland rainforest.

For those visiting, do not miss the coastal views and the amazingly scenic outlooks that are found around every bend of Noosa Headland.

GPS Coordinates
-26.38192, 153.09854 (Noosa Headland)
-26.50635, 153.08654 (Emu Mountain)
-26.48044, 153.09028 (Peregian)
-26.44018, 153.07388 (East Weyba)

Getting There
Drive north from Brisbane via the

Bruce Highway/M1 (140km). From Mooloolaba along the Sunshine Motorway/State Route 70 (55km), or if coming from the north, drive south from Gympie via Sunshine Motorway/ State Route 70 (95km).

Tracks & Trails
A range of hikes provides the opportunity to see all sides of the park. The *Coastal Walk* (5.4km) is scenic and provides the opportunity to see whales at the right time of year. This popular walk along the coast is wheelchair friendly and offers a beautiful way to finish your afternoon. For rainforest walks the *Tanglewood Walk* (8km) and *Palm Grove Walk* (1.1km) venture through thickets of rainforest, or visit the East Weyba section of the park to walk along fire-management tracks through the giant Hoop *Araucaria cunninghamii* and Kauri Pines *Agathis australis* dominating the rainforest.

Fees & Permits
Fees are payable for camping in Queensland national parks.

Facilities
Situated on the Sunshine Coast, the park is close to many towns, all of which have facilities. Throughout the various sections of the park there are toilets, picnic tables and day-use facilities such as barbecues and lookouts, but no camping is permitted in the park.

Services Nearby
All major services (fuel, mechanical repairs, banks, post office, supermarkets, restaurants, chemists, hospital and dental clinics) are located in Noosa and Brisbane.

Conondale National Park

Established in 1977 and covering an area of 358.8km², the national park protects more than 30 vegetation types, including wet and dry sclerophyll forests, open woodland, vine thickets and subtropical rainforest. The park is subject to significant seasonal changes in conditions, with temperatures varying between 0 °C (winter) and 35 °C (summer) and fluctuating with topography and vegetation cover. Annual rainfall can exceed 1,500mm, peaking during the November–April period and dropping during the winter months.

Like many of Queensland's parks, Conondale National Park and the surrounding area was subjected to logging (Red Cedar, Blackbutt and Tallowwood), mining (gold) and agriculture, and currently acts as a refuge for many species that have been cleared from the surrounding landscape.

Approximately 800 flora species have been recorded here, including stands of the Bunya Pine *Araucaria bidwillii*, Hoop Pine *A. cunninghamii* and Richmond Birdwing Vine *Pararistolochia praevenosa,* which is critical in the life-cycle of the Richmond Birdwing. More than 70 mammal species, 250 birds, 50 reptiles and 30 amphibians have been recorded in the park. Unfortunately, two species that once lived here are now considered extinct, the Southern Gastric Brood Frog and the Southern Dayfrog. Their deaths, like those of

Darren McMillan (CC)

Booloomba Creek

many amphibians, were due to the Chytrid Fungus, which continues to affect amphibian populations throughout Australia.

Although inhabitants of the park are legally protected, they are still threatened by changes to fire regimes, overgrazing and predation by feral animals, particularly cats and foxes, poison baiting and Cane Toads.

GPS Coordinates
-26.74337, 152.73145

Getting There
Head north from Brisbane via the M1 towards the Sunshine Coast before a left turn inland at Beerwah (108km). From the Sunshine Coast it is directly west via Maleny-Kenilworth Road (56km). It is a scenic drive south from Gympie via Maleny-Kenilworth Road (78km). Roads in the park are gravel

and there are a number of creek crossings that require a four-wheel-drive vehicle. Access is via either Maleny or Kenilworth.

Tracks & Trails
There are a number of walking tracks, including the short *Peters Creek Walk* (500m), *Booloumba Falls Walk* (3km) and *Strangler Cairn* (6.5km), or for the more physically inclined the four-day *Conondale Range Great Walk* (56km), beginning at the Booloumba day-use area. Walks vary in intensity but allow you to discover the creeks, cascades, waterfalls, rainforest and rock formations with great wildlife-watching opportunities. The park also offers mountain biking (vehicle tracks), horse riding (SEQ horse-trail network), swimming and scenic driving (in four-wheel-drive vehicles) and viewpoints such as the Mt Allan Fire Tower.

Fees & Permits
Fees are payable for camping in Queensland national parks.

Facilities
The Booloumba day-use area has picnic tables and camping areas, toilets, barbecues and public pay-phone facilities. Camp grounds include Booloumba Creek, which can take tents and campervans, but you will need a four-wheel-drive vehicle to access these sites due to river crossings. There is free camping at the nearby Charlie Moreland camping area, which is accessible by four-wheel-drive vehicles.

Services Nearby
Most major services (fuel, mechanical repairs, banks, post office, supermarkets, restaurants, chemists, hospital and dental clinics) are located in Caboolture and Caloundra.

Main Range National Park

Often overlooked due to the popularity of Lamington National Park, the less-visited Main Range National Park has just as much to offer, with the added benefit of fewer people to share it with. Covering an area of 348km², the park encompasses mountains, scenic views and a diverse array of walks, all within the Gondwana Rainforest of Australia World Heritage Area. The park is divided into four main sections: Cunninghams Gap, Spicers Gap, Queen Mary Falls and Goomburra; each has something different to offer.

This area is part of the western section of the Scenic Rim, a group of mountains that continues into northern New South Wales. It is subjected to a range of topographical changes that influence diversity of habitats in the park, which vary significantly and include subtropical and cool temperate rainforests, wet and dry sclerophyll forests and montane heath. This allows for a diversity of fauna, which includes more than 80 mammal species, 270 birds, 50 reptiles and 30 amphibians.

The park is home to some significant frogs and is considered a special area for Fleay's Barred Frog and the Red and Yellow Mountain Frog, which inhabit the streams of

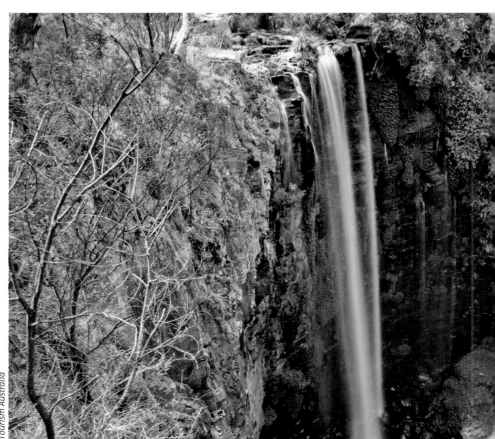

Tourism Australia

Queen Mary Falls

the park. Your cooperation in keeping away from streams will help to protect them. There are also a number of other threatened species. You may be lucky enough to see the Spotted-tailed Quoll or Hastings River Mouse *Pseudomys oralis* when visiting. While these threatened species may be difficult to find, the Queen Mary Falls are not and this magnificent waterfall is worth the visit.

GPS Coordinates
-28.04864, 152.38721

Getting There
A 112km drive south-west of Brisbane along National Highway 15 will get you to the centre of the park. From Warwick it is a 47km drive to the centre of the park or a 54km drive to the Goomburra section.

Tracks & Trails
A range of walks depart from each section of the park, providing opportunities for everyone. Highlights include *Araucaria Falls* (3.6km), the *Dalrymple Creek Circuit* (1.2km) and the walk through subtropical rainforest to *Sylvesters Lookout* (940m). For the more enthusiastic, the *Cascade Circuit* (6.5km) is a good warm-up for the *Scenic Rim Trail* (completed in 2020–2021), a four-day (three-night) hike through the park and private property.

Fees & Permits
Fees are payable for camping in Queensland national parks.

Facilities
There are three main camping areas in the park: Spicers Gap, and Poplar Flat and Manna Gum camping areas at Goomburra. These camping areas have toilets, but there are only barbecues at the Goomburra sites. There is little to no mobile telephone reception at the camping and day-use/picnic areas. Throughout the park there are numerous remote bush-camping areas that can be hiked to, but there are no facilities at any of these sites and they must be booked online before arrival. During wet conditions camp grounds may not be accessible.

Services Nearby
All major services (fuel, mechanical repairs, banks, post office, supermarkets, restaurants, chemists, hospital and dental clinics) are located in Warwick, Toowoomba and Ipswich.

Lamington National Park

Situated on the Queensland–New South Wales border, this area was once home to the Yugambeh people. Now, Lamington National Park is one of the best-known parks in eastern Australia. Established in 1915, the park contains the largest tract of subtropical rainforest in Australia and retains the magnificent Antarctic Beech *Nothofagus moorei* trees that define our connection with Gondwana and Antarctica. As was usually the case, this area was heavily logged before being given protection. Covering an area of 212km² and extending up to 1,100m elevation along the McPherson Range, the park is part of a UNESCO World Heritage Area and has more than 70 mammal species, 240 birds, 60 reptiles and 30 amphibians.

The lush green rainforest can be weaved through via the extensive network (160km) of trails that wind between numerous waterfalls and, while doing so, you are almost tripping over the wildlife. From the car park to the heart of the forest, you are constantly surrounded by the calls of parrots, riflebirds, catbirds, thornbills and scrubwrens, while the ever-watchful eyes of forest dragons peer from the trees and nocturnal fauna hides awaiting the sunset before coming out to forage.

The park is divided into two sections. The western side of the Lamington Plateau is called Green

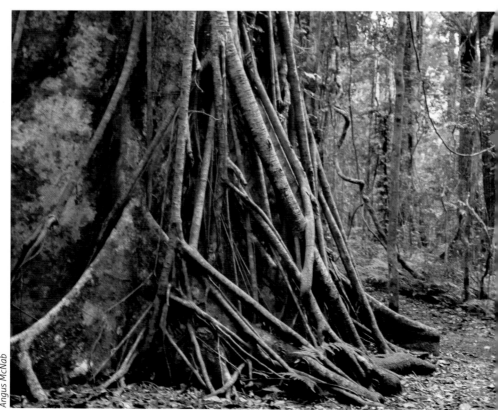

Angus McNab

Lamington National Park has an extensive network of walking trails

Mountains (also known as O'Reilly's, the family name of the owners of the resort that is located there), while the eastern side of the plateau is named Binna Burra, which is the local Aboriginal term for 'where the beech tree grows'. Unfortunately, the Binna Burra side of the park was subjected to significant fire damage during the 2019 summer and will take many years to recover.

GPS Coordinates
-28.23039, 153.13173 (O'Reilly)
-28.19878, 153.18520 (Binna Burra)

Getting There
From Gold Coast follow M1 and Beechmont Road to Binna Burra (65km), or M1 and Lamington National Park Road to Green Mountains (O'Reilly's) (87km). From Brisbane head south on the M3, to the M1, and towards Beaudesert-Beenleigh Road before turning on to Lamington National Park Road (114km).

Tracks & Trails
The park has an extensive network of walking trails, including a wheelchair-friendly 1km boardwalk at O'Reilly's and the *Python Rock Walk* (3.4km). It also contains a large number of waterfalls, camping and bird feeding at O'Reilly's. A 22km border track joins the two sections of the park and runs along the state border. Other spectacular walks include the *Picnic Rock, Elabana Falls, Moran Falls*, the *Wishing Tree* and *Box Forest Circuit*. Several walks from Binna Burra (most starting near the kiosk) are enjoyable hikes. The main walks are *Coomera Circuit* (17.4km, return), a moderately hard walk that can be shortened to an easier 1km by taking the *Tullawallal Loop* back to the *Border Track*, the *Lower Bellbird Circuit* (12km, return), *Rainforest Circuit* (1.2km, return) and *Bellbird Lookout* (2km, return).

Fees & Permits
Fees are payable for camping in Queensland national parks.

Facilities
Both Green Mountains and Binna Burra have toilets, picnic facilities, barbecues, cafe/kiosk and public telephone.

Services Nearby
Fuel is available at Canungra and shops are found at Beaudesert, Tamborine Mountain and Nerang. The closest hospital is located at Robina on the Gold Coast if you are at Binna Burra, or at Beaudesert if you are at O'Reilly's.

Border Ranges National Park

The Border Ranges National Park is part of the shield volcano group and is home to a section of the UNESCO World Heritage-listed Gondwana Rainforests of Australia (inscribed in 1986 and added to the Australian National Heritage List in 2007). The Gondwana Rainforests of Australia contain the most extensive areas of subtropical rainforest in the world. They also have large areas of warm temperate rainforest and the world's largest area of Antarctic Beech *Lophozonia moorei* cool temperate rainforest. The Gondwana Rainforests extend from southeastern Queensland to Barrington Tops National Park, New South Wales. The majority of the 317.3km² park is located in northern New South Wales, with a small portion extending into southeastern Queensland. The Bandjalang people of north-east New South Wales and south-east Queensland have strong cultural and spiritual connections to the Border Ranges region.

More than 4,000 plant species have been recorded in the region, including over 160 that are of major conservation significance, such as Davidson's Plum *Davidsonia pruriens,* Ormeau Bottletree *Brachychiton* sp. *Ormeau* and Springbrook Pinkwood *Eucryphia jinksii.* Vertebrate fauna of conservation significance that occurs in the region includes 22 bird species, 22 mammals, 17 reptiles and nine frogs. Of these, a number are largely

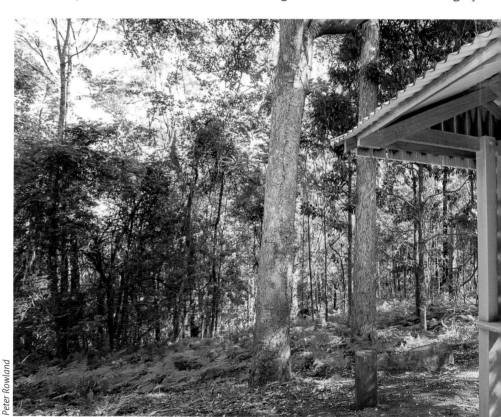

Peter Rowland

The majority of the Border Ranges National Park is located in New South Wales

restricted to the local area, including Albert's Lyrebird, Fleay's Barred Frog and the Richmond Birdwing butterfly.

Cane Toads have been recorded in rainforest in the park and pose a significant threat to its native fauna. The introduced wood-decaying Orange Pore Fungus *Favolaschia calocera* has also been recorded in the park and has the potential to spread rapidly, displacing the native fungi of the region.

GPS Coordinates
-28.46790, 153.14210

Getting There
The park is located 150km south of Brisbane, Queensland, and 32km north of Kyogle, New South Wales. From Queensland, follow the Mount Lindesay Highway and Running Creek Road. From Kyogle, follow Summerland Way, Lynches Creek Road and Forest Road.

Tracks & Trails
Border Loop Track (1.5km) is an easy walk that passes through the rainforest. *Bar Mountain Circuit* (4km) winds up to the Bar Mountain lookout. *Falcorostrum Loop* (650m) passes through ancient stands of Antarctic Beech, the trunks and branches of which are adorned with locally endemic Falcorostrum Orchids *Dendrobium falcorostrum*. Albert's Lyrebird can be seen foraging in the leaf litter among the beech trees. The *Red Cedar Loop* (750m) is an easy loop that passes a giant Red Cedar *Toona ciliata*. The *Helmholtzia Loop* (1km) passes through stands of Antarctic Beech and Hoop Pine *Araucaria cunninghamii* and crosses over Brindle Creek, a good place to search for the Rufous Scrub-bird. The longer *Brindle Creek Track* (6km, one way) passes through stands of Antarctic Beach and Hoop Pine and is a good place to see the regionally endemic Stream Lily *Helmholtzia glaberrima*, which grows in tall clumps along the track.

Fees & Permits
Park entry fees apply.

Facilities
There are many picnic areas, barbecues and toilets scattered throughout the park, and drinking water is available at *Falcorostrum Loop* and *Helmholtzia Loop* walking tracks. Camping is also available at Sheepstation Creek and Forest Tops.

Services Nearby
Kyogle, Woodenbong, Nimbin and Rathdowney are the best places to fuel up before heading out to the national park. Kyogle has most services.

Wollumbin National Park

Formerly known as Mount Warning National Park, Wollumbin is a sacred place to the Bundjalung Peoples, and was declared an Aboriginal Place in 2015. The name Mt Warning was given to Wollumbin, the remnant central vent of an extinct volcano, by Captain James Cook in 1770. Cook intended the 1,157m mountain to serve as a warning to sailors of the dangerous Point Danger reefs near Tweed Heads. Wollumbin, means 'cloud catcher'. The park was originally gazetted on 22 February 1928 as a recreation reserve; it was gazetted as the Mount Warning National Park on 14 January 1966. It has had some additions to its land area since then and now covers around 24km².

The national park is part of the ancient Mt Warning (Wollumbin) shield volcano of far northern New South Wales. The park's present-day land form is the result of large-scale erosion of the basalt rocks that formed the bulk of the original shield volcano and the slower erosion rate of the rhyolite that forms the central vent.

The park contains subtropical rainforest and is home to a rich diversity of animals and an even richer number of plant species. These include the Giant Stinging Tree *Dendrocnide excelsa,* Giant Spear Lily *Doryanthes*

Peter Rowland

Wollumbin is a sacred place to Bundjalung People, including the Galibal, Gidhabul, Nganduwal and Widja

palmeri, Lawyer Vine *Calamus muelleri*, maidenhair ferns *Adiantum* spp., Milky Silkpod *Parsonsia dorrigoensis*, Prickly Shield Fern *Polystichum vestitum*, Stinging Nettle *Urtica incisa*, Turpentine *Syncarpia leptopetala*, Water Vine *Cissus antarctica*, Wilkiea *Wilkiea huegeliana*, Wollumbin Dogwood *Ozothamnus vagans* and Wollumbin Zieria *Zieria adenodonta*.

GPS Coordinates
-28.38320, 153.33900

Getting There
Travel south-west from Murwillumbah (towards Uki) for about 12km and take a right turn on to Mount Warning Road. The car park is about 3.5km from the turn-off.

Tracks & Trails
The *Wollumbin (Mount Warning) Summit Track* (8.8km, return) is a sacred place to the Bundjalung People, and since 2015 visitors have been asked to respect the wishes of the Bundjalung Elders and avoid climbing it. If you do choose to climb this difficult track, take extreme care. It takes at least five hours to climb, is very steep and ends with a 100m vertical rock scramble to reach the exposed summit. *Lyrebird Track* (600m, return) is a short, easy walk that passes through subtropical rainforest to a stunning lookout. Along the way it crosses over Breakfast Creek. The rainforest along this track contains a huge diversity of plants and animals, so allow plenty of time to see everything that this short-but-sweet track offers. A few of the park's residents that can be encountered are the Australian Brush Turkey, Carpet Python, Eastern Whipbird, Koala, Lace Monitor, Land Mullet, Long-nosed Potoroo and Noisy Pitta.

Fees & Permits
Entry to the park is free.

Facilities
Toilets are located in the Breakfast Creek car park. Visitors must take their own rubbish away with them.

Services Nearby
The nearest town, Uki (10km), has some services, including post office, general store, cafe, bakery, pharmacy, guesthouse and laundromat. Murwillumbah (15km), located on the beautiful Tweed River, is larger and has more services, including markets, accommodation and a hospital.

eclared an Aboriginal Place in 2015

Nightcap National Park

This park's rainforests are part of the Shield Volcano group of Australia – UNESCO World Heritage-listed Gondwana Rainforests. The 81km² conservation area was established in 1983 and is approximately 70 per cent rainforest communities, with the remainder being mainly wet sclerophyll forest and some dry sclerophyll forest. The major occurrence of warm temperate rainforest in the bioregion is found on the rhyolitic soils of the Nightcap Range. The region is of significant cultural importance to the Bundjalung People of the Galibal, Githabul, Nganduwal and Widjabal language groups, and the national park contains many sacred sites.

The park protects a number of vulnerable and threatened animal species, as well as a large selection of those that are more secure. Some of the animal species you might encounter here include Albert's Lyrebird, Australian Brush Turkey, Australian Logrunner, Fleay's Barred Frog, Green Catbird, Lace Monitor, Pale-yellow Robin, Paradise Riflebird, Regent Bowerbird and Satin Bowerbird.

The national park is also home to a huge diversity of plant species, including the recently described and Critically Endangered Nightcap Oak *Eidothea hardeniana*, a member of the Proteaceae (banksia and grevillea) family. These trees can grow to 40m

Peter Rowland

Start of the Big Scrub Loop, which can become inaccessible after heavy rains

tall, but most are smaller and no living trees have been recorded outside the Nightcap Range. Other significant trees species in the park include the Blueberry Ash *Elaeocarpus reticulatus*, Coachwood *Ceratopetalum apetalum*, Minyon Quandong *Elaeocarpus sedentarius*, Peach Myrtle *Uromyrtus australis* and Southern Ochrosia *Ochrosia moorei*.

GPS Coordinates
-28.63970,153.33720

Getting There
The park is located around 35km north of Lismore and has several entry points: Gibbergunyah Range Road, Newton Drive and Terania Creek Road.

Tracks & Trails
Big Scrub Loop (1.5km, return) passes

through some of the most spectacular subtropical rainforest anywhere in New South Wales. The start of this track requires you to walk through a shallow waterway that can become impassable after heavy rainfall. *Boggy Creek Walk* (4km, return) is an easy winding trail through the rainforest between Minyon Falls and Rummery Park camp ground. *Minyon Falls Walking Track* (8km, return) is a moderately difficult walk that descends into the rainforest valley on its way to the base of the 100m-high waterfall (best to start at the *Minyon Falls Lookout*). *Mount Matheson Loop* (3km) takes you through lush rainforest to eucalypt forest on the dramatic cliff edges. The walk is challenging in places. *Pholis Gap* (4km, return) starts at Mt Nardi and winds through lush rainforest on its way to Pholis Gap and its spectacular views across to Wollumbin and over the rugged Nightcap escarpment. *Protesters Falls* (2.8km) is an easy walk through rainforest rich with palms and the massive buttress-rooted Yellow Carabeen *Sloanea woollsii* on its way to Protesters Falls and the rock pool at its base.

Fees & Permits
Entry to the park is free.

Facilities
Camping (Rummery Park), cycling trails (Whian Whian), picnic areas, barbecues, drinking water (Goorgana Walking Track) and toilets are available throughout the park.

Services Nearby
Nimbin (11km) has some services, including camping, but the town of Lismore (27km) is a major town with all commercial, cultural and administrative services.

NEW SOUTH WALES

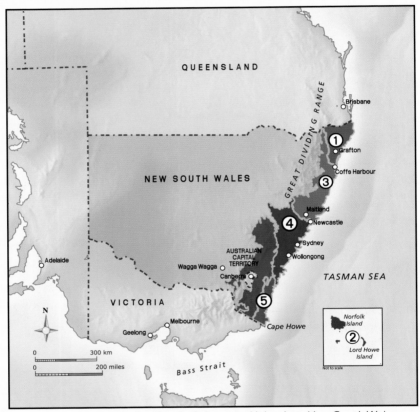

1. South East Queensland 2. Pacific Subtropical Islands 3. New South Wales North Coast 4. Sydney Basin 5. South East Corner

State Overview

The state of New South Wales covers 801,212.68km², of which 708,46.83km² is held in its 867 reserves. The state's 6,060km² of rainforests are the most diverse of any in Australia. They are widely distributed in the state's east, from the ancient, lush World Heritage listed subtropical Gondwana Rainforests that occur extensively within the Border Ranges National Park on the Queensland border, to the isolated pockets of dry temperate (littoral) rainforest of Mimosa Rocks National Park in the far south-east of the state.

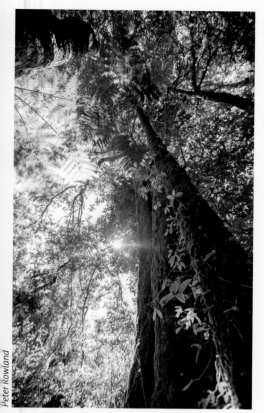

Iluka Nature Reserve

and open woodland found in the east. The uplands of the far west, the western plains in the central area and the Great Dividing Range in the east form the three main topographical regions. These regions contain a combined total of 17 bioregions, which support a huge number and diversity of plant and animal species.

Although generally regarded as having a mild temperate climate, the north-west of the state can experience much higher temperatures than the alpine areas of the south-east. Rainfall averages also show a gradual increase from west to east, with the north-west at around 200mm per year, compared with an annual mean of 1,500mm in the north-east.

The ancient Gondwana Rainforests (conserved in 28 separate reserves) and the Greater Blue Mountains Area are on the UNESCO World Heritage List of areas with natural and/or cultural values of global significance.

New South Wales is Australia's most populous state, with more than 7.8 million residents, and is the country's fifth largest state or territory. It is bordered by Queensland in the north, South Australia and the Northern Territory in the west, Victoria in the south and the Pacific Ocean along the east coast. Cape Byron is the state's (and the country's) most easterly mainland point. New South Wales surrounds the Australian Capital Territory, which contains the country's capital, Canberra, and has 41 offshore islands, although almost all of these are small and have either small or no resident human populations.

The state's landscape varies greatly from west to east, with sandy deserts, rocky ranges and plains dominating the west, and rainforests, mountain ranges

Myall Lakes National Park

Pacific Subtropical Islands

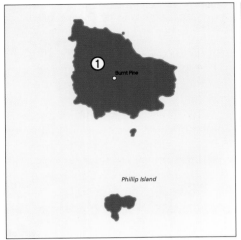

1. Norfolk Island 2. Lord Howe Island

The Pacific Subtropical Islands bioregion is one of four new oceanic bioregions added to IBRA7 (p. 6). It contains the Lord Howe and Norfolk Island groups. About 1,400 species of animal have been recorded in the bioregion, including 150 birds, nine mammals, five reptiles, three amphibians and more than 100 endemic land snails, the remainder consisting of insects and other invertebrates. Around 1,300 species of plant and fungus have also been recorded. The Lord Howe Island group covers an area of 19.09km², with about 11.75km² of that held in protected areas, including the island's gnarled mossy cloud forest on Lord Howe Island, which is classed as Critically Endangered. The Norfolk Island group covers 39.08km², of which 6.86km² are within protected areas. The key rainforest type found in this bioregion is subtropical.

Tourism Australia

Mt Gower, Lord Howe Island

Kathryn Himbeck

Norfolk Island

Key Species

BIRDS

Australian Golden Whistler, Channel-billed Cuckoo, Fan-tailed Cuckoo, Grey Fantail, Lord Howe Woodhen, Magpie-lark, Australian Masked Owl, Norfolk Gerygone, Morepork, Norfolk Parakeet, Pacific Emerald Dove, Pied Currawong, Providence Petrel, Shining Bronze-cuckoo, Silvereye.

MAMMALS

Gould's Wattled Bat, Large Forest-bat, Lord Howe Long-eared Bat (presumed extinct).

REPTILES

Delicate Skink (introduced), Lord Howe Island Gecko, Lord Howe Island Skink.

AMPHIBIANS

None.

INVERTEBRATES

Australian Wood Cockroach, Campbell's Keeled Glass Snail, Caper Gull, Helicarionid Land Snail, land snails *Allenoconcha basispiralis*, *Cryptochropa exagitans* and *Roybellia platystoma*, Lord Howe Flax-snail, Lord Howe Island Phasmid, Magnificent Helicarionid Land Snail, Mount Lidgbird Pinwheel, Norfolk Swallowtail, Phillip Island Centipede, Poinciana Longicorn, Slug-like Pinwheel Snail, Small-sculptured Glass Snail and Whitelegge's Pinwheel.

The Norfolk Island group lies 1,412km east of the Australian mainland and supports a population of about 1,750 people. It has a subtropical climate with average maximum temperatures at 18–19 °C in winter and 23–25 °C in summer. Temperatures rarely exceed 28 °C. The island's mean annual rainfall is 1,312mm.

Lord Howe Island lies some 900km south of Norfolk Island and 600km east of mainland Australia, and has a population of under 400 people. It experiences mild to warm summers with fairly regular rain. Its mean annual temperature ranges from lows of 12 °C in winter to highs of 27 °C in summer, and it receives mean annual rainfall of 1,463mm.

Winters are significantly wetter than the rest of the year on both island groups and the driest months on average are in November–February. El Niño weather events can cause extended periods of lower than average rainfall or droughts.

John Harris

Red-tailed Tropicbird on nest, Norfolk Island

Lord Howe Woodhen *Hypotaenida sylvestris*

Patrick Kavanagh (CC)

This flightless bird is endemic to Lord Howe Island, where it lives on the ground and feeds on insects and other invertebrates. It was almost hunted to extinction by visiting sailors, early settlers and introduced feral predators, and it is estimated that fewer than 30 individuals existed by the 1970s. Within a short period of time it had withdrawn to just two remote mountain locations. A captive-breeding programme was established in the early 1980s in an attempt to resurrect the species, and numbers have increased dramatically. Today these chicken-sized brown birds, with moderately long, slightly decurved bills and short, robust legs, are a familiar sight on the island. The species forms lifelong pair bonds and maintains an established territory of about 3ha. Nesting takes place in burrows or under tree roots.

Norfolk Gerygone *Gerygone modesta*

John Harris

This 'little brown bird', known locally as the 'peurty', is endemic to Norfolk Island. It is closely related to and treated by some authors as conspecific with the Grey Warbler *G. igata* of New Zealand and the now extinct Lord Howe Gerygone *G. insularis*. It is olive-brown above, the tail with a broad blackish tip. The face is pale grey with a broken white eye-ring, pale eyebrow and small dark patch in front of the eye. The underparts are pale with a yellow wash. It inhabits rainforests, adjacent vegetation, pastureland and gardens, and forages for insects in the canopy area, either by actively investigating concealed areas or by gleaning prey from foliage while hovering. It has a melodic, warbling song.

Norfolk Parakeet *Cyanoramphus cookii*

John Harris

The Norfolk Parakeet is treated by some authorities as a subspecies of the Red-crowned Parakeet *C. novaezelandiae*. It is primarily green with a blue leading edge to the wings, and a red crown and spot behind the eye. At the time of the first British settlement, it was described as occurring in destructive plagues of very large flocks that wreaked havoc on planted crops. However, by the late 1980s there were reported to be only 32 birds, comprising four breeding pairs. The current estimate of the population is around 400 birds. This parrot primarily occurs in Norfolk Island Pine *Araucaria heterophylla* tall closed rainforest, as well as in other native vegetation, eucalypt plantations and areas adjacent to native forest. It primarily eats seeds, fruits, flowers and leaves of native and introduced trees and shrubs.

Providence Petrel *Pterodroma solandri*

Peter Rowland

An unusual bird to include as a rainforest species, this robust seabird relies heavily on the rainforests of Mt Lidgard and Mt Gower, where it nests in burrows or rock crevices. It is dark grey-brown with a paler head, brown eye and off-white triangular patches under the wing. Its face and forehead are marked with fine white scalloping, and its bill is short and black. Its legs are brownish black and the webbing between the toes is grey to black. The species was once numerous on Norfolk Island, but its population there was decimated by hunting in the late eighteenth century, although it still breeds in small numbers on the nearby Phillip Island.

135

Gould's Wattled Bat *Chalinolobus gouldii*

Angus McNab

This bat has predominantly dark brown fur on the back, and almost black shoulders, neck and head. The 'wattled' part of the name refers to the fleshy lobe or wattle that sits between the base of the ear and corner of the mouth. Gould's Wattled Bat can be found in nearly every climatic zone in Australia and in most habitats with trees. It roosts in hollows of old trees and in some cases in old buildings. In southern parts of Australia it is usually one of the first bats to emerge from winter hibernation, and one of the first bats to emerge at dusk each evening. A capable flier, much of its hunting is done above the canopy but individuals will use 'flyways' and paths within the forest to ease their movement through the landscape. It feeds on a rich diversity of flying and non-flying insects.

Lord Howe Island Gecko *Christinus guentheri*

Steve Wilson

Found on Lord Howe Island and islands of Norfolk Island, this heavily built reptile exhibits a broad habitat preference, which includes lowland and montane rainforests, and shows a marked preference for rocky areas with crevices and similar shelter. It is pale grey to dark brown above, finely spotted with darker brown and with six paler 'W'-shaped transverse markings and paler yellow-brown to whitish on the flanks and underparts. The tail has a reddish stripe, but this is often lost before reaching maturity. Females lay 1–3 eggs in rock crevices and tunnels, and several females may lay eggs in the same nest site. Food consists of nectar, fruits, leaves, seeds and a range of invertebrates.

Lord Howe Island Skink *Oligosoma lichenigera*

Steve Wilson

This medium-sized skink is endemic to the Lord Howe and Norfolk Island groups, although it is considered to be extinct in Norfolk Island, but still occurs on the nearby Phillip Island; its distribution on Lord Howe Island is much reduced. It is rich metallic-bronze to olive-brown above, variably marked with brownish flecks and stripes, with a pale yellowish stripe from above the eye to the tail. The underparts are grey to white, typically with darker markings on the throat. It inhabits a range of habitats, including rainforest, where it shows a preference for basalt boulder fields. It shelters during the day in rock crevices, under rocks and in tree hollows, and emerges at night to forage in leaf litter for insects and other invertebrates.

Lord Howe Island Phasmid *Dryococelus australis*

Rohan Cleave (Zoos Victoria)

This Critically Endangered, flightless stick insect is found only on Balls Pyramid, off Lord Howe Island. It was formerly abundant on Lord Howe Island, but became extinct shortly after the introduction of the Black Rat, which was most likely to have occured in 1918 following the shipwreck of the SS *Makamba*. The House Mouse had already invaded the island some 58 years earlier and may also have had some impact. The species is dark golden-brown with a pale creamish stripe along the abdomen. Females (12cm) are larger than males (10cm), but males have longer, thicker antennae and a more slender abdomen, which also lacks the ovipositor possessed by the female. Juveniles are bright green. Adults are mainly nocturnal, but juveniles are active during the day.

137

Norfolk Island

When Captain Cook sighted Norfolk Island in 1774, little did he realize that human history here dated back to the Polynesian seafarers 700–800 years before. The first British settlement was established in 1788 and hoped to make use of the island's natural resources, including the Norfolk Island Pine *Araucaria heterophylla* and 'harakeke' or New Zealand Flax *Phormium tenax*. Much of the island was cleared for agriculture, with the rich volcanic soils helping to sustain the fledgling colony of New South Wales. In the winter of 1790, at least 172,000 Providence Petrels were slaughtered in four months to feed the island's increased population following the shipwreck of HMS *Sirius*. Along with these early settlers came the introduction of feral animals, such as the Polynesian Rat, Feral Pig, Feral Goat, European Rabbit and Domestic Cat, which have all had a devastating impact on the island's wildlife and continue to be a major threat.

Norfolk Island covers approximately 35km² and has a population of nearly 1,800 people. Nearly 120 bird species have been recorded here, including 17 Australian endemic species or subspecies (only eight are confirmed as still extant). The island group has two native reptiles, the Lord Howe Island Skink and Lord Howe Island Gecko. There are no

Kathryn Himbeck

Palm Glen Circuit Track passes through lush rainforest gullies containing the world's tallest tree ferns and I

endemic mammals or frogs.

In addition to its vertebrate fauna, the island has a large number of endemic invertebrates, including about 30 moths, 65 beetles, up to 70 land snails and the 150mm-long, 17mm-wide Phillip Island Centipede. About 50 endemic plant species have been described.

GPS Coordinates
-29.02529, 167.93826

Getting There
Air New Zealand flies from Sydney and Brisbane. Norfolk Island Airlines also flies from Brisbane.

Tracks & Trails
There are 10 walking tracks throughout Norfolk Island National

Park that, with some planning, can be undertaken as loops. Some are listed here. *Palm Glen Circuit Track* (910m, return) is a circuit track that begins at the Palm Glen picnic area, which has tables and a toilet. It passes through lush rainforest gullies containing the world's tallest tree ferns and Norfolk Palms. The botanic gardens have a series of trails with some, such as the *Garden Trail* and *The Boardwalk*, being easy walks also suitable for wheelchairs. The *Rainforest Gully Circuit* is the longest trail in the gardens, totalling about 800m from the parks and gardens visitor centre.

Fees & Permits
While there is no charge to visit the national park, visitors can buy a parks pack from the visitor information centre or national parks office. The pack includes a walking track map, and bird, plant and Phillip Island pamphlets. The funds raised from the sales go towards protecting and managing the park and botanic gardens.

Facilities
The national park and botanic gardens have a variety of facilities such as toilets, barbeques, tourist information and boardwalks. Elsewhere on the island there are numerous lookouts with seating and picnic tables.

Services Nearby
Burnt Pine, the largest community on the island, has a variety of accommodation, cafes, restaurants and food/drink outlets, as well as a bank, postal services, tourist information, tour companies and hire-car outlets.

Lord Howe Island

The UNESCO World Heritage listed Lord Howe Island group is a subtropical paradise, boasting the most southerly coral reef in the world. Two towering mountains named Lidgbird (777m) and Gower (875m) sit at one end of the island. Lieutenant Lidgard Ball, commander of the First Fleet ship *Supply*, happened on the island in 1788, while en route between Sydney Cove and the penal settlement of Norfolk Island.

Dramatic volcanic sea-cliffs, rainforest with many rare native plants and a diversity of land and seabirds make this a unique and compelling place to visit. Although considered part of the state of New South Wales, its distance offshore makes it very difficult to access other than by air.

Across the entire summits of Mt Lidgbird and Mt Gower, the rainforest consists of a dense growth of small trees and an abundance of bushes, palms and tree ferns rarely exceeding 4m in height. Epiphytic ferns, lichens and orchids cover almost every available trunk and branch. Ancient flowering plants like the Island Apple *Dysoxylum pachyphyllum,* Lord Howe Tea Tree *Leptospermum polygalifolium* and Mountain Rose *Metrosideros nervulosa* grow readily in the mountain mists.

As is the case with many remote islands, the fauna of Lord Howe Island

Marcello Saponaro (CC)

A large number of oceanic rainforest communities are widely distributed across low- to high-altitude areas

has been negatively impacted by human disturbance and the associated introduction of feral animals. The introduction of the Black Rat, which was most likely to have occured in 1918 following the shipwreck of the SS *Makamba,* has caused much destruction to the local fauna. The House Mouse had already invaded the island some 58 years earlier.

GPS Coordinates
-31.59510, 159.07120

Getting There
There is a two-hour flight from Sydney via Qantas link most weekdays; Brisbane flights (1 hour 50 minutes) are available on weekends.

Tracks & Trails

A large number of rainforest communities are widely distributed across low- to high-altitude areas throughout the island. Patches of these can be accessed from a number of locations throughout the island. Some of these include:

Lowlands *Transit Hill, Middle Beach Common, Moseley Park, Stevens Reserve, Ned's Beach Common* and *Capella South.*

Montane *Erskine Valley, Goat House Track, Rocky Run* and parts of the lower road on the western shoreline.

Cloud Forest Summits of Mt Lidgard and Mt Gower.

Fees & Permits
Entry is free to any part of the island, via the walking tracks or roads.

Facilities
A variety of accommodation types is available (no camping). Picnic areas and barbecues are found at the Aquatic Club, Cobby's Corner, Ned's Beach, North Bay, Old Settlement, the Pines and the Playground. Most barbecues are wood fired, but those at Ned's Beach and North Bay are gas powered. Public toilets are available at Ned's Beach, North Bay, Old Settlement, the Playground and the Public Hall. A swimming pontoon is located at the Pines.

Services Nearby
Lord Howe Island has all essential services, including schools, bank, supermarket, liquor store, cafes, restaurants, bowling club and golf club, kayak hire, diving gear, guided tours and boat trips, which include fishing and general trips.

e island

New South Wales North Coast

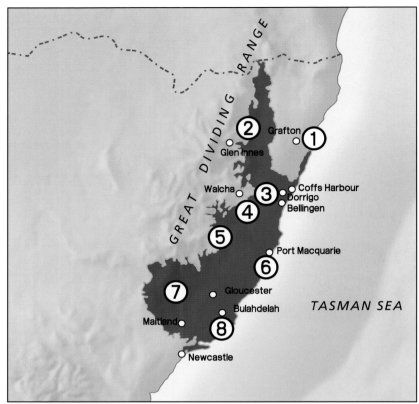

1. Iluka Nature Reserve 2. Washpool National Park 3.Dorrigo National Park 4. New England National Park 5. Oxley Wild Rivers National Park 6. Sea Acres National Park 7.Barrington Tops National Park 8.Myall Lakes National Park

The New South Wales North Coast bioregion covers 39,966km² and encompasses 19 subregions. It extends from the Queensland border to just north of Newcastle, New South Wales, although about 20,000km² of north-east New South Wales, previously included within this bioregion, are now within the South East Queensland bioregion. The bioregion supports more than 8,000 described animal species, including 450 birds, 100 mammals, 135 reptiles, 60 amphibians and over 5,100 insects and 600 spiders. In addition to this impressive fauna total, it supports more than 6,000 described plants and fungi. It contains several rainforest types, including dry, littoral, cool temperate, northern warm temperate and subtropical rainforests. Several rainforest communities are considered threatened, including some that are Critically Endangered.

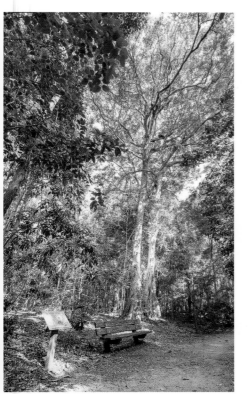

Iluka Nature Reserve

Key Species

BIRDS

Australasian Figbird, Australian Golden Whistler, Australian Logrunner, Barred Cuckoo-shrike, Bassian Thrush, Black-faced Monarch, Cicadabird, Eastern Whipbird, Eastern Yellow Robin, Green Catbird, Lewin's Honeyeater, Noisy Pitta, Pacific Emerald Dove, Pale-yellow Robin, Paradise Riflebird, Regent Bowerbird, Rose Robin, Rufous Scrub-bird, Russet-tailed Thrush, Scarlet Myzomela, Spectacled Monarch, Superb Fruit-dove, Superb Lyrebird, Topknot Pigeon, White-eared Monarch, White-throated Treecreeper, Wompoo Fruit-dove, Wonga Pigeon, Yellow-throated Scrubwren.

MAMMALS

Black-striped Wallaby, Brown Antechinus, Eastern Falsistrelle, Eastern Ring-tailed Possum, Golden-tipped Bat, Long-nosed Potoroo, Northern Free-tailed Bat, Parma Wallaby, Platypus, Red-legged Pademelon, Sugar Glider, Swamp Wallaby, Yellow-bellied Glider.

REPTILES

Black-bellied Swamp Snake, Burton's Legless Lizard, Carpet Python, Eastern Water Dragon, Eastern Water-skink, Golden-crowned Snake, Gully Skink, Land Mullet, Murray's Skink, Orange-tailed Shadeskink, Red-bellied Snake, Red-tailed Calyptotis, Rose's Shadeskink, Scute-snouted Calyptotis, Southern Angle-headed Dragon, Southern Dwarf Crowned Snake, Stephens' Banded Snake, Three-clawed Worm-skink.

AMPHIBIANS

Cascade Tree Frog, Dainty Green Tree Frog, Davies' Tree Frog, Giant Barred Frog, Glandular Frog, Great Barred Frog, Hip Pocket Frog, Loveridge's Frog, Mountain Stream Frog, Pugh's Mountain Frog, Red and Yellow Mountain Frog, Sandpaper Frog, Sphagnum Frog, Stuttering Frog, Tusked Frog, Wilcox's Frog.

INVERTEBRATES

Australian Land Leech, Four-barred Swallowtail, Giant King Cricket, Jezebel Nymph, Leafwing, Poinciana Longicorn, Purple Crow, Regent Skipper, Rhinoceros Beetle, Vampire Moth.

Peter Rowland

Paradise Riflebird (female)

Dry rainforests are scattered in gorges, on foothills and in riparian corridors in the east of the state. Examples of these occur in Barrington Tops and Oxley Wild Rivers National Parks. Littoral dry rainforest types occur in coastal areas. Iluka Nature Reserve has the largest area of this in New South Wales. Cool temperate rainforest is found in small isolated stands in New South Wales, mainly at higher altitudes, mostly in the higher ranges, such as Barrington Tops National Park. Northern warm temperate rainforests grow mainly in sheltered areas of hilly regions. New England National Park contains a large area of this rainforest type. Subtropical rainforests typically occur in regions that receive more than 1,300mm of annual rainfall. They are more extensive in sheltered gully areas up to about 900m above sea level. These occur in Dorrigo and Barrington Tops National Parks.

Australasian Figbird *Sphecotheres vieilloti*

Frequently associated with the Olive-backed Oriole (p. 146), the Australasian Figbird shares much of the same range and the two are often confused. Females are superficially oriole-like but have dark brown upperparts, more heavily streaked underparts, and a short dark bill and dark eye. Males are easier to identify; the back is olive-green, the head black and the eye surrounded by bare red skin. Southern males have grey underparts and collar; northern males are bright yellow below and lack the grey collar. This species largely eats soft fruits. It lives in flocks in rainforest and eucalypt forest, where its downwardly inflected *tcher* is a characteristic sound.

Australian Golden Whistler *Pachycephala pectoralis*

This bird is a melodic whistler. Males have a black hood that wraps below the throat forming a breast-band that separates the white throat from the vibrant yellow underparts. The nape is also yellow, while the remaining upperparts are olive yellow-brown. The upperwings are dark grey-brown with olive-yellow edging and the tail is grey. Females are duller, with grey-brown upperparts, a brown head and a white throat. The underparts are tan-brown with a slight rufous-yellow wash. The young resemble females but have a rufous wash to the wings and a pale base to the bill. The call is strong, musical and varied, including a *we-we-we-whit*, the last note strongly emphasized.

Angus McNab

Angus McNab

Azure Kingfisher *Ceyx azureus*

Peter Rowland

This beautiful small kingfisher has striking violet-blue upperparts, rufous-orange underparts (paler on the throat) and bright coral-pink legs and feet. A large buff-white patch is visible on the neck-sides. The long black bill has a small white spot at the tip of each mandible and is adapted to catch fish, crustaceans and aquatic insects. This is the second smallest of Australia's kingfishers, after the Little Kingfisher *C. pusillus*, but the two are easily distinguished by breast colour. The Azure Kingfisher is found in stream-side vegetation in both dry and wet forests and mangroves throughout northern and eastern Australia, including Tasmania and offshore islands. The common call is a loud, high-pitched *seeeeeeep*.

Lewin's Honeyeater *Meliphaga lewinii*

Peter Rowland

This honeyeater has dark greenish-grey colouration, interrupted only by the creamy yellow of the gape and the yellowish crescent-shaped patch on the ear-coverts. The sexes are similar in appearance. It is mostly frugivorous, eating berries and small fruits, but also takes insects and some nectar. Its strong rattling notes carry over long distances and instantly confirm its presence in an area. It is common in wetter parts of eastern Australia, frequenting both rainforest and wet sclerophyll forest, and often wandering into more open woodland. Some similar species are found in north Queensland, but can be distinguished by the combination of size, voice and shape of the ear-covert patch.

Noisy Pitta *Pitta versicolor*

Angus McNab

This bird has a distinctive chestnut cap, black eye-stripe, green back, iridescent blue wing-patch, buff-yellow underparts, black belly-patch, red undertail-coverts and short, stumpy tail. In flight, it reveals large white wing-patches. Despite this striking plumage pattern, it can be difficult to see and is more often heard than seen. Its call is loud and well known, resembling the words 'walk to work', and often betrays an individual's presence. The species lives primarily in the rainforests of Australia's east coast, but also enters mangroves and spends much of its time on the ground. It eats various terrestrial vertebrates, particularly snails.

Olive-backed Oriole *Oriolus sagittatus*

Peter Rowland

Although similar in size to several other species that gather together in fruiting trees, the Olive-backed Oriole is distinguished by the combination of olive-green upperparts, white underparts with dark teardrop-shaped streaks and, in particular, the salmon-coloured bill and red eye. The Green Oriole (p. 333), which overlaps with this species in tropical Australia, is yellow-green and more finely streaked below. The Olive-backed Oriole's pleasant *olly ole* call is a familiar sound in the wooded habitats that it occupies in northern and eastern Australia, which range from rainforests to drier inland scrubland. It also visits urban parks and gardens, as well as commercial orchards.

Pacific Baza *Aviceda subcristata*

This beautiful bird of prey with a distinctive erectile black crest has an alternative name of Crested Hawk, although the boldly barred underparts and large yellow eyes might catch the observer's attention first. The head is pale blue-grey, the wings darker and the back brownish. Despite its bold appearance the species often goes unnoticed as it conceals itself in the foliage of trees or flies slowly over the canopy. During the breeding season, however, its tumbling acrobatic courtship flight and *whee-chou* call readily attract attention. It inhabits the edges of eucalypt forests and rainforests, particularly along watercourses, where it snatches insects from close to the foliage and in mid-air.

Peter Rowland

Rainbow Lorikeet *Trichoglossus moluccanus*

This aptly named lorikeet of many colours has one of the most beautiful plumages of all Australian parrots. The head and belly are blue, the breast is red-orange, and the upperparts and tail are green. Both the bill and the eyes are red. The underwing has large red patches, a yellow stripe and grey wing-tips. Young birds have an orange-brown bill and dark brown eyes. This bird frequents rainforests, open forests and urban parks and gardens in eastern and southeastern Australia. It has been introduced in other parts of Australia, most notably around Perth, Western Australia, and Tasmania, originally due to escaped aviary birds. The Red-collared Lorikeet (p. 344) of northern Western Australia, the Northern Territory and northwestern Queensland was formerly considered a subspecies of this species.

Angus McNab

Rose-crowned Fruit-dove *Ptilinopus regina*

Peter Rowland

Although seasonally abundant and beautifully coloured (female duller than male), this small dove often goes unseen in the densely vegetated canopy areas of the rainforests that it inhabits. The rich rose-coloured crown, edged with yellow, and orange-yellow belly and vent, distinguish it from the Superb Fruit-dove (p. 150), which has a mainly white belly and vent. The species overlap in range in eastern Australia. The Rose-crowned Fruit-dove is nomadic, following the availability of the fruits on which it feeds. Where food is plentiful, it can form large flocks. Its most common calls are a loud *coo-coo-coo-coo-coo,* which is uttered faster towards the end, and a soft, three-note *boo-uk-boo.* It is found in a broad coastal band through northern and eastern Australia, from the Kimberley, Western Australia, to just north of Sydney, New South Wales.

Rufous Fantail *Rhipidura rufifrons*

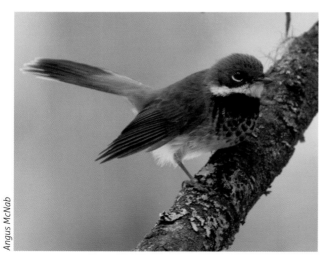

Angus McNab

The Rufous Fantail is the most colourful of Australia's five fantails. Its long grey-brown tail, with bright rufous base, is fanned out as it busily flits from tree to tree. The rump and forehead are also rufous in colour, while the remaining plumage is brown above and white below, with black mottling on the throat. Its range extends in a broad coastal band from the Kimberley, Western Australia, through northern and eastern Australia, to western Victoria. It prefers wetter forests and woodland and is a familiar sight in rainforest, dense eucalypt forest and mangroves. It actively forages among the foliage for insects and is confiding and inquisitive around humans. It is a migratory species, especially in southern areas of its range.

Rufous Scrub-bird *Atrichornis rufescens*

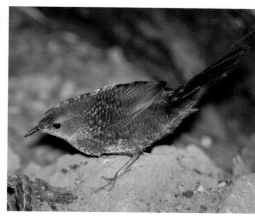

David Stowe

This stocky, ground-dwelling bird is very elusive. It has a restricted range between Barrington Tops and the Border Ranges, New South Wales, above 600m in altitude. It has quite specific habitat requirements. Although largely associated with subtropical, warm temperate and cool temperate rainforests, it can also be found in wet and dry sclerophyll forests, provided that there is a dense layer of leaf litter and the vegetation is moist, dense and around 1m high. Both sexes are brown above and rufous below, with fine barring and a white malar stripe. The male has more extensive black plumage on the throat, breast and flanks. The male's variety of calls and mimicry, given most often during the breeding season, can betray its presence, but the dense vegetation renders it almost invisible, even at close quarters.

Russet-tailed Thrush *Zoothera heinei*

Angus McNab

This heavily mottled, ground-dwelling thrush occurs in rainforests and wetter lowland forests, where it forages in leaf litter in clearings and along tracks for invertebrates. It has a white eye-ring, which contrasts with the large dark bill. The upperparts are rufous-brown with black scalloping, and the throat, breast and flanks are white with dark brown-black scalloping. The legs are pinkish-brown. The tail is slightly shorter than that of the very similar Bassian Thrush (p. 90) and has broader white tips on the outer feathers. This species generally occurs at lower altitudes than the Bassian Thrush (down to 250m above sea level), but the ranges of the two species do overlap in south-east Queensland and eastern New South Wales (north of Newcastle). The song, a two-note *wheee-dooo*, provides the easiest way to differentiate the species. The song of the Bassian Thrush is a more complex warble.

Scarlet Myzomela *Myzomela sanguinolenta*

Peter Rowland

The Scarlet Myzomela is diminutive in size, but not in colour or voice. The male has a vibrant scarlet head, breast and central back, with a black rump, wings and tail and white belly and flanks. The female and young are brown, with adult females having varying amounts of red on the face. The bill is long and downwardly curved and, like most other honeyeaters, it feeds on nectar, insects, fruits and sugary excretions from certain insects. The voice is a pleasant short, high-pitched warble. It inhabits forests, riverine areas and nearby urban parks and gardens, from northeastern Queensland to southern Victoria, although it is an uncommon visitor in the south of its range.

Superb Fruit-dove *Ptilinopus superbus*

Michael Schmid

Similar in size to the Rose-crowned Fruit-dove (p. 148) and equally difficult to spot in the canopy of the rainforest, the Superb Fruit-dove occupies much of the same range in eastern Australia. Unlike the Rose-crowned, the male and female show strong sexual dimorphism. The adult male has a purple crown, reddish-orange nape, olive-green back and wings, grey throat and black breast-band (tinged with blue in some individuals). The female and young males are predominantly green, the adult female with some darker spots on the back. Both sexes have a white belly, with large green patches. The species is known to feed on more than 50 species of rainforest fruits. Its call is a double note *coo-coo* and a low *oom*.

Yellow-throated Scrubwren *Neosericornis citreogularis*

Angus McNab

This bird's yellow throat and dark mask, fringed with white or yellow, are distinctive characteristics, easily seen in the darkness of the forest floor, where individuals move about in pairs or small family groups as they forage for food. The remaining plumage is primarily olive-brown. The nest is a large, pendulous structure suspended from a branch, typically over a stream within the rainforest. The call is a pleasant series of tucking notes, and the song includes melodious whistles interspersed with excellent mimicry of the vocalizations of other birds. Two discontinuous populations occur in the east of Australia, one in the Wet Tropics, Queensland, the other extending from southern Queensland to southeastern New South Wales.

Brown Antechinus *Antechinus stuartii*

Ryan Francis

Often taken for a mouse or rat, the antechinus is a small dasyurid, a relative of quolls and Tasmanian Devils (p. 267). It is a tiny carnivore, greyish-brown above washed with reddish-brown and paler brown below. Extremely active, it spends the nights hunting for small invertebrates in the leaf litter and cracks and crevices of trees. It regularly takes on comparatively large prey. Individuals sleep during most days in a communal nest in a tree hollow, crevice or hollow log. Due to its semelparous lifestyle, the life span of this species is usually restricted to less than one year. After the breeding season males die off, leaving pregnant females to give birth and raise young before passing away themselves.

Eastern Falsistrelle *Falsistrellus tasmaniensis*

Angus McNab

Also known as the Eastern False Pipistrelle, this bat is relatively large and has long, fine, dark brown to reddish-brown fur (paler and more greyish below). The ears are long, slender and narrow, and set well back on the head. There is some scattered hair on the nose. The species occurs in southeastern Australia, from far southeastern South Australia, through Victoria, Tasmania (including islands of Bass Strait), and eastern New South Wales, to southeastern Queensland. It inhabits rainforests, wet sclerophyll and tall open eucalypt forests, generally with a dense understorey. It roosts mainly in hollow eucalyptus tree trunks, under loose bark on trees, but has also been recorded in caves, in small to medium-sized colonies of up to 80 individuals. It forages nocturnally through the forest canopy, along creeks and tracks, for large moths, beetles, weevils and other insects.

Long-nosed Potoroo *Potorous tridactylus*

Angus McNab

This species is grey or brown above and paler below, with a naked patch of skin extending along the long, pointed nose and on to the snout. It is smaller, with proportionally smaller feet than the Long-footed Potoroo (p. 211). The hindfoot is shorter than the length of the nose. It occurs from southeastern Queensland, to far southeastern South Australia and Tasmania (including islands of Bass Strait). It is found in moist areas with dense groundcover in a range of habitats, including rainforests, wet sclerophyll forests, woodland, shrubland and heathland. In New South Wales it favours coastal heath and forests east of the Great Dividing Range, where the annual rainfall is greater than 760mm. This species is predominantly nocturnal and rests by day in groundcover of thick vegetation. It is omnivorous and feeds mostly on subterranean fungi and roots.

Parma Wallaby *Notamacropus parma*

Brian Gratwicke (CC)

This wallaby is reddish-brown above, with a darker longitudinal dorsal stripe and white cheek-stripe. The underparts are whitish, paler on the chest and throat, and the tail is often tipped with white. This species is known from the ranges and slopes of eastern New South Wales, from the Queensland border, south to around Gosford. Its habitat is moist eucalypt forest with a thick, shrubby understorey, often with nearby grassy areas, rainforest margins and occasionally drier eucalypt forest. It feeds at night on grasses and herbs in more open eucalypt forest and the edges of nearby grassy areas, and also uses runways to move through the dense understorey. During the day individuals shelter in dense cover.

Platypus *Ornithorhynchus anatinus*

Angus McNab

The Platypus has a streamlined body covered with dense, dark greyish to reddish-brown, waterproof fur above, and a flat, paddle-shaped tail and broad, greyish-brown 'duck-like' bill that extends over the forehead and chin. It also has short limbs with webbed feet. Males possess a poisonous horny spur on the ankle of each hindleg. The species is distributed throughout eastern and southeastern Australia. It is found in regularly flowing river systems and associated billabongs, where it hunts along the bottom of the waterway for a variety of large aquatic invertebrates. The bill has electrosensors and mechanoreceptors to detect electrical pulses and movement of prey. The nesting chamber is at the end of a long burrow with an entrance just above the water level. Up to three (usually two) soft-shelled eggs are incubated for about 12 days before they hatch.

Red-legged Pademelon *Thylogale stigmatica*

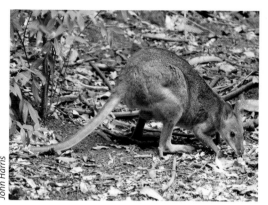

John Harris

This small macropod has soft, thick fur and is greyish-brown above, more rufous on the hindlegs, flanks, forearms and cheeks, and has a pale brownish stripe on the hip. The underparts are off white to greyish. The rainforest-dwelling individuals are darker than those living in vine thickets. The tail is short, about 75–85 per cent of the head-body length. The species is distributed on ranges and slopes from Cape York, Queensland, to the Wyong area on the central coast of New South Wales. It is found in dense understorey and groundcover in rainforests, wet sclerophyll forests and vine thickets. It is active in the late afternoon to the early morning, but stays in dense vegetation by day and forages in more open areas at night, feeding on native grasses, herbs, seedlings and stem leaves, fungi, ferns, and fruits.

Swamp Wallaby *Wallabia bicolor*

Peter Rowland

This wallaby is dark reddish-brown to black above, with a light pale yellowish-brown cheek-stripe (more prominent in northern individuals), light brown to rufous-orange on the chest, and pale yellowish to orange-brown below. Its extremities, such as the tail, forearms and legs, show a darker, almost black colouring, and the tail occasionally has a white tip. The species is broadly distributed in coasts, slopes and ranges of eastern and southeastern Australia (including Fraser Island), from northern Cape York Peninsula, Queensland, through eastern New South Wales and southern Victoria, and possibly into far southeastern South Australia. It is found in forests, woodland and heaths with a dense understorey. It shelters during most of the day in dense vegetation, often in moist areas, and emerges at night to feed on grasses, shrubs, ferns and seedlings. When disturbed, it bounds away with head held low and tail held straight.

Yellow-bellied Glider *Petaurus australis*

This glider is grey above with a conspicuous black vertebral stripe, and white (young) or yellow (adults) below. The feet are black, and the tail is long and black, edged with grey at the base. The gliding membrane is large and edged with black. The species occurs from northeastern Queensland, through eastern New South Wales, eastern and southern Victoria, to far southeastern South Australia. It inhabits mainly mature wet eucalypt forests in an ecotone between rainforest and drier woodland ecosystems in temperate, subtropical and tropical areas. In the south-east, it can occur in dry, open eucalypt forests. It sleeps by day in pairs or small family groups in tree hollows, and feeds in trees at night on sap, nectar, pollen, honeydew and invertebrates, gliding between trees as it forages within its large home range.

Angus McNab

Black-bellied Swamp Snake *Hemiaspis signata*

This snake is slender and olive to grey-brown or blackish above, with darker forms having a paler head; it is dark grey to black underneath. The face has narrow, pale yellowish-white lines from the eyes to the neck, and along the upper lip from the snout to the corner of the mouth; the latter is often spotted and flecked with darker brown. The species occurs in coastal and near-coastal areas, from southern New South Wales to northern Queensland, although it is more patchily distributed in the north. It occupies marshy areas of wet and dry forests and woodland, including rainforests, coastal heaths and well-watered gardens. It is mostly diurnal and crepuscular, sheltering at night under rocks, dense leaf litter, logs and sheets of iron, but may be active on warmer nights. It forages in thick vegetation for frogs, tadpoles and skinks. VENOMOUS

Angus McNab

Burton's Legless Lizard *Lialis burtonis*

This is a robust, smooth-scaled, 'snake-like' lizard, with an elongated head with a long, pointed, wedge-shaped snout. It is highly variable in colour, including grey, yellow, reddish-brown or blackish above, with or without longitudinal stripes or broken lines on the body, and a conspicuous white or cream stripe on the sides of the head and neck. The underparts are covered with variable amounts of small dark and pale flecks. The forelimbs are absent and the hindlimbs are reduced to tiny flaps. The eyes have vertical pupils. The species is distributed throughout mainland Australia and islands of Torres Strait, but is absent from the far south-west and far south-east. It occupies a wide range of habitats, including rainforest, dry forests, woodland, heaths, shrubland and deserts. Active by day and night, it forages on the ground almost exclusively for small lizards, which are supplemented with invertebrates.

Angus McNab

Carpet Python *Morelia spilota*

A highly variable large python, this snake is generally, blackish, brownish or olive-green above, with greenish-yellow spots, irregular bright yellow stripes, or pale brown to olive-grey, dark-edged blotches, transverse bands and longitudinal lines. It is yellowish, cream or white on the undersurface. The head is large and triangular and visibly distinct from the neck, with a row of deep heat-sensory pits along the lower jaw. The species occurs throughout mainland Australia, except the arid interior, western Western Australia and southern Victoria, in a range of habitat types, including rainforests, open forests and woodland, riverine areas, coastal heaths, shrubland, rocky outcrops, and suburban parks and gardens. It is generally nocturnal and semi-arboreal, becoming more diurnal during cooler months. It feeds mostly on small to medium-sized mammals and birds, but also on frogs and lizards.

Angus McNab

Golden-crowned Snake *Cacophis squamulosus*

Angus McNab

This snake is grey or brown above and pink below, with a golden-yellow marking on top of the head. The yellowish-brown crown on either side of the head and on the nape converges slightly but does not meet. The pupils are elongated and vertical. The species occurs along the east coast and ranges from around Sydney, New South Wales, to southeastern Queensland, where it inhabits denser forests in northern parts of its range and sandstone areas in the south, sheltering by day under logs and rocks and in leaf litter. It hunts mainly for sleeping lizards, which are detected largely by scent, but also takes blind snakes and frogs. It lays an average of six eggs in a clutch in midsummer. If threatened, it flattens its neck and makes striking actions, but rarely bites. VENOMOUS

Gully Skink *Saproscincus spectabilis*

Angus McNab

This smooth-scaled, slender skink has long, well-developed limbs, five digits on each hand and foot, and a slender, tapering tail. It is brown to reddish-brown above, with scattered lighter and dark flecks and blotches forming a complex variegated pattern. It has a broad, ragged dark brown dorsolateral stripe and flanks with a variegated pattern of lighter and darker brown with, at times, a cream midlateral stripe. The tail is reddish-brown, and the underparts are white to yellow with longitudinally aligned brownish flecks. It occurs in coastal and near-coastal southeastern Queensland and ranges of northeastern New South Wales, in wetter forests, including rainforests, where it is active from dawn to dusk, foraging on the ground for small insects and other invertebrates, and often being seen basking in patches of sunlight.

157

Murray's Skink *Karma murrayi*

Angus McNab

This is a robust skink with an attractive variegated pattern. It is rich brown to coppery-brown above, with dark-edged scales giving a flecked transverse pattern. The sides and neck are paler, with numerous black flecks that combine to form larger blotches on the neck. The lips are creamish with black blotches, and the underparts are creamish with darker flecking towards the outer edges. The species is distributed along the coast and ranges of southeastern Queensland and northeastern New South Wales. It occurs in rainforests and wet, open forests, where it is active by day, foraging on logs and in leaf litter in open areas, or patches of native or exotic shrubs. It is normally found sheltering under rotting logs or in crevices, or basking partially exposed in filtered sunlight. It produces 3–5 live young in a litter.

Orange-tailed Shadeskink *Saproscincus challengeri*

Angus McNab

This smooth-scaled, slender skink has long, well-developed limbs, five digits on each hand and foot, and a slender, tapering tail. It is yellowish-brown to greyish-brown or reddish-brown above, with light brown flecks and scattered black spots. There is a blackish-brown dorsolateral stripe, often fragmented and occasionally with paler reddish margin, and the tail has conspicuous creamish blotches. The sides of the neck and face are paler, with darker brown spots and a blackish streak behind the eye. Females have a pale-edged, dark brown dorsolateral stripe. The underparts are white to yellowish with brown spots. The species occurs in far southeastern Queensland and far northeastern New South Wales, where it occupies wetter forests, including rainforests. It is active from dawn to dusk, foraging on the ground or in leaf litter for insects and other small invertebrates, and sheltering at other times in moist areas under rocks and logs, or in dense leaf litter.

Red-bellied Black Snake *Pseudechis porphyriacus*

This snake is uniformly glossed black above, often with a paler brownish snout. It has crimson on the lower flanks, fading to duller red, orange-pink or pale pinkish-cream on the middle of the belly, and black under the tail. The eye is dark. It is widely distributed in the eastern and southeastern Australian mainland, from Adelaide, South Australia, through central and southeastern Victoria, central and eastern New South Wales and eastern Australian Capital Territory, with populations becoming more isolated in the north. It favours moist areas, normally near watercourses, lagoons, swamps, drainage ditches and farm dams, but also occurs in rainforest, forests, woodland, heaths and grassland. It is predominantly diurnal, sheltering by day in thick grass tussocks or disused animal burrows, or under logs or large rocks. Foraging on land or in water for frogs, tadpoles, fish, small mammals, lizards and snakes (including its own species), it can stay underwater for up to 20 minutes. VENOMOUS

Angus McNab

Red-tailed Calyptotis *Calyptotis ruficauda*

This is a smooth, glossy-scaled skink with a light brown, medium-length tail. It is brown above with dark brown to black spots forming longitudinal lines and a darker line from snout to tail, along both edges of the dorsal surface. The sides are whitish to light brown, with small white and black spots. The limbs are small with five digits on each hand and foot and a pinkish-orange flush to the hindlimbs and tail-sides. There are dark bars on the lips, the belly is whitish, and the ear opening is large and vertical. The species occurs in the lower north coast and adjacent ranges of New South Wales. It is found in wet and dry forests and rainforests, where it burrows in moist soil under logs, rocks and leaf litter. It lays up to six (average three) eggs in a clutch, with clutch sizes relating to body size.

Angus McNab

Rose's Shadeskink *Saproscincus rosei*

Angus McNab

This smooth-scaled, slender skink has long, well-developed limbs, five digits on each hand and foot, and a slender, tapering tail. It is greyish-brown to reddish-brown above, either with a short, blackish vertebral line, bordered with broad bronze to orange stripes and with numerous scattered spots and flecks of lighter and darker brown, or largely unpatterned. There is a broad, fragmented blackish-brown dorsolateral stripe and paler greyish flanks, spotted with lighter and darker brown. Females have strong blackish sides with a broad white or yellow midlateral stripe. This skink occurs in coastal southeastern Queensland and northeastern New South Wales, where it inhabits wetter forests, including rainforests and dense thickets. It is active from dawn to dusk, foraging on the ground or in leaf litter for insects and other small invertebrates, including cockroaches and moths.

Scute-snouted Calyptotis *Calyptotis scutirostrum*

Angus McNab

This glossy, smooth-scaled skink has an elongated body and medium-sized, tapering tail. It is brownish above and sometimes has four rows of small black dorsal spots. It is brown on the flanks, with white spots and lips with dark barring. The limbs are small, with five digits on each hand and foot, and a pinkish-orange wash on the hindlimbs and tail-sides. The belly is whitish or yellow, with brown spotting on the throat. It occurs in coastal and near-coastal southeastern Queensland and northeastern New South Wales, inhabiting rainforests and wet sclerophyll forests, preferring moist soils, where it burrows under logs and surface litter, foraging for small invertebrates. It lays 2–5 (average four) eggs in a clutch, with clutch sizes relating to female body size.

Southern Angle-headed Dragon *Lophosaurus spinipes*

This large dragon has a long tail that is about twice as long as the body, a large, angular head, enlarged nuchal crest and raised, 'saw-like' vertebral crest. It is grey to greenish or rich brown above, with numerous raised spinose scales, arranged in transverse rows along the body. There is a dark band from the ear to the eye and dark bars on the jaw. The back and tail have yellow flecks or spots, and the belly is whitish to pale brown. The species occurs in southeastern Queensland and northeastern New South Wales, typically in rainforests and wet forests, where it is active by day, feeding mostly on invertebrates that are pounced on from perches in the trees. Although largely arboreal, it is more commonly seen foraging on the ground in clearings, often freezing and relying on camouflage for protection if disturbed.

Angus McNab

Southern Dwarf Crowned Snake *Cacophis krefftii*

This snake is steely-grey to black above, with a narrow yellowish-cream collar on the nape of the neck, flecked darker as it extends along the sides of the head towards the snout. The underside is pale yellow, with each scale distinctly edged with black. It is found in coastal regions east of the Great Dividing Range, from central New South Wales to south-east Queensland, occurring in rainforests and moist areas of open forests. It is terrestrial and nocturnal, sheltering by day under rocks, rotting logs and moist leaf litter, and emerging to feed on small skinks and other lizards. It is venomous, but not considered dangerous to humans and is reluctant to bite. If threatened it rears up and makes striking motions with a closed mouth. VENOMOUS

Angus McNab

Three-clawed Worm-skink *Anomalopus verreauxii*

Angus McNab

An elongated, smooth-scaled, 'snake-like' burrowing skink, this species has a cylindrical body and medium-length tail that tapers at the tip. It is brown to grey above with a creamy-yellow band on the head, which is more distinctive on the darker juveniles, resembling the markings of young crowned snakes *Cacophis* spp. It has small limbs, with three digits on the hands and greatly reduced styliform hindlimbs, each with a single toe. It occurs in central eastern Queensland and northeastern New South Wales, where it is typically secretive, spending most of its time under foliage, rocks or logs on the ground, in wet forests, rainforest margins and coastal shrubland. It forages at night, on the ground or in ground litter, for invertebrates, including worms. When disturbed, it burrows deeply into soft soil. It lays soft-shelled eggs in spring.

Davies' Tree Frog *Litoria daviesae*

Angus McNab

The colouration of this frog varies, but it is usually brown on top with green and white to cream, with a dark stripe edged with white-cream that extends from the snout, along the sides to just above the front legs. The flanks are orange to pink, mottled black and white on the rear. Some individuals are flecked with black or dark brown. The species occurs in the Hastings River catchment in northeastern New South Wales, where it lives around creeks and streams in forests. It breeds in ephemeral pools beside creeks and streams, and in the slower part of the main waterway. The male's call, a rapidly repeated *waahh rarr*, is made from the water's edge, on rocks in the water or from overhanging vegetation during spring and early summer.

Giant Barred Frog *Mixophyes iteratus*

Angus McNab

This species is reddish-brown to dark brown above, with a mainly smooth back and legs with black bands. The eyes are golden and the underparts yellow. It is found from mid-eastern New South Wales to southeastern Queensland, where it lives along watercourses, in rainforest and wet sclerophyll forest, and feeds at night on invertebrates and small vertebrates. The male's call, a single *wharrrk*, is made from the edge of a waterbody, or occasionally from burrows or beneath leaf litter. The species breeds in ephemeral pools beside streams, with up to 4,200 eggs laid in the water, which are kicked on to an overhanging bank above the water once fertilized. They hatch 8–10 days later, the tadpoles falling into the water after wriggling free.

Glandular Frog *Litoria subglandulosa*

Angus McNab

The colouration of this species is variable, but it is usually brown above with green and white to cream on the flanks, becoming orange to pink on the lower flanks and mottled black and white towards the rear. A dark stripe edged with white-cream extends from the snout, along the sides to just above the front legs. Some individuals are flecked with black or dark brown. The underside is white. The frog occurs from Walcha in northeastern New South Wales to Stanthorpe, Queensland. It lives around creeks and streams in forests and montane heaths, where it feeds on invertebrates. The male's *waahh rarr* call, repeated every second or so, is given from the water's edge, on rocks in the water, or from overhanging vegetation in spring to early summer.

Great Barred Frog *Mixophyes fasciolatus*

Angus McNab

This frog is tan or light brown to dark brown above with black bands on the legs, and white underparts. Juveniles resemble adults, but can have bright red or orange irises that fade to brown as they mature. The species occurs from eastern New South Wales to central eastern Queensland, where it lives around watercourses in rainforest and wet sclerophyll forests. It is active at night, feeding on invertebrates and small vertebrates. The male's call is a single *wharrrup*, repeated often, and is given from the edge of a waterbody, or occasionally from burrows or beneath leaf litter. It breeds in pools beside streams, and about 800 eggs are laid into the water. Once fertilized, the female kicks the eggs on to an overhanging bank above the water. When hatching, the tadpoles wriggle free and fall into the water below.

Mountain Stream Frog *Litoria barringtonensis*

Ryan Francis

Individuals of this species are bright green above, sparsely covered with small black flecks on the back, with a dark-edged gold or yellow stripe extending from the snout, through the eye and on to the flanks. It is found in eastern New South Wales, from the Barrington Tops, north to the Gibraltar Range, where it inhabits creeks and streams in forests. It breeds in pools beside creeks and streams and in the slower parts of the main waterway, and feeds on invertebrates. The male's call is made in two parts: the first is a *wrekik-wrekik* and the second a loud *eeep*, which is not always repeated. The female lays about 450 eggs, and the tadpoles take around 8–10 weeks to become frogs.

Pugh's Mountain Frog *Philoria pughi*

Angus McNab

This frog is brown or yellow above. The legs and hips are usually reddish-brown, with a prominent dark stripe from the nostril, through the eye and on to the shoulder. There is typically a large dark spot on the lower flank, in front of the hindlimbs. The underside is yellow with darker markings. Found in a few upland locations in northern New South Wales near Washpool National Park, the species lives in seepages in wet sclerophyll forests and rainforests and feeds on invertebrates. The male's call, a guttural *wrok*, sometimes with a low, descending growl, is made from a chamber of mud, usually beneath rocks and leaf litter. The species is endangered and little is known about its reproductive behaviour.

Sandpaper Frog *Lechriodus fletcheri*

Angus McNab

The colouration of this frog is tan to dark brown above, with darker bands on the legs. The back is rough, like sandpaper, with a black band from the back of the eye to the shoulder. The underparts are mainly white, with dark grey undersides to the hands and feet. The species is found from Mt Tamborine, Queensland, to the Watagan National Park, New South Wales, where it lives around water courses in rainforests, feeding at night on arthropods. The male's call is a bobbling *roc roc roc roc*, given while floating in the water. The species breeds in pools and about 450 eggs are laid in a foam nest. Tadpoles start to develop into frogs after four weeks.

Sphagnum Frog *Philoria sphagnicola*

Stephen Mahony

This species occurs in variable shades of grey or brown above, but can be reddish, orange or yellow, usually with a dark stripe from the rear of the eye to above the shoulder that continues down on to the lower flank. It often has darker mottling. and occasionally 'V'- or 'W'-shaped black marks on the back. It is white to pale brown below, with or without heavy brown mottling. Found in a few upland locations in north-east New South Wales, from Glen Innes to Comboyne, it lives in beds of sphagnum moss, and seepages in wet sclerophyll forests and rainforests, where it feeds on invertebrates. The male's call, a guttural *wrocc*, repeated in short bursts, is made from a chamber of mud, usually beneath rocks and leaf litter.

Stuttering Frog *Mixophyes balbus*

Akash Samuel

This species is tan to light brown or dark brown above, with black bands on the legs and white below. The upper iris is metallic blue. It is found in New South Wales on the eastern slopes of the Great Dividing Range south of the Timbarra River catchment, near Drake, and, historically, south to the Cann River catchment, Victoria, but is now presumed extinct in that state. It lives around watercourses, where it feeds at night on invertebrates and small vertebrates. The male's call, a single *wha-rr-rup*, repeated frequently, is made from the edge of a waterbody, or occasionally from burrows or beneath leaf litter. It breeds in shallow riffles of permanent streams.

Four-barred Swordtail *Protographium leosthenes*

This beautiful butterfly has matt white wings, the upperside with four black bands. The hindwings have a slender black tail, and the remainder of the wing is white with two black bars lined with orange spots on both wing surfaces. It has a patchy distribution in coastal and sub-coastal areas from north Queensland to eastern NSW. There is also a second, darker, subspecies endemic to Kakadu National Park, NT. It is associated with vine thicket, monsoon forest and lowland rainforest, with populations reaching large numbers after heavy summer rains. There is some evidence the Four-barred Swordtail participates in migratory flights. Males often patrol hilltops or territories along forest margins, and may puddle on hot days. Larvae feed on the Zig-zag Vine *Melodorum leichhardtii*, whose fruit are a source of bush tucker for indigenous Australians.

Angus McNab

Jezebel Nymph *Mynes geoffroyi*

The upper surface of the adult butterfly's wings are grey (female) to white (male), with black margins (broader in females) and white spots at the tips of the forewings. The underwing surface is banded with black and white, with yellow and red markings. The rear edge of each hindwing is irregularly shaped. Caterpillars are orange to brown or black, covered with fine white spots, and have black or pink branched projections all over the body. The species occurs through coastal Queensland and north-east New South Wales, where it inhabits tropical and subtropical rainforests and wet scrubland. Host plants are typically in the nettle family (Urticaceae), and include the Gympie-Gympie *Dendrocnide moroides*, Shining-leaved Stinging Tree *D. photinophylla* and Native Mulberry *Pipturus argenteus*.

Angus McNab

167

Leafwing *Doleschallia bisaltide*

Garry Sanbowski (CC)

At rest this butterfly resembles a dead leaf. The upperwing surface is orange with brown to black margins, and with small white spots at the forewing wing-tip. The underwing is brown, with light and dark markings and spots, and a dark line down the middle of the wings (giving the appearance of a leaf midrib). The hindwings have a short 'tail'. Caterpillars are black with pale yellow spots down the back and sides, with orange-red tubercles, and blue-black branched projections over the body. The species occurs in coastal Queensland and northeastern New South Wales, where it is locally common in rainforests, wet sclerophyll forests and wet scrubland. Host plants include species in the acanthus family (Acanthaceae), including *Pseuderanthemum* spp. Adults typically fly near the ground, using the dead-leaf appearance of their underwings for camouflage while resting.

Purple Crow *Euploea tulliolus*

John Tann (CC)

The upperwings of adult butterflies are dark brown to black with an arc of white spots along the margins; smaller on the hindwing. The undersurface of the wing is similar, but with large spots also on the hindwing. The wings appear to have a purple sheen in some lights, hence the common name. The body is dark with white spots. Caterpillars have contrasting black and white stripes, orange markings down the sides, and long black projections at each end of the body. The species occurs in coastal Queensland to the north-east New South Wales coast, but is also found in Torres Strait Islands, Papua New Guinea, south-east Asia, Fiji, New Caledonia, the Solomon Islands and Vanuatu. It occurs in a range of habitats, from rainforest margins to subtropical gardens. It uses the Burny Vine *Trophis scandens* as a host species.

Regent Skipper *Euschemon rafflesia*

Garry Sanbowski (CC)

Adult butterflies are blackish with bright yellow patches on the wings, larger on the hindwings, and have a red-tipped abdomen. Females are larger than males. Caterpillars are green with black and white longitudinal stripes, a black head, and short, fleshy projections on the thorax. The species occurs from central eastern New South Wales to northeastern Queensland. It inhabits both upland and lowland rainforests and the fringes of adjacent open forests. Adults are most active late in the afternoon, settling frequently with outstretched wings. Caterpillars construct a shelter made of two leaves joined together with silk, and feed nocturnally on magnoliid *laurales*, including *Tetrasynandra pubescens* in the north of the range and *Wilkiea huegeliana* in the south.

Rhinoceros Beetle *Xylotrupes ulysses*

Joshua Prieto

This large (70mm), shiny, dark brown to black beetle occurs in near-coastal rainforests of eastern Queensland and northeastern New South Wales. Adult beetles feed on nectar and rotting fruits. Males have horn-like projections on the head and pronotum, which they use to battle each other. The losing beetle may be flipped on to its back and be unable to right itself. The larvae are pale grubs with a thick, soft body and reddish head. They live in soil rich in decomposing organic matter, and are sometimes found in garden compost heaps. Adults are typically encountered during the wet season, often attracted to lights at night, and are capable of making a hissing or squeaking noise if disturbed.

Iluka Nature Reserve

Located on the coast on the north-east bank of the Clarence River mouth, this reserve is only 1.3km² in size, but contains the largest remaining stand of littoral rainforest in New South Wales (about 1km²). (Smaller remnants are found in the vicinity of Woody Head camping area and Gumma Garra picnic area in the north of the adjacent Bundjalung National Park. This is a remnant of what was once an extensive coastal rainforest. The littoral rainforest contains more than 180 species of flora, including banksias *Banksia* spp., Broad-leaved Lilly Pilly *Syzygium hemilamprum*, Riberry *Syzygium luehmannii*, strangler figs *Ficus* spp., Tuckeroo *Cupaniopsis anacardioides* and an assortment of epiphytes, ferns and vines. The reserve is part of the traditional homelands of the Bundjalung and Yaegl Nations.

Iluka Nature Reserve was gazetted in 1976 and the littoral rainforest was inscribed on the UNESCO World Heritage List in 1986. In the 1990s, however, the nature reserve was overrun by weeds, including the Asparagus Fern *Asparagus aethiopicus*, Bitou Bush *Chrysanthemoides monilifera*, Brazilian Nightshade *Solanum seaforthianum*, Cape Ivy *Delairea odorata*, Climbing Asparagus *Asparagus plumosus*, Coral Berry *Rivina humilis*, Dutchman's Pipe *Aristolochia elegans*, Madeira Vine

Peter Rowland

The Iluka Rainforest Walk is an easy self-guided walk

Anredera cordifolia, Mother of Millions *Bryophyllum delagoense,* Ochna *Ochna serrulata* and White Passionflower *Passiflora subpeltata,* and was in danger of being removed from the UNESCO World Heritage List. The local Iluka Landcare and Duncare Group restored the nature reserve to its former beauty through a dedicated regime of weed removal, planting and restoration. The reserve was added to the Australian National Heritage List in 2007.

GPS Coordinates
-29.39910,153.36440

Getting There
From Grafton, follow the Pacific Highway north for about 45 minutes and take a right turn on to Iluka Road,

which leads to Iluka township. From Ballina, follow the Pacific Highway south for about 60 minutes and take a left turn on to Iluka Road, leading to Iluka township. The nature reserve is accessed off Long Street or via the Iluka Bluff picnic area.

Tracks & Trails
Iluka Rainforest Walking Track (2.6km, one way) is an easy walk through lush rainforest from the car park to Iluka Bluff Lookout and picnic area. The walk is self-guided, with a number of information signs that give an insight into the World Heritage Gondwanan rainforest. Look along here for the Barred Cuckoo-shrike, Black Flying-fox, Common Wombat, Eastern Whipbird, Grey-headed Flying-fox, Koala, Noisy Pitta, Short-beaked Echidna, Varied Triller and White-eared Monarch. The Common Blossom-bat has also been recorded here. Spring sees the most bird activity. *Gummigurrah Walk* (3.5km, return) in Bundjalung National Park is part of a traditional winter camping ground for the Bundjalung people. The walk starts at the picnic area and passes through open woodland, heath and rainforest to an ancient midden adjacent to the Evans River.

Fees & Permits
Entry to the reserve is free.

Facilities
Camping and accommodation is available at the neighbouring Bundjalung National Park.

Services Nearby
Iluka is a small town but has all essential services. The nearest hospital is in Maclean.

Washpool National Park

Northern warm temperate rainforests are the predominant rainforest type in this region, due to its large areas of acidic soils, and it contains some of the least-disturbed forest in New South Wales. In addition to the huge Red Cedar trees, the region is home to the world's largest tract of Coachwood *Ceratopetalum apetalum*. Eucalypt tall open forests are also extensively distributed in the region. From the 1800s until the establishment of the park, the area was selectively logged for its valuable Red Cedar *Toona ciliata*. As the logging industry became more automated, the increasing rate of logging placed unsustainable pressure on the ecology of the forests. The 587km² Washpool National Park was formed in 1983 following recommendations from a study that identified a number of local endemic plant and animal populations and a number of other natives, which were not adequately conserved elsewhere. The region is sacred to the Bundjalung, Gumbaingirri and Ngarrabul people, who have a long connection with the land.

The fauna of the park includes the Eastern Ring-tailed Possum, Long-nosed Potoroo, Parma Wallaby,

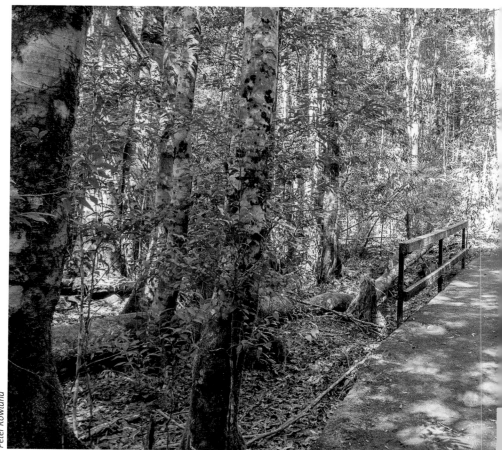

Peter Rowland

Northern warm temperate rainforest along the Coombadjha Nature Stroll

Powerful Owl, Rufous Scrub-bird, Spotted-tailed Quoll, Stuttering Frog, Superb Lyrebird and Swamp Wallaby.

A number of feral animal species have been identified in the park, including the Eastern Gambusia (Mosquitofish), European Red Fox, European Rabbit, Domestic Cat, Feral Donkey, Feral Horse, Feral Pig, Red-eared Slider Turtle and Dog.

GPS Coordinates
-29.43620, 152.33400

Getting There
The park entry is off the Gwydir Highway, between Grafton (90km) and Glen Innes (75km).

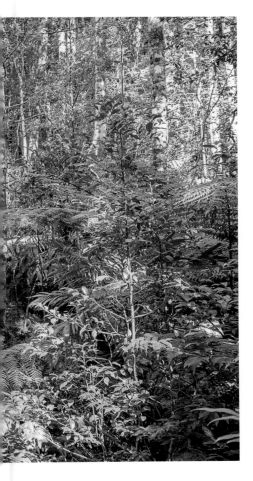

Tracks & Trails
The *Gibraltar/Washpool World Heritage Walk* (45km, loop) is a 3–4-day walk that passes through a range of environments, including wetlands, dry sclerophyll forest, rocky granite outcrops and Gondwana rainforest. Indigenous sacred sites and the remains of tin mining and grazing activities from early colonial times are encountered along the way. *Coombadjha Nature Stroll* (1.4km, loop) is a short walk through the UNESCO World Heritage listed rainforest. The walk departs from Coachwood Picnic Area along a bitumen path that leads to a viewing platform over the creek (this 400m section is wheelchair accessible). From there you can either return along the same path or take the loop track. At the end of the walk is the refreshing Coachwood Pool swimming spot.

Fees & Permits
The park is always open (except during high public risk periods), but entry fees apply.

Facilities
Camping is permitted at Bellbird and Coombadjha camp grounds, and Four Bull Hut is a two-bedroom, six-berth cabin in the north-west. Picnic areas are located at Coachwood and Granite. There are toilets, barbecues and picnic tables at all camp grounds and picnic areas. Drinking water, showers and power are available at Four Bull Hut. There are numerous horse-riding trails in the north-west section of the park.

Services Nearby
Both Grafton and Glen Innes are major towns and have all essential and tourism services. The closest fuel is at the Jackadgery Station in the Mann River Caravan Park (40km), which also has food, gas and accommodation.

Dorrigo National Park

Dorrigo National Park is part of the Gondwana Rainforests of Australia World Heritage Area, which includes reserves in both New South Wales and Queensland and contains the largest expanse of subtropical rainforests in the world. The mosaic of soil types in the Dorrigo region supports a range of forest types, including subtropical and cool temperate rainforest. A small area of the rainforest was first protected in 1901 and the Dorrigo National Park was established in 1974, before being incorporated in the UNESCO World Heritage List in 1986. The park currently protects an area of 119km².

Canopy species in the subtropical rainforest areas include the Black Booyong *Heritiera actinophylla,* Giant Stinging Tree *Dendrocnide excelsa* and Yellow Carabeen *Sloanea woollsii,* while the cool temperate rainforest is dominated by the Antarctic Beech *Nothofagus moorei.*

The views from the elevated deck at the rear Rainforest Centre are stunning, but the rainforest floor and lower tree levels are where the bulk of the action takes place. The Australian Brush Turkey, Australian Logrunner, Noisy Pitta and Superb Lyrebird rake through the leaf litter, looking for food, the Australian Golden Whistler, Eastern Yellow Robin, Green Catbird and Paradise Riflebird move from tree to tree, and the Satin Bowerbird maintains bowers decorated with bright blue objects.

Peter Rowland

View from the end of the Skywalk elevated boardwalk at the rear of the rainforest centre

Spotlighting the park at night can be good for nocturnal animals, including the Australian Boobook *Ninox boobook,* Brown Antechinus, Bush Rat, Eastern Ring-tailed Possum, Glandular Tree Frog, Greater Sooty Owl, Hip Pocket Frog, Powerful Owl, Red-legged Pademelon, Spotted-tailed Quoll and Yellow-bellied Glider.

Numerous stunning waterfalls can be accessed by some of the many walks through the rainforest.

GPS Coordinates
-30.36354, 152.72879 (Rainforest Centre)

Getting There
Accessed via the Waterfall Way from either Bellingen (30km) in the east or Armidale (130km) in the west. Coffs Harbour (63km) has the closest airport and the nearest railway station is Raleigh (41km).

Tracks & Trails
Skywalk is an elevated boardwalk located at the rear of the rainforest centre, projecting out over the canopy of the rainforest. Numerous canopy-feeding birds can be viewed from here. *Lyrebird Link Track* (800m, return) starts from behind the rainforest centre and is an easy walk that descends into the rainforest via a sloping boardwalk. You can either return along the same track or follow the *Wonga Track* at the 'T' section. The *Satinbird Stroll* (600m, loop) is a great short rainforest walk from Glade Picnic Area that links up with the elevated walk with the *Birds' Boardwalk* (200m, return). The *Satinbird Stroll* and *Birds' Boardwalk* are wheelchair accessible. *Wonga Walk* (6.6km, loop) branches off from the *Satinbird Stroll* and heads in a large loop past Crystal Shower and Tristania Falls. *Rosewood Creek Track* (5.5km, loop) is accessed from the Never Never Picnic Area and links up with the *Blackbutt Walking Track.*

Fees & Permits
Entry to the national park visitor centre is by gold coin donation, but the remainder of the park is free.

Facilities
Wheelchair-accessible toilets (including Glade Picnic Area), cafe, shop, drinking water, picnic area, barbecues and free WiFi at Rainforest Centre. The centre is open every day from 9.00 a.m. to 4.30 p.m. (except Christmas Day).

Services Nearby
Dorrigo (4km) is the closest town that has various shops, cafes, pubs, supermarkets, restaurants and health clinic.

New England National Park

New England National Park was gazetted in 1931 and was incorporated in the UNESCO World Heritage List in 1986 as one of the subtropical and warm temperate rainforest parks of eastern Australia. The current gazetted area covers 673km². The park contains the largest area of northern warm temperate rainforests in Australia. Warm temperate rainforests have a canopy height of up to 30m and predominantly grow in sheltered areas of hilly regions. The park also has patches of subtropical and cool temperate rainforest, heathland (mainly at Wrights Lookout), sclerophyll forest, subalpine woodland and swampland. Current estimates suggest that about 1,000 plant species are found in these habitats within the park.

More than 110 species of bird have been recorded in the park, including the Australian King Parrot, Rufous Scrub-bird, Superb Lyrebird, and Topknot and White-headed Pigeons.

Mammal species include the Brush-tailed Phascogale, Little Bent-winged Bat, Parma Wallaby, Platypus, Red-necked Pademelon, Spotted-tailed Quoll and Swamp Wallaby.

The Carpet Python, Delicate Skink, Golden-crowned Snake, Lace Monitor

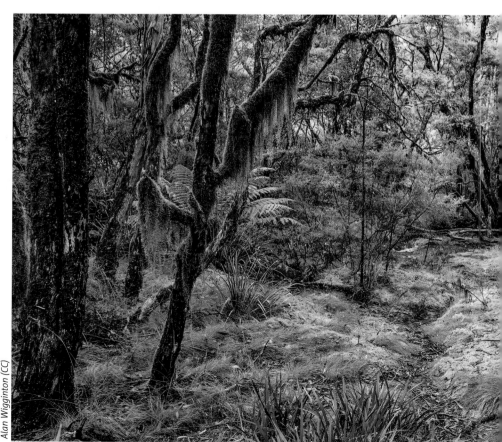

Alan Wigginton (CC)

On the Tea Tree Falls Walking Track

and Southern Leaf-tailed Gecko are among the commonly encountered reptiles.

Frog fauna includes the endangered Spagnum Frog. The male of this variably coloured species gives his guttural *wrocc* call from within leaf litter or from under a patch of moss.

Of the large number of invertebrates found in the park, the velvet worm, or 'peripatus', is among the most curious and ancient.

GPS Coordinates
-30.67991, 152.47219

Getting There
The park is located 75km east of Armidale and 50km west of Coffs Harbour along the Waterfall Way.

Tracks & Trails
Cascades Walking Track (5.7km, loop) descends into the valley below Wrights Lookout. The track can be rough in places and has some steep sections. It follows Five Day Creek through lush rainforest burgeoning with vivid green moss, liverworts and magnificent ferns. *Eagles Nest Walking Track* (2.2km, loop) has rich sections of Antarctic Beech *Nothofagus moorei*, decorated with orchids and covered in fungi. It also gives walkers the opportunity to pass through some spectacular Snow Gum *Eucalyptus pauciflora* woodland. *Lyrebird Walking Track* (5.5km loop) passes through cool temperate rainforest and wet sclerophyll forest. *New England Wilderness Walk* (33km, one way) is a challenging three-day walk that descends from the New England Tableland to the Bellinger River; a drop in altitude of about 1,000m. *Tea Tree Falls Walking Track* (4km, return) is the easiest walk in the park and links Thungutti camp ground and Tom's Cabin. The track passes through Antarctic Beech forest; a range of mosses, including sphagnum moss and tall moss, can be seen along the way.

Fees & Permits
Entry to the park is free, but camping fees are payable.

Facilities
Toilets, barbecues, picnic facilities and drinking water are available at various locations throughout the park. Self-contained accommodation is available at the Chalet, the Residence and Tom's Cabin; camping is permitted at Thungutti Campground.

Services Nearby
Bellingen (39km), Dorrigo (39km) and Armidale (78km) have a range of services.

Oxley Wild Rivers National Park

This park was gazetted in 1986, but has had more land added to the original boundaries and now covers 1,452km². It was inscribed on the UNESCO World Heritage List as part of the Central Eastern Rainforest Reserves of Australia (CERRA) World Heritage Area in 1991. The national park and immediate surroundings contain dry, cool temperate and, to a lesser extent, subtropical rainforest types. The dry rainforest is widespread across the slopes and gullies of the park and was one of the principal reasons for its inclusion on CERRA. The subtropical patches within Oxley Wild Rivers are unusual, due to the absence of figs *Ficus* spp. The cool temperate rainforest occurs in a restricted area in the vicinity of Pinnacle Creek.

The national park and immediate surrounding area is thought to support more than 170 native bird species, 55 mammals, 38 reptiles, 19 amphibians and 14 fish. A number of these are at the western limits of their distribution, including the Fawn-footed Melomys, Great Barred Frog, Green Catbird, Mountain Brush-tailed Possum and White-headed Pigeon. The Little Bent-winged Bat is at the southern limits of its range at the park.

John Tann (CC)

Wollomombi Falls

The majority of Oxley Wild Rivers National Park lies within an area of significant cultural value for the Dunghutti Aboriginal people. A number of burial sites have been discovered in the region and violent confrontations occurred between cedar loggers, settlers and the local Aboriginal people during the 1830s.

GPS Coordinates
-30.971521,152.0095548

Getting There
The southern entrance to the park is 36km east of Walcha along Emu Creek and Moona Plains Roads. The northern entrance is 22km east of Armidale along Castledoyle Road.

Tracks & Trails
Budds Mare to Riverside Walking Track (7km, one-way) is a moderately difficult walk that descends from heathland into ancient rainforest, dominated by the Sassafras *Doryphora sassafras* and Coachwood *Ceratopetalum apetalum. Apsley Gorge Rim Walking Track* (1.2km, loop) has a formed track and some steps. It is a good place to see the Brush-tailed Rock Wallaby. *Threlfall Track* (5.5km, loop) has some steep sections and some steps, but is good for birdwatching. The challenging *Green Gully Track* (65km, loop) is a 4–5-day trek with cabins along the way. The cabins have power, water, beds and toilets (Cedar Creek has an emergency phone). Bookings are required.

Fees & Permits
Entry to the park is free, but day-use permits are required for Halls Peak camp ground and picnic area, Riverside camp ground and picnic area, and Youdales Hut camp ground and picnic area. Permit fees are included in the camping fee, if staying overnight.

Facilities
Picnic facilities are available at Apsley Falls, Blue Hole, Dangar Falls and Wollomombi. Swimming can be done in the Apsley River. Drinking water is available at Blue Hole. Camping is available at Apsley Falls, Budds Mare, Dangars Gorge, Riverside and Wollomombi. Self-contained accommodation is available at East Kunderang Homestead, and huts are located along the Green Gully Track.

Services Nearby
Walcha is a reasonably sized town with all essential and tourist services. It has medical services, but the closest major hospitals are Armidale (65km) and Tamworth (90km).

Sea Acres National Park

Sea Acres National Park is the traditional country of the Birpai People, who used to make travel aids from the Walking Stick Palm *Linospadix monostachya* and weapons from the Python Tree *Gossia bidwillii,* reputed to be one of the hardest timbers in the world. The reserve was established in 1987.

Other common plant species include (trees) the Coogara *Arytera divaricata,* Flintwood *Scolopia braunii,* Pepperberry *Cryptocarya obovata,* Red Olive Berry *Elaeodendron australe,* Sour Cherry *Syzygium corynanthum,*

strangler figs *Ficus* spp. and Tuckeroo *Cupaniopsis anacardioides.* Vines include the Austral Sarsaparilla *Smilax australis,* Supplejack *Flagellaria indica* and Water Vine *Cissus hypoglauca*; palms the Bangalow Palm *Archontophoenix cunninghamiana*; epiphytes the Staghorn *Platycerium superbum* and Elkhorn *Platycerium bifurcatum* and climbers the interesting Hare's Foot Fern *Davallia solida.*

Despite its relatively small size (0.76km²), the park has a rich diversity of animals including the Australian

Peter Rowland

Main entrance to Sea Acres National Park visitor centre

Brush Turkey, Carpet Python, Eastern Water Dragon, Green Catbird, Lace Monitor, Land Mullet, Little Bent-winged Bat, Rose-crowned Fruit-dove, Scarlet Robin and Wompoo Fruit-dove. Koalas have also been recorded here, but are uncommon. They are not regular rainforest visitors – the best chances to see them occur within the eucalypts along the park's western boundary.

The Sea Acres Rainforest Centre is located at the entrance of the national park and is open every day of the year (9.00 a.m.–4.30 p.m.) except Christmas Day. A ranger-guided walk is available from here and will help you get the most from your visit.

GPS Coordinates
-31.46100, 152.92970

Getting There
The national park is located next to Shelly Beach, on Pacific Drive, 5km south of Port Macquarie.

Tracks & Trails
The *Sea Acres Rainforest Boardwalk* (1.3km), located adjacent to the Sea Acres Rainforest Centre, is an easy walk through the rainforest canopy. It can be undertaken independently or as part of a guided walk. The boardwalk is wheelchair accessible. *Port Macquarie Coastal Walk* (9km, one way) is a long walk that can be steep in places and has many steps. It can be accessed from Sea Acres National Park or from Westport Park in Port MacQuarie's town centre. The walk follows the coast and as well as passing through areas of rainforest, cliff and beach views can be afforded from the many lookouts. September is the driest month and February is typically the wettest. More than 1,500mm of rain has been recorded in a single 24-hour period in the park, and temperatures can exceed 43 °C, so ensure you carry water and sun protection when walking in the park.

Fees & Permits
Entry to the park is free, but fees apply for the Rainforest Boardwalk.

Facilities
Cafe and kiosk facilities, including toilets and drinking water, are available at the rainforest centre.

Services Nearby
Port Macquarie (5km) is the closest town and has all major services, including restaurants, motels, shops, service stations, hospitals and airport.

Barrington Tops National Park

This incredible 765km² area was declared as a national park on 3 December 1969, with the last gazetted amendment occuring in June 2010. The park contains the southernmost part of the Gondwana Rainforests of Australia World Heritage Area, along with a range of other habitats. It is located on the Mount Royal Range, the highest point (1,586m) of which is at the summit of Brumlow Tops. The region contains significant areas of subtropical rainforest and cool temperate rainforest, around a third of which occurs at higher altitudes (>1,000m). Warm temperate rainforest also occurs, but to a much lesser extent. The region was the traditional home of the Biripi, Geawegal, Wonaruah and Worimi people.

The impressive diversity of animal species in the park includes the Eastern Pygmy-possum, Giant Barred Frog, Glandular Frog, Golden-tipped Bat, Greater Sooty Owl, Grey-headed Flying-fox, Long-nosed Potoroo, Australian Masked Owl, Olive Whistler, Parma Wallaby, Rufous Scrub-bird, Spotted-tailed Quoll, Stephen's Banded Snake, Stuttering Frog and Wompoo Fruit-dove.

Barrington Tops also supports the largest mainland captive-breeding programme for the Tasmanian Devil. This was set up by Aussie Ark (then Devil Ark) in 2011 to help protect the

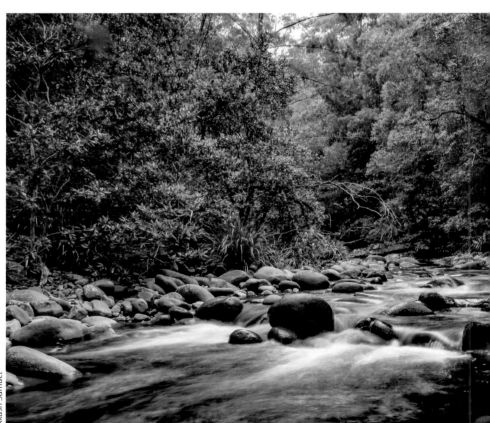

Akash Samuel

Gloucester River

species, which was once widespread on the mainland, but now restricted to Tasmania. The Tasmanian population was decimated by Devil Facial Tumor Disease (DFTD).

Rare or threatened rainforest plant species in the national park include the Craven Grey Box *Eucalyptus largeana,* Rainforest Cassia *Senna acclinis,* Slender Marsdenia *Marsdenia longiloba* and Spade-lipped Wasp Orchid *Chiloglottis palachila.*

GPS Coordinates
-32.02154, 151.49603

Getting There
South Dungog (27km) via Chichester Dam and Salisbury Roads. **East** Gloucester (30km) via Bucketts Way and Gloucester Tops Road.

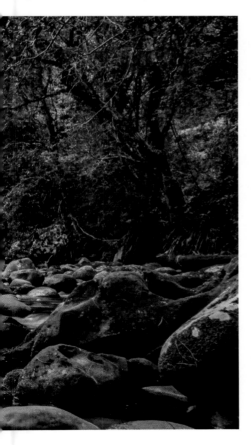

North Gloucester (45km) but via Thunderbolts Way (later Scone Road) and Barrington Tops Forest Road.

Tracks & Trails
The Gloucester Tops Circuit (8km) is a relatively easy track through rainforest gullies and past stunning cascading swimming holes on its way to Andrew Laurie Lookout. The *Antarctic Beech Forest* section (2.5km) passes the ancient temperate rainforest, dominated by the Antarctic Beech *Nothofagus moorei,* and is a favourite haunt of the Rufous Scrub-bird. *Blue Gum Loop* (3.5km) crosses William River before passing through stunning rainforest and blue gum forest. *Devils Hole Lookout Walk* (300m, return) is a wheelchair-friendly track near a picnic area, with a wonderful lookout at the end. *Barrington Trail* (15km) is a four-wheel-drive vehicle or mountain-bike trail through a range of forests, with remote campsites along the way. *Honeysuckle Forest Track* (1km, loop) is an easy walk that passes through Antarctic Beech rainforest, interspersed with tree ferns and decorated with epiphytic orchids.

Fees & Permits
Access to the park is free, but camping fees are payable. Fees are payable for Aussie Ark tours.

Facilities
Numerous toilets, picnic areas, barbecue sites and car parks are located across the park. Camping is permitted at Black Swamp, Devils Hole, Gloucester River, Junction Pools, Little Murray, Polblue and Wombat Creek.

Services Nearby
Many small towns in the region have some services, but Gloucester is the closest major town with all essential and tourism services.

Myall Lakes National Park

This national park was established in 1972, but the last gazetted amendment occurred in 2009. The diverse, largely unmodified lakes, river systems, wetlands and swamps of Myall Lakes were listed under the Ramsar Convention in 1999. The site provides habitat for 12 nationally or internationally threatened bird species. It covers 448km², although only a small percentage of this is rainforest, including dry and subtropical rainforest. The dominant rainforest type is littoral (dry) and the largest patch is located at Mungo Brush (0.67km²). The area now covered by the park was occupied by the Worimi Aboriginal people and the Dark Point Aboriginal place is a sacred area for them.

Rainforest plants include the Broad-leaved Paperbark *Melaleuca qinquenervia*, Coogara *Arytera divaricata*, Cabbage Tree Palm *Livistona australis*, Magenta Lilly Pilly *Syzygium paniculatum*, Mock Olive *Notelaea longifolia*, Plum Pine *Podocarpus elatus*, Rainforest Cassia *Senna acclinis*, Scentless Rosewood *Dysoxylum fraserianam*, Shining-leaved Stinging Tree *Dendrocnide photinophylla* and Yellow Tulip *Drypetes lasiogyna*.

More than 350 vertebrate species have been recorded in the park, including 280 birds, 40 mammals, 20 reptiles and 15 amphibians. Of

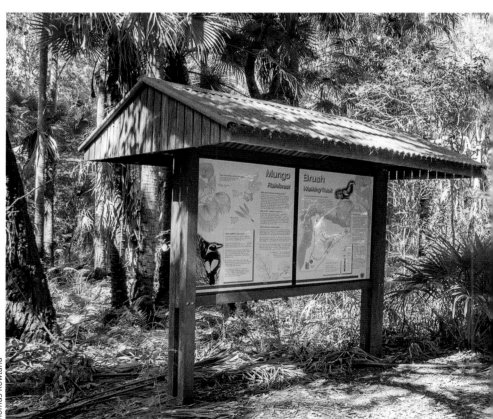

Thomas Rowland

Information sign along the Mungo Brush Walking Track

these the key species that utilize the various rainforest patches include the Australian Brush Turkey, Australian Golden Whistler, Carpet Python, Golden-tipped Bat, Powerful Owl, Satin Bowerbird, Short-beaked Echidna, Stephen's Banded Snake, Stuttering Frog and Wompoo Fruit-dove.

In addition to these, the rainforest gullies of the adjacent Cabbage Tree Island (viewable from Yacaaba Headland) are a valuable nesting site for the endangered Gould's Petrel.

GPS Coordinates
-32.44927, 152.36230

Getting There
Myall Way/Tea Gardens Road and Mungo Brush Road from Tea Gardens (30km) give access to the Myall River

and Bombah Broadwater sections, including Mungo Brush. Bombah Point Road from Bulahdelah (10km) gives access to the Boolambayte and Bombah Broadwater regions. Seal Rocks Road (off Lakes Way) from Forster (46km) via Elizabeth Beach (27km) gives access to Sugarloaf Point and Shelley Beach.

Tracks & Trails
Mungo Brush Walking Track (23km, one way) starts at the Mungo Brush Campground, and passes through coastal rainforest on the *Mungo Brush Rainforest Walk* (1.5km, loop) section before continuing all the way to Hawks Nest. Large Cabbage Tree Palms are seen along the walk. These giants can reach 30m in height. The *Cabbage Palm Loop* (1.7km) in the nearby Wallingat National Park is a haven for rainforest birds and is well worth a visit.

Fees & Permits
Park entry fees apply and camping fees are also payable. The Bombah Point ferry across the lake has varying charges for pedestrians and each vehicle type.

Facilities
Numerous picnic grounds, toilets and campsites are located in the park. The Boomeri Campground is closest to the Mungo Brush rainforest area. The NRMA Myall Shores Holiday Park is also close to Mungo Brush and has villas, cabins, powered sites, toilets, showers, barbecues, kiosk, cafe, boat ramp and cycling trails.

Services Nearby
Bulahdelah (10km) has a range of services, including fuel, hospital, bowling club, pub, shops, restaurants, cafes and accommodation.

Sydney Basin

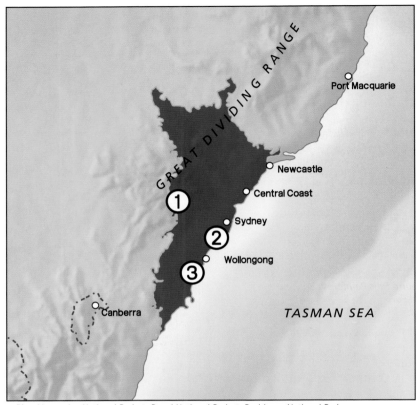

1. Blue Mountains National Park 2. Royal National Park 3. Budderoo National Park

The Sydney Basin bioregion covers 36,229.39km² and comprises 13 subregions. Just over 40 per cent of the bioregion, 14,505.45km², is held in 160 reserves, with more than 70 per cent of the protected area occurring in national parks. The bioregion supports over 3,600 described animal species, including about 350 birds, 100 mammals, 125 reptiles, 60 amphibians, and 2,800 insects and spiders, in addition to more than 4,800 described plant and fungi species. The bioregion extends from Nelson Bay in the north to Batemans Bay in the south, and almost as far west as Mudgee. It lies on rocky, sandy and clay soils on plateaus of sandstones and shales. These support a range of vegetation types, including northern warm temperate rainforest, subtropical rainforest and dry rainforests (including littoral).

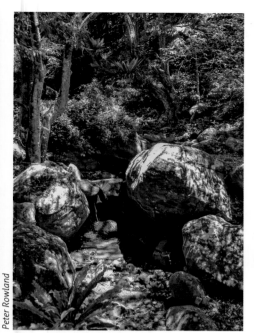

Minnamurra Falls Rainforest, Budderoo National Park

Key Species

BIRDS

Australasian Figbird, Australian Golden Whistler, Australian King Parrot, Bassian Thrush, Black-faced Monarch, Brown Cuckoo-dove, Channel-billed Cuckoo, Cicadabird, Pacific Koel, Eastern Whipbird, Eastern Yellow Robin, Fan-tailed Cuckoo, Greater Sooty Owl, Green Catbird, Grey Goshawk, Grey Shrikethrush, Large-billed Scrubwren, Lewin's Honeyeater, Olive Whistler, Olive-backed Oriole, Rose Robin, Rufous Fantail, Satin Bowerbird, Scarlet Myzomela, Shining Bronze-cuckoo, Silvereye, Spangled Drongo, Superb Lyrebird, Topknot Pigeon, Varied Sittella, White-browed Scrubwren, White-headed Pigeon, White-throated Treecreeper, Wonga Pigeon, Yellow-throated Scrubwren.

MAMMALS

Brush-tailed Phascogale, Brush-tailed Rock Wallaby, Chocolate Wattled Bat, Eastern Forest-bat, Eastern Pygmy-possum, Eastern Ring-tailed Possum, Golden-tipped Bat, Greater Broad-nosed Bat, Koala, Large Bent-winged Bat, Large-eared Wattled Bat, Large Forest-bat, Long-nosed Potoroo, Platypus, Red-necked Pademelon, Southern Forest-bat, Squirrel Glider, Sugar Glider.

REPTILES

Bandy-bandy, Barred-sided Skink, Broad-tailed Gecko, Delicate Skink, Eastern Small-eyed Snake, Eastern Water Dragon, Eastern Water-skink, Highlands Forest Skink, Pale-flecked Garden Sunskink, Pink-tongued Lizard, Swamp Snake, Three-toed Skink, Tiger Snake.

AMPHIBIANS

Blue Mountains Tree Frog, Heath Frog, Leaf-green Tree Frog, Red-crowned Brood Frog.

INVERTEBRATES

Australian Land Leech, Black Jezebel, Blue Triangle, Bronze Flat, Caper Gull, Chequered Sedge-skipper, Common Red-eye, Dingy Shield-skipper, Macleay's Swallowtail, Narrow-banded Awl, Southern Grass-skipper, Spotted Sedge-skipper, Splendid Ochre, St Andrew's Cross, Vampire Moth, Varied Swordgrass Brown, Wonder Brown.

The Sydney Basin bioregion has a temperate climate with warm summers. Temperatures vary across the bioregion, with warmer conditions recorded in the east, along the coast, and cooler conditions in the higher altitude of the west. The highest temperature on record is 48.9 °C (recorded at Penrith Lakes on 4 January 2020). Rainfall can occur throughout the year and ranges between 522 and 2,395mm per year. Monthly averages range from 26 to 245mm. Rainfall varies depending on altitude and proximity to the coast, with more rain falling at higher altitudes and closer to the coast. Montane areas can also experience snowfall.

A number of the region's rainforests are classed as Threatened Ecological Communities (TECs), such as Illawarra subtropical rainforest in the Sydney Basin bioregion, littoral rainforest in the New South Wales North Coast, Sydney Basin and South East Corner bioregions and Robertson rainforest in the Sydney Basin bioregion.

Australian King Parrot (female)

Eastern Yellow Robin *Eopsaltria australis*

Angus McNab

This medium-sized robin with a grey back and head and yellow underparts is usually first seen perched on the side of a tree trunk or other low perch, as it inquisitively inspects passers-by. It will readily approach humans, often accepting handouts of food from picnickers. If not seen, however, a bird is often easily attracted by making a squeaking noise with your lips and hand. The superficially similar Pale-yellow Robin (p. 54) is smaller, and has pale lores and lighter underparts. The Eastern Yellow Robin is a delight to observe in its wide choice of habitat types, mostly dry woodland and rainforests, as well as parks and gardens. Its characteristic calls are an assortment of high, bell-like piping, some harsh scolding notes and a repeated *chop chop*.

Fan-tailed Cuckoo *Cacomantis flabelliformis*

Angus McNab

Throughout eastern Australia and southwestern Western Australia and Tasmania, the descending mournful trill of this bird is a familiar sound, particularly during the breeding season, which is in August–December in the east and June–October in the west. Host species of this parasitic nest brooder include flycatchers, fairy-wrens, scrubwrens and thornbills, particularly the Brown Thornbill. The species inhabits open wooded areas, where it is often seen perching on a low, exposed branch. When sighted, it can be identified by its dark grey upperparts and soft buff underparts. The black tail is notched with white above and barred black and white below. It can be distinguished from the superficially similar Brush Cuckoo *C. variolosus* by its bright yellow eye-ring.

Large-billed Scrubwren *Sericornis magnirostra*

The light brown plumage of this species is almost uniform and unremarkable, but the large black bill is distinctive. The legs are long and pinkish and it has a thick off-white eye-ring. Individuals in the far north of its range have a white wing-spot. It forages for invertebrates individually or in small family groups in mid-level vegetation and on the trunks of trees within rainforests and wet eucalypt woodland. It forages higher than other scrubwrens and rarely descends to the ground. The bird often takes over the nests of other similarly sized passerines, favouring those of the Yellow-throated Scrubwren (p. 151). It occurs in eastern Australia from Cooktown, Queensland, to southern Victoria.

Owen Lishmund

Rose Robin *Petroica rosea*

The Rose Robin is an inhabitant of moist forests, where it feeds on insects, which are either pursued and caught in flight or gleaned from foliage. The adult male plumage is pink below, grey above, with white sections on the outer tail feathers. The female is paler than the male and the young are brownish. The Pink Robin (p. 281), which overlaps in distribution with the Rose Robin in the south, is darker above and has paler pink on the undersurface that also extends to the lower belly. The Rose Robin is found from southeastern Queensland, through eastern New South Wales, and all bar the north-west of Victoria to southeastern South Australia. Its call is a soft trill, rising in pitch and volume towards the end of each phrase.

Peter Rowland

Varied Sittella *Daphoenositta chrysoptera*

Angus McNab

This species shows considerable plumage variation across its range, which covers the majority of the Australian mainland. Depending on its location, a bird can have white, black, grey or mottling on its head, white or orange wing-stripe, and plain or streaked underparts. All birds have yellow, upturned bills with black tips, short tails and legs, and large feet. The species feeds in active flocks of up to 20 birds on the trunks of trees and branches, often walking on the undersides of the limbs as it goes. The commonly heard call is a high-pitched *chip-chip*. It can be found in a range of habitats, including rainforests, eucalypt woodland and inland scrubs.

White-headed Pigeon *Columba leucomela*

John Haris

This pigeon has a white head and neck and white underparts, but lacks the dark breast-band and white tail-tip of the Black-banded Fruit-dove (p. 316). The wings, back and tail are dark grey to black, and males can have a greenish or russet-brown iridescent wash. The eye-ring, bill-base, legs and feet are reddish-pink. The species is endemic to the coast and adjacent highlands of eastern Australia, from around Cooktown, Queensland, to the New South Wales–Victoria border. It was once solely dependent on rainforests and was initially severely impacted by loss of habitat, but managed to adapt somewhat to the changing landscape. These days it nests in rainforests, but feeds on fruits and seeds of both native and exotic plants in a range of adjacent habitats.

Chocolate Wattled Bat *Chalinolobus morio*

The fur of this bat is soft and thick, chocolate-brown above and below, and sometimes paler on the belly in the inland population. The top of the head is rounded, and the ears are broad and relatively short. It is broadly but patchily distributed through coastal and inland Australia, including Tasmania and several offshore islands, from around Townsville, Queensland, in the north-east, to the Pilbara region, Western Australia, in the north-west. It is found in large rainforests, sclerophyll forests, woodland and shrubland, mostly along watercourses in drier areas inland, roosting mainly in trees, including in hollows and under loose bark, but also in caves and inside buildings. It forages mostly between the understorey and canopy, mainly for moths and beetles, hunting at speeds of about 28km/h.

Angus McNab

Eastern Pygmy-possum *Cercartetus nanus*

This is one of the smallest possums in the world. It is pale brown to grey above and pale greyish below, with white tips on the hairs. The tail is brownish, almost naked and prehensile. It occurs in southeastern Australia, from far southeastern Queensland to southeastern South Australia and Tasmania (including islands of Bass Strait). The Little Pygmy-possum (p. 274), with which it overlaps in range in the south, is similar, but smaller and less than half the weight. The Eastern Pygmy-possum inhabits rainforests, forests, woodland and heathland. It feeds largely on nectar and pollen, supplemented with insects and spiders. Individuals shelter by day in a nest of shredded bark and leaves placed in a hollow or under bark. They emerge shortly after dusk to forage both in trees and on the ground.

Lachlan Hall

191

Gould's Long-eared Bat *Nyctophilus gouldi*

Angus McNab

The fur of this bat is greyish-brown to dark grey above, and paler grey with a light brown wash below. The head is blunt, with a medium-sized ridge across the snout, and very long ears that fold down when at rest, with a small, triangular lower lobe that extends over the ear opening. The wings are short and wide. It occurs in eastern and southwestern Australia, from northeastern Queensland, through coastal and inland New South Wales and Victoria, including along Murray River, to far southeastern South Australia; also in southwestern Western Australia. It inhabits rainforests, forests and woodland, preferring wetter areas, where it roosts by day, either solitarily (mainly males) or in small colonies in tree hollows and tree crevices, and under loose bark. It emerges at dusk to forage for insects, mainly moths, and other invertebrates, which it catches either by sight or by using echolocation.

Sugar Glider *Petaurus breviceps*

Angus McNab

This glider is brownish-grey to blue-grey above, with a blackish stripe running from between the eyes to the centre of the back, and cream to greyish below. The tail is blackish and bushy, occasionally tipped with white, the snout is short and rounded, and the ears are broad. The large gliding membrane (edged with blackish and white) is attached at the wrists and ankles (able to glide up to 90m). The black beady eyes are large, prominent and protruding. The Sugar Glider is found in southeastern Queensland and far eastern New South Wales. It was recently split from a wider ranging species complex, which also included the Savanna Glider *P. ariel* of northern Australia, from the Kimberley region, Western Australia, through the northern Northern Territory, to northwestern Queensland, and the Krefft's Glider *P. notatus*, which occurs from northern Queensland, through New South Wales, Victoria and Tasmania, to far southeastern South Australia. It inhabits rainforests, wet and dry sclerophyll forests and woodland. It is nocturnal, sheltering by day in a hollow tree lined with leaves, and feeds arboreally on nectar, pollen, honeydew and arthropods. Individuals chew the bark from trees to feed on sap when other food sources are rare.

Bandy-bandy *Vermicella annulata*

This slender snake has alternating black and white cross-bands wrapping completely around the body, with up to 75 black rings evident. The snout is black, the eyes small, and the tail short and blunt. It does not overlap with any other members of the genus, all of which have similar colour patterns. It is widespread through eastern and far northern Australia, from the central northern Northern Territory, northern and eastern Queensland, to New South Wales, northern Victoria and southeastern South Australia. It occurs in a range of habitats, from wet coastal rainforest to sandy spinifex desert, where it can be found sheltering under rocks and logs. Nocturnal and fossorial, it is presumed to feed exclusively on blind snakes, some as large as itself, and is able to go for extended periods without food or water. When threatened it loops parts of its body high off the ground. VENOMOUS

Angus McNab

Broad-tailed Gecko *Phyllurus platurus*

Also known as the Southern Leaf-tailed Gecko, this lizard is brown or grey above with cryptic darker brown and black speckling, and whitish-grey below. The original tail is darker and occasionally has a number of bands towards the tip. The head, body and tail are flattened and covered with numerous small, raised tubercles. The tail is wide and either heart- or leaf-shaped. The species is confined to Sydney Hawkesbury sandstone along the central coast and ranges of New South Wales, in sandstone caves and crevices and nearby houses, within forests and heaths. It shelters, often communally, in rock crevices by day and emerges at night to forage. It is insectivorous, feeding on small insects and spiders; extra fat reserves are stored in the tail. The tail keeps moving when dropped, distracting potential predators while the gecko makes its escape; it is then regrown.

Angus McNab

Eastern Water-skink *Eulamprus quoyii*

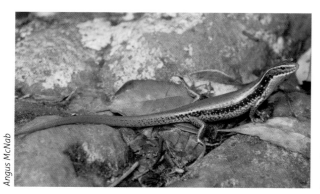

Angus McNab

This is a glossy, robust skink with a long, slightly laterally flattened tail and relatively long rear legs. It is metallic-brown to olive-brown above, with scattered black flecks on the back and tail-base, and a yellowish dorsolateral stripe from above the eye to the rump. The sides are black with scattered cream flecks, bordered below by yellowish-cream with dark grey spotting and marbling. It occupies ranges, slopes and lowlands of eastern Australia, from coastal northeastern Queensland, to southern New South Wales and through central New South Wales along the Murray-Darling river drainage systems, to southeastern South Australia. It inhabits most wet habitats, including rainforests, wet and dry sclerophyll forests, woodland and heaths, particularly in rocky areas around edges of creeks, rivers and swamps, and is usually seen basking on rocks or foraging among riverine vegetation for invertebrates, small frogs, fish and small lizards.

Highlands Forest Skink *Anepischetosia maccoyi*

Angus McNab

This smooth, glossy-scaled skink has an elongated body and narrow, tapering tail that is equal in length to the body. The forelimbs and hindlimbs are short, all with five digits. The colouration is rich brown to dark greyish-brown, with light and dark flecks on the dorsal and a narrow blackish-brown vertebral stripe, usually broken or obscure and sometimes with a yellowish-brown bar above. The sides are light grey or brown, with light and dark mottling, and there are brown spots on the white throat. The lips are white with black bars and the belly is cream to yellow. It occurs in the southeastern Australian mainland, from western Victoria to southeastern New South Wales, inhabiting rainforests and wet forests, where it is found in dense leaf litter or under rocks and logs. It is nocturnal, emerging at dusk to feed in moist soil.

Three-toed Skink *Saiphos equalis*

This robust, smooth-scaled, long-bodied skink has shortened, widely spaced limbs, each with three very short digits. It is rich brown to greyish-brown above with dark brown, longitudinally aligned spots and sharply contrasting blackish-brown sides. It has a dark brown face, with yellowish spots on the cheeks and flanks, no external ear openings,

Angus McNab

and movable lower eyelids. The underparts are yellow to orange, with dark brown spots on the throat. The underside of the tail is black. It occurs in coastal lowlands and adjacent ranges of the eastern mainland, including southeastern Queensland and eastern New South Wales, in rainforests, forests, woodland, heaths, grassland and adjacent suburban gardens. It is active at night, foraging under rocks and logs, or in dense groundcover, for invertebrates that include beetles and their larvae, worms and centipedes.

Bleating Tree Frog *Litoria dentata*

The colouration of this tree frog varies from cream to dark brown, with a darker irregular stripe running from the nose, over the shoulders and down to near the hips. The underside is cream to white. The species is found along the coast and adjacent ranges from Gympie, Queensland, to Mallacoota, Victoria, where it occurs in moist habitats such as swamps, rainforest, eucalypt forest, heaths and

Angus McNab

wallum. It also enters urban areas, where it can be seen in bathrooms, roadside ditches, cattle troughs and dams. It feeds on arthropods. The male's call, a prolonged sheep-like bleating, is made from vegetation and at the bases of grass clumps around a waterbody. An average clutch consists of 1,100 eggs, which once hatched take about eight weeks to turn into frogs.

Blue Mountains Tree Frog *Litoria citropa*

Angus McNab

The colouration of this tree frog is variable, but it is usually brown above with green and white to cream on the flanks, and pinkish-red between the shoulders to the base of the hips. A cream-edged dark stripe extends from the snout, along the side to just above the front legs. It is white below. Some individuals are flecked with black or dark brown. It inhabits creeks and streams in forests in southeastern Australia, from Wollemi National Park, New South Wales, to Gippsland, Victoria. It breeds in pools beside creeks and streams and in slower parts of a main waterway, where it also feeds on invertebrates. The male's call is made in two parts, the first a *waaark* and the second a gurgling bobble, repeated quickly.

Heath Frog *Litoria littlejohni*

Stephen Mahoney

The colouration of this frog varies from light grey to dark brown, with or without a broad dark brown stripe that extends over the head, from behind the eyes and down the back. Some individuals can have additional stripes and dark flecks. The insides of the armpits and the groin are pale orange. This species occurs in eastern New South Wales from the Watagan Ranges to Wollongong. It feeds on invertebrates around natural or artificial slow-moving or still watercourses in a variety of habitats, including warm temperate rainforest. The male's call, a pulsed *creeeet creeeet creeeet*, repeated frequently, is made from grass tussocks, reeds, low overhanging branches and aquatic vegetation, from autumn to early spring.

Leaf-green Tree Frog *Litoria phyllochroa*

This tree frog is bright green to dark brown above with a dark-edged gold or yellow stripe extending from the nostril, above the eye to the armpit. The underside is white. It is found in eastern New South Wales, from Sydney to near Bellingen, where it occurs around creeks and streams in forests. It breeds in pools and in slower parts of the main waterway, and feeds on invertebrates. The male's call, a loud *eeech*, repeated reasonably frequently from spring to early summer, is given from vegetation overhanging the water, especially after heavy rain. It breeds in pools beside streams, and eggs are laid in loose clusters attached to sticks or other plant material.

Angus McNab

Red-crowned Brood Frog *Pseudophryne australis*

This species is light grey to almost black above, with bright orange to red spots and flecks on top of the head and along the back and sides. There is usually a red triangle from the snout, across the top of the head, to the rear of the eyes. The underparts are white with black marbling. It is found around Sydney, New South Wales, and although not common in rainforest areas, has been recorded in this habitat within Royal National Park. It is most commonly found in moist gutters and seepages, formed between layers of sandstone where water gathers and is held after rain, where it feeds mainly on ants. The male's call is a short squelch, given from below leaf litter or under rocks. The eggs are guarded by the male until the nest is inundated by rain.

Angus McNab

Australian Land Leech *Chtonobdella limbata*

Scott Eipper

A brownish to blackish leech, with a paler longitudinal stripe along the tapering body. Restricted to the coast and near inland of southern New South Wales, although isolated records of this species have recently come from the border of northern New South Wales and southern Queensland. Found in forested areas, where it occurs on or close to the ground, and is generally most active following rain. Feeds on the blood of mammals, including humans, using its two jaws to pierce the skin of its host, leaving a V-shaped mark. It injects a secretion called hirudin into its victim to prevent the blood from clotting. The wound can bleed and stay itchy and inflamed for several hours after the leech has dropped off.

Blue Triangle *Graphium choredon*

Peter Rowland

The adults are virtually unmistakable for any other butterfly species in Australia. The uppersides of the wings are black with a central matt blue band, the hindwings have submarginal lunules. The underside is paler with a silvery submarginal band and several red spots on hindwing. Males have a dense tuft of hairs that are popped open while hovering over the female during courtship. This species occurs in coastal eastern Australia from near the Victoria-New South Wales border north to Cape York Peninsula, Queensland. Further north in the Torres Strait it is replaced by the similar *G. isander*. The species is common along forest margins, including rainforests, and in suburban gardens. Adults actively feed and drink during the day, seldom resting long in any one place. Host plants are laurels (Lauraceae), including the introduced camphor laurel *Cinnamomum camphora*.

Bronze Flat *Netrocoryne repanda*

John Tann (CC)

Butterflies of this species are brown with narrow dark margins on the wings. Each forewing has several pale spots and there is a single small pale spot on each hindwing. Females are slightly larger than males. Caterpillars start yellow with a black head, but become greenish-grey with yellow and black at each end as they age. The species occurs throughout eastern Australia, from northern Victoria, through the Australian Capital Territory and eastern New South Wales, to northern Queensland. It is mainly found in rainforests, but also occurs in eucalypt woodland. In flight, adults alternate between rapid flight and gliding on outstretched wings. At rest, the wings are held outstretched and moth-like. Caterpillars initially form a shelter by cutting a small circle from a leaf of their host plant and attaching it to the rest of the leaf with silk. This is replaced with a curled-over leaf as they mature.

Caper Gull *Cepora perimale*

Jean & Fred Hort (CC)

The upperwing surfaces of adult butterflies are white, with broad black margins with white spots. The underside is much like the upper surface, except that the hindwing base colour is yellow to brown (depending on the season). Caterpillars are green with small yellow tubercles and short white setae. The species is distributed through northern and eastern Australia, including Norfolk Island, but also occurs in Papua New Guinea, Indonesia, Fiji, New Caledonia, Vanuatu and the Solomon Islands. It typically occurs in coastal forest, rainforest margins, gardens and drier inland forest. Caterpillars are known to feed on species of capparis (Capparaceae), lying along the midrib of a leaf when resting. Adults are fast fliers.

Blue Mountains National Park

The Blue Mountains National Park, together with Gardens of Stone, Kanangra-Boyd, Nattai, Thirlmere Lakes, Wollemi and Yengo National Parks and the Jenolan Karst Conservation Reserve, combine to form the Greater Blue Mountains World Heritage Area. The extensive Greater Blue Mountains World Heritage Area covers a massive million hectares of wilderness. It supports a huge biodiversity and is dominated by eucalypt woodland. It exhibits incredible geological features, as well as being an important cultural area for six Aboriginal tribes. The park is a short drive from Sydney and well worth visiting for a few days if you have the time. Its sheer size (2,690km^2) and rugged terrain make it difficult to enjoy its full wildlife-watching potential without a dedicated long stay.

About 45 per cent of the national park's vegetation is dry forests, 40 per cent woodland, 11 per cent heathland and 2 per cent moist forests and rainforests. Northern warm temperate rainforests are the dominant rainforest type, due to the park's large areas of acidic soils.

The national park is an important refuge for more than 200 bird species, 46 mammals, 58 reptiles and 32 frogs, many of which are threatened. Some of these are the Greater Sooty

Thomas Rowland

Katoomba Cascades Round Walk

Owl, Large-footed Myotis, Pink Robin, Powerful Owl, Red-crowned Brood Frog, Southern Brown Bandicoot, Spotted-tailed Quoll and Yellow-bellied Glider.

The park also conserves a huge diversity of plant communities and species. More than 1,000 species of flowering plant are estimated to occur here.

GPS Coordinates
-33.63107,150.30573 (Blue Mountains Heritage Centre)

Getting There
The park comprises six areas: Katoomba, Blackheath, Glenbrook, Lower Grose Valley, Mount Wilson and Southern Blue Mountains. It is accessed via the Great Western

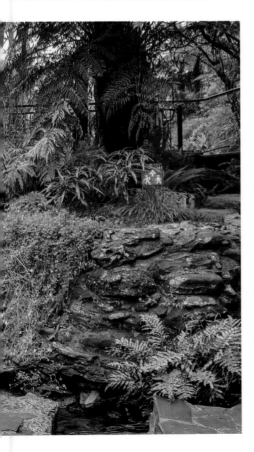

Highway or the Bells Line of Road.

Tracks & Trails
The *Grand Canyon Track* (6km, loop) near Blackheath winds beneath waterfalls and across streams as it meanders through the rainforest. It is one of the most beautiful walks in the Blue Mountains and is best tackled anticlockwise to finish at the top of Evans Lookout. The *Katoomba Falls Round Walk* (4km, loop) is a short and relatively easy walking trail for all fitness levels, although there are some steep sections. The track starts at Scenic World and passes through lush rainforest on its way to Katoomba Falls. The waterfall starts about 150m above the spectacular Jamison Valley. *Dardanelles Pass Circuit Walk* (5km, loop), including the historic Giant Stairway, is a challenging walk through Leura Forest. The scenic waterfalls, panoramic valley views and sights, sounds and smells of the lush rainforest give frequent opportunities to rest during the steeper parts of the walk. The *Leura Cascades Circuit* (4.5km, loop) is a moderately difficult walk with amazing rainforest views. The track winds downstream for 100m before climbing some steep stairs on its way to the halfway point that overlooks a natural amphitheatre.

Fees & Permits
Entry to the park is free, but some attractions are charged.

Facilities
The park has numerous facilities, including camp grounds, public toilets, picnic areas, barbecue areas, kiosks/cafes and drinking water points.

Services Nearby
There are numerous large towns in the vicinity of the park.

Royal National Park

This is Australia's oldest national park. When first gazetted in 1879, it was called 'The National Park' but it was renamed with its current title in 1955, after Queen Elizabeth II saw the park from a train during her 1954 tour. The park was added to the Australian National Heritage List in December 2006. Today, it covers an area of about 151km², rising from sea level to 300m. Situated along the coast of southern Sydney, the park is easily accessible by road and water, both of which provide access to numerous walking trails and sites.

The canopy of the northern warm temperate and subtropical rainforest that occurs in the park includes the Coachwood *Ceratopetalum apetalum*, Giant Stinging Tree *Dendrocnide excelsa* and Red Cedar *Toona ciliata*. The park is also home to littoral rainforest. Dominant species include the Tuckeroo *Cupaniopsis anacardioides*, with emergent species like the Coastal Tea Tree *Leptospermum laevigatum* and an undergrowth of the Long-leaf Matrush *Lomandra longifolia*.

The park and adjacent area support almost 350 native fauna species, more than 40 of which are threatened. As many as 230 bird species have been recorded in the park, as well as 38 mammals, 42 reptiles and 21 frogs. Commonly encountered

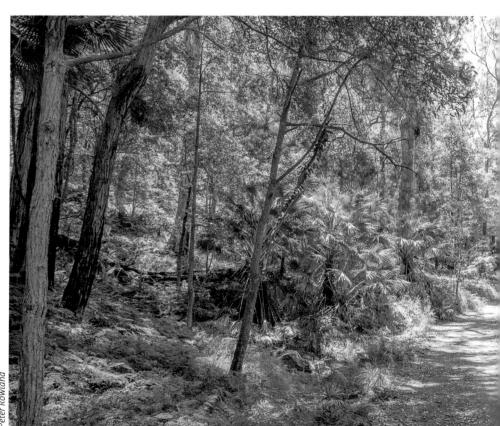

Peter Rowland

Along the Forest Path walking trail

species include the Australian Golden Whistler, Black-faced Monarch, Brown Gerygone, Brown Thornbill, Crimson Rosella, Delicate Skink, Eastern Spinebill, Eastern Whipbird, Eastern Yellow Robin, Eastern Water-skink, Leaf-green Tree Frog, Lewin's Honeyeater, Sugar Glider, Superb Lyrebird, Swamp Wallaby, White-browed Scrubwren and White-throated Treecreeper.

GPS Coordinates
-34.05329, 151.04870 (Main entry)
-34.07531, 151.05640 (Information Centre)

Getting There
The park can be accessed via Farnell Avenue, Loftus (main entrance); Lady Wakehurst Drive, Otford; McKell

Avenue, Waterfall. The closest major airport is Sydney Airport, and trains on the Illawarra and South Coast lines stop at Sutherland, Loftus and Waterfall.

Tracks & Trails
The *Forest Path* (4.4km, loop) is an easy walking trail and can be accessed from Lady Carrington Drive or via the stone gates on Sir Bertram Stevens Drive. A variety of native plants, including giant Cabbage Tree Palms *Livistona australis* and Gymea Lilies *Doryanthes excelsa*, which have a tall flower spike and large red flowers during winter, can be seen along the walk. *Lady Carrington Drive* (10km, one way) is open to traffic, but is also a popular cycle track. It follows the Hacking River south from Audley to Sir Bertram Stevens Drive (near McKell Avenue). Along the way it passes through wet sclerophyll forest and rainforest. *Palm Jungle Loop* (10km) is a challenging walk that contains littoral rainforest. It is located at the southern end of the 26km Coast Track, which stretches between Bundeena and Otford.

Fees & Permits
A park entry fee is payable and camping fees are payable if staying overnight.

Facilities
Toilets, drinking water, cafes, picnic tables, barbecues, boating and public phones are available in the park. River swimming and patrolled beaches are also nearby.

Services Nearby
Numerous shops, fuel outlets and cafes are within a short drive of park entrances, including in the towns of Heathcote, Sutherland, Engadine, Maianbar and Bundeena.

Budderoo National Park

This park is located on top of the Illawarra escarpment. The winding road up the mountain from the village of Jamberoo passes through towering rainforest with an understorey of large tree ferns. The park covers 72.19km² and its mosaic of soil types supports a range of forest types, including subtropical and northern warm temperate rainforest.

The temperate rainforest patches support large trees, such as the Brown Beech *Pennantia cunninghamii*, Giant Stinging Tree *Dendrocnide excelsa*, Silky Beech *Citronella moorei*, Moreton Bay Fig *Ficus macrophylla*, Red Cedar *Toona ciliata* and Sassafras *Doryphora sassafras* which dominate the canopy.

Shrubs, ferns, epiphytes and vines are common.

The main patches of moist subtropical rainforest occur below Minnamurra Falls, Carrington Falls and Gerringong Falls. These species rich forests are characterized by a high density of subtropical species, a dense shrub understorey and a dense ground cover of ferns. Vines and epiphytes are plentiful. Tree species include the Brown Beech, Cabbage Tree Palm *Livistona australis*, Featherwood *Polyosma cunninghamii*, Giant Stinging Tree, Red Cedar, Silky Beech and Silver Quandong *Elaeocarpus kirtonii*.

While few comprehensive wildlife surveys have been conducted in the

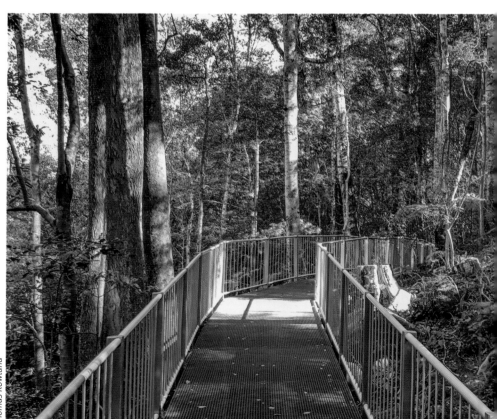

Thomas Rowland

Minnamurra Rainforest Loop & Falls Walk

park, the area is known to support a rich assemblage of bird, mammal, reptile and frog species, including the Australian Brush Turkey, Eastern Whipbird, Short-beaked Echidna, Spotted-tailed Quoll, Superb Lyrebird, Topknot Pigeon and Wonga Pigeon. Platypus have been recorded in creeks in the Minnamurra Rainforest area.

GPS Coordinates

-34.64515, 150.70374 (Budderoo Plateau Road)
-34.63454, 150.72762 (Minnamurra Falls Main entry)

Getting There

From Wollongong (33km) take the Princes Highway (A1) and Jamberoo Mountain Road. Albion Park Rail (25km) has a regional airport and train service.

Tracks & Trails

Minnamurra Rainforest's Falls Walk (4.2km, return, moderately difficult) is located about halfway along the *Rainforest Loop Walk* (1.6km). The *Rainforest Loop Walk* has well-maintained walkways and the first 500m, up to the first suspension bridge, is suitable for wheelchairs. The remainder of the walk crosses suspension bridges and meanders its way up through the rainforest to the Falls Walk turn-off, then winds back down through the rainforest to the Rainforest Centre and gift shop. The Falls Walk is steep in sections, but the viewing platforms at the lower and upper Minnamurra Falls give spectacular views.

A rich diversity of plants, including native orchids and ferns, and animals can be seen along both walks. Keep an ear out for the expert mimicry of the Superb Lyrebird as it weaves the calls of other animals and mechanical sounds into its incredible song.

Fees & Permits

There are no entry fees to the national park, but fees are payable for the Minnamurra Falls Rainforest Centre.

Facilities

Toilet and handwashing facilities, picnic tables (some undercover) and barbecues are located at Minnamurra Falls and Carrington Falls. Camping is available at Carrington Falls and the Minnamurra Falls Rainforest Centre has a shop and cafe.

Services Nearby

Jamberoo has shops, cafes, pub, post office and newsagency. Albion Park and Robertson, both moderately short drives, have fuel, banks and other services. Kiama has the closest hospital.

South East Corner

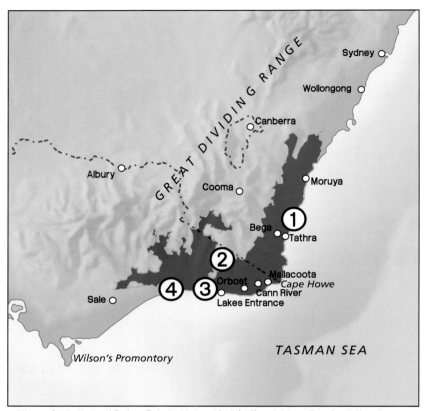

1. Mimosa Rocks National Park 2. Errindra National Park (VIC) 3. Cabbage Tree Creek Flora Reserve (VIC) 4. Lake Tyers State Park (VIC)

Within New South Wales, the South East Corner bioregion covers 12,064.79km². Of this total area, 41.8 per cent (5,043.18km²) is protected within the bioregion's 52 reserves. A further 13,255.73km² of the bioregion occurs in Victoria and 27.02 per cent (3,581.92km²) of this is protected in a further 118 reserves. The bioregion supports more than 4,700 described animal species, including about 360 birds, 80 mammals, 65 reptiles, 35 amphibians and 3,300 insects and spiders, as well as over 5,400 described species of plant and fungi. This bioregion includes both cool and warm temperate and dry rainforests. It has a largely temperate climate, characterized by warm summers and no dry season. The higher montane areas in the bioregion's south and south-west have mild summers.

Angus McNab

Cabbage Tree Palms Flora Reserve

South East Corner

Key Species

BIRDS
Australian Golden Whistler, Australian King Parrot, Australian Masked Owl, Bassian Thrush, Black-faced Monarch, Brown Gerygone, Brown Thornbill, Cicadabird, Crimson Rosella, Eastern Spinebill, Eastern Whipbird, Eastern Yellow Robin, Fan-tailed Cuckoo, Flame Robin, Greater Sooty Owl, Grey Fantail, Grey Goshawk, Grey Shrikethrush, Large-billed Scrubwren, Lewin's Honeyeater, Olive-backed Oriole, Olive Whistler, Pacific Koel, Red-browed Finch, Rose Robin, Rufous Fantail, Satin Bowerbird, Silvereye, Scarlet Myzomela, Shining Bronze-cuckoo, Spangled Drongo, Superb Lyrebird, Topknot Pigeon, White-browed Scrubwren, White-headed Pigeon, White-throated Treecreeper, Wonga Pigeon, Yellow-throated Scrubwren.

MAMMALS
Brush-tailed Phascogale, Brush-tailed Rock Wallaby, Chocolate Wattled Bat, Common Wombat, Eastern Pygmy-possum, Eastern Ring-tailed Possum, Golden-tipped Bat, Grey-headed Flying-fox, Koala, Krefft's Glider, Long-footed Potoroo, Long-nosed Potoroo, Mainland Dusky Antechinus, Mountain Brush-tailed Possum, Southern Brown Bandicoot, Squirrel Glider, Sugar Glider, Water Rat, Yellow-footed Antechinus.

REPTILES
Bandy-bandy, Carpet Python, Delicate Skink, Eastern Small-eyed Snake, Eastern Water Dragon, Eastern Water-skink, Highland Copperhead, Highlands Forest Skink, Lace Monitor, Mainland She-oak Skink, Pale-flecked Garden Sunskink, Swamp Snake, Three-toed Skink, Tiger Snake, Water Dragon, Weasel Skink, Yellow-bellied Water-skink.

AMPHIBIANS
Booroolong Frog, Narrow-fringed Frog.

INVERTEBRATES
Orbost Spiny Crayfish, Varied Swordgrass Brown, Wonder Brown, Yellow-spotted Jezebel.

The bioregion is split into three subregions. The East Gippsland Lowlands subregion has 892.26km² in New South Wales (319km² protected) and 5,342.90km² in Victoria (1,191.51km² protected); the South East Coastal Ranges has 9,432.26km² in New South Wales (4,448.71km² protected) and 7,912.91km² in Victoria (2,390.41km² protected); and Bateman 1,740.20km² (2,753.8km² protected) is wholly contained in New South Wales.

Rainforests have a patchy distribution across this bioregion, generally occurring within protected gullies and along waterways. In New South Wales, rainforest patches occur in Mimosa Rocks National Park, and along the Sandy Creek Loop track in Bournda National Park and the Goodenia Rainforest Walk in the South East Forests National Park. Rainforest areas in the Victorian part of the bioregion include Errinundra National Park, Cabbage Tree Creek Flora Reserve, Bemm River Scenic Reserve (McKenzie River) and Lake Tyers State Park.

Angus McNab

Satin Bowerbird (female)

Australian Masked Owl *Tyto novaehollandiae*

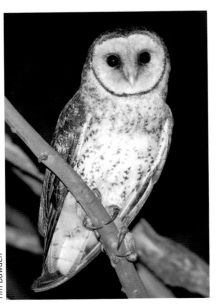

Tim Bawden

The Australian Masked Owl is a large, robust owl with variable plumage across its range. Females have a dark rufous-brown face and dark-mottled rufous underparts, while males are generally whitish in comparison. The face is enclosed within a dark-rimmed facial disk. The upperwings are varying shades of dark brown with faint bands and silver flecking throughout. The pale legs are fully feathered, giving an appearance of the owl wearing trousers; the feet have massive talons. Females are much larger than males. These owls are elusive but may be heard calling during the breeding season. Calls include a loud, deep, hissing screech and variable cackling by the males. Nests are in large old trees with substantial hollows. The bird's diet consists almost entirely of small to medium-sized terrestrial mammals.

Flame Robin *Petroica phoenicea*

Angus McNab

The orange breast and throat of the male of this aptly named species with a grey back and white wing-bar distinguish it from other robins. The female is largely warm grey-brown, the wing-bar is pale buff, and only the outer tail feathers are extensively white. Both sexes have a characteristic upright stance, which also helps to distinguish the species from other similarly coloured robins. The Flame Robin pounces on prey from a prominent, exposed lookout, returning to the perch to eat. The attractive song has been interpreted as 'you may come if you wish to the sea'. In summer it can be observed in forests and woodland up to 1,800m above sea level, but it disperses to lower altitudes in winter.

Greater Sooty Owl *Tyto tenebricosa*

Both the Greater and Lesser Sooty Owl are dusky-grey. They are both confined to the eastern coast of Australia, but do not overlap in distribution. The main range of the Greater is from southeastern Queensland to Victoria's central highlands, but there is also a population in the Clarke Range, Queensland. The Lesser is found only in north Queensland, from around Townsville to just north of Cooktown. The Greater is dark sooty-grey, heavily spotted with white, with a dark facial disk. Its talons are heavy set and used to forage for both arboreal and terrestrial prey. It roosts during the day in dense foliage or in a large tree hollow or cave.

Owen Lishmund

Red-browed Finch *Neochmia temporalis*

Like a fiery dart as it flies, this medium-sized finch is distinguished from other Australian finches by the combination of its bright red rump and eyebrow. The remainder of the upperparts are olive-green, and the underparts and head are grey. The bill is red with a broad black wedge on the top and bottom mandibles. The species is distributed in a broad coastal band along the east and south-east coasts, from Cape York Peninsula, Queensland, to Adelaide, South Australia. Small populations are also recorded near Perth and Albany, Western Australia. It is found in a variety of habitats, especially shrubland and open grassy areas, and enters the fringes of rainforests where these meet. Its call is a high-pitched *seee* or *ssitt*.

Angus McNab

209

Topknot Pigeon *Lopholaimus antarcticus*

Chris Farrell

This large rainforest pigeon is predominantly grey, with slate-grey upperparts with black wing feathers and silvery-grey underparts. The tail is blackish with a grey subterminal band. It gets its common name from the distinctive double crest on its head. The front crest is grey and curls forwards over the bill and back over the crown, while the hind-crest is a rusty colour and droops down the neck to the nape; males have a longer crest than females. These pigeons can form large, nomadic flocks moving between patches of rainforest looking for fruiting trees. They are quite acrobatic, clambering among foliage in search of fruits. The species was first seen in East Gippsland during the 1990s and is now a regular summer visitor, although in small numbers.

Brush-tailed Phascogale *Phascogale tapoatafa*

Tim Bawden

This small arboreal dasyurid is grey above, streaked with silvery-white, and white to creamish below, with a long, brushy, black bottlebrush tail. It has a pointed snout, with large naked ears and large protruding eyes. It is patchily distributed in the southwestern and Kimberley region, Western Australia, northeastern and southeastern Queensland, eastern New South Wales, and central and southwestern Victoria. It prefers dry sclerophyll open forests with herbs, shrubs, grass and leaf litter, but also occurs to a lesser degree in rainforests, wet sclerophyll forests, heaths and swamps. Generally most numerous in moist gullies, it shelters in tree hollows and emerges at night to forage almost exclusively in trees for invertebrates concealed under loose bark, supplemented with nectar. This species is the most arboreal of the dasyurids.

Long-footed Potoroo *Potorous longipes*

First recorded by scientists in the late 1960s, the Long-footed Potoroo was not formally described until 1980. Its fur is greyish-brown above and grey below. The hindfoot is longer than the head and has a small raised pad between the heel and base of the fused second and third toes. Occurring in a fragmented range in far southeastern New South Wales and eastern Victoria, it is found in dry and wet forests, including rainforests, with a dense understorey used for shelter, and more open areas for feeding. Primarily nocturnal, it feeds mainly on subterranean fungi and invertebrates, supplemented with seeds and other plant material. The animals are normally solitary and monogamous, with home ranges only overlapping with their mate and subadult young. This species is listed as Endangered under Commonwealth legislation.

Dave Watts

Mountain Brush-tailed Possum
Trichosurus cunninghami

This possum is usually dark silvery-grey above, occasionally tinged with reddish-brown and pale cream or white below; some individuals are entirely blackish. The tail is black and bushy, tapering towards the tip, with a section of naked skin towards the tip on the underside. The ears are short and rounded, and the eyeshine is red when reflected in a spotlight. The species occurs in southeastern Australia, from around Ulladulla, New South Wales, to central Victoria, with an isolated population in western Victoria. It inhabits a variety of wooded habitats, including tall open and closed forests, rainforests and adjacent pine plantations, where it sleeps by day in tree hollows or rocky crevices. The female gives birth to a single young, which is suckled in her pouch for up to six months.

Angus McNab

211

Southern Brown Bandicoot *Isoodon obesulus*

Appearing greyish-brown above from a distance, this species is more brown when viewed at closer range. The underparts are cream to yellowish-grey. The snout is pointed, and the small, rounded ears and tail are short, brownish above and creamish-yellow below. The female has a rear-facing pouch. The species occurs from southeastern South Australia (including Kangaroo Island) and southern Victoria, to southeastern New South Wales. It inhabits forests, rainforests, wetlands and moist heathland with dense vegetation, where it sleeps by day in nests under vegetation, or occasionally in disused burrows of other animals, emerging at night to forage in the ground litter or dig in topsoil for a variety of invertebrates, fungi, and plant roots and tubers.

Angus McNab

Eastern Small-eyed Snake *Cryptophis nigrescens*

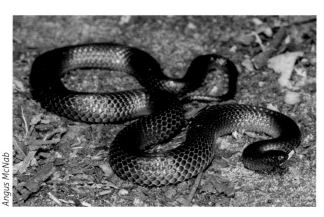

Uniformly glossy blue-black or dark grey on the back and sides, this snake has a cream belly with grey blotches in the south, reddish-pink with dark grey flecks in the north. The head is flattened and the eyes are small and dark. Males are larger than females, with larger heads. The species occurs along the coast and ranges of eastern Australia between southern Cape York Peninsula, Queensland, and southeastern Victoria. It inhabits rainforests, wet and dry sclerophyll forests, woodland, coastal heaths and suburban gardens, and is nocturnal, sheltering by day beneath stones, rock crevices, loose bark and fallen logs, and emerging to forage for small terrestrial lizards and their eggs, blind snakes and small snakes. It produces up to 7–8 live young in a litter. VENOMOUS

Angus McNab

Eastern Water Dragon *Intellagama lesueurii*

This large, very distinctive dragon has an angular head, large nuchal crest, vertebral crest running the length of the body and long, laterally compressed tail. The subspecies in this region, referred to as the Gippsland Water Dragon *I. l. howittii*, is usually brownish to grey-green. Breeding males have blue-green and yellow-orange stripes on their throats. This

John Harris

subspecies ranges from around Kangaroo Valley in southern New South Wales to eastern Victoria. It occurs in varied habitats, from alpine streams to rainforests, but always in association with water, where it is omnivorous, feeding on flowers, fruits, invertebrates and small vertebrates. It is often seen basking on branches overhanging water or on banks of waterways, and may dive into the water when approached. A strong swimmer, it can remain submerged for long periods.

Highland Copperhead *Austrelaps ramsayi*

Highland Copperheads are variable in colour, from dark grey to black, through to shades of brown or reddish-brown on the back, often with a faint pale and dark collar. The head is often paler than the body, and the upper 'lips' have white triangles on each scale. The snake can grow to about 1.3m, but is usually smaller. It is found in upland areas of Victoria, the Australian

Angus McNab

Capital Territory and New South Wales, along the Great Dividing Range and to the coast, in cool and cold temperate areas. It is normally diurnal although it can be active on warm nights, hunting for frogs and lizards. It is active at lower temperatures than other snakes in the same areas. Females give birth to 5–30 live young. VENOMOUS

Mainland She-oak Skink *Cyclodomorphus michaeli*

Lachlan Hall

This species has an elongated body with short limbs and a moderately long tail, up to about one and a half times the length of the body. Individuals are generally greyish to dark reddish-brown above, and paler with grey on the head, and obscure longitudinal lines or transverse bars on the back. The sides have darker vertical barring, with some paler spots or an obscure reticulated pattern. The underparts are generally grey or greenish, occasionally with a yellowish wash and with darker transverse barring from chest to tail. Some individuals are unpatterned. The species occurs in the southeastern mainland, from northeastern Victoria, to the northern tablelands, New South Wales. It inhabits wet forests, woodland, coastal heathland and moist grassland, and is crepuscular and diurnal, foraging on the ground in open areas and around edges of vegetation for small invertebrates.

Yellow-bellied Water-skink *Eulamprus heatwolei*

Akash Samuel

This glossy, moderately robust skink has relatively long rear legs. It is coppery-brown to olive-brown above with numerous black flecks on the head, back and tail-base. The sides are black with many cream blotches, becoming more concentrated on the tail, and the flanks are yellowish-cream with dark grey marbling. The cheeks normally have white spots, and the limbs are olive-brown with black blotches and lines. The belly is yellowish and the throat white with black blotches. The species occurs in uplands of southeastern mainland Australia, from central Victoria to New England Plateau of northeastern New South Wales, although this may be a distinct species. It is a terrestrial inhabitant of forests, rainforests, woodland and grassland, and is usually found in association with moist habitats such as margins of swamps, lagoons and creeks. It feeds on a variety of invertebrates and small vertebrates such as fish, frogs and small reptiles.

Narrow-fringed Frog *Litoria nudidigita*

Angus McNab

Also known as the Southern Leaf Green Frog, the colouration of this species is bright green with a dark-edged gold or yellow stripe extending from the nostril, above the eye, and broadening over the flanks. The underside is white. The species is found in southeastern Australia, from just south of Sydney, New South Wales, to Gippsland in northeastern Victoria, living around creeks and streams in forests, and breeding in pools beside creeks and streams and in slower parts of a main waterway. The male's call is made from overhanging vegetation or branches and consists of two parts – the first a *wrekik-wrekik* and the second a loud *eeep*, which is not always repeated. It feeds on invertebrates.

Orbost Spiny Crayfish *Euastacus diversus*

Ian Bool

This small, spiny crayfish is widely distributed across East Gippsland in tributaries of the Snowy River (250–1,400m above sea level), but is typically found in low densities compared with other crayfish species (averaging 1–2 per 10–50m of stream). It is territorial, defending its section of a waterway, and is fast moving and agile, weighing to 47g and with an occipital-carapace length of to 44mm. Its colour varies between populations in different watercourses, and in the same watercourse at different altitudes, but it is generally dark or light green to brown on the dorsal surface, with green to grey-black abdominal or thoracic spines. The lower surface is creamish to orange. The claws (chelipeds) are brown to rusty, tipped with green/blue, and the legs have a bluish tint. Any spines on the legs and claws are generally cream or yellow. Females carry less than 30 large eggs in May–June.

215

Mimosa Rocks National Park

The 57km² Mimosa Rocks National Park is located on the far south coast of New South Wales between Bermagui and Tathra. The western section is dominated by dry sclerophyll forest with pockets of temperate littoral rainforest, while the eastern section has wetlands, heathland and coastal scrub. More than 200 native animal species have been recorded in the park, including 115 birds, 39 mammals, 21 reptiles and 12 amphibians. The park lies within the traditional country of the Yuin people, and its rugged landscape is strongly connected to Dreaming stories. It is named after the paddle steamer *Mimosa* that ran aground here in 1863.

The underlying geology of the park is dominated by folds, faults and intrusions of sedimentary rocks, such as shale, siltstone and slate. The formations have a castle-like appearance.

The Bunga Head Rainforest is only 0.07km² in extent. It has a low canopy (<10m tall) due to shearing effects of the coastal winds. The dominant canopy trees are the Kurrajong *Brachychiton populneus*, Lilly Pilly *Syzygium smithii*, Rusty Fig *Ficus rubiginosa* and Sweet Pittosporum *Pittosporum undulatum*, and the Bangalay *Eucalyptus botryoides* is the main emergent species. Other rainforest plants around the park include the Blueberry Ash *Elaeocarpus*

Peter Rowland

Temperate littoral rainforest pocket on the way to the Mimosa Rocks Walking Track

reticulatus and Wonga Vine *Pandorea pandorana*. The vulnerable Chef's Cap Correa *Correa baeuerlenii* is at the southern limit of its distribution here.

The park provides refuge for a range of animals, including the Long-nosed Potoroo, a regular nocturnal visitor to Gillards camp ground, and the Yellow-bellied Glider. Aragunnu camp ground is as good as any place to find the gliders (just listen for their distinctive cackling calls).

GPS Coordinates
-36.5828, 150.0514

Getting There
Access to the park is via gravel roads that lead off from the Bermagui–Tathra Road. Some roads may not be suitable for conventional vehicles after rain.

Tracks & Trails
Mimosa Rocks Walking Track (2km, return) is an easy walk and has wheelchair access. It is located in the northern section of the park and starts at Aragunnu car park. From the car park follow the track linking the section's two picnic areas, then continue north towards Bunga Head along the paved path and boardwalk. The boardwalk crosses over the largest Aboriginal midden in the park. The walk ends at a lookout, which affords scenic views over the rocks and the site where the paddle steamer *Mimosa* ran aground, and steps leading down to the beach. In spring migrating Humpback Whales *Megaptera novaeangliae* may be seen from the lookout. The coastal rock platforms and beaches are important breeding locations for native waders, including Hooded Plovers *Thinornis cucullatus* and Pied Oystercatchers *Haematopus longirostris*, and are feeding grounds for migratory waders such as the Bar-tailed Godwit *Limosa lapponica*.

Fees & Permits
Entry to the park is free and it is always open, but camping fees apply at all campsites.

Facilities
Camping and toilet facilities can be found at Aragunnu Beach, Gillards (caravan access), Middle Beach (walk-in only) and Picnic Point (bring your own drinking water). Accomodation is available at Myer House. Picnic facilities and barbecues are available at Aragunnu, Gillards, Middle Beach and Picnic Point. Aragunnu also has a wheelchair-accessible boardwalk and lookout. There is a public phone at Myer House.

Services Nearby
The closest towns are Tathra (5km) and Bega (23km). Both have a number of essential and tourism services.

Errinundra National Park

This national park was gazetted in 1988 following protests and a concerted effort to stop logging over many years. The park now encompasses 268.75km², rising to 1,000m above sea level on the Errinundra Plateau.

The park has the largest area of cool temperate rainforest, botanically unique to East Gippsland, consisting of the Southern Sassafras *Atherosperma moschatum oblongifolia,* Black Oliveberry *Elaeocarpus holopetalus* and Mountain Plum Pine *Podocarpus lawrencei.* The Mountain Plum Pines are believed to be more than 400 years old and are giants to around 17m, while they are usually small alpine shrubs in other areas. Goonmirk Range is the best place to see these giants. The Banyalla *Pittosporum bicolor,* Soft Tree Fern *Dicksonia antarctica,* Mountain Clematis *Clematis aristata* and Bat's Wing Fern *Histiopteris incisa* are some of the most recognizable understorey species.

More than 90 bird species have been recorded in the park, many of them inhabiting the rainforest patches, including the Australian King Parrot, Bassian Thrush, Brown Gerygone, Crimson Rosella, Gang-gang

Roderick Eime (CC)

The Errinundra National Park protects the largest remaining cool temperate rainforest in Victoria

Cockatoo, Greater Sooty Owl, Grey Fantail, Powerful Owl, Superb Lyrebird and Yellow-tailed Black Cockatoo. A number of small skinks may be found basking in sunny spots among the leaf litter or on exposed granite, while the Common Wombat, Southern Greater and Yellow-bellied Gliders, microbat species and the elusive Long-footed Potoroo may be found after dark with the aid of a spotlight or thermal imaging device.

GPS Coordinates
-37.28543, 148.87044

Getting There
From Orbost, take the Bonang Road (C612) for 85km. Turn right on to the

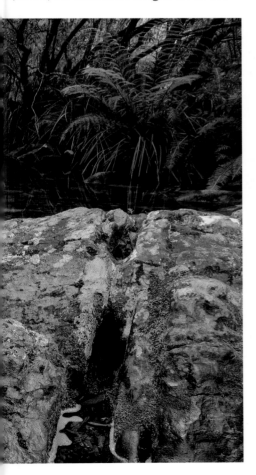

Bendoc-Orbost Road for about 5km to Gunmark Track, take this track south until Errinundra Track, turn left, then travel about 2.5km to the rainforest walk. Be aware that roads in this region are used by logging vehicles.

Tracks & Trails
Errinundra Saddle Rainforest Walk (1km, 45 minutes, return) is an easy walk that meanders through the rainforest in the shade of the Sassafras and Black Oliveberry canopy. Most of the walk is on a raised boardwalk that helps to protect the delicate flora, such as ferns and mosses, and the soil underneath. A series of information signs along the walk helps explain the forest, fauna and history of the area. *Errinundra Old Growth Forest Walk* (2.5km, 3 hours, return) is within the Gap Scenic Reserve, adjacent to Errinundra National Park. The walk starts on the Bendoc-Orbost Road, roughly 4.5km from the Bonang Road. It takes you through stands of Errinundra Shining Gum *Eucalyptus denticulata* before the elevated boardwalk takes you to an area of cool temperate rainforest dominated by Southern Sassafras and Australian Blackwoods, and some huge shining gums. This walk is quite steep in parts.

Fees & Permits
Entry to the park is free.

Facilities
Car park, raised boardwalk, information signs, picnic tables and toilets.

Services Nearby
Bendoc is the nearest (although small) town, with limited services about 30km north via Gunmark Track. Orbost, the biggest town in the area, is to the south and has a supermarket, accommodation, fuel and a variety of other services.

Cabbage Tree Creek Flora Reserve

This reserve is named after the Cabbage Fan-palm or Cabbage Tree Palm *Livistona australis* that is found in this area. Victorian Government Botanist Baron von Mueller first observed Cabbage Fan-palms in the area in 1854. In 1886 Tambo Shire set aside 100 acres to preserve them. There are only three naturally occurring locations for these palms in Victoria, here and in two nearby locations at Brodribb River and Caleys Creek, making them the most southerly distributed palms in Australia. They are listed as a threatened species in Victoria. The leaves of the palm were used to make sun hats back in the 1800s. The young shoots are considered edible, hence the name 'cabbage'.

This reserve features warm temperate rainforest consisting of the threatened Yellow-wood *Acronychia oblongifolia*, Blue Oliveberry *Elaeocarpus reticulatus*, and vines like the Austral Sarsaparilla *Smilax australis* and Pearl Vine *Sarcopetalum harveyana*. The McKenzie River Rainforest Walk is also warm temperate rainforest but with a different assembly of plants, including the Lilly Pilly *Syzygium smithii* and Kanooka *Tristaniopsis laurina*.

More than 120 bird species have been recorded in the reserve, some of them migrants arriving to

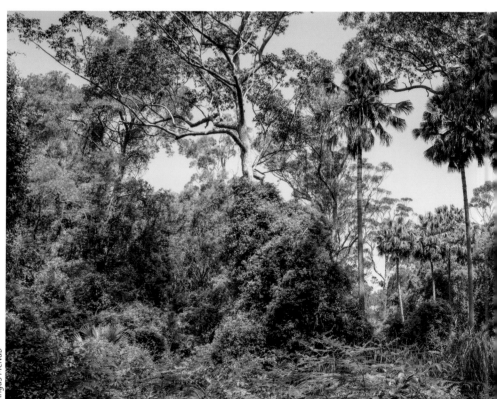

Angus McNab

The reserve is named after the Cabbage Fan-palm or Cabbage Tree Palm

take advantage of the fruiting trees. Rainforest species that are likely to be seen across the year are the Bassian Thrush, Black-faced Monarch, Brown Gerygone, Brown Thornbill, Eastern Whipbird, Grey Fantail, Large-billed Scrubwren, Superb Lyrebird, and Topknot and Wonga Pigeons. Eastern Water Dragons may be seen on sunny days basking on logs near the creek, while Grey-headed Flying-foxes, Southern Long-nosed Bandicoots, and the threatened and wary Long-nosed Potoroo may be found after dark feeding on the palm fruits and digging among the soil and leaf litter for food.

GPS Coordinates
-37.74397, 148.64709

Getting There
From Orbost head towards Marlo on

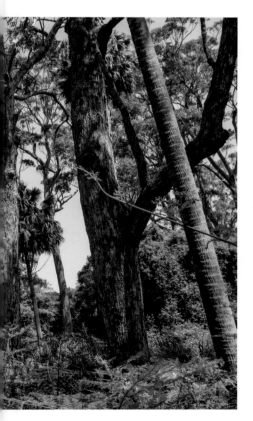

the Marlo Road (C107). Once there, continue for another 5km, then turn left and follow the Marlo-Cabbage Trees Road for 10km. Arriving at the aptly named Palm Track, turn left and go a further 2km to the car park.

Tracks & Trails
Cabbage Tree Creek Flora Reserve Walk (250m, 0.5 hour, return) is a gentle stroll through the warm temperate rainforest. Keep a look out for the Cabbage Fan-palms while listening for the musical repertoire of the local male lyrebirds. There are benches that enable you to sit and take in the sounds of the rainforest, or watch as Cabbage Tree Creek flows softly by. You can return the same way, or if time is short, walk back along *Palm Track* to the car park. *McKenzie River Rainforest Walk* (1km, 1 hour, return) is a half-hour drive to the east. It is just off the Princes Highway (A1), 45km to the east of Orbost. The walk starts at the end of the dirt track, 300m from the highway. Parts of this walk, including infrastructure (bridges and boardwalk), were burnt during the bushfires in early 2020.

Fees & Permits
Entry to the park is free.

Facilities
Car park, information signs and picnic tables at Cabbage Tree Creek Flora Reserve. McKenzie River Rainforest Walk has a picnic area, and a large parking area nearby, suitable for all vehicles, on the southern side of the highway, has toilets.

Services Nearby
The towns of Orbost and Cann River have supermarkets, cafes and other services. Marlo, which is smaller, has a variety of accommodation options, fuel and general supplies.

Lake Tyers State Park

Lake Tyers State Park was gazetted in 1984 and officially handed back to the local traditional owners in 2010, and is jointly managed with Parks Victoria. The state park covers 86.93km² from Lake Tyers beach in the south to Mt Nowa Nowa to the north, with parts of the park bordering Lake Tyers itself.

The park only has small patches of warm temperate rainforest, with the Lilly Pilly *Syzygium smithii* and Brush Muttonwood *Myrsine howittiana* providing the canopy, and the Hazel Pomaderris *Pomaderris aspera,* Blanket-leaf *Bedfordia arborescens* and Soft Tree Fern *Dicksonia antarctica* included in the understorey. The Common Milk Vine *Marsdenia rostrata* is a climber that is most visible during flowering.

Nearly 70 birds species have been seen from the Marsdenia walk, including rainforest species such as the Superb Lyrebird, Brown Gerygone, Yellow-tailed Black Cockatoo, Black-faced Monarch, Large-billed Scrubwren, Eastern Whipbird, Rose Robin, Eastern Yellow Robin and Lewin's Honeyeater. The Australian Masked Owl has been recorded in the

John Harris

Marsdenia Rainforest Walk

general vicinity. The Common Wombat and Swamp Wallaby have been recorded in the park.

Other small areas, totalling about 2.4km², of warm temperate rainforest can be found in the adjacent South East Coastal Plain bioregion to the west of Lakes Entrance. These rainforests occur on drainage lines flowing into the Gippsland Lakes, although many of them are on private land or inaccessible by vehicle, so have not been included here.

GPS Coordinates
-37.80638, 148.04527 (Marsdenia Walk)

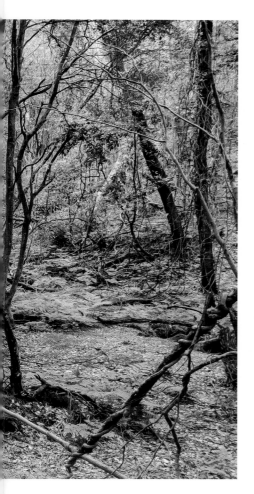

Getting There
Head east out of Lakes Entrance towards Nowa Nowa on the Princes Highway (A1) for 8km, then turn right into Burnt Bridge Road and follow for 1.5km before turning left into Cherry Tree Track. The Marsdenia walk starts about 700m along, on the left.

Tracks & Trails
Marsdenia Rainforest Walk (1.2km, 30 minutes, loop) named after the Common Milk Vine *Marsdenia rostrata*, begins at Cherry Tree Track. The walk begins in eucalypt forest, making its way downslope to a patch of rainforest along a tributary of Stony Creek that runs parallel to the Princes Highway. Along the creek is a relatively open understorey, although vines, ferns and mosses are still present. Once through the rainforest the walk returns to the start through more eucalypt forest. The track is not formed but does have simple bridges and a boardwalk over the wetter areas.

Fees & Permits
Entry to the park is free.

Facilities
Just off the highway, at the start of Burnt Bridge Road, are picnic shelters, tables and information signage about the local area. There are also picnic tables at the end of Cherry Tree Track and Burnt Bridge Track. The end of Cherry Tree Track has basic toilet facilities.

Services Nearby
Lakes Entrance, at the mouth of the Gippsland Lakes, is 10 minutes south of Lake Tyers State Park. It is a large town and fishing port with various accommodation options, cafes, supermarkets, takeaway food, fuel, medical facilities and visitor information centre.

VICTORIA

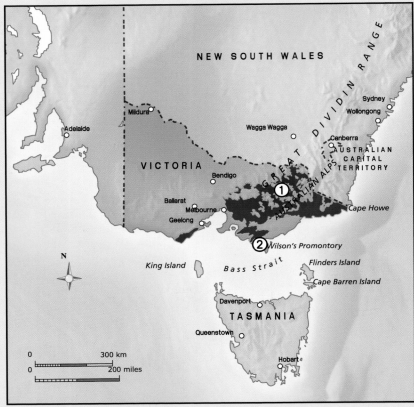

1. South Eastern Highlands 2. Furneaux

State Overview

Victoria is Australia's smallest mainland state, covering an area of 227,444km², although it is the second most populous state after New South Wales. The state contains about 200km² of rainforest (0.55 per cent of Australia's rainforest), comprising both cool temperate and warm temperate rainforests. These rainforests are scattered across four bioregions (Furneaux, South East Coastal Plain, South East Corner and South Eastern Highlands). The most southerly extension of warm temperate rainforest in Australia can be found at Wilsons Promontory, the southernmost part of the Australian mainland.

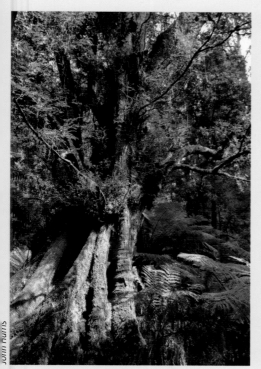

Tarra Valley, Tarra-Bulga National Park

There are 11 IBRA bioregions in the state, with the Murray Darling Depression making up nearly 30 per cent and the Furneaux only about 0.2 per cent. Ecosystems within the bioregions range from alpine to tall forests, grassland, woodland and mallee.

The total protected area of Victoria is quite low, with nearly 17 per cent set aside in national parks and other reserves. The three bioregions featured here rank in the top five for protected areas within the state, with Furneaux having almost 100 per cent due to Wilsons Promontory National Park, while the South East Corner has 27 per cent and South Eastern Highlands 22 per cent.

The South East Coastal Plain bioregion has just over 2.4km^2 of rainforest in many small patches around the very eastern part of the Gippsland Lakes system, but has limited public access.

Victoria, the most southern mainland state, shares a border with New South Wales to the north and South Australia to the west. The entire southern boundary is coastline, with the Bass Strait separating Victoria from Tasmania and the Tasman Sea to the south-east.

The state was initially part of the Colony of New South Wales following European arrival in 1788. The first settlement was established in Port Phillip Bay in 1803. In the 1850s there was a gold rush across many areas of the state that lasted a few decades. Timber logging began around the same time to meet the needs of a growing population, and industry and still occurs today in the bioregions discussed below.

Despite its size, Victoria has a diverse climate, with the highest annual rainfall being more than 1,900mm in the Otway Ranges to under 300mm in the dry inland.

Otway Ranges

225

South Eastern Highlands

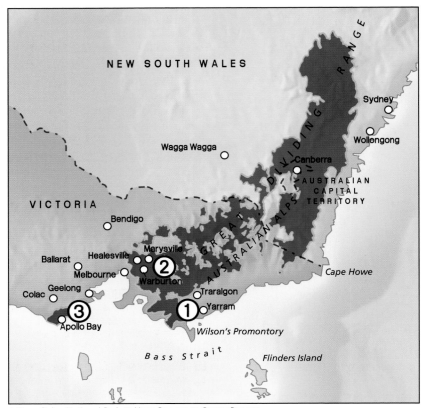

1. Tarra-Bulga National Park 2. Yarra Ranges 3. Otway Ranges

The South Eastern Highlands IBRA bioregion consists of 16 subregions, four of which only occur in Victoria, with the remainder in New South Wales. Victoria's subregions cover 32,492km² of the total area, which equates to a little under 39 per cent of the entire bioregion. The South East Highlands contains 549 protected areas (434 in Victoria and 115 in New South Wales). Rainforest communities are only found in Victoria, with the majority being cool temperate and some small areas warm temperate. Combined, the rainforest makes up <1 per cent of the total area of this bioregion in Victoria. The bioregion as a whole has nearly 350 birds, 110 mammals, 95 reptiles, 38 frogs, more than 4,000 insects, at least 33 freshwater crayfish, 6,300 plus plants and 2,000 plus fungi.

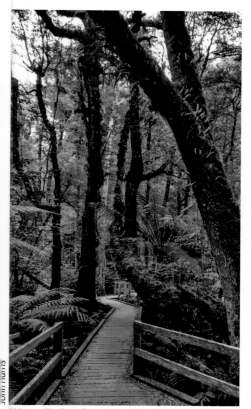

Wirrawilla Rainforest Walk, Toolangi

Key Species

BIRDS

Australian King Parrot, Bassian Thrush, Brown Thornbill, Crescent Honeyeater, Crimson Rosella, Eastern Whipbird, Eastern Yellow Robin, Forest Raven, Gang-gang Cockatoo, Greater Sooty Owl, Grey Fantail, Grey Goshawk, Large-billed Scrubwren, Olive Whistler, Pilotbird, Pied Currawong, Pink Robin, Powerful Owl, Rose Robin, Rufous Fantail, Satin Bowerbird, Silvereye, Superb Lyrebird, White-browed Scrubwren, White-throated Treecreeper, Wonga Pigeon, Yellow-tailed Black Cockatoo.

MAMMALS

Agile Antechinus, Bush Rat, Common Brush-tailed Possum, Common Wombat, Eastern Pygmy-possum, Eastern Ring-tailed Possum, Lesser Long-eared Bat, Leadbeater's Possum, Little Forest Bat, Long-nosed Potoroo, Mainland Dusky Antechinus, Mountain Brush-tailed Possum, Platypus, Southern Greater Glider, Southern Long-nosed Bandicoot, Swamp Antechinus, Swamp Wallaby.

REPTILES

Blotched Blue-tongue, Coventry's Skink, Delicate Skink, Highland Copperhead, Metallic Skink, Southern Water-skink, Spencer's Skink, Weasel Skink, White-lipped Snake.

AMPHIBIANS

Brown Tree Frog, Common Eastern Froglet, Victorian Smooth Froglet, Whistling Tree Frog.

INVERTEBRATES

Central Highlands Spiny Crayfish, Fungus Gnat, Macleay's Swallowtail, Otways Black Snail, Otways Stonefly, South Gippsland Spiny Crayfish, Strzelecki Burrowing Crayfish.

Chimneys made by the Strzelecki Burrowing Crayfish

In Victoria, the South East Highlands bioregion stretches from the New South Wales border to the Yarra Ranges just east of Melbourne, with a disjunct portion in the Otway Ranges, some 140km to the south-west of the Melbourne CBD. Elevations are generally from about 150–200m extending to 900m, above which snow-covered ground is a regular occurrence.

Average temperatures vary across the bioregion, with rainfall averages generally higher than in other parts of Victoria. Weeaproinah in the Otway Ranges has Victoria's highest average yearly rainfall of 1,937mm.

Forestry has significantly influenced the higher elevations of this bioregion over the last 150 years, and continues to do so, although logging is no longer permitted on public land in the Otways.

Crimson Rosella *Platycercus elegans*

Angus McNab

A robust parrot with blue cheeks and a pale bill that contrasts against the crimson head, its underparts are crimson, as are the mantle and back, which has black streaking. The leading edge of the wing and the inner wing are bright blue, while the wing-tips are black. The long tail is dark blue in males and dark blue with a green wash to the central tail feathers in females. The young are predominantly green and have a pale wing-bar in the underwing; they gradually attain the adult plumage over a period of 15 months. The species is commonly associated with the tall eucalypt and wetter forests of southeastern Australia, and its harsh, ringing *cussik-cussik* is a familiar sound in these areas.

Eastern Whipbird *Psophodes olivaceus*

Angus McNab

Adults of this species are olive-green, with a black head and breast, and a broad white patch on the sides of the face. The head bears a crest, the eye is pale and the tail is long. The species is more often heard than seen. Its explosive whipcrack call is one of the most characteristic sounds of the Australian bush. The male gives the long whipcrack, which is usually followed quickly by a sharp *choo-choo* from the female. The bird occupies dense vegetation in wetter habitats, typically near the ground. Although usually secretive, it is also curious and, with patience, an observer can obtain good views.

Forest Raven *Corvus tasmanicus*

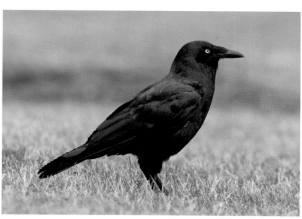

Angus McNab

The Forest Raven is one of three ravens found in Victoria; it can be distinguished from the others by its harsh, low-pitched call. It is a large, thickset black bird with a deep, massive bill and heavily feathered legs, giving it the appearance of wearing trousers, and a relatively short tail. Its throat hackles are short, forming a small 'beard' when expanded during calling. Immature birds lack the pink skin around the face that the other species have. Pairs form breeding territories while non-breeding birds can be found in nomadic flocks of up to 100 birds in winter. While the species is omnivorous, its diet consists mainly of insects, lizards, and small birds and their eggs; it will also eat dead animals, including roadkill.

Gang-gang Cockatoo *Callocephalon fimbriatum*

Angus McNab

This cockatoo is readily identified by its general grey plumage, with adult males having a conspicuous orange-red head, while the female's head is grey. The tail is short and square. The bird only ventures to the ground to drink or pick up fallen food. It is easily overlooked when feeding on the seeds and nuts of trees and shrubs, with only the cracking of seed pods and occasional growls and crackles betraying its presence. In flight, its prolonged creaky screech quickly draws attention. It inhabits wetter forests, woodland, and suburban parks and gardens in southeastern mainland Australia. Some birds have an annual migration, moving to lower altitudes in winter, although individuals can be found at lower altitudes all year round.

Grey Goshawk *Accipiter novaehollandiae*

This sleek goshawk has a black bill, and bright yellow legs, feet and cere. Adults have a deep red eye and young have a greenish-yellow eye. Occurring in two colour morphs, grey-phase individuals have grey upperparts and white underparts mottled with light grey, with a grey tail and grey wings that darken towards the tips. White-phase individuals are completely white. The white phase is dominant in southern Australia and is the only colour morph in Tasmania; it is relatively rare the further north you go in Australia. Grey Goshawks can be found flying among white cockatoos, potentially hiding before launching into a hunt. This species occurs in tall, wet forests and has a diet predominantly consisting of medium-sized mammals and birds, taken from the ground or trees and shrubs.

Pilotbird *Pycnoptilus floccosus*

The Pilotbird is a plump bird with a long, often erect tail. It is found in wet forest and rainforest in southeastern Australia. It is dark rufous-brown, with a buff face, and throat and underparts that are a deep rufous colour, mottled with brown. Some individuals have a white patch in the centre of the belly. The iris is dark red. A territorial species that often gives its loud, ringing and far-reaching call of 3–5 syllables, it moves about the forest floor scratching among the leaf litter for invertebrates. It can often be seen in the company of the Superb Lyrebird (p. 289), catching food that is disturbed by the lyrebird's scratchings. Its common name is an indicator of such associations, but it follows the lyrebird instead of being its 'pilot'.

Powerful Owl *Ninox strenua*

The Powerful Owl, Australia's largest owl species and among the world's largest, is found in tall eucalypt forest and fringes of rainforest in southeastern Australia. It is almost unmistakable with its intense yellow eyes set in a smallish dark facial disc. The facial disc contrasts with a whiter forehead and body, appearing to form a mask. The upperparts are grey-brown with whitish barring; the underparts are white with dark chevrons. The feet are dull yellow. Young birds are predominantly white with a darkish mask, streaking on the underparts and grey barring on the upperparts. The deep, slow *woo-hoo* call usually indicates the presence of this elusive species. Its roost is usually a tree, and individuals can be seen at roosts clutching the leftovers from the previous night's meal. Whitewash on the ground indicates a regular roosting spot. The species feeds on medium-sized arboreal mammals and birds.

Angus McNab

Wonga Pigeon *Leucosarcia melanoleuca*

This is a large, plump bird that feeds on seeds and fruits on the forest floor. It is primarily slatey-grey with a white slash forming a broad 'V' on the breast. The underparts are white with black markings on each feather. Bare skin on the legs and face is pink, especially during the breeding season. This pigeon's distinctive, continuous *whoo* call can be heard throughout the forest, even if the bird is not close by. While birds spend most of their time on the ground in search of food, they will quickly fly to a branch, often in the canopy, if disturbed. They are often flushed from beside walking tracks or roadsides in suitable habitats.

Angus McNab

Agile Antechinus *Antechinus agilis*

Angus McNab

This antechinus is pale brownish-grey above and greyish below, with a pale eye-ring. The snout is pointed and the large, rounded ears are pinkish-grey. The tail is thin and lightly furred, and the same length as the head–body length. Males are larger than females. The species is found in highlands of the southeastern mainland, from southeastern New South Wales to western Victoria, occurring to about 2,000m above sea level. It favours a range of forests, woodland and heathland, where it forages in trees and on the ground, in leaf litter and around fallen logs, for insects and small vertebrates. It shelters communally in tree hollows. Females breed from 11 months of age and mate within a synchronized 2–3 week period each year. Males die shortly after breeding, and some females survive to breed a second year. This antechinus was formally described as a separate species in 1998.

Leadbeater's Possum *Gymnobelideus leadbeateri*

Angus McNab

Leadbeater's Possum is Victoria's only endemic mammal species and is its faunal emblem. It is grey to brownish above, with a black vertebral stripe, and cream-white below. The tail is long and club shaped. It is confined to fragmented areas, mainly above 500m, in the Victoria central highlands, inhabiting tall forests with a dense shrubby understorey, and subalpine woodland, with an isolated population in lowland swamps. It sleeps by day in small groups in tree hollows lined with shredded bark. Emerging at dusk, it feeds arboreally on tree exudates, invertebrates and nectar. Females produce 1–2 young in a litter, normally with two litters in a year. The species is Critically Endangered, threatened by loss of habitat from logging and bushfires, and associated competition for available tree hollows.

Mainland Dusky Antechinus *Antechinus mimetes*

Jono Dashper

This antechinus is predominantly brownish, paler on the belly, with a broad head, pointed snout and tail shorter than the head–body length (generally about 75 per cent). It occupies wetter areas, including rainforests, woodland and alpine heaths, and in New South Wales also coastal sand dunes and swamps, where it feeds on invertebrates. Females have up to 10 teats, with upland populations having more than those in lowland areas, and breeding takes place in May–September. Males die shortly after mating. Two subspecies are found in Australia, *A. m. mimetes* in the eastern Great Dividing Range, southeastern New South Wales and southern Victoria, and *A. m. insulanus* in the Grampians, western Victoria. This species was found to be taxonomically different from the Tasmanian Dusky Antechinus (p. 282) and elevated to species level in 2015.

Southern Greater Glider *Petauroides volans*

Lachlan Hall

This glider has variable colouration above, uniformly white, or grey or black, or a combination of these, and large, furry ears, a short snout and a pale spot behind the ears. The tail is very long and bushy. The gliding membrane extends from the elbows to the ankles. The species is found in eastern Victoria, reaching central Victoria; also New South Wales and southern Queensland. It occurs mainly in eucalypt forests and woodland with abundant large tree hollows for shelter, but also enters rainforests. It feeds at night almost exclusively on young eucalyptus leaves and buds, which are supplemented with flowers. It is arboreal, moving between trees in its small home range by gliding through the canopy. Females produce a single young each year, in March–June. It was recognized as a separate species in 2011, and is listed as Vulnerable under Commonwealth legislation.

233

Swamp Antechinus *Antechinus minimus*

Angus McNab

This antechinus is metallic-greyish on the head and shoulders, becoming more yellowish-brown on the back, sides and thickset rump, and darker brown on the short tail. The underparts are pale brown to yellowish, tinged with grey. *A. m. maritimus* occurs in coastal Victoria and far southeastern South Australia, in rainforests and open habitats, including heathland, tussock grassland, swamps and shrubland, where it shows a preference for wetter areas. It sleeps in a nest beneath dense leaf litter or in a short underground burrow. While this species is partly diurnal, it forages mainly at night in leaf litter on the forest floor for a range of insects. Males die off shortly after breeding, and some females survive to breed a second year. Population sizes appear to increase during wetter periods.

Coventry's Skink *Carinascincus coventryi*

Akash Samuel

This slender skink has slightly keeled scales, well-developed limbs with five digits on the hindlimbs and four on the front limbs, and a movable lower eyelid containing a clear transparent disc. It is uniform dark brown above, occasionally with blackish or paler flecks, with a pale coppery-brown dorsolateral stripe, over a black lateral stripe, from neck to tail. The underparts are creamish with scattered blackish flecks. It is distributed in southeastern Australia, from around Sydney, New South Wales, to central western Victoria, and is normally associated with wet forests, rainforests and woodland, but also occurs in mixed forests and grassland. It is active by day in both shaded and sunny areas, foraging within fallen tree litter for small invertebrates. Females bear up to seven (average three) live young in a litter.

Delicate Skink *Lampropholis delicata*

Angus McNab

This smooth-scaled skink has moderately sized limbs, with five digits and a movable lower eyelid containing a transparent disc. It is greyish-brown to rich coppery-brown above, more copper coloured on the head and nape, with a thin, pale yellowish-brown dorsolateral stripe from neck to tail. The underparts are whitish. It occurs in Tasmania and the eastern and southeastern mainland from eastern Queensland, through eastern New South Wales and southern Victoria, to southern South Australia. It utilizes a variety of habitats, from rainforests, dry and wet forests, and open woodland, to coastal heaths, moist grassland and suburban gardens. It is diurnal, actively foraging on the ground for insects and other small invertebrates, including ants, spiders, flies, moths and worms. It lays about 3–4 eggs in a communal nest with other females; such nests can contain more than 200 eggs.

Southern Water-skink *Eulamprus tympanum*

Angus McNab

A glossy, moderately robust skink with a slightly depressed tail and relatively long rear legs, this species is olive-brown above with numerous black flecks on the head, back and tail-base. The sides, including the tail, are black with scattered olive-brown blotches, becoming more concentrated on the tail and flanks. The limbs are olive-brown with black blotches. The belly and throat are grey, marbled and spotted with black. The species is found in southeastern Australia, from northeastern New South Wales, through central and southern Victoria, to southeastern South Australia and the Fleurieu Peninsula. It occurs in rainforests, open forests, woodland and grassland, and is most commonly encountered in moist habitats along small creeks, basking on rocks and logs and taking refuge in the water when alarmed. It is diurnal, feeding on invertebrates including spiders and snails, tadpoles, small frogs, other lizards and a small amount of plant matter.

235

Spencer's Skink *Pseudemoia spenceri*

Unusual among its genus due to its arboreal habits, this species has been found up to 75m above the ground, on large dead trees. Unlike the rest of the genus *Pseudemoia,* this skink has a broad, flattened head and body with long limbs and toes, making it well suited for life high above the ground. The back, head and tail are dark grey-brown to black, with numerous brown or pale grey flecks. It is distributed throughout the heavily forested areas of eastern Victoria, with scattered occurrences to the west of Melbourne and into similar areas in the Australian Capital Territory and eastern New South Wales. It can live in dense colonies of up to 50 individuals, mostly feeding on flies but also other insects. Females give birth to live young.

Angus McNab

Weasel Skink *Saproscincus mustelinus*

This smooth-scaled, slender skink has long, well-developed limbs with five digits on each one, and a long, slender, tapering tail. It is grey-brown, pale brown or dark coppery-brown above, with or without a variegated pattern of light and dark brown flecks, and with an indistinct pale yellowish-brown to orange-brown dorsolateral stripe. It is paler with darker brown streaks on the flanks, and a short white 'teardrop' behind the eye, edged with blackish-brown above. The underparts are whitish to yellowish with long, dark streaks. The species occurs along the coast and adjacent ranges of southeastern Australia, from northern New South Wales to southern Victoria, inhabiting wetter forests, including rainforest, woodland, heaths and adjacent pastures or gardens, where it shelters under logs or within timber and other vegetation. It feeds on small invertebrates, and lays about 3–4 eggs in a communal nest, with several other females.

Akash Samuel

Victorian Smooth Frog *Geocrinia victoriana*

Angus McNab

This relatively smooth-skinned frog is tan, dark brown or grey above, usually plain with darker flecking. Some individuals have a paler triangle, starting from in front of the eyes to the snout. The underside is bluish-grey with dark speckling and pinkish around the groin; the throat of males is usually yellowish. The species is found across Victoria and into the border region of southern New South Wales, where it lives in a range of habitats, including alpine bogs, rainforest, wet and dry forests, and open shrubland. It is usually found in moist pockets such as drainage lines, and feeds at night on invertebrates. Its call is a series of single *raaak,* followed by a series of rapid *pip pip pip pip* notes. About 120 gelatinous eggs are laid, attached to vegetation in depressions; males are often found with eggs once these are laid.

Whistling Tree Frog *Litoria verreauxii*

Angus McNab

The nominate subspecies *L. v. verreauxii* is light grey to red-brown, with a dark brown to tan stripe that extends from the snout, through the eye and along the flanks. The insides of the hip and groin are light orange and almost always have black markings. The frog is found around slow-moving or still watercourses from Victoria to south-east Queensland, where it feeds on invertebrates. The subspecies *L. v. alpina* from alpine ponds and bogs is mostly green above with two brown dorsal stripes. The male's call, a pulsed *creeee creeee creeee* that is repeated frequently, is made from grass tussocks, low overhanging branches and emergent vegetation. Eggs are laid in small, floating groups, sometimes attached to plant material, with a clutch of about 720 eggs spread over a dozen or more floating groups.

Central Highlands Spiny Crayfish
Euastacus woiwuru

Kate Stevenson

This crayfish is found across a wide area of Victoria to the east of Melbourne, occurring in river systems both north and south of the Great Dividing Range, including the Ovens, Goulburn, Yarra and La Trobe Rivers and their tributaries (150–1,400m above sea level). Its colouration varies between populations, with the dorsal surfaces being brown, greenish or red-brown, to vivid blue or bright red. Most individuals have bright blue highlights on the claws and other parts of the body. The abdominal spines are cream, while the cervical spines can be yellow, orange or cream. The maximum occipital–carapace length size is approximately 75mm. Females carry up to 90 eggs, with breeding commencing in May–June. The species is often found in good numbers in highly modified areas, such as farmland and urbanized land.

Otways Black Snail *Victaphanta compacta*

Akash Samuel

The Endangered Otway Black Snail is the only endemic carnivorous snail of the five snail species located in the Otway Ranges. It is found in patches of cool temperate rainforest and wet forests across the region. The body is grey-blue to black; the spherical shell with four whorls ranges from glossy dark brown to black, with tinges of yellow-brown on the inner whorl. The shell, positioned towards the tail of the body, has a maximum diameter of 28mm. It is thin, lightweight and moderately flexible. The species can be distinguished from other snails in the genus by its range, globulous shell, absence of an orange frill around the foot and lack of orange mucus. It is partially nocturnal, feeding on other snails, slugs, earthworms and soft-bodied insect larvae. Its preferred micro-habitat is at the bases of trees and tree ferns and in deep leaf litter.

South Gippsland Spiny Crayfish
Euastacus neodiversus

This small, spiny crayfish is one of the most colourful Victorian species, found on the southern side of the Strzelecki Ranges in tributaries of rivers, including the Tarra River and Wilsons Promontory waterways. Its body is brown with underlying green colouration that lightens towards the light blue, cream and green ventral surface. The spines on the thorax are dark green, while other spines on the body are blue. The edges of the tail are iridescent blue
with white-tipped spines. The claws are brown and green with blue spines, while the legs are blue. The maximum occipital-carapace length is 45mm. The species is mostly nocturnal, although it can be found walking around in waterways in mid-afternoon. It can survive extended dry periods in its moist burrows. Females carry 30–90 large, crimson-coloured eggs after breeding commences in May–July. This crayfish is currently listed as Endangered in Victoria.

Aaron Jenkin, Aquatica

Strzelecki Burrowing Crayfish
Engaeus rostrogaleatus

This Victorian endemic burrowing crayfish is listed as Endangered and protected under the Flora and Fauna Guarantee Act. Like other *Engaeus* species, it has a restricted distribution (about 600km²), in this case in areas more than 400m above sea level in the eastern Strzelecki Ranges. Its colouration ranges from dark purple with olive tones to bright orange or red, with orange to red legs. The claws may be the same
or of different sizes, with orange to olive and blue colouring and orange tips. The rostrum, the key identification feature, is lumpy, ends bluntly and is downcurved. The adult carapace measures to 30mm and the total length is about 60mm. The species is found on clay and clay-loam soils along creek banks, boggy seepages and other wet areas away from main waterways, in primary habitat (wet forests), including the cool temperate rainforest of Tarra-Bulga National Park. It builds characteristic mud chimneys, to 100mm, above its burrows.

Beverley Van Praagh

239

Tarra-Bulga National Park

This park has many links to the history of South Gippsland. In 1840 Strzelecki, the Polish explorer, and his party, along with indigenous guide Charlie Tarra, explored this area of southern Victoria. Gippsland was named after Strzelecki's friend, New South Wales Governor Gipps. This area of South Gippsland was opened up to farming, especially dairying, in the 1870s. The western areas were prosperous, but in the 1890s, when the eastern areas were opened up, this was not the case, so many cleared areas went to waste. The beginnings of the national park occurred at the turn of the twentieth century, when the local Alberton Council asked the state government to set aside some fern gullies in the Balook area. Twenty hectares were reserved and given the indigenous name 'bulga', meaning mountain. A few years later the council set aside further land and named it Charlie Tarra. The two reserves eventually combined to form Tarra-Bulga National Park, which now covers 15.22km².

Yarram's water supply comes from the rainforest-lined Tarra River. The park's cool temperate rainforest is dominated by the Myrtle Beech, Southern Sassafras, Banyalla and Austral Mulberry, and giant tree ferns, various ground ferns, creepers and more than 200 fungi species.

The fauna is diverse and includes the Crimson Rosella, Eastern Whipbird, Eastern Yellow Robin,

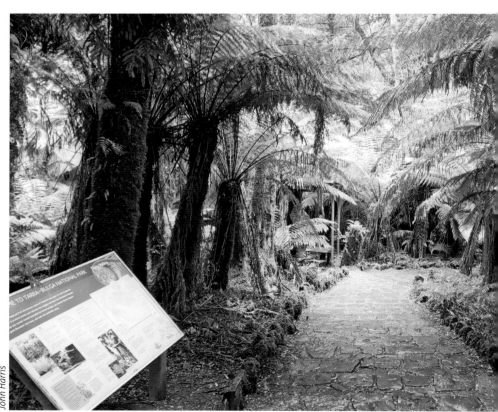

John Harris

Tarra Valley Rainforest Walk

Pilotbird, Pink Robin, Superb Lyrebird and Yellow-tailed Black Cockatoo, with the Common Wombat, Krefft's Glider, Platypus, Southern Long-nosed Bandicoot and several species of microbat also being recorded. Two crustaceans that dwell in the waterways and wet areas of the park are the South Gippsland Spiny Crayfish and the Strzelecki Burrowing Crayfish.

GPS Coordinates

-38.44766, 146.53818 (Tarra Valley Section)
-38.42890, 146.56634 (Balook Section)

Getting There

Tarra-Bulga is about 220km south-east of Melbourne, being accessed by the South Gippsland Highway and Yarram to the Tarra Valley section (27km), or

the Princes Highway to Traralgon, then south to the Balook section (37km).

Tracks & Trails

There are a number of tracks that feature rainforest in this park. *Tarra Valley Rainforest Walk* (1.4km, 45 minutes, loop) begins at the Tarra Valley picnic area. The track follows the Tarra River for a short distance before splitting into the West and East Tracks. The *East Track* is the most direct way to Cyathea Falls, named after the local tree fern. On your way back along *West Track,* look for the chimney entrances to Strzelecki Burrowing Crayfish holes. If it has recently rained you may even spot a crayfish among the leaf litter. *Corrigans Suspension Bridge Walk* (2.5km,1 hour, return) is located in the Balook section of the park. It starts at the visitor centre car park via parts of *Lyrebird, Ash* and *Wills Tracks. Fern Gully Nature Walk* (500m, 30 minutes, loop) starts at the Bulga Picnic Area and also takes in Corrigans Suspension Bridge. This self-guided walk has brochures available at the start. The bridge gives you the opportunity to be in the canopy with some of the rainforest trees, Myrtle Beech and Southern Sassafras.

Fees & Permits

There are no fees payable.

Facilities

In both sections of the park there are toilets, shelters and picnic facilities.

Services Nearby

Yarram, the largest town in South Gippsland, offers a wide range of services, while Traralgon, the largest city in Gippsland, offers all services you would expect from a large regional city. Pet-friendly accommodation is available on the Tarra Valley Road between Yarram and the park.

Yarra Ranges

The Yarra Ranges are about an hour east of Melbourne and are sometimes referred to as the Central Highlands. The ranges are important to the well-being of Melbourne, Australia's second largest city, as the headwaters of the Yarra River are protected catchments providing most of Melbourne's water supply. On the way to the Yarra Ranges from Melbourne, you pass through the Yarra Valley, famous for its wines. A significant part of the Yarra Ranges was badly burnt in the 'Black Saturday Fires' of February 2009, with the town of Marysville being almost wiped out in one day. Fortunately, Marysville has been rebuilt. The Yarra Ranges National Park was established in 1995, consisting of 760km² of primarily forested mountainous areas. It is positioned between Melbourne and the Victorian Alps, and is a major tourist destination. The Yarra Ranges is the traditional country of the Wurundjeri People

The flora of this area is diverse, from the Mountain Ash *Eucalyptus regnans,* the world's tallest flowering plant with some trees growing to at least 100m, to the tallest free-standing moss, *Dawsonia superba,* which can grow to 600mm, looking like a miniature pine tree. The Myrtle Beech *Nothofagus cunninghamii,* Southern Sassafras *Atherosperma moschatum* and Australian Blackwood *Acacia melanoxylon* are the dominant cool temperate rainforest trees, with a range of smaller shrubs, tree ferns, epiphytes, ground ferns and mosses living below.

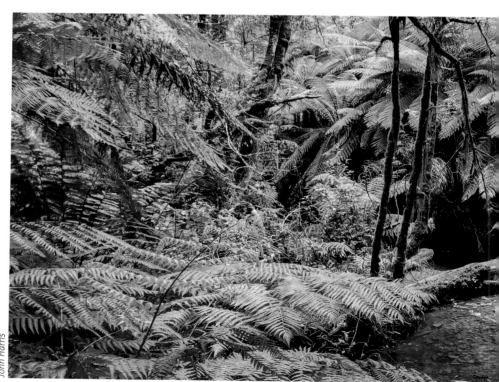

John Harris

Wirrawilla Rainforest Walk

Iconic fauna like the Australian King Parrot, Central Highlands Spiny Crayfish, Common Wombat, Powerful Owl, Southern Greater Glider, Superb Lyrebird and Swamp Wallaby live in this area. It forms part of the limited habitat for Victoria's faunal emblem, Leadbeater's Possum, a nationally Critically Endangered species.

GPS Coordinates
-37.71047, 145.70940 (Mt Donna Buang Rainforest Gallery)
-37.56320, 145.87699 (Cora Lynn Falls)
-37.52757, 145.52183 (Wirrawilla Rainforest Walk).

Getting There
From the Melbourne CBD, take the Eastern Freeway and Maroondah Highway to Lilydale, then the Warburton Highway to Warburton, about 80km.

Tracks & Trails
Mt Donna Buang Rainforest Gallery (350m, 45 minutes, loop) has two parts, a 40m 'skywalk' that is accessible to all, and a 350m loop that takes you to the rainforest floor. The 'skywalk' is a flat, aerial walkway taking you into the canopy of Mountain Ash and Myrtle Beech, with some trees more than 400 years old. The loop walk has you descending from road level to a boardwalk that then loops around Cement Creek before ascending again back to the start. This walk is 10 minutes north of Warburton. *Cora Lynn Falls Walk* (1.1km, 30 minutes, return) begins in the Cumberland Falls car park about 17km from Marysville on the Woods Point Road. Cross the road and follow the *Cumberland Walk* to an intersection, then turn right to the falls, an additional 100m. This area was burnt during the 'Black Saturday Fires' (p. 367), so this rainforest patch is still recovering. There is more mature rainforest nearer the falls. *Wirrawilla Rainforest Walk* (1.15km, 45 minutes, loop) is near Toolangi. This walk starts in an old quarry off Sylvia Creek Road. The loop is a boardwalk, protecting the fragile soils and leaf litter of the rainforest floor. Keep your eyes open for the *Dawsonia superba* moss and the aptly named Beech Orange *Cyttaria gunnii* fungus, found growing only on Myrtle Beech.

Fees & Permits
No fees are payable.

Facilities
All three walks have car parks, while the rainforest gallery and Wirrawilla have toilets. Wirrawilla also has picnic tables.

Services Nearby
Warburton, Healesville and Marysville all have accommodation, supermarkets, meals, fuel and medical services.

Otway Ranges

The Otways were opened up to settlement from the 1870s. With the abundance of towering Mountain Ash *Eucalyptus regnans*, logging and milling grew rapidly. Many relics of this time, such as boilers and tramways, can be found in the area. Logging ceased on public land in 2008 but there are still numerous private plantations throughout. Great Otway National Park was declared in 2005, incorporating a number of former reserves, including Otway National Park, several state parks and state forest, with 2010 being the last gazetted update. The park covers an area of 1,032km², located alongside the world-famous Great Ocean Road. Cool temperate rainforest makes up about 64km² of the park, the adjacent Otway Forest Park another 6.24km². The Otway Ranges are part of the traditional lands of the Gadubanud people.

The Otways are the most westerly distribution of cool temperate rainforest in Australia. This is dominated by the Myrtle Beech *Nothofagus cunninghamii* and Australian Blackwood *Acacia melanoxylon*, with emergent Mountain Ash in some parts. Fallen orange beech leaves along the tracks look like rainforest confetti.

The region supports a huge diversity of native fauna and flora, including a number of threatened species such as the Powerful Owl, Long-nosed Potoroo, Southern Brown Bandicoot, Swamp Antechinus and endemic Otways Black Snail.

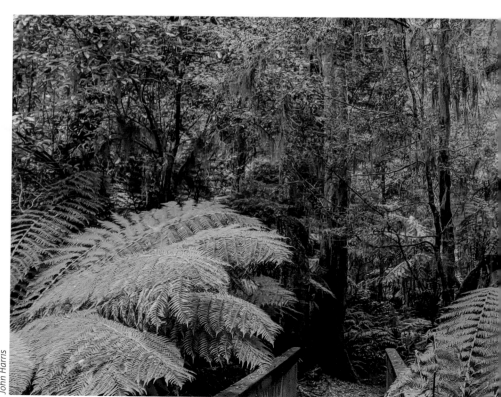

Melba Gully along Madsen's Track Nature Trail

John Harris

The Otways contain an extensive network of walking tracks, from the spectacular short rainforest walks at Maits Rest and Melba Gully, to the multi-day 100km Great Ocean Walk along the region's scenic coastline. A stroll along the Madsen's and Maits Rest walks after dark is a delight on any visit to the Otways due to the 'magic' of glow worms, the larvae of fungus gnats *Arachnocampa* spp.

GPS Coordinates

-38.75581, 143.55458 (Maits Rest)
-38.69759, 145.36973 (Melba Gully)

Getting There

The park is about 210km south-west from Melbourne's CBD. There are numerous access points, most of which are via the Great Ocean Road, between Torquay and Princetown. Colac is to the north on the Princes Highway (A1).

Tracks & Trails

Maits Rest Rainforest Walk (800m, 30 minutes, loop) combines timber boardwalks and gravel paths, starting at the Maits Rest car park. You walk through lush cool temperate rainforest with tree ferns, mosses and majestic beeches, some more than 300 years old. There are many spectacular waterfalls in the Otways, including Triplet and Beauchamp Falls. Each is surrounded by rainforest dominated by Myrtle Beeches and Australian Blackwoods. The *Triplet Falls Rainforest Walk* (2km, 1 hour, loop) and *Beauchamp Falls Walk* 2.5km, 1.5 hours, return) have steep sections culminating in viewing platforms near the falls. *Madsen's Track Nature Trail* (1.2km, 1 hour, loop) in the stunning Melba Gully, passes through tall wet forest and lush rainforest, dominated by beech and Australian Blackwoods.

Fees & Permits

Camping fees apply at some sites. Entry fees are payable for the Otway Fly Treetop Walk, a private tourist attraction.

Facilities

Detailed information is available at www.visitotways.com. Barbecue and picnic areas are located throughout the park, with most sites having toilets. Camping sites are spread throughout the park. Some, like Dando's, Beauchamp and Stevenson Falls, are free. Paid sites like Aire River (east and west) and Blanket Bay need to be booked in advance. Visitors with mobility difficulties can book all-terrain wheelchairs through the Colac Otway and Surf Coast Shires.

Services Nearby

The larger towns in the region are Apollo Bay, Colac and Lorne. All have most services, including restaurants, cafes, shops, accommodation, fuel and hospitals.

Furneaux

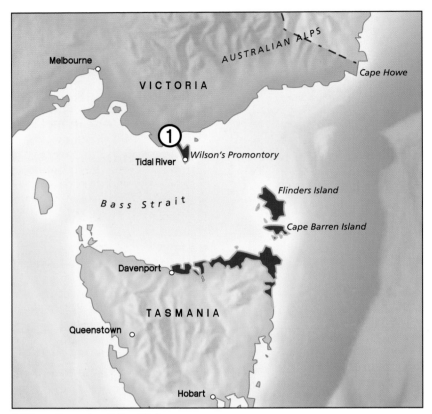

1. Wilsons Promontory National Park

The Furneaux bioregion is the smallest IBRA bioregion in Victoria, covering only 410km². All of it is found on Wilsons Promontory, with the majority of the bioregion occurring in the Furneaux Island group and coastal north-east Tasmania. These two subregions of the Furneaux bioregion were joined before the last ice age, but as sea levels rose they became separated. Within Victoria, this bioregion is almost entirely protected (99.5 per cent) as it occurs within the Wilsons Promontory National Park. Both warm temperate rainforest and cool temperate rainforest combined make up only 3 per cent of the bioregion in Victoria. The Furneaux bioregion as a whole has over 220 birds, 58 mammals, 24 reptiles, 11 frogs, 27 butterflies, 19 terrestrial crayfish, 1,900 plus plants and 600 plus fungi.

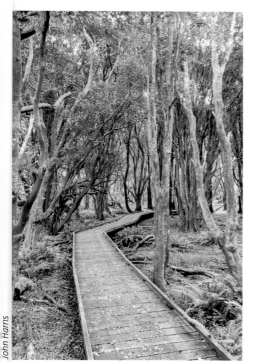

Lilly Pilly Gully Nature Walk

Key Species

BIRDS

Australian King Parrot, Bassian Thrush, Beautiful Firetail, Brown Gerygone, Brown Thornbill, Crescent Honeyeater, Crimson Rosella, Eastern Spinebill, Eastern Whipbird, Eastern Yellow Robin, Forest Raven, Gang-gang Cockatoo, Grey Fantail, Grey Goshawk, Grey Shrikethrush, Olive Whistler, Pink Robin, Powerful Owl, Red Wattlebird, Rose Robin, Rufous Fantail, Satin Flycatcher, Silvereye, Southern Boobook, White-browed Scrubwren, White-throated Treecreeper, Yellow-tailed Black Cockatoo.

MAMMALS

Agile Antechinus, Bush Rat, Common Wombat, Eastern Pygmy-possum, Eastern Ring-tailed Possum, Grey-headed Flying-fox, Koala, Krefft's Glider, Little Pygmy-possum, Mainland Dusky Antechinus, Mountain Brush-tailed Possum, Southern Long-nosed Bandicoot, Swamp Antechinus, Swamp Wallaby.

REPTILES

Blotched Blue-tongue, Lace Monitor, Metallic Skink, Southern Water-skink, Spencer's Skink, Tiger Snake, Weasel Skink, White-lipped Snake.

AMPHIBIANS

Brown Tree Frog, Common Eastern Froglet, Victorian Smooth Froglet.

INVERTEBRATES

Bogong Moth, Forest Brown, Lilly Pilly Burrowing Crayfish, Macleay's Swallowtail, Narracan Burrowing Crayfish, South Gippsland Spiny Crayfish, Splendid Ochre, Varied Swordgrass Brown.

The Wilsons Promontory National Park was proposed in 1898, but gazetted in 1905 and has since had additional areas added to it. The promontory and surrounding islands are granitic bedrock with some localized areas of sedimentary rock. The geology of the promontory makes for spectacular landscapes compared to the alluvial plains to the north, which are linked by the Yanakie Isthmus formed from sand. Mt Latrobe at 754m is the highest point on the promontory.

Wilsons Promontory has a mild climate with moderate temperatures characteristic of a coastal environment. February is the warmest month, with an average temperature of 24 °C, dropping to 13 °C in July. Average rainfall, recorded at Tidal River, is 1,014mm per year, with more than 40 per cent falling in May–August. As an exposed coastal area, strong fluctuating westerly winds (north-west to south-west) are a regular feature.

Gang-gang Cockatoo (female)

247

Australian King Parrot *Alisterus scapularis*

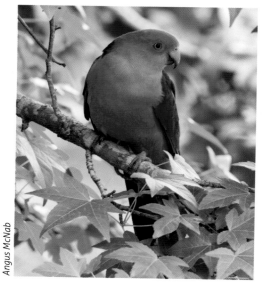

Angus McNab

Found in rainforest and wet eucalypt forest along the east coast and ranges of Australia, the Australian King Parrot is a striking bird. Adult males have an entirely red head, orange bill and pale green shoulder-stripe. The female (p. 187) has a dark grey bill and green head. The species feeds on seeds, nectar, fruits and some insects, usually high in the canopy of the forest, but will enter suburban parks and gardens to feed, often becoming quite tame. Its most common call is a shrill *crassak-crassak*. It occurs in a coastal and subcoastal belt throughout eastern Australia, from the Atherton Tableland, Queensland, to southern Victoria.

Brown Gerygone *Gerygone mouki*

Angus McNab

This is the smallest (~10cm) of the Australian gerygones. Like other gerygones, it lacks the coloured rump and marked forehead or breast of the thornbills, but differs from other gerygones in its range by its grey-brown upperparts, white eyebrow, grey face, buff flanks and black subterminal tail-band. It is an active species that forages for insects by gleaning or hovering among the foliage of trees and shrubs in the rainforests and wet eucalypt woodland of eastern Australia. As it moves through the foliage it repeatedly gives a *which is it, which is it* call. Although often seen alone, it will join mixed feeding parties of small birds.

Grey Shrikethrush *Colluricincla harmonica*

Peter Rowland

The Grey Shrikethrush is a common and familiar bird. Its alternate names of Harmonious Shrikethrush and Whistling Shrikethrush stemmed from its beautiful whistling song, which typically includes phrases such as *pip-pip-pip—pip-hoee* and a sharp *yorrick*, but also includes some that are often unique to individual birds. The song makes up for the rather drab plumage, which varies throughout its extensive range. Birds are mostly grey in the east, with an olive-grey back and pale grey-white cheeks and underparts. In the north, the plumage is mainly brown. Western birds are grey with buff underparts. This species ranges throughout Australia, and can be found in a variety of wooded habitats.

White-browed Scrubwren *Sericornis frontalis*

Angus McNab

The white eyebrow distinguishes this mostly fuscous-brown bird from other scrubwrens and similarly sized small brown birds. The underparts are slightly paler than the upperparts. Subtropical and tropical populations are more yellow underneath, and males have an almost black facial mask. Other populations along the southern coastline have dark streaking on the throat. Females have duller and less well-defined facial markings of the male. The call is an almost persistent chattering of notes uttered as if being disturbed, but the bird is also an accomplished mimic. This insectivorous species usually occurs in pairs low down in thick vegetation. It is common and widespread, inhabiting rainforest, open forest, woodland and littoral scrub in eastern, southern and southwestern Australia.

White-throated Treecreeper *Cormobates leucophaea*

Angus McNab

Treecreepers, like sittellas, forage on trees for insects and other invertebrates, prying under loose bark or within crevices. Sittellas can walk along the undersides of tree branches but treecreepers cannot, instead sticking primarily to the trunks of the trees, foraging in an upwards direction. This species has dark brown upperparts, a white throat and upper breast, and flanks with white streaks edged with black. In flight, a buff wing-bar is visible. The bird is common in rainforests, eucalypt forests and woodland of eastern and southeastern Australia. The call, a repeated, high-pitched piping, betrays its presence, often before it is seen.

Common Wombat *Vombatus ursinus*

Peter Rowland

This stocky wombat has a large, flattened head, short limbs and powerful claws for digging. It is greyish-brown to blackish above and paler below, and has a bare nose and short, slightly rounded ears. The female has a rear-facing pouch. The species is found from southeastern Queensland, through ranges of eastern New South Wales, to central Victoria. It also occurs in Tasmania and far southeastern South Australia. It inhabits rainforests, forests, woodland and grassland, where it sleeps by day in often extensive underground burrows. It feeds on the ground, mostly at night, on native grasses, sedges and roots of shrubs. The female has two teats, but usually gives birth to a single young, which may be born at any time of the year.

Grey-headed Flying-fox *Pteropus poliocephalus*

This large flying-fox has greyish-black fur on the back, paler grey fur on the head and belly, generally heavily flecked or dusted with silvery-grey and with some reddish-brown on belly. It has a full collar of reddish-brown fur. It occurs on the coast, ranges and slopes of southern and eastern Australia, from around Mackay Queensland, through New South Wales and Victoria, to south-eastern South Australia. It roosts in trees in large colonies of up to tens of thousands of individuals, favouring wetter areas and gullies. Nocturnal, it forages over a wide area of native forests, gardens and orchards, for fruits, nectar, pollen and occasionally leaves. Some roost sites have been used for over 100 years. It is one of the largest bat species in the world and Australia's only extant endemic flying-fox. It is an important pollinator of native forest species.

John Harris

Koala *Phascolarctos cinereus*

The Koala is a tree-dwelling arboreal marsupial with thick greyish fur (shorter and paler in north Australia, and longer and more grey-brownish in the south). The ears are round and woolly, and the prominent nose is smooth, black and vertically oval. The Koala has long, sharp claws adapted to climbing trees and has no tail. It is found in eastern Australia, from south of Cape York Peninsula, Queensland, through central and eastern New South Wales and Victoria (and along the Murray River), to far southeastern South Australia, and has been introduced to Phillip Island, Victoria, and Kangaroo Island, South Australia. It inhabits eucalypt forests and woodland in lowland areas and along river systems, and can be seen along rainforest fringes. It is arboreal, feeding exclusively on eucalypt

Angus McNab

leaves and occasionally non-eucalypt leaves. A young Koala is not born with the gut bacteria needed to digest eucalypt leaves, and obtains them by eating its mother's pap (faeces).

Lace Monitor *Varanus varius*

Angus McNab

A robust goanna with a long, laterally compressed tail that extends to a thin, 'whip-like' end, this species is generally bluish-black above with numerous variably sized, creamish-yellow spots, arranged in transverse bands, becoming less intense with age and almost absent in older adults. The snout and chin have yellow and black barring. In parts of its range, some individuals have a pattern of wide yellow and black bands, known as Bell's phase. It is wide ranging in eastern Australia from southern Cape York Peninsula and eastern Queensland, through central and southeastern New South Wales and eastern and northern Victoria, to southeastern South Australia. Found in rainforests, forests, woodland and inland ranges, it is largely arboreal, but often forages on the ground for food, which includes carrion, mammals, birds and their eggs, reptiles, invertebrates and frogs. It lays up to 19 parchment-shelled eggs in termite nests.

Common Eastern Froglet *Crinia signifera*

Angus McNab

This species is one of the most commonly encountered frogs throughout its range, from southeastern Queensland through to South Australia and Tasmania. It inhabits almost every habitat within this range, from rainforest creeks to beach dune soaks, dams and much drier areas. It is very variable in colouration and pattern, even within a single waterbody. The back can range from light grey, fawn or brown to dark grey-brown, while the skin can be warty or smooth. Patterning can be uniform grey or brown with irregular blotches, to heavily striped. Common features are dark, triangular markings on the upper lips and darker bands on the back legs. The belly ranges from 'salt and pepper' to broad black and white marbling. Males have dark throats. Some liken the call to the sound of a Geiger counter. The frogs breed all year following rains.

Lilly Pilly Burrowing Crayfish *Engaeus australis*

This crayfish is endemic to this bioregion, only being found in the Wilsons Promontory National Park. The type specimen was from a patch of warm temperate rainforest in Lilly Pilly Gully. The species is listed as Vulnerable in Victoria. Its colouration ranges from orange to red, fading to white on the underside. An adult carapace can be to 26mm in length. The claws appear large  in comparison to the rest of the body. The rostrum is short with a swollen area at the tip that is surrounded by a tuft of long setae. The antennae do not extend past the back of the carapace. The eyes are relatively large, protruding forwards to about two-thirds the length of the rostrum. Burrows can be about 100–750mm deep, depending on soil type, and some have rim-shaped chimneys.

Alan Henderson

Macleay's Swallowtail *Graphium macleayanum*

The uppersides of this butterfly's wings are white with a black margin with matt green subapical spots; the anterior edge of the forewings is also matt green. Both the fore- and hindwings have a row of submarginal white spots that vary from large in alpine populations to smaller or almost totally obscured in lower altitude populations. The underside of the wings is green with a silvery-brown margin. The species occurs along the peaks of the Great Dividing Range from southern Queensland south through  New South Wales and the Australian Capital Territory to Victoria and Tasmania; an isolated population occurs on the Atherton Tablelands near Cairns. It is associated with upland tropical and subtropical rainforests, as well as subalpine forests in the south of its range. Males defend territories around hilltops, while females are usually seen feeding or searching for the host plants, which include Sassafrass (Atherospermataceae), Laurels (Lauraceae) and Mountain Pepper (Winteraceae).

Angus McNab

Wilsons Promontory National Park

The promontory is the southernmost part of the Australian mainland. The first Europeans to sight it were the explorers Bass and Flinders in 1798. Only a small percentage of the total park area of 490km² is rainforest. Warm temperate rainforest covers just over 11km² and cool temperate rainforest only 1.42km². The warm temperate rainforest is the most southerly distribution of this rainforest type in Australia. The largest patches are tucked in behind 5 Mile Beach (4.45km²) and near Sealer's Cove (2.08km²). About 500,000 visitors each year make the drive to 'The Prom' (Wilson's Promontory National Park). The area is spiritually significant to the local indigenous people, with shell middens dating back thousands of years located behind many beaches.

During the Second World War, Wilsons Promontory was used by Australian and New Zealand commandos as a training ground for guerrilla warfare.

The dominant warm temperate rainforest trees are the Lilly Pilly *Syzygium smithii* and Australian Blackwood *Acacia melanoxylon*, which grow to upwards of 25m. Other plants include the Blanket-leaf *Bedfordia arborescens*, Musky Daisy-bush *Olearia argophylla*, White Elderberry *Sambucus gaudichaudiana* and a variety of ferns including tree ferns, Fishbone Water Fern *Blechnum nudum* and Weeping Spleenwort *Asplenium flaccidum*.

Approximately 300 animal species have been recorded in the park, including roughly 220 birds, 40 mammals, 17 reptiles, 11 amphibians

John Harris

Sealers Cove

and four freshwater crayfish. Fauna that is likely to be found in the rainforest includes the Bassian Thrush, Brown Gerygone, Brown Thornbill, Crescent Honeyeater, Crimson Rosella, Eastern Whipbird, Eastern Yellow Robin, Grey Fantail, Olive Whistler, White-browed Scrubwren, Yellow-tailed Black Cockatoo, Agile Antechinus, Common Wombat, Victorian Smooth Froglet and the endemic Lilly Pilly Burrowing Crayfish.

GPS Coordinates
-38.85805, 146.24873

Getting There
Tidal River is 230km from Melbourne. Follow the Monash Freeway (M1) to join the South Gippsland Highway (M420) to Meeniyan. Take the Meeniyan-Promontory Road (C444) to the Wilsons Promontory entrance. Tidal River is 30 minutes' drive from the entrance. Drive carefully and look out for wildlife, especially between dusk and dawn.

Tracks & Trails
Lilly Pilly Gully Nature Walk (5.2km, 2 hours, loop) starts on the Wilsons Promontory Road, about 2km before Tidal River. You walk through heathland before finding yourself among tall eucalypts. A boardwalk loop takes you through the shady rainforest, dominated by the Lilly Pilly, where you can admire lush ferns and a trickling creek, and take in the natural beauty. It is perfect for families and people with limited mobility. *Sealer's Cove Walking Track* (20km, return) starts at the Telegraph Saddle Car Park, 3.3km from Tidal River, along the Mt Oberon Car Park Road. This track meanders through a variety of vegetation communities along the way. As you near the cove, you pass through about 2km of warm temperate rainforest in the Sealers Swamp area, with its abundance of Australian Blackwoods and Lilly Pilly, ferns and mosses.

Fees & Permits
Camping fees apply.

Facilities
Numerous picnic grounds, showers, toilets and campsites are located in the park. Tidal River also has other accommodation options for those not camping. Bookings are essential for December–January, long weekends and Easter; at other times it is a first-come basis. A range of mobility equipment is for hire in the park. The Tidal River General Store offers a cafe and range of grocery items and ice, some camping equipment and gas refills.

Services Nearby
The nearest fuel is at Yanakie (37km) or Fish Creek and Foster.

TASMANIA

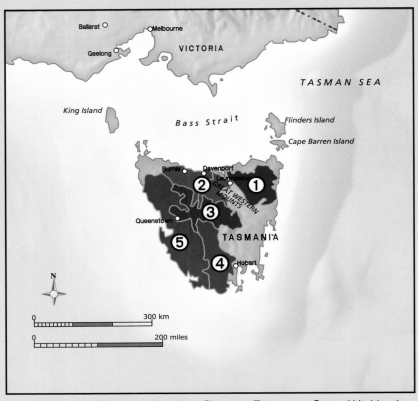

1. Ben Lomond 2. Tasmanian Northern Slopes 3. Tasmanian Central Highlands
4. Tasmanian Southern Ranges 5. Tasmanian West

State Overview

The southernmost Australian state, Tasmania is an island separated from the mainland by Bass Strait. Including King and Flinders Islands, as well as more than 200 other small islands, Tasmania is Australia's smallest state (68,401km²). Although not commonly associated with rainforest, due to the latitude and cooler climate, Tasmania has the highest ratio of rainforest to any other forest type of any state, with 20 per cent of native forest being rainforest (7,000km²). The dominant forest type here is eucalypt forest (76 per cent) but there is a diversity of other habitat types throughout the state, such as buttongrass plains, alpine herbfields, rocky beaches, coastal scrub, wetlands and beautiful underwater environments.

John Lynch Creek, Tarkine

Although a small land mass compared with mainland Australia, proportional to any other state a considerable amount of the state is protected, with 50 per cent being within reserves (34,000km²). The Tasmanian Parks and Wildlife Service manages 823 reserves (about 29,000km²), which cover more than 42 per cent of Tasmania. With a small population of just over 515,000 humans, it is easy to get away from the cities, towns and people to explore the wilderness areas, which are never far away.

Hobart is Australia's second driest capital city (after Adelaide), despite areas on the west coast of the state receiving an annual rainfall of 2,800mm. With nothing but ocean for thousands of kilometres to the west, oceanic storms and heavy rains blown in from the Indian and Southern Oceans drop large amounts of rain along the mountainous west coast, before it reaches Hobart.

Subsequently, almost all of Tasmania's rainforest occurs on the west coast. This area, with its giant trees, ancient ferns, mosses and endemic species, and in many cases threatened rainforest, is considered of such significance that the Tasmanian Wilderness World Heritage Area was added to the UNESCO World Heritage List. The Tasmanian Wilderness World Heritage Area covers 15,800km², or almost 20 per cent of Tasmania through the Tasmanian southern ranges, Tasmanian west and Tasmanian central highlands bioregions. Some of the remaining six bioregions contain rainforest, particularly in the north-west.

Cephissus Creek, Pine Valley

Ben Lomond

1. Blue Tier Forest Reserve

Situated in the north-east corner of the state, the Ben Lomond bioregion is landlocked and does not quite reach the coast due to the Furneaux bioregion covering the northern and eastern coastlines. It is a small bioregion, encompassing an area of 6,570km², of which 68 per cent is native vegetation. Many habitat types are present, including heaths, dry sclerophyll forest, wet sclerophyll forest, rainforest and alpine habitats on the mountain tops. A large amount of the bioregion and east coast of Tasmania is agricultural land – being relatively flat, open and notably drier than the west coast, the area was quickly modified for human cultivation. A cooler region, temperatures vary from about -2 °C to 23 °C, and up to 1,500mm of rain falls annually.

Helen Robertson

Tree fern

Key Species

BIRDS
Crescent Honeyeater, Eastern Spinebill, Fan-tailed Cuckoo, Forest Raven, Green Rosella, Grey Goshawk, Morepork, Pink Robin, Shining Bronze-cuckoo, Tasmanian Scrubwren, Tasmanian Thornbill, Yellow-tailed Black Cockatoo.

MAMMALS
Chocolate Wattled Bat, Gould's Wattled Bat, Krefft's Glider, Rufous-bellied Pademelon, Southern Forest Bat, Swamp Rat, Tasmanian Devil, Tasmanian Long-eared Bat.

REPTILES
Metallic Skink, Ocellated Skink, Tasmanian Tree Skink.

AMPHIBIANS
Brown Tree Frog, Common Eastern Froglet, Tasmanian Froglet.

INVERTEBRATES
Australian Wood Cockroach, Common Albatross, Delicate Xenica, Giant Velvet Worm, Green Mantid, Macleay's Swallowtail, Simson's Stag Beetle.

A large number of forest reserves and some national parks occur throughout the area, but rainforest does not occur in many of them. Rainforest is largely restricted due to the overall dryness of east Tasmania and is often associated with rivers, creeks and gullies, which are full of large ferns and mosses.

The rainforest in the bioregion is dominated by the Myrtle Beech *Nothofagus cunninghamii* with components of the Southern Sassafras *Atherosperma moschatum,* Australian Blackwood *Acacia melanoxylon,* Celery-top Pine *Phyllocladus aspleniifolius,* Dwarf Leatherwood *Eucryphia milliganii,* King Billy Pine *Athrotaxis selaginoides,* Tasmanian Leatherwood *Eucryphia lucida* and Woolly Tea Tree *Leptospermum lanigerum,* depending on the location.

Ben Lomond is easily accessible from the small, historic town of Derby, and there are a number of scenic drives, walks and mountain-bike tracks throughout the local rainforest.

Peter Rowland

Yellow-tailed Black Cockatoo

Crescent Honeyeater *Phylidonyris pyrrhopterus*

Angus McNab

Males of this loud, sexually dimorphic honeyeater have dark grey-black upperparts and a white breast with a thick black crescent down either side. Females have the same pattern, but are light grey-brown rather than grey-black. Both sexes have yellow patches in the wings, bright red eyes surrounded by a dark mask and a streaked throat. An altitudinal migrant, the Crescent Honeyeater spends the cooler months at lower elevations and the warmer months at higher elevations, utilizing varying habitats on the way. Regularly seen alone or in pairs, these birds form loose flocks and can be very loud and raucous when competing for flowering resources.

Tasmanian Scrubwren *Sericornis humilis*

Angus McNab

This is a small, stocky brown bird with a dark grey head, thin, pale stripe above the yellow eye and thicker pale stripe below the eye. Its upperparts are brown, with a small white mark on the shoulder. The throat is off white streaked with grey, and the breast is pale yellow with faint mottling. The flanks, vent and short tail are rufous-brown, with dark tips to the tail feathers. The species is usually heard before being seen – pairs and small groups of scrubwrens are quick to give 'angry-sounding' defensive calls from the undergrowth. Although capable of flying, individuals tend to bound across the ground in search of food, rarely moving very high into the trees.

Swamp Rat *Rattus lutreolus*

Angus McNab

Although beautifully soft and referred to as the velvet-furred rat, for all intents and purposes this still looks like a typical rat. It is quite chubby, particularly on the face, with brown fur, sometimes with a reddish wash, and pale white on the belly. Although difficult to see, it is often one of the most abundant small mammals within its range. Like most rodents, it is nocturnal and rarely spend time in the open, preferring shelter in the undergrowth. Individuals can be very active at night, and by repeated use of an area create small tunnels through the vegetation that aid with moving in the landscape. The diet consists of seeds and vegetation.

Tasmanian Froglet *Crinia tasmaniensis*

Angus McNab

You could understandably be confused in thinking that you can hear the bleating of a lamb coming from a rainforest pond or roadside ditch, but you are actually hearing the call of the Tasmanian Froglet, a very small froglet that is highly variable in colour and pattern. The ventral surfaces are speckled black and white, becoming more heavily mottled on the hindlimbs, but this colouration is highly variable. A reddish wash covers the ventral surfaces of the lower abdomen and the hindlimbs, which separates this species from the Common Eastern Froglet (p. 253). The upper surfaces are as varied as the underparts, but often have two broad, reddish-orange-brown stripes running down the back. A poor climber, the Tasmanian Froglet spends its days hiding under debris or vegetation. When conditions are suitable, it will call throughout the day.

Blue Tier Forest Reserve

The region is well known for its world-famous mountain-bike trails and the 'Derby River Derby', and this reserve contains some amazing rainforest valleys that are filled with the sound of birds.

North-east Tasmania was made famous with the discovery of tin and subsequent mining boom, which saw people flock to the area. This was not the only threat to the area as clear fell logging was started in the region. However, in 1958 the Blue Tier was designated as a forest reserve protecting the tree-fern filled cool temperate rainforest and wet myrtle forest. It provides an area for everyone to enjoy the scenic views from the top of the Blue Tier plateau, which is 600m above sea level. Throughout the reserve there are views of the river and numerous waterfalls can be visited.

Along the Ringarooma River the mountainsides are densely covered in the Myrtle Beech *Nothofagus cunninghamii*, Woolly Tea Tree *Leptospermum lanigerum*, and the wet forests with the Mountain Ash *Eucalyptus regnans* and a diversity of other temperate rainforest species.

The reserve is home to the state's three large native predators, the Eastern Quoll, Spotted-tailed Quoll and Tasmanian Devil, as well as

Ryan Francis

Blue Tier Forest Reserve protects tree-fern filled cool temperate rainforest

Tasmania's least-seen nocturnal bird, the predatory Australian Masked Owl. More specific to the region are Simson's Stag Beetle, a small, flightless, black ground-dwelling beetle that is restricted to the region, and the Blue Tier Giant, a 70m-tall Mountain Ash *Eucalyptus regnans* and Australia's widest tree.

GPS Coordinates
-41.14759, 147.80107

Getting There
From Launceston it is a 94km drive via Scottsdale on the Tasman Highway/ A3. Coming from the east coast, head north towards Scamander and follow the A3 for 86km.

Tracks & Trails
There is a large number of trails throughout the reserve, some for walking, some for mountain biking and some for dual use (always watch out for bikes). *Goblin Forest Walk* (20 minutes) is a nice short walk through forest that has been regenerating since mining finished. Along the walk a number of interpretive signs help to explain the region's history. There are a number of other tracks, including *Australia Hill Loop Walk* (2 hours), *Mt Michael Loop Walk* (2 hours), which heads through the rainforest and provides some magnificent views from the summit of Mt Michael, *Wellington Loop Walk* (3 hours) and *Moon Valley Rim Loop Walk* (2 hours), which takes you to the summit of Mt Poimena. *Three Notch Walk* (6 hours) is the most difficult of the walks in the reserve and is a return trail to McGoughs Lookout. For those with time, the region is home to the 'The Trail of the Tin Dragon' a historical mining experience that moves from Launceston through Branxholm, Derby, Moorina, Pyengana and St Helens.

Fees & Permits
Park-entry permits must be purchased for all of Tasmania's national parks. Additional fees are payable for camping in national parks.

Facilities
There are some facilities including a picnic area, barbecues and an emergency shelter at the beginning of the *Goblin Forest Walk*. Other sections of the park also have picnic facilities.

Services Nearby
The Derby township and surrounding townships are small and have limited facilities. All major facilities are available in Launceston.

Tasmanian Northern Slopes

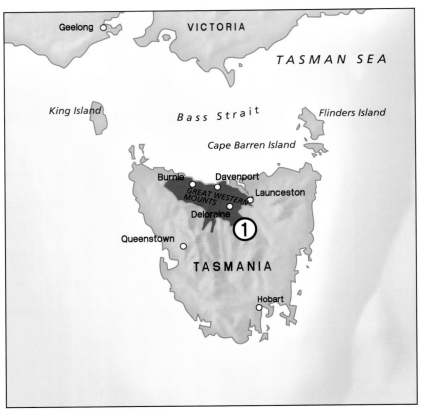

1. Liffey Falls State Reserve

Situated in northern central Tasmania, the Tasmanian northern slopes bioregion encompasses 6,231.03km². Located between six other bioregions, the area contains a number of different habitat types, including wetlands, coastal heath, wet and dry sclerophyll forests and even small patches of lowland grassland. Rainforest areas are restricted to the southern sections of the bioregion with mountains, slopes and gullies, closer to the Tasmanian central highlands bioregion. The coastal lowlands areas are drier and do not contain any rainforest. There are a number of reserves and protected areas in the bioregion, including Dial Range Forest Reserve, Laurel Creek Forest Reserve, Leven Canyon Regional Reserve and Gog Range Regional Reserve. These are just some of the areas that make up the 14.7 per cent (876.10km²) of the bioregion that occurs within protected areas.

Tourism Australia

Liffey Falls Forest Reserve

Key Species

BIRDS
Black Currawong, Brush Bronzewing, Eastern Spinebill, Fan-tailed Cuckoo, Forest Raven, Green Rosella, Olive Whistler, Pink Robin, Scrubtit, Swift Parrot, Tasmanian Scrubwren, Yellow-tailed Black Cockatoo.

MAMMALS
Large Forest Bat, Lesser Long-eared Bat, Little Pygmy-possum, Long-nosed Potoroo, Platypus, Spotted-tailed Quoll, Tasmanian Devil, Tasmanian Dusky Antechinus, Tasmanian Long-eared Bat.

REPTILES
Metallic Skink, Tasmanian She-oak Skink, Tasmanian Tree Skink, White-lipped Snake.

AMPHIBIANS
Brown Tree Frog, Common Eastern Froglet, Tasmanian Froglet.

INVERTEBRATES
Australian Wood Cockroach, Delicate Xenica, Green Mantid, Macleay's Swallowtail, Tasmanian Pill Beetle.

There are a number of towns throughout the region, Penguin, Bernie and Nietta all providing the services required for access to the rainforest areas and the highly coveted Narawntapu National Park, which is sited in an essentially isolated section of the Furneaux bioregion that is accessed via the Tasmanian Northern Slopes.

A huge diversity of wildlife can be seen throughout the bioregion, particularly birds, which vary significantly with habitat. Within the cool temperate rainforest there is significant overlap in species composition with the Tasmanian central highlands, with the Pink Robin, Scrubtit, Tasmanian Scrubwren and Tasmanian Thornbill commonly seen. The area is also home to all eight of Tasmania's bat species and the majority of its reptile and amphibian species.

Chris Farrell

Swift Parrot

265

Scrubtit *Acanthornis magna*

Angus McNab

Some birds, including the Scrubtit, spend much of their time hidden from view. Tending to prefer denser, wetter habitats than most Tasmanian birds, the Scrubtit can be a challenge to see. As its environments are poorly lit, its dark brown colouration, white throat, grey face and ear-coverts, partial white eye-ring, off-white underparts and buff flanks all contribute to its camouflage. Its high-pitched call can be difficult to hear, and as individuals are shy and nervous about coming out from cover, they are often overlooked. At times they can be seen clinging to tree trunks as they pop up out of the vegetation. The King Island subspecies of Scrubtit *A. m. greeniana* is listed as Critically Endangered.

Spotted-tailed Quoll *Dasyurus maculatus*

Lachlan Hall

Sleek, fast and elusive, this mammal is restricted to rainforest habitats along much of the east coast of Australia. This is not its preferred habitat, but introduced predators, particularly foxes, compete with and predate upon it, limiting its distribution in open woodland and dry forests. A formidable predator, it can prey on macropods that are larger than itself. Dark reddish-brown fur covers its body; it is interspersed with white spots, including on the legs and long tail. Usually solitary, individuals have large ranges that cover many hectares, making them difficult to find. Unfortunately, Spotted-tailed Quolls are regularly found in chicken coops, or stalking around them in attempts to take an easy feed. This does not do them any favours and in many cases results in individuals being shot.

Tasmanian Devil *Sarcophilus harrisii*

Angus McNab

The largest carnivore in Tasmania, this species has a reputation for being aggressive, bitey and pugnacious. A stocky black, short-legged predator, it spends much of its day in wombat burrows or under dense undergrowth, coming out to feed at night. Devils have long been known to remove much of the roadkill that litters Tasmania's roads, despite being capable of killing prey. Their noisy battles for food are well documented and scared many early settlers. However, these sounds no longer echo through the forests at the same ferocity that they once did. This is because Devil Facial Tumour Disease has reduced devil numbers by up to 90 per cent across most of the state. Conservation efforts continue to try and save the species and limit its decline.

Tasmanian She-oak Skink *Cyclodomorphus casuarinae*

Angus McNab

A large, elongated skink with short legs and a long tail, this species could readily be confused for a snake. Sliding through the leaf litter or basking on a rock, the long, slim body is often moved in a snake-like fashion without the use of the legs (which are tucked up and out of the way). Unlike snakes, which have a forked tongue, she-oak skinks have a thick, fleshy tongue that is often flicked out of the mouth. Highly variable in pattern, their body can be grey, brown, reddish-bronze or black, and patterns (including banded, unbanded, mottled or variegated) can vary substantially. While the upperparts are often coloured in earthy tones, the ventral scales can be beautifully patterned and vary from olive-grey to bright yellowish-orange. The young are live-born and may be finely banded.

Liffey Falls State Reserve

Occurring in a very 'green' space, Liffey Forest State Reserve adjoins or is in close proximity to a number of other reserves, including Dry Bluff Forest Reserve, Jackeys Creek Forest Reserve, Quamby Bluff Forest Reserve and Liffey Forest Reserve, all of which are just to the north of the large Central Plateau Conservation Area and Great Lakes. These areas are on the eastern edge of the Great Western Tiers and provide a boundary for a continuous patch that continues all the way to the west coast of Tasmania. The large area of forest provides an example of what forest may have looked like pre-European settlement, and protects a considerable amount of land and the flora and fauna that occur here. Once a significant logging area, the reserve became part of the Tasmanian Wilderness World Heritage Area in 1989.

Named after the magnificent three-tiered Liffey Falls, the reserve contains wet and dry sclerophyll

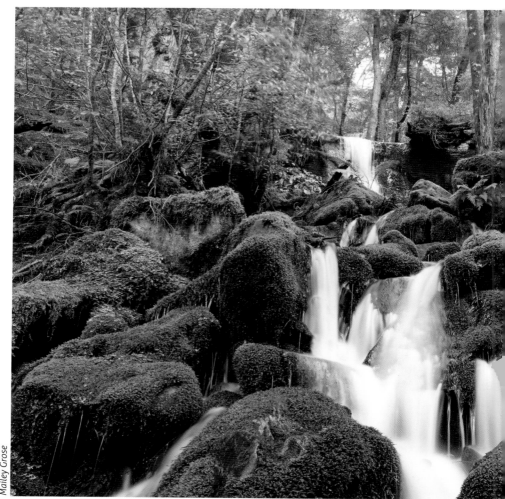

Mailey Grose

Liffey Falls National Park is named after the magnificent three-tiered falls

forests, cool temperate rainforest gullies and sandstone overhangs. The area is home to threatened species like the Wedge-tailed Eagle and Grey Goshawk, Tasmanian Devil, Eastern Barred Bandicoot and other fantastic species like Pink Robins, Green Rosellas and Platypus.

When visiting the reserve it is easy to see why it was protected – the huge trees and moss-covered forest floor alongside the slow-flowing Liffey River provide a magnificent backdrop to any day out.

GPS Coordinates
-41.70002, 146.75934 (upper car park)
-41.68310, 146.78223 (lower car park)

Getting There
Leaving Hobart you can take either Highland Lakes Road/A5 (203km), or the National Highway 1 (213km). From Launceston it is a short drive via National Highway 1 and C513 (54km).

Tracks & Trails
The *Liffey Falls Walk* (2–3 hours) is amazingly scenic and takes you through beautiful tall eucalypt forest, past giant trees and tree ferns, across the river as well as past four smaller falls (Alexandra Falls, Hopetoun Falls, Albert Falls and Victoria Falls) before you reach the 70m tall, three-tiered Liffey Falls. Be aware that this walk has a large number of stairs. Liffey Falls can also be reached from the upper car park (2km, return) along a much shorter and flat track. *Big Tree Stroll* (100m) makes its ways through a glade of gigantic Messmate Stringybarks *Eucalyptus obliqua*.

Fees & Permits
Park-entry permits must be purchased for all of Tasmania's national parks.

Facilities
Picnic facilities, including barbecues and toilets (wheelchair accessible at upper Liffey Falls car park), are available at both the upper and lower sections of the park. Free camping is available in the lower section of the park – camp fires are not allowed.

Services Nearby
Deloraine is the closest town with facilities including hospital, banks, schools, mechanical and tyre repair, post office, bakery, cafe, restaurants, bars and shops. Launceston is only an hour's drive away and has all major facilities.

Tasmanian Central Highlands

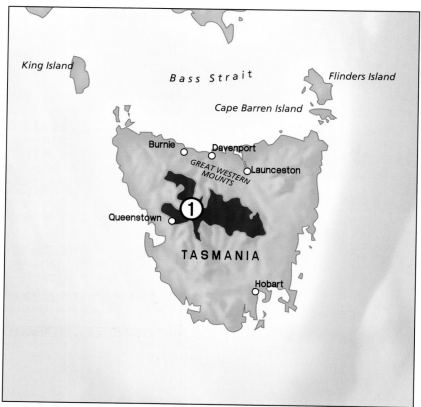

1. Cradle Mountain-Lake St Clair National Park

One of the most awkwardly shaped bioregions in Australia, the Tasmanian central highlands bioregion sits on the central plateau and covers an area of 7,678.49km². Containing the best-known national park in the state, Cradle Mountain-Lake St Clair National Park, this bioregion is home to many species that are restricted to high elevations, such as the Southern Snow Skink *Carinascincus microlepidotus* and Northern Snow Skink *C. greeni*. There are many habitat types across the plateau, including eucalypt forest, grassland, rainforest and alpine heath. Overall, about 86 per cent of the bioregion is covered by native vegetation, although like most of Tasmania the area was once logged for timbers such as the Tasmanian Myrtle *Nothofagus gunnii*, Southern Sassafras *Atherosperma moschatum*, Tasmanian Leatherwood *Eucryphia lucida* and Celery-top Pine *Phyllocladus asplenifolius*.

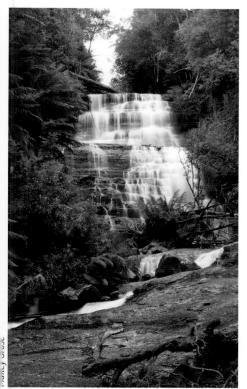

Westmorland Falls

Key Species

BIRDS

Bassian Thrush, Black Currawong, Brush Bronzewing, Crescent Honeyeater, Eastern Spinebill, Forest Raven, Golden Whistler, Green Rosella, Morepork, Olive Whistler, Pink Robin, Scrubtit, Shining Bronze-cuckoo, Spotted Pardalote, Striated Pardalote, Strong-billed Honeyeater, Tasmanian Native-hen, Tasmanian Scrubwren, Tasmanian Thornbill, Yellow-throated Honeyeater.

MAMMALS

Chocolate Wattled Bat, Common Wombat, Eastern Quoll, Krefft's Glider, Large Forest Bat, Lesser Long-eared Bat, Little Pygmy-possum, Long-nosed Potoroo, Long-tailed Mouse, Platypus, Short-beaked Echidna, Southern Forest Bat, Spotted-tailed Quoll, Tasmanian Devil, Tasmanian Dusky Antechinus, Tasmanian Long-eared Bat.

REPTILES

Metallic Skink, Northern Snow Skink, Tasmanian Tree Skink, Tiger Snake, White-lipped Snake.

AMPHIBIANS

Brown Tree Frog, Common Eastern Froglet.

INVERTEBRATES

Australian Wood Cockroach, Common Albatross, Delicate Xenica, Green Mantid, Macleay's Swallowtail.

Annual rainfall can be very high, with up to 2,500mm per year, while temperatures can be very low (-2–3 °C) in winter. Although temperatures can get up to 22 °C in summer, conditions can change quickly, so it is important to be aware of this and to always be prepared when outdoors. Large expanses of the Tasmanian central highlands bioregion consists of elevated undulating plateau, with a series of rocky mountain ranges towards the west.

The area is very scenic, with beautiful vegetation like the King Billy Pine *Athrotaxis selaginoides*, native 'fagus' or Deciduous Beech *Nothofagus gunnii*, waratahs, orchids, banksias, hakeas and leatherwoods. The region contains numerous lakes that entice many anglers, both beginners and experts, and the bioregion is well known for its camping, hunting and adventure sports.

Shining Bronze-cuckoo

Angus McNab

Black Currawong *Strepera fuliginosa*

Angus McNab

At first glance you might think that this is a crow or raven, as the Black Currawong is a large, slender and almost completely black bird. The only colour is in the small white tips to the flight feathers, the white tail-tips and the yellow eyes. Endemic to Tasmania, this large bird has a large, thick black bill with a slightly hooked tip. During the cooler winter months, it may form large flocks of more than 50 individuals. It does this at lower elevations where it spends the winter, while during the warmer summer months it tends to move to higher elevations and spend more time alone.

Eastern Spinebill *Acanthorhynchus tenuirostris*

Peter Rowland

The small, fast and agile Eastern Spinebill is usually seen racing between flowers in search of nectar, which it eats through a long, fine, black slightly downcurved bill. Nectar is an important resource for spinebills and it is common to see individuals chasing competitors from their patch of flowers. Similarly, small flying invertebrates are chased away through the forest. As the birds fly, white margins on the outer tail feathers flash brightly. The grey-black wings contrast against the white throat and breast, which adjoin buff-orange underparts. A small, dark rufous throat-patch matches the mantle. Juveniles are similar in shape to adults, but have uniformly buff-coloured underparts and are duller in the wings – and are thus a source of confusion to many a birdwatcher.

Green Rosella *Platycercus caledonicus*

Angus McNab

Endemic to Tasmania, this solidly built rosella is Australia's largest (33–37cm). More yellowish-green than green when mature, it has a blue throat-patch and reddish forehead and face, the red wash extending below the throat-patch in adult females. The wings and tail are dark blue and the back is dark green, with a darker blackish centre to each feather. Young birds are predominantly green. Widespread throughout Tasmania in most habitats, the species forms small groups outside the breeding season. During the breeding season, the female lays 4–8 eggs in a tree hollow, which she incubates while being fed by the male. This rosella feeds on fruits, flower buds, nectar and some insects.

Tasmanian Thornbill *Acanthiza ewingii*

Angus McNab

Thornbills can be a challenge to identify, as they have many shared features among species. The Tasmanian Thornbill, which is endemic to Tasmania, looks very similar to the Brown Thornbill *A. pusilla,* which also occurs in Tasmania, although the latter prefers drier, more open habitats. Both have small red eyes with an off-white, grey-brown mottled throat and breast, and a rufous, faintly scalloped forehead. The rump and tail are chestnut-brown with a dark subterminal tail-band. However, the Tasmanian Thornbill has less streaking on the breast and throat, white flanks, a longer tail, a shorter bill and rufous edges to the primaries. Usually in small flocks, the birds forage in the middle to high canopy. They are easily disturbed, and it is not uncommon to have angry-sounding calls directed at you as you walk through the rainforest.

Little Pygmy-possum *Cercartetus lepidus*

Angus McNab

Also referred to as the Tasmanian Pygmy-possum, this tiny marsupial is not restricted to rainforest, but occurs in a variety of habitat types. Smaller than its eastern counterpart, this dainty little possum is also a lighter tan-brown than its grey-brown relative. Feeding on invertebrates, nectar and flowers, it can be difficult to spot as it moves through the mid-canopy. Relatively shy, it is quick to retreat when lights are shone in its direction, running into a clump of leaves or thicker vegetation that provides it with more safety than exposed perches. During the cooler months pygmy-possums go into hibernation, sleeping in a nest that they have built from dry bark, leaves and grasses.

Short-beaked Echidna *Tachyglossus aculeatus*

Angus McNab

One of Australia's most famous animals, emblazoned on the 5-cent coin, the Short-beaked Echidna is unlike anything else in Australia, although it does have relatives in Papua New Guinea. Of the five subspecies in Australia, the Tasmanian subspecies is the smallest and fluffiest. Although the back is covered in short, straw-coloured spikes, these are separated by dense fur that is less obvious in other subspecies. This fur layer is thought to compensate for the cooler climate in the habitats it occupies, many of which are snow covered in winter. Regularly seen wandering along tracks, you may notice the large, stocky front claws that are used for digging, and the curved back claws that aid in clearing dirt as the animal digs for ants to eat or a burrow to live in.

White-lipped Snake *Drysdalia coronoides*

The smallest and slimmest of the Tasmanian snakes, this species is also the least commonly encountered. There is considerable variation in its dorsal colouration, which can be pale olive, grey, reddish-brown or dark brown. A narrow white stripe runs along the upper lip and on to the neck. Similar to the Tasmanian She-oak Skink (p. 267), the upper tones are earthy colours but the ventral scales can be bright red-orange. Although not regarded as being as venomous or as dangerous as the Tiger Snake (p. 283) or Lowland Copperhead *Austrelaps superbus*, bites can still require medical attention. A live-bearing elapid, females can give birth to 2–10 young. VENOMOUS

Angus McNab

Brown Tree Frog *Litoria ewingii*

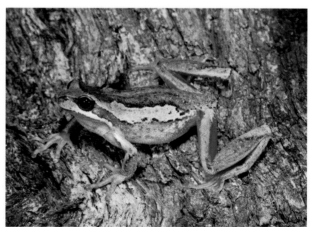

This smooth, slender, medium-sized tree frog is the most commonly heard frog in Tasmania. It is is varying shades of cream to brown, and has a wide dark dorsal stripe flanked by paler dorsal-lateral edges, which runs from between the eyes down the length of the back. The brown canthal stripe passes through the eye and brown tympanum, and becomes paler as it joins the flanks. The ventral surfaces are pale with some mottling, and the upper thighs are reddish-orange. The sticky toe-pads make the Brown Tree Frog an excellent climber. Males climb to call from an elevated position, allowing their calls to project further. Females are not particularly fussy where they lay their eggs, depositing them in almost any still waterbody.

Angus McNab

Cradle Mountain-Lake St Clair National Park

This area of almost 640km² was gazetted as a Scenic Reserve in 1922. In 1971 it was declared a State Reserve and in 1982 it became part of the Tasmanian Wilderness World Heritage Area. Cradle Mountain-Lake St Clair National Park gives the visitor a taste of the rugged beauty of the broader Tasmanian Wilderness World Heritage Area, with the jagged contours of the mountains, old-growth rainforest, smaller stands of beech and pine forests, and extensive heathland and buttongrass meadows. A park to be visited in all seasons, during winter the snow-covered landscape is different from the greens of summer, the flowers in spring and the shades of brown with the 'turning of the Fagus' Deciduous Beech *Nothofagus gunnii* in autumn. Much of the park is largely undisturbed and you can hike through its centre along the world-famous Overland Track. In addition to birds, many endemic mammals, reptiles and invertebrates can be found here.

Located at the northern end of the larger Cradle Mountain-Lake St Clair National Park, Cradle Mountain rises to just over 1,500m above sea level and can be a challenging environment if you are not properly prepared for its changeable weather. The popular glacial Dove Lake is 950m above sea level.

The park is home to the iconic Tasmanian Devil, the world's largest

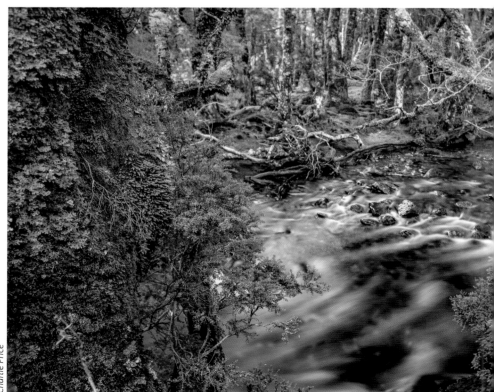

Charlie Price

Along the Enchanted Walk

living marsupial carnivore, two quoll species, both Australian monotremes (egg-laying mammals) and the iconic Common Wombat. Although the total number of bird species recorded here is not huge (just over 75), it has 10 of Tasmania's 12 endemic species.

GPS Coordinates
-41.82758, 146.00023

Getting There
From Hobart take either the National Highway 1 (319km) or the more scenic Highland Lakes Road/A5 (319km), both of which pass through Deloraine. From Launceston take National Highway 1 (141km).

Tracks & Trails
Rainforest Walk (20 minutes, circuit) contains a short, wheelchair-friendly

boardwalk that passes through a section of rainforest to the Pencil Pine Falls. *Weindorfers Forest Walk* (20 minutes, circuit) climbs a short distance up through pine forest and myrtles. *Dove Lake Circuit* (2 hours, circuit) starts at the car park and loops around the lake and through the Ballroom Forest, a section of cool temperate rainforest. *Enchanted Walk* (20 minutes), meanders through the moorland and patches of rainforest. The walk passes waterfalls and icy pools along the way. The *Overland Track*, one of the most famous Tasmanian hikes, is a 5–6 day hike, walking through the park from Cradle Mountain to Lake St Clair (or vice versa), with huts and some facilities. This hike must be booked well in advance and is definitely not for the faint-hearted or poorly equipped.

Fees & Permits
Park-entry permits must be purchased for all of Tasmania's national parks. Additional fees are payable for camping in national parks.

Facilities
Wheelchair-accessible toilets are located at the information centre, visitor centre, Waldheim Chalet and Dove Lake. Shop, restaurant, cafe, picnic shelters, electric barbecues, public phone and 24-hour fuel are all available within the park boundary. All-terrain wheelchairs are also available for hire at the visitor centre (bookings essential). Rubbish bins are not provided.

Services Nearby
Cradle Mountain is located in a remote area, with limited services available between the park and the nearest major city of Devonport (77km).

Tasmanian Southern Ranges

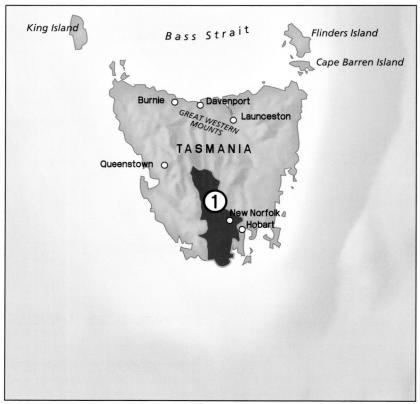

1. Mount Field National Park

From the border of the central highlands to the southern beaches of Cockle Creek, the Southern Ranges bioregion covers an area of 7,572.28km² between the Tasmanian West and Tasmanian South East bioregions. Hartz Mountain, Mount Field National Park, Hasting's Caves, Cockle Creek and the Styx are major areas visited throughout the bioregion, along this north–south running range, much of which remains relatively inaccessible. Generally a cooler, wetter region with significant rainfall and snow cover in winter (at higher elevations), it contains a diversity of habitat types, much of which are subalpine heaths, rainforest and wet forest. Beautifully scenic, filled with quaint little towns, logging and history and plenty of opportunities for enjoying the outdoors, this bioregion contains some of Tasmania's most fantastic wildlife opportunities.

Tree ferns along the road to Mt Field summit

Most of Tasmania's rainforest fauna can be found within the bioregion, as it encompasses the higher elevation mountains and coastlines, and is situated between the wetter west coast and drier east coast. The vast majority of the bioregion is within protected areas, although this can only do so much to protect the inhabitants, and the region is home to at least 15 threatened vertebrates and 120 threatened plants.

Key Species

BIRDS
Australian Masked Owl, Bassian Thrush, Beautiful Firetail, Black Currawong, Black-headed Honeyeater, Brown Goshawk, Brown Thornbill, Crescent Honeyeater, Green Rosella, Grey Goshawk, Grey Shrikethrush, Morepork, Olive Whistler, Pink Robin, Scrubtit, Shining Bronze-cuckoo, Striated Pardalote, Strong-billed Honeyeater, Tasmanian Scrubwren, Yellow-tailed Black Cockatoo.

MAMMALS
Eastern Barred Bandicoot, Eastern Pygmy-possum, Eastern Quoll, Large Forest Bat, Lesser Long-eared Bat, Long-tailed Mouse, Platypus, Southern Forest Bat, Tasmanian Dusky Antechinus. Note: the last Tasmanian Tiger *Thylacinus cynocephalus* held in captivity at the Beaumaris Zoo in Hobart had been trapped in the Florentine Valley in 1933.

REPTILES
Metallic Skink, Northern Snow Skink, Southern Snow Skink, Tasmanian She-oak Skink, Tasmanian Tree Skink, Tiger Snake, White-lipped Snake.

AMPHIBIANS
Brown Tree Frog, Common Eastern Froglet, Tasmanian Froglet.

INVERTEBRATES
Delicate Xenica, Forest Scorpion, Green Mantid, Lake Fenton Trapdoor Spider, Macleay's Swallowtail, Slender Save Beetle, Tasmanian Redspot.

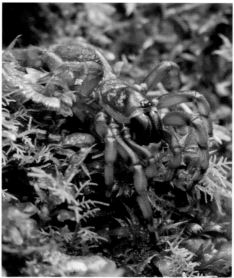

Lake Fenton Trapdoor Spider

279

Brown Goshawk *Accipiter fasciatus*

Peter Vaughan

This species is stocky, with a grey head, long bill, yellow eyes, a strong, pronounced eyebrow, rufous collar, and grey-brown upperparts and tail. The pale underparts, including the underwing-coverts, undertail and trousers, have fine rufous barring. The tail is long with a rounded tip and the legs are long, thick and yellow. Juveniles have broadly mottled and barred underparts, with the barring becoming thinner with age; the rufous collar appears with adult plumage. An agile flier, the Brown Goshawk spends much of its time in closed forests waiting in ambush to predate on smaller birds. There is a considerable difference in size between males and females (females are larger). A large stick nest is constructed in the forest and may be used repeatedly for many years.

Morepork *Ninox novaeseelandiae*

Angus McNab

Recently split from the Australian Boobook *N. boobook* of mainland Australia, the Morepork is a small owl with large yellow eyes surrounded by large, pale-edged, dark grey eye-patches. The head and upperparts are dark brown with small white spots and mottling. The breast is heavily mottled, or roughly streaked, in brown and white. Like the commonly heard Australian Boobook, the Morepork has a very similar onomatopoeic call that can be heard from dusk to the early morning, ringing through the forests. During the day, Moreporks roost in a tree with significant foliage or a tree hollow, avoiding diurnal birds that harass and annoy them while sleeping. A nocturnal hunter, the Morepork can often be seen perched in low branches searching for prey such as small mammals, amphibians and moths.

Pink Robin *Petroica rodinogaster*

Angus McNab

A beautiful little inhabitant of the southern rainforests, the male Pink Robin adds a spark of colour to what can be very dark forests. Although the upperparts are dark grey-black, the bright pink breast and underparts stand out as males perch on small branches. The females are less conspicuous and are shades of brown with orange wing-bars and a buff forehead-patch that separate them from other local robins. Often seen in male-female pairs, the two can regularly be heard making soft contact calls to each other. The nest is a beautiful mixture of stripped bark, spider webs, hair, lichens and mosses that are wound together and hidden in a tree.

Long-tailed Mouse *Pseudomys higginsi*

Angus McNab

Hiding in the rocky rainforest floor, the Long-tailed Mouse is very rarely seen. It has a long tail, up to a third longer than the length of the body (which is very uncommon in small native rodents). Not only is the tail long, but it is also bicoloured; dark above and pale below, matching with the body, which is grey above and white below. The nose is rounded and the eyes have a dark grey eye-ring. Quick and agile, the Long-tailed Mouse is able to move across uneven surfaces and into small cracks and crevices in search of food and shelter. During the winter, individuals at higher elevations may be snowed under and must be prepared for the cold conditions; they can survive under the snow for substantial lengths of time.

Tasmanian Dusky Antechinus *Antechinus swainsonii*

Tim Bawden

One of three antechinus in Tasmania, this species is equivalent to the Mainland Dusky Antechinus (p. 233), and looks and behaves in a similar fashion. It is predominantly nocturnal, but it is not uncommon to see these small, dark-furred, pointy-snouted dasyurids moving around during the day. A ferocious little hunter, you would not want to be a potential prey item, as antechinus will chase down invertebrates, lizards and baby birds and at times even eat them alive. The semelparous lifestyle reduces the detectability of this species for much of the year, as males die off after the breeding season, leaving only females to give birth and raise the young before the following breeding season.

Metallic Skink *Carinascincus metallicus*

Angus McNab

The Metallic Skink is the most commonly seen of Tasmania's skinks, as it is common in gardens and is the first skink to emerge from hibernation in early spring. Only growing to about 60mm, this small, moderately robust, brown-backed snow skink is highly variable in colour and pattern, with keeled scales. Some features are present in some but not all individuals, including a black vertebral stripe, fine longitudinal back stripes and a midlateral stripe. Living communally, many individuals may be seen basking together, often sitting on top of each other next to a retreat site. Quick to withdraw to cover, Metallic Skinks will equally quickly return to basking when conditions are suitable. Like all snow skinks young are born live, with up to eight (average four) in a litter.

Tiger Snake *Notechis scutatus*

Angus McNab

The Tiger Snake is the largest, most robust and most commonly seen of Tasmania's snakes. While many individuals have bands or stripes like a tiger, many do not. Tiger Snakes are not always black and yellow, but can be greys, dull reds or varying shades of black, and have varying amounts of patterning. A venomous snake, bites do require immediate medical attention. However, maintaining a safe distance between yourself and any snake reduces the likelihood of a bite. Tiger Snakes prefer to bite frogs, reptiles, and on occasion small mammals that they can eat, rather than expend venom defending themselves. The species is live-bearing, and an adult female can produce up to 45 young in a single clutch, which are left to fend for themselves as soon as they are born. VENOMOUS

Forest Scorpion *Cercophonius squama*

Charlie Price

This species is variably coloured, from yellowish-brown to dark brown, with reddish-brown patterning. Its body is moderately thick-set, with small pedipalps. It is widespread in southern eastern Australia, from southeastern South Australia to eastern New South Wales, with an isolated population in southwestern Western Australia. It is the only scorpion species in Tasmania, occurring in moist habitats, where it lives in a burrow, emerging at night to feed on small invertebrates. The female gives birth to live young, which are carried on her back for the first few weeks of their lives. The species is capable of inflicting a painful sting, which is accompanied by swelling and redness that can last for some hours. A single human fatality, a small infant, has been recorded from this species.

Mount Field National Park

One of Tasmania's best-known national parks and among its first, Mount Field National Park was initially proclaimed as the Russell Falls Reserve in 1885, before becoming a national park in 1916. The lower slopes of the park contain the picture-perfect rainforests seen in most of the advertising for Tasmanian tourism. Part of the Tasmanian Wilderness World Heritage Area, the park contains amazing rainforest, streams and the spectacular Russell Falls that cascades down over three tiers.

Containing some of Tasmania's largest eucalypt forests, on a visit do not restrict yourself to the rainforest. As one of the state's most diverse national parks, it is highly recommended that you visit its alpine tarns, subalpine heathland and Deciduous Beech *Nothofagus gunnii,* higher up into the park above the rainforest. The mountains, covered by snow in winter, rise to more than 1,400m and disappear into the distance, far into the park (which covers an area of about 162km^2).

The park is regularly green, but the 'turning of the Fagus' as the Deciduous Beeches prepare to drop their leaves (late April–May) is one of the biggest botanical events of the year. With a network of trails for both beginners and the more adventurous, you can move through a region that has a diversity

Anders Zimny

Russell Falls

of geological substrates, a range of vegetation types, an extreme diversity of fungi and lichen (290 plus species) and multiple waterfalls. If you are lucky you could also find a range of fauna, including the Eastern Quoll and Eastern Barred Bandicoot, both of which have gone extinct in the wild on mainland Australia. The region was home to potentially the last wild-caught Thylacine and remains the home of the ever-elusive Platypus.

GPS Coordinates
-42.66357, 146.64942

Getting There
Considerably closer to Hobart than Launceston, there are beautiful winding roads via National Highway 1, Lyell Highway/A10 and B62 (64km).

From Launceston you can travel via the more scenic Highland Lakes Road/A5 (204km), or via the midlands and National Highway 1 (226km).

Tracks & Trails
The park has short and long walks leaving from both the lower car park, including *Russell Falls* (wheelchair accessible – an all-terrain wheelchair may be hired from the information centre). The multi-tiered falls can be viewed from below and above (involves stairs) and this is highly recommended. Additional walks include *Horseshoe Falls, Lady Barron Falls Circuit* and the *Tall Trees Walk.* From the top car park at Lake Dobson, walks are predominantly through subalpine heath, and all the walks have magnificent tarns and provide scenic views of the mountains. There are a number of other walks, including *Seagers Lookout, Mount Field East via Lake Nicholls, Tarn Shelf* and *Lake Seal Lookout.*

Fees & Permits
Park-entry permits must be purchased for all of Tasmania's national parks. Additional fees are payable for camping in Tasmanian national parks.

Facilities
The park has many facilities, including barbecues, camping, a cafe, an information centre, huts, hiking, skiing (winter), picnic tables and toilets. Phone reception is very limited and cannot be relied upon.

Services Nearby
The park is remote and other than the facilities listed above does not have any services. Many major services are available in New Norfolk and all major services are available in Hobart.

Tasmanian West

1. Tarkine 2. Franklin-Gordon Wild Rivers National Park 3. Southwest National Park

This is the largest bioregion in Tasmania, and also the most remote and least accessible. Covering an area of 15,650.77km² and encompassing the majority of the west coast of Tasmania, the bioregion has some of the most magnificent mountain ranges and the most scenic multi-day walks. Within its 52 reserves, 13,252.15km² (84.67 per cent) of the Tasmanian West bioregion is protected – the largest area of any of Tasmania's 10 bioregions and almost 20 per cent of the entire state. It is also a major refuge for the Myrtle Beech *Nothofagus cunninghamii* dominated temperate rainforest. The region has a long indigenous history, which is visible through the huge middens seen along the coast, and a dark European history with Macquarie Harbour Penal Station.

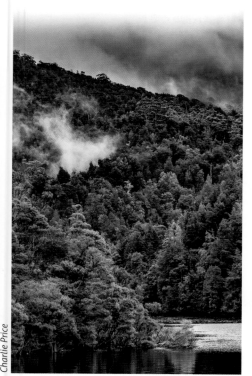

Charlie Price

Franklin-Gordon Wild Rivers National Park

Key Species

BIRDS

Australian Golden Whistler, Beautiful Firetail, Black Currawong, Brown Goshawk, Crescent Honeyeater, Eastern Spinebill, Fan-tailed Cuckoo, Forest Raven, Green Rosella, Grey Fantail, Grey Goshawk, Grey Shrikethrush, Olive Whistler, Orange-bellied Parrot, Pink Robin, Scrubtit, Superb Lyrebird, Tasmanian Thornbill, Tasmanian Scrubwren, Yellow-tailed Black Cockatoo, Yellow-throated Honeyeater.

MAMMALS

Chocolate Wattled Bat, Eastern Pygmy-possum, Eastern Barred Bandicoot, Eastern Quoll, Gould's Wattled Bat, Krefft's Glider, Large Forest Bat, Little Pygmy-possum, Long-nosed Potoroo, Long-tailed Mouse, Southern Forest Bat, Spotted-tailed Quoll, Tasmanian Devil, Tasmanian Dusky Antechinus, Tasmanian Long-eared Bat, Tasmanian Pademelon.

REPTILES

Southern Snow Skink, Tasmanian Mountain Skink, Tasmanian She-oak Skink, Tasmanian Tree Skink, Tiger Snake.

AMPHIBIANS

Common Eastern Froglet, Tasmanian Tree Frog.

INVERTEBRATES

Australian Wood Cockroach, Delicate Xenica, Green Mantid, Macleay's Swallowtail, Tasmanian Pill Beetle.

The bioregion lies within the wettest region of the state and the long, isolated beaches are subjected to the full force of storms that drop rain on the first mountain range they hit. Most of the region receives an average annual rainfall above 1,250mm, and rainfall can exceed 2,500mm in some places. This provides the perfect conditions for extensive areas of rainforest. The diversity of habitats allows for giant trees to tower over the landscape, while button-grass plains extend as far as the eye can see. Heathland covers the mountain tops during summer, but the peaks become blanketed with snow in winter. Average temperatures range from a minimum of -2 to 6 °C in winter, to an average maximum of 13 to 21 °C in summer. No matter how you access this bioregion (on foot, or by car, bike or plane), be prepared for an adventure.

Peter Rowland

Beautiful Firetail

Grey Fantail *Rhipidura albiscapa*

Peter Rowland

Small, flittery and highly active, this species has a beautifully glassy yet piercing call that can be heard Australia-wide. Not considered a cryptic species, the Grey Fantail regularly occurs along walking tracks and forest edges, sallying for small invertebrates. It also gives away its presence through the regular fanning of its long and erect tail. Predominantly grey in colour, the upperparts are paler than the head, which has a contrasting white eyebrow, white throat and mark behind the eye. The narrow wing-bar, outer tail-shafts and tail-tips are also white. The underparts are white and fade to buff-white with a black breast-band. Many subspecies occur across Australia, and each utilizes a range of habitat types.

Olive Whistler *Pachycephala olivacea*

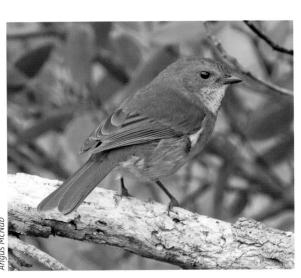

Angus McNab

Much chunkier than the other whistlers, the Olive Whistler has a thick grey head, neck and breast, with a finely barred white throat. The upperparts are olive-brown, the underparts rufous-brown. Females are duller brown than males, with a browner head and smaller grey breast-band. As in all whistlers, the call is a beautiful drawn-out whistle that carries through the rainforest. Birds usually occur alone, but can be seen as pairs. The Olive Whistler tends to remain in the cover of dense foliage so it is uncommon to see it in the open. It spends very little time on the ground as it is usually in the canopy, but on occasion it can be seen to forage low to the ground.

Superb Lyrebird *Menura novaehollandiae*

Angus McNab

The head, breast and underparts of this lyrebird are dark grey, while the wings are brown. Males have wispy, filamentous tail feathers that are dark above and pale below. Adjoining these are two large, lyre-shaped outer tail feathers that are banded in rufous and pale brown, with dark tips. The excellent conditions of the southern forests have allowed for large numbers of lyrebirds to breed and spread. To ensure foxes would not wipe out the species on the mainland, the Superb Lyrebird was introduced to Tasmania in the 1920s. Its continuous scratching and moving of leaf litter is damaging to the forest and the flora that grows in it. An awkward flier, the species is an incredible mimic, a talent males use to impress females from their display platforms.

Eastern Quoll *Dasyurus viverrinus*

Angus McNab

A smaller relative of the Spotted-tailed Quoll (p. 266), this is a dainty quoll that is less arboreal than its relatives. Once occurring on the Australian mainland, it is now restricted to Tasmania. One of the few mammals to have two colour morphs, it may be tan brown with white spots, or black with white spots. Both colour morphs have an unspotted tail and legs. It is carnivorous and there is little that it will not eat, including frogs, reptiles, birds, invertebrates and even other roadkill quolls. Although one of the larger predators in Tasmania, it is small enough for feral cats to be a threat, predating on fully grown quolls. There have been suggestions that the decline of Tasmanian Devils has negatively impacted on Eastern Quolls, which appear to be declining for reasons that remain unclear.

Tasmanian Long-eared Bat *Nyctophilus sherrini*

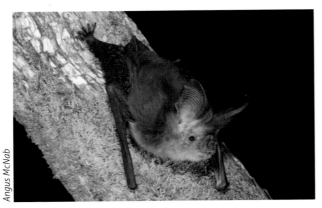

Angus McNab

It is hard to ignore the bizarre face and huge ears on the head of this bat. The largest of Tasmania's eight resident bat species, it is very similar to the Lesser Long-eared Bat *N. geoffroyi*, which is smaller and has a slightly differently shaped noseleaf. The long-eared bats are well known to be excellent fliers in cluttered environments and can move through dense vegetation with ease where other bats cannot. They are also capable of taking off from the ground, which not all bats can do. During the day, individuals tuck themselves away into tree hollows, or even under bark on the outsides of trees. During winter they hibernate, like all Tasmanian bats, coming out in late September–October when temperatures are slightly warmer and insect activity has increased.

Tasmanian Pademelon *Thylogale billardierii*

Angus McNab

Possibly the most common mammal in Tasmania – at least the most commonly seen – the Tasmanian Pademelon spends its days hidden in the undergrowth of forests. During the late afternoon and early evening it moves to the forest edges and grazes on grasses adjoining the rainforest. A robust macropod that stands at about knee height, its fur is dark brown on the back, while the breast and belly are rufous, giving rise to another common name of Rufous-bellied Pademelon. Breeding occurs year round, so it is common to see joeys at their mother's feet. Quite a confiding species, it is often possible to watch individuals feeding from close proximity. When disturbed, you can often hear the loud thump of their feet as they bound away.

Tasmanian Tree Skink *Carinascincus pretiosus*

This beautiful, moderately sized snow skink has a brown or grey back that is covered in pale and black flecks, and a narrow black vertebral stripe. It is the pale flecks that contrast with the dark body and really make this skink stand out from its close relatives. The pale flecks are also present on the dark reddish-brown to black upper lateral zone, which has a white midlateral stripe. Living in dense

Angus McNab

forest, sunlight patches can be a prime resource for this species, and multiple individuals can be seen scampering from the same sunspots as you walk past boulder piles in the forest. A most unusual trait of this skink is its affinity for nectar, which it includes in its diet along with small invertebrates.

Tasmanian Tree Frog *Litoria burrowsae*

This large and beautiful, smooth-skinned tree frog is varying shades of green and brown. A thin brown canthal stripe passes through the golden-brown eye, enclosing the upper tympanum before merging into the mottled flank-stripe. The ventral surfaces are pale brown, with darker mottling and a granular texture. Individuals can change colour and are considerably brighter at night when calling from around still waterbodies, or searching

Angus McNab

for mates. The fingers and toes have large pads, which allow for a highly arboreal lifestyle, and individuals are usually seen sitting in small shrubs or trees, or on any other elevated platform. Unfortunately, this rainforest- and heath-dwelling frog has suffered significant declines due to the amphibian Chytrid Fungus reducing its area of occupancy statewide.

Tarkine

Unlike most well-known rainforest sites in Australia, the Tarkine has no defined boundaries, but covers an area of roughly 4,500km². It is considered one of the most extraordinary places in Tasmania, yet remains unprotected. The area is made up of a variety of tenures and contains a national park, state reserves and conservation areas, among others. Protection of the region has been debated since the 1960s and continues to be debated today, with significant sections of the area still open to logging and mining (gold and tin) on certain tenures. Although some protections have been given, removed and denied, the IUCN (International Union for the Conservation of Nature) has recommended that the area should be considered for World Heritage status.

Loosely bordered by the Arthur River, Pieman River and Murchison Highway, the region is filled with some of the largest patches of ancient cool temperate rainforest in Australia, some of which sits on Tasmania's most extensive basalt plateau. It includes myrtle-dominated rainforest dating back to Gondwana, but also eucalyptus forest, dry sclerophyll forest, buttongrass plains, sand dunes containing Aboriginal middens, long, beautiful empty beaches, magnesite and dolomite cave systems, rivers and forest-covered mountains.

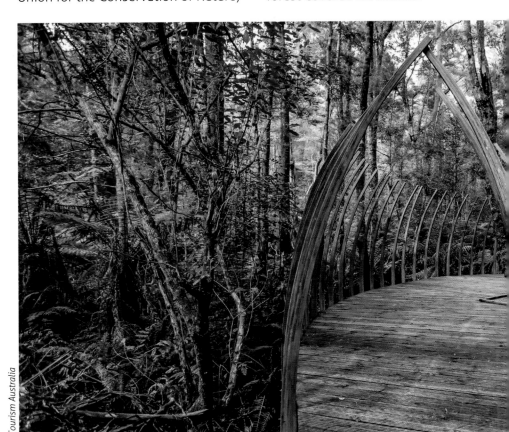

Tourism Australia

Dismal Swamp Forest Reserve

The region contains a significant number of Aboriginal sites and the remnants of a mining industry, with Corrina being the only settlement that remains. Corrina offers river cruises along the Pieman River, where patches of Huon Pine (one of the best boat-building timbers) remaining in the region can be seen, while the Tasmanian Giant Freshwater Crayfish lives beneath the surface, and Tasmanian Devils that remain free of the Tasmanian Devil Facial Tumour Disease continue to inhabit it.

GPS Coordinates
-41.41666, 145.13333

Getting There
A long drive north from Hobart via National Highway 1, through the

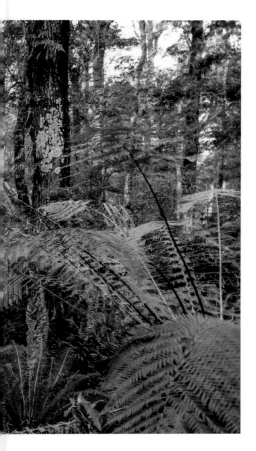

midlands and along the northern coast passes through many well-known Tasmanian towns (381km). From Launceston drive west along the northern coast via National Highway 1 (202km).

Tracks & Trails
The region has many large reserves offering numerous walks that pass through a variety of different habitat types. Walks include the *Philosopher Fall Walk, Bluff Hill Point, Arthur River Coastal Walk, Sarah Anne Walk, Balfour Packhorse Track* and *Sumac Lookout*. There are also long expanses of open beach that can be walked for kilometers in either direction. To see more of the region consider taking the Tarkine drive, a loop drive that takes you through old myrtle forest, rainforest and eucalypt forest, and past lakes, walking tracks and picnic areas where you can stop for a break.

Fees & Permits
There are no fees to enter the Tarkine region, although park-entry permits must be purchased for entry into the Tasmanian national park sections of the Tarkine. Additional fees are payable for camping in Tasmanian national parks.

Facilities
Facilities vary throughout the region but some of the walks have picnic tables, public toilets and associated camp grounds.

Services Nearby
The Tarkine region has limited services but includes small towns such as Corrina and Arthur River, which have some supplies. Larger towns to the north – Burnie, Stanley and Wynyard – and to the south – Strahan, Queenstown and Zeehan – have more services.

Franklin-Gordon Wild Rivers National Park

Wild and rugged is how this national park is often described, yet a cruise along the Gordon River can be tranquil, peaceful and a magical experience. For the adventurous, the rivers can be an experience like no other, with kayak trips that can last for weeks. The Franklin and Gordon Rivers form the heart of this park. A legal and conservation battle in the 1970s and '80s to preserve the Franklin River and stop a proposed hydroelectric power scheme are what really put this part of the world on the map.

Although the park has snow-capped peaks, long, expansive beaches and everything in between, most of it is impenetrable, yet what can be accessed provides an unforgettable experience. The inaccessibility to much of the region is probably a factor in the survival of the Huon Pines *Lagarostrobos franklinii* that still stand in the forest, where many if not most of their relatives were historically logged. The rivers provide access into the 4,463km^2 of remote wilderness. The water trickles from the mountain tops, crystal clear as it cascades through the rapids, and becoming deeply stained from vegetation as it collects tannins on

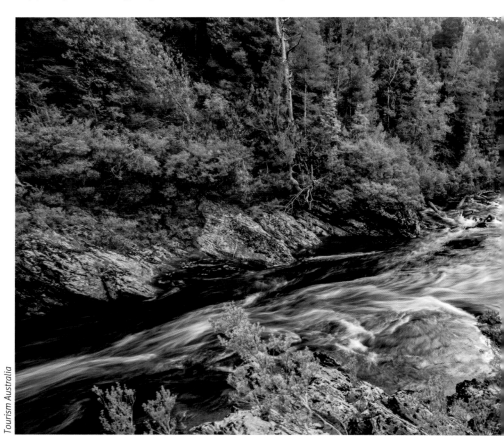

Tourism Australia

The Franklin and Gordon Rivers form the heart of this park

its way to the sea. The high rainfall causes everything to be wet for much of the year, providing the perfect environment for moss, lichens, liverworts and fungi that thrive in the rainforest environments. These dense environments provide cover for a diversity of rainforest creatures, including the three large carnivorous marsupials, the Eastern Quoll, Spotted-tailed Quoll and Tasmanian Devil, which hunt in the forest at night, while all of Tasmania's bats hunt through the forest above them.

GPS Coordinates
-42.47204, 145.96430

Getting There
This large national park is mostly inaccessible by vehicle. Sections

of it can be driven through on the Lyell Highway/A10 on the way to Queenstown from Hobart, or if heading to Strathgordon from Hobart, then via the B61 (155km). From Launceston head to Queenstown via National Highway 1 (244km).

Tracks & Trails
Walking tracks can be found all along the Lyell Highway, and tracks such as *Nelson Falls, Franklin River Nature Trail* and *Donaghy's Hill* are recommended. The longer multi-day *Frenchman's Cap Hike* to the top of Frenchman's Cap (1,443m) is highly recommended as one of Tasmania's most scenic walks through the subalpine heath. This is just one of the many locations that have scenic lookouts within the park. For more easily accessible lookouts try King William Saddle and Surprise Valley Lookout, which overlooks the glacially carved landscape.

Fees & Permits
Park-entry permits must be purchased for all of Tasmania's national parks. Additional fees are payable for camping in them.

Facilities
The remoteness of the park limits the access to facilities, although Strahan and Queenstown offer a range of services. Camping sites are available, but rustic with no facilities. Picnic facilities and toilets are limited, but available at some locations.

Services Nearby
Strahan and Queenstown offer most major services, such as food and accommodation, although they are small towns and do not have all major services.

Southwest National Park

Forming a large part of the Tasmanian Wilderness World Heritage Area, this very large park was a scenic reserve in 1968 and become a national park in 1971. It covers about 6,182km², making it the largest national park in Tasmania. It encompasses a diverse range of habitats, including snow-capped mountains, heathland, sedgeland, buttongrass plains, beautiful beaches and dense rainforest, and provides access to the most remote regions of the state. Bordered by the Franklin-Gordon Wild Rivers National Park, Hartz Mountain National Park and the ocean to the south, the park is home to 20 per cent of Tasmanian flora, 118 endemic species and Tasmania's most famous flora and fauna, the Huon Pine *Lagarostrobos franklinii*, Orange-bellied Parrot *Neophema chrysogaster* and Tasmanian Devil.

Best accessed by air from the north (Strathgordon), the south (Cockle Creek) and the west (Melaleuca) or by sea (Port Davey), the vast majority of the park is inaccessible. For those who venture into the park via the South Coast Track or the Arthurs Traverses, the remoteness does have some dangers, as the weather is highly changeable and often inhospitable. Cold temperatures, strong winds and rain (2,000mm per year) are the norm. While it may be sunny in the morning

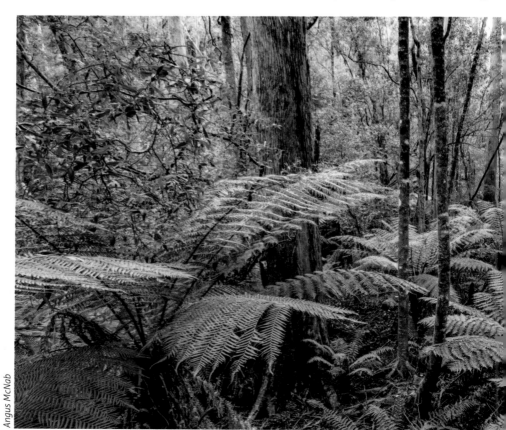

Angus McNab

Dense rainforest in the Southwest National Park

it can quickly turn to rain, sleet or snow by lunchtime, so visits to the park's remote areas require sufficient knowledge and preparation.

You can experience the magic of the park from your vehicle, driving west of Maydena via the Gordon River and Scott's Peak Road, which was built as part of the controversial Middle Gordon hydroelectric power scheme, but now forms a scenic, winding drive that provides access to numerous walks and amazing scenic viewpoints.

GPS Coordinates
-43.17109, 146.22044

Getting There
From Hobart access to walking trails is via Strathgordon on the B61 (115km) or via Cockle Creek using the B61

(121km). Flights to Melaleuca are from Hobart's Cambridge Airport with Par Avion.

Tracks & Trails
Numerous walks occur throughout the park and can be accessed from many different areas. Some, like the *Mt Anne Circuit, Huon Track, Creepy Crawly Walk, Eastern Arthurs Traverse, Western Arthurs Traverse, Lake Judd Track* and *Needles Track,* are best accessed from the Strathgordon side of the park, while the *Port Davey Track* leaves from Melaleuca, and the best-known of them all, the *South Coast Track,* is accessed from either Melaleuca (by flight) or Cockle Creek. This multi-day hike follows the coast, heading over the Ironbounds and through the button-grass plains to the summer home of the Orange-bellied Parrot.

Fees & Permits
Park-entry permits must be purchased for all of Tasmania's national parks. Additional fees are payable for camping in them.

Facilities
Due to the remoteness of the park most facilities are associated with roads and not available beyond the start of walking tracks, but include picnic facilities, toilets, barbeques, camping, caving, swimming, fishing, kayaking, boating (Lake Pedder and Lake Gordon) snorkelling, scenic drives and flights.

Services Nearby
There are no services in proximity to the park. Cockle Creek and Maydena have very limited services but should be contacted if help is required.

NORTHERN TERRITORY

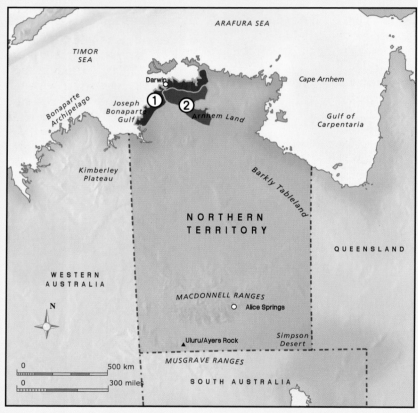

1. Darwin Coastal 2. Pine Creek

State Overview

The Northern Territory lies in the centre of Australia's north. It is the largest of Australia's two mainland territories, the other being the Australian Capital Territory. It has a population of just under 250,000 people, about 27 per cent of them of Aboriginal or Torres Strait Islander descent. Its landscape ranges from the arid deserts of its southern regions to the lush tropical wetlands and monsoon vine forests (rainforests) in the north.

Berry Springs

Pitjantjatjara and Yankunytjatjara (APY) people, and forms part of the traditional belief system of one of the oldest human societies in the world. Climbing Uluru was banned in 2019.

The Northern Territory covers an area of 1,347,787.62km² and comprises 20 bioregions. The largest of these are the arid desert bioregions of Tanami (229,811.37km²), Great Sandy Desert (112,587km²) and Simpson Strzelecki Dunefields (105,747.62km²). The Territory's 105 reserves protect 146,967.53km², including about 2,600km2 of monsoon vine forest. Its Kakadu National Park is listed on the UNESCO World Heritage List of areas with natural and/or cultural values of global significance. Uluru-Kata Tjuta National Park is also on the list.

The Northern Territory's capital city, Darwin, is located on the northern coastline. It was named in 1839 after Charles Darwin, the well-known English naturalist, although it was not proclaimed as a city until 1959. Before European settlement in 1869, the Darwin region was home to the Aboriginal people of the Larrakia language group, who lived off of the land and from the sea, as well as trading with south-east Asia. The tropical climate and 'small' city atmosphere of Darwin make it a popular visitor destination.

Australia's largest monolith, Uluru, is located in the Alice Springs region of the Territory's far south. This giant sandstone structure rises to a height of 348m above the surrounding ground (863m above sea level) and has a perimeter distance of 9.4km. Uluru is sacred to the Aboriginal Anangu,

Nitmiluk National Park

Darwin Coastal

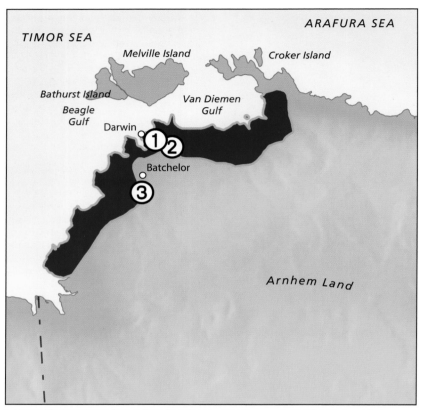

1. Howard Springs Nature Park 2. Fogg Dam Conservation Reserve 3. Litchfield National Park

More than 2,300 animal species and over 2,700 described plant and fungi species have been recorded in this bioregion, which covers 28,431.99km². Currently 8,282.33km² (29.13 per cent) of it is protected in about 27 protected areas, although some of these have not been formally gazetted. The main conservation areas that form part of this bioregion are Kakadu National Park, Litchfield National Park, Mary River National Park (proposed) and Nitmiluk National Park. The bioregion's fauna list includes about 320 birds, 90 mammals, 150 reptiles and 30 frogs. More than 2,200 plant taxa have also been recorded. The main land-use activity is farming and about 25 per cent of the bioregion has been subject to grazing.

Buley Rockholes, Litchfield National Park

The climate of the Darwin Coastal bioregion is tropical monsoonal, and has a distinct wet and dry season. High temperatures occur throughout the year and average annual rainfall exceeds 1,350mm.

Bushfires are a feature of the Northern Territory dry season (mainly in March–October). The territory has the most frequent vegetation fires of any part of the Australian continent, and although 90 per cent of vegetation fires typically burn less than 1ha each, single intense fires have burnt up to 9,000km² in the past decade. Weed species like the Gamba Grass *Andropogon gayanus,* which was introduced to the Northern Territory in 1931 as a potential pasture crop, is spreading through the north-west Top End. It increases fuel loads and, consequently, changes fire trends.

The Mimosa *Mimosa pigra* is also a major weed in regional areas of the Darwin Coastal bioregion. Extensive weed-management programmes undertaken over the past two decades have reduced its occurrence.

Key Species

BIRDS

Arafura Fantail, Australian Masked Owl, Australasian Figbird, Azure Kingfisher, Bar-shouldered Dove, Black-banded Fruit-dove, Brown Honeyeater, Cicadabird, Dusky Myzomela, Great Bowerbird, Green Oriole, Green-backed Gerygone, Grey Shrikethrush, Grey Whistler, Northern Fantail, Olive-backed Oriole, Orange-footed Scrubfowl, Pacific Baza, Pacific Emerald Dove, Peaceful Dove, Rainbow Pitta, Red-winged Parrot, Rose-crowned Fruit-dove, Rufous Fantail, Rufous Owl, Shining Flycatcher, Spangled Drongo, Torresian Imperial Pigeon, Varied Triller.

MAMMALS

Agile Wallaby, Arnhem Land Rock-rat, Arnhem Leaf-nosed Bat, Arnhem Long-eared Bat, Black Flying-fox, Brush-tailed Phascogale, Common Planigale, Delicate Mouse, Dusky Leaf-nosed Bat, Gould's Wattled Bat, Grassland Melomys, Hoary Wattled Bat, Large Bent-winged Bat, Little Red Flying-fox, Northern Blossom-bat, Northern Brown Bandicoot, Northern Free-tailed Bat, Rock Ring-tailed Possum, Water Rat.

REPTILES

Brown Tree Snake, Burton's Legless Lizard, Bynoe's Gecko, Carpet Python, Common Tree Snake, Northern Bandy-bandy, Northern Bar-lipped Skink, Northern Dtella, Northern Giant Cave Gecko, Shaded-litter Rainbow-skink, Slaty-grey Snake, Spotted Tree Monitor, Zigzag Velvet Gecko.

AMPHIBIANS

Copland's Rock Frog, Green Tree Frog, Masked Frog, Northern Territory Frog, Ornate Burrowing Frog, Rockhole Frog, Roth's Tree Frog.

INVERTEBRATES

Atlas Moth, Blue Tiger, Caper Gull, Chrome Awl, Dark Ciliated-blue, Glasswing, Green Mantid, Green Tree Ant, Pale-blue Triangle, Purple Cerulean, Shining Oak-blue, Two-brand Crow.

Lemon-bellied Flycatcher at Fogg Dam Conservation Reserve

Darwin Coastal

Tourism Australia

Peter Rowland

Northern Fantail *Rhipidura rufiventris*

Peter Rowland

Also known as the Timor Fantail, this species has a large range that includes Australia, Papua New Guinea and Indonesia. In Australia it is found in lowland tropical and subtropical forests, dense vine thickets, mangrove fringes and some woodland from northwestern Western Australia to northeastern Queensland. Unlike other fantails it does not display the typical fanned tail and constant activity; instead the tail is squarish and the bird sits motionless for periods of time between foraging flights. The plumage is grey to blackish above, with a small whitish eyebrow, cream belly and white vent. The breast is paler grey with numerous vertical 'tear-drop' streaks, and the throat is white.

Orange-footed Scrubfowl *Megapodius reinwardt*

Angus McNab

This large, mainly terrestrial bird is easily identified by its bright orange legs and feet, brown back and wings, and dark slate-grey head, neck and underparts. The head has a small brown crest. Its calls consist of a combination of loud clucks and screams. Although it is the smallest of the megapodes found in Australia, this species builds the largest incubation mound, up to 3m high and 7m wide. The mound is used to incubate the eggs that are laid beneath the rotting vegetation matter, and after hatching the newborn chicks must fend for themselves. Inhabiting rainforests and dense vine forests, individuals defend exclusive feeding territories but several pairs may use the same incubation mound.

Rainbow Pitta *Pitta iris*

This colourful, ground-dwelling bird with a short, square tail is readily identified. It is black on the face, black and brown on the crown, black on the neck, breast and flanks, and green on the back and wings. The wings also have a blue patch and a large white patch (visible in flight). Immature birds and adults have red on the lower belly and undertail, while juveniles are yellowish. This species is sedentary in the monsoon vine forest, riverine scrubs and mangroves of northern Western Australia and the Northern Territory's Top End. No other pittas regularly occur within this range. The call is a pair of double-whistles, *tewo-whit teo-whit,* and a short *keow* is given in alarm. The short sequence of footsteps of birds foraging for earthworms in the leaf litter readily draws attention.

Angus McNab

Rufous Owl *Ninox rufa*

This large owl is dark rufous-brown above, barred paler and orange-buff below, with conspicuous darker reddish-brown horizontal barring; the tail is broadly barred. It is found in northern Australia and Papua New Guinea, and it roosts by day among the dense foliage of rainforests. At night it forages in more open habitats for mammals, birds and large insects, and can travel up to 4km when hunting. Its large talons and powerful feet are able to catch and subdue quite large prey. Its call is a drawn-out *whooo-hoo,* which is most often given at the onset of the breeding season. Rufous Owls pair for life and maintain a territory throughout the year. Two young are typically raised in a year and eggs are laid in a hollow tree.

John Harris

Brown Tree Snake *Boiga irregularis*

Anders Zimny

Slender, with a narrow neck, distinct head and bulging yellow eyes with vertical pupils, this snake occurs in two distinct colour patterns. Eastern Australian individuals are orange to reddish-brown above with irregular dark cross-bands on the back and sides, and cream or orange underparts. Northern Australian individuals are cream above and below, with bold reddish-brown bands. The species is distributed through coastal and subcoastal northern and eastern Australia, from the Kimberley region, Western Australia, through the northern Northern Territory, and northern and eastern Queensland, south to Sydney, New South Wales. It occurs in a broad range of habitats, including open forests, rainforests, mangroves, rock escarpments, coastal heaths and urban areas. It is nocturnal and arboreal, sheltering coiled up in tree hollows, caves and buildings by day, but may also hunt on the ground. It preys mainly on birds, and also birds' eggs, reptiles, frogs and small mammals.

Bynoe's Gecko *Heteronotia binoei*

Angus McNab

Commonly found in a variety of wooded habitats, this large-headed lizard occurs in most of Australia, being absent only from the south-east and south-west. It is nocturnal, sheltering by day in crevices or under rocks or logs, hunting during the night for insects and small invertebrates. Its bumpy skin, which gives rise to its alternative common name of Common Prickly Gecko, can vary in colouration from grey to brown, and is liberally covered in dark and pale flecks, which can merge together to form broad stripes. Its tail is long and cylindrical, and its toes are slim with non-expandable pads. This species is considered to be part of a largely unexplored species complex.

Rockhole Frog *Litoria meiriana*

This small, agile frog differs from most other Australian species by being mainly active by day. Its bumpy skin is mottled grey or brown above, depending on the colour of the rock substrate it occurs on; the limbs are irregularly banded. Some individuals are reddish-tan with a yellow stripe. The underparts are white to cream. It occurs from the Arnhem Plateau of the northern Northern Territory across and into the Kimberley region of Western Australia, where it is restricted to rocky gorges with permanent or seasonal watercourses. It presumably feeds on invertebrates. Its call is a rapidly repeated *pop-pop-pop-pop-pop*. The female lays about 60 eggs, and tadpoles take about four weeks to become frogs after hatching.

Angus McNab

Roth's Tree Frog *Litoria rothii*

The colouration of this tree frog varies, but is usually cream to tan by day, and dark brown with black speckling, giving a mottled appearance, at night. The webbing on the hands, the insides of the thighs, and the rear of the legs are bright yellow and black. The upper part of the eye is bright red. The back has tiny 'wart-like' bumps. Found from Maryborough, Queensland, across northern Australia, to the Kimberley region, Western Australia, the species occurs in watered areas in a range of habitats, including rainforests and wet coastal forests, but shows a preference for cane fields and pandanus, where it feeds on invertebrates. The male's call, a series of closely spaced *arc*s, slowing towards the end of the call, is given from floating vegetation, on emergent plants or shrubs surrounding a waterbody.

Angus McNab

Blue Tiger *Tirumala hamata*

John Tann (CC)

Adults of this butterfly are black with numerous conspicuous pale blue streaks and blotches. Caterpillars are grey with horizontal bands of black and orange, and with pairs of long, fleshy filaments front and back. The head is black and white. The species is found mainly in northwestern Western Australia, the northern Northern Territory and eastern Queensland, but adults disperse in spring to other areas, including eastern New South Wales and northeastern Victoria. It inhabits rainforests and vine thickets, where adults feed on the Monkey Rope Vine *Parsonia straminea,* and obtain pyrrolizidine alkaloids (mainly males) from plants such as the Blue Heliotrope *Heliotropium amplexicaule.* The eggs are laid on members of the dogbane family (Apocynaceae), particularly the Corky Milk Vine *Secamone elliptica.*

Chrome Awl *Hasora chromus*

Bernard DuPont (CC)

Adults of this butterfly are brownish with a white band across the underside of each hindwing. Females have a pair of transparent spots on each forewing. Caterpillars are pinkish-brown to greenish, with longitudinal white stripes, sparse white hairs and black spots along the sides. The species is patchily distributed in coastal and near-coastal areas of New South Wales, Queensland, the Northern Territory and northern Western Australia. Also in India, Japan, New Guinea and Taiwan. It occurs in rainforests and vine thickets, where adults actively feed from flowers and hang upside down below leaves when at rest. Caterpillars feed on the leaves of the pea *Millettia pinnata,* and construct shelters of folded leaves within which to feed and pupate.

Pale-blue Triangle *Graphium eurypylus*

Garry Sanbowski (CC)

In adult butterflies the outer margins of the upperwing surfaces are black with numerous pale spots and blotches, forming a single row towards the outer edge. The inner panels are pale and broken into separate blotches on the forewings. The undersurface of the wings is paler but similarly patterned, and with red markings on the bases and subterminal edges of the hindwings. The sexes are similar in size but females are slightly larger. The species is found in a broad coastal band from northeastern New South Wales to northern Queensland, and from northwestern Queensland, through the northern Northern Territory, to northern Western Australia, but migrates further south to southeastern New South Wales and the Australian Capital Territory. It typically occurs in drier vine thickets and the fringes of adjacent rainforests, where adults are most active in the canopy area.

Shining Oak-blue *Arhopala micale*

Donald Hobern (CC)

In adult butterflies the upperwing surface is electric dark blue with a black margin; females are lighter than males and with a thicker margin. The underside of the wing is brown with bands of light and dark markings, some edged in white. There is a short 'sword' on the hindwing. The species is distributed through the tropical Northern Territory and Queensland, and further north through Torres Strait Islands, Papua New Guinea and Indonesia. It is locally common in wet forested areas, from rainforest to littoral forest, where individuals use a wide variety of native host plants, including lilly-pillies *Syzygium* spp. and the Cottonwood *Hibiscus tiliaceus*. The caterpillars are attended by Green Tree Ants (p. 347), which protect them as they feed in the open by day. Adults fly fast and low.

Howard Springs Nature Park

Howard Springs Nature Park was the Northern Territory's first reserve, declared in 1957. Before then the site served as a recreation area for Australian and American Second World War service personnel. The weir was constructed in 1944 to improve access to the waterhole for swimming. The park provides easy access to lush monsoon vine forest that is just a short drive from the state's capital city of Darwin. Permanent water is present within the rainforest, although it is surrounded by savannah grassland and can be affected by fires from time to time. The park is located in the traditional homelands of the Larrakia people and contains one documented sacred site. Its permanent natural spring emerges at the head of an area of monsoon vine forest and would no doubt have been of significant importance to the local Aboriginal people. The water flows year round, but slows during the dry season.

This small (2.83km²) reserve is home to about 175 bird species, including Orange-footed Scrubfowl, Rainbow Pitta and Shining Flycatcher.

Thirteen mammal species have been recorded in the park, including the Agile Wallaby, Black Flying-fox,

Thomas Rowland

Aerial view of the nature park following Cyclone Marcus in 2018

Common Brush-tailed Possum, Little Red Flying-fox, Northern Brown Bandicoot and Critically Endangered Northern Quoll.

Of the 15 amphibians recorded here, notable ones include Copland's Rock Frog and the Green Tree Frog and Roth's Tree Frog.

The park is also home to 34 reptile and 17 fish species. Look in the large pools for the Barramundi, Arafura File Snake, Mertens' Water Monitor, Northern Snake-necked Turtle, Northern Snapping Turtle and Yellow-faced Turtle.

GPS Coordinates
-12.46161, 131.05090

Getting There
The park is located 27km south of Darwin off the Stuart Highway. Turn on to Howard Springs Road. Darwin has an international airport that is serviced daily from all major Australian airports and Indonesia. Darwin is also serviced by rail from Alice Springs and Adelaide.

Tracks & Trails
Spring Walk (100m, one way) is an easy stroll through lush monsoon vine forest. It is one of the most reliable places to see the Rainbow Pitta close to Darwin. *Howard Creek Walk* (1.8km, loop) follows the spring-fed Howard Creek through the park. It is an easy walk, suitable for all fitness levels, and passes through a range of vegetation types. Note that the park was affected by Tropical Cyclone Marcus in March 2018 and a lot of the vegetation along the walking tracks was severely damaged.

Fees & Permits
The park is open year round, normally between 7.30 a.m. and 7.00 p.m. each day, and has free entry.

Facilities
Picnic areas, free barbecues, swimming (including toddler pool), playground and toilets. Wheelchair access. Camping is not permitted in the park.

Services Nearby
Camping and self-contained accommodation is available at Howard Springs Big 4 (4km), and there is a tavern and restaurant within walking distance of there. Palmerston (11km) has all essential services, including retail outlets, cafes, restaurants, health services, hotels, mechanical services and a bus service to Darwin.

Fogg Dam Conservation Reserve

The Fogg Dam Conservation Reserve is located 69km east of Darwin near the township of Humpty Doo, and between the Adelaide River and Mary River floodplains. The reserve forms part of the traditional lands of the Wulna people. The 2.2km-long dam was constructed by the RAAF Airfield Construction Squadron in the 1950s to provide water to irrigate the local rice fields of Humpty Doo, although the farming of rice was short-lived in the area. The importance of the dam to waterbirds and other wildlife was recognized shortly afterwards and the dam was declared a Bird Protection Area in 1959, before becoming established as a conservation area in 1982. In 2005 the wider Adelaide and Mary River Floodplains were recognized as an Important Bird Area, and in the same year the traditional owners were given joint management (with the Northern Territory Government) of the conservation reserve. In May 2009 Fogg dam was declared a heritage site.

The conservation area now covers an area of 15.69km². Although the area of monsoon vine forest that is protected within it is quite small, the site is a must for anyone who wants to

Peter Rowland

Aerial view looking back over Beatrice Lagoon towards Fogg Dam Conservation Reserve

get easy access to a site that has a rich number of rainforest species.

The protected wetland is a haven for birdlife, with more than 220 species recorded here. The wetlands are located in the Adelaide River Floodplain and are a permanent water source for the region's wildlife, and a vital refuge as other smaller lagoons and waterways dry out.

Estuarine Crocodiles occur in the park, so always be aware of this and obey all signs. Pedestrians are not permitted to walk along the dam wall. Biting insects are also prevalent and can spread disease, including Ross River Virus, Barmah Forest Virus, Dengue Fever and Zika Virus.

GPS Coordinates
-12.55760,131.29647

Getting There
The reserve is accessed via the Arnhem Highway, about 69km east of Darwin. Darwin has an international airport that is serviced daily from all major Australian airports and Indonesia. Darwin is also serviced by rail from Alice Springs and Adelaide. Note that the best time of year to visit is December–July, although access can be difficult at the height of the wet season.

Tracks & Trails
Monsoon Forest Walk (2 km, return) is an easy walk through monsoon vine forest, paperbark forest and on to the floodplains (parts of the walk have been closed due to fire damage). Bird species to look out for include the Dusky Myzomela, Green Oriole, Lemon-bellied Flycatcher, Northern Fantail, Orange-footed Scrubfowl, Rainbow Pitta and Rose-crowned Fruit-dove. The Agile Wallaby, Black Flying-fox, Dusky Rat, Northern Blossom-bat and Northern Quoll have also been recorded here.

Fees & Permits
The reserve is open year round, but may be closed during periods of excessive rain or high bushfire risk. Entry is free.

Facilities
Shaded and unshaded picnic tables, comfortable viewing areas with seating and wheelchair accessible toilets are provided.

Services Nearby
Nearby Humpty Doo has most services, including fuel, vehicle repairs and servicing, cafe, supermarket and medical clinic. Palmerston Hospital is the closest hospital.

Litchfield National Park

This park was gazetted in 1986 and is perhaps most famed for the incredible 1–4m-tall mounds constructed by some the park's smallest inhabitants, Magnetic (or Compass) Termites *Amitermes meridionalis*. The mounds are all oriented in the same direction, with the wide, flattened walls facing east and west, in order to receive the warmth of the morning and afternoon sun, and the north, south and top edges are kept thin to minimize heat retention. Other conspicuous invertebrate structures that are visible in the park include the enormous mounds of the Cathedral Termite *Nasutitermes triodiae* and the ball-shaped leaf nests of Green Tree Ant colonies.

The park covers an area of about 1,456km², most of which is sandstone plateaus, melaleuca woodland and alluvial plains, but it also contains an area of monsoon vine forest. It is part of the Wagait traditional indigenous lands and is important to the Koongurrukun, Mak Mak, Marranunggu, Warray and Werat Aborignal people.

About 180 birds, 52 mammals, 80 reptiles and 22 frogs have been recorded in the park.

In addition to the incredible fauna, the park features stunning waterfalls, crystal-clear swimming holes and

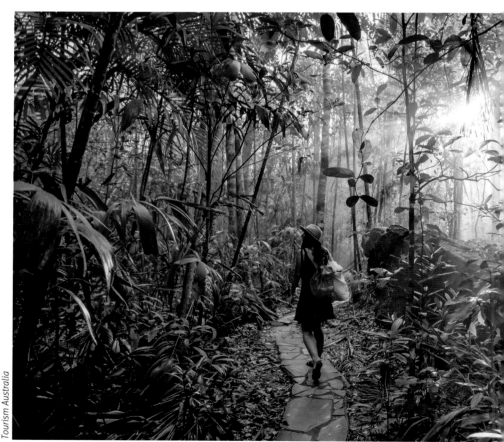

Tourism Australia

Florence Falls Walk

numerous walking tracks. Florence Falls is a spectacular twin waterfall surrounded by monsoon vine forest and is a great spot to enjoy the local wildlife and cool off with a swim.

Estuarine Crocodiles occur in the park, so always be be alert for them and only swim where permitted and signposted.

Scrub typhus is transmitted by microscopic bush mites on grasses and bushes, so sitting on bare ground or grass is discouraged.

GPS Coordinates
-13.25693, 130.84889

Getting There
The park is located 120km south-west of Darwin (via Batchelor). Follow the Stuart Highway south from Darwin (or north from Adelaide River), and take the Batchelor Road turn-off. The park is also accessible via the Cox Peninsula Road (dry season only) and the Reynolds Track (four-wheel drive vehicles).

Tracks & Trails
Shady Creek and Florence Falls Walk (2km, return) is an easy walk, although there are 160 stairs along the way. It passes through cool monsoon vine forest and open woodland. Look out for the Mertens Water Monitor *Varanus mertensi*. This semi-aquatic lizard is a strong swimmer and is seldom found far from water. *Wangi Falls Walk* (1.6km, return) starts at the Wangi plunge pool and passes through monsoon vine forest on the way to the viewing platform at the top of the escarpment. The walk is steep in some sections and has a number of stairs along the way. The Bar-shouldered Dove and Brown Honeyeater are among the more conspicuous rainforest birds along this walk.

Fees & Permits
The park is open year round and has free entry, but camping fees apply.

Facilities
These include camping (Florence Falls, Wangi Falls), kiosk and cafe (Wangi Centre, Wangi Falls), picnic facilities, barbecues, fire pits, swimming holes (there are a number of these designated through the park, but they may be closed after heavy rains), toilets, hot showers, public phone and emergency call devices.

Services Nearby
Batchelor has accommodation, fuel, shops, restaurants, medical clinic, police station, post office and other essential services.

Pine Creek

1. Kakadu National Park 2. Nitmiluk National Park

Some 4,600 species of described plant, animal and fungi have been recorded in the 28,517.77km² that this bioregion covers, including more than 275 bird species, 80 mammals, 145 reptiles and about 35 frogs. The bioregion contains sections of two of the Northern Territory's most popular tourism destinations: the 2,920km² Nitmiluk National Park and the much larger (almost 20,000km²) Kakadu National Park. In fact, 12,160.38km² (42.64 per cent) of this bioregion is held across the eight current and one proposed protection areas. In addition to Kakadu and Nitmiluk National Parks, the other main conservation areas are Litchfield National Park and Mary River National Park (proposed), which borders Kakadu National Park to the east.

Edith Falls

The climate in the bioregion is tropical, with two distinct seasons. The 'dry' season (May–October) receives an average rainfall of 75mm, most of it in May–October. The tropical summer 'wet' season (November–April) sees large amounts of rain falling on the region, with the wettest month typically being January, although 1,141.6mm of rainfall was recorded in March 2007. The driest month is typically June, with a long-term average of 1mm. The temperature is less variable, with average maximums of just under 32 °C in the coolest month (June) and just under 38 °C in the hottest month (October).

The bioregion consists largely of rugged ridges and undulating plains, with scattered patches of monsoon vine forests. The major land uses outside conservation areas include grazing (about 40 per cent), horticulture and mining. The major population centres are Adelaide River, Batchelor, Jabiru and Pine Creek.

Key Species

BIRDS

Arafura Fantail, Australian Masked Owl, Australasian Figbird, Azure Kingfisher, Bar-shouldered Dove, Black Butcherbird, Black-banded Fruit-dove, Brown Honeyeater, Brush Cuckoo, Cicadabird, Dusky Myzomela, Great Bowerbird, Green Oriole, Green-backed Gerygone, Grey Whistler, Northern Fantail, Olive-backed Oriole, Orange-footed Scrubfowl, Pacific Baza, Pacific Emerald Dove, Peaceful Dove, Rainbow Pitta, Red-winged Parrot, Rose-crowned Fruit-dove, Rufous Owl, Shining Flycatcher, Spangled Drongo, Torresian Imperial Pigeon, Varied Triller.

MAMMALS

Agile Wallaby, Arnhem Land Rock-rat, Arnhem Long-eared Bat, Black Flying-fox, Brush-tailed Phascogale, Common Planigale, Delicate Mouse, Dusky Leaf-nosed Bat, Eastern Long-eared Bat, Golden-backed Tree-rat, Gould's Wattled Bat, Grassland Melomys, Hoary Wattled Bat, Large Bent-winged Bat, Little Red Flying-fox, Northern Blossom-bat, Northern Brown Bandicoot, Rock Ring-tailed Possum, Short-beaked Echidna, Water Rat.

REPTILES

Brown Tree Snake, Burton's Legless Lizard, Bynoe's Gecko, Common Tree Snake, Estuarine Crocodile, Northern Bandy-bandy, Northern Giant Cave Gecko, Oenpelli Rock Python, Shaded-litter Rainbow-skink, Spotted Tree Monitor, Zigzag Velvet Gecko.

AMPHIBIANS

Australian Woodfrog, Green Tree Frog, Masked Frog, Northern Territory Frog, Ornate Burrowing Frog, Rockhole Frog, Roth's Tree Frog.

INVERTEBRATES

Blue Tiger, Caper Gull, Chrome Awl, Dark Ciliated-blue, Dingy Bush-brown, Fuscous Swallowtail, Glasswing, Green Mantid, Green Tree Ant, Pale-blue Triangle, Purple Cerulean, Purple Oak-blue, Shining Oak-Blue, Two-brand Crow.

Peaceful Dove

Black-banded Fruit-dove *Ptilinopus alligator*

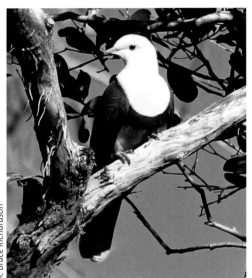

R. Bruce Richardson

The white head and neck, contrasting black back and wings, and coral-pink legs and feet of this bird make it hard to confuse with any other species in its range. The tail is black with a grey tip and the underparts are grey, with the exception of the black breast-band from which its common name is derived. The common call is a low, booming *coo*. The species is endemic to Australia, where it is restricted to gully rainforests on sandstone escarpments in western Arnhem Land, and is largely sedentary within this range. Food consists of rainforest fruits. Breeding takes place in May–September, with a single egg laid in a stick nest.

Black Butcherbird *Melloria quoyi*

Angus McNab

The Black Butcherbird is almost entirely deep bluish-black, except for the large, silver-grey bill with a black tip. The species has a large range. Three subspecies are found in Australia, from the western Northern Territory to the Gulf of Carpentaria, in northern Queensland, from Cape York Peninsula to Cooktown, and from Cooktown to around Mackay, Queensland. It is also found in Papua New Guinea and Indonesia. The species inhabits rainforests and mangroves, including adjacent parkland and urban gardens, where it is diurnal and largely sedentary, with pairs occupying permanent territories. Food consists of lizards, small birds and their eggs, mammals, crustaceans and insects, and the birds also scavenge. Breeding takes place early in the wet season; both sexes perform nest-building and incubation duties and both feed the young.

Dusky Myzomela *Myzomela obscura*

The Dusky Myzomela is darker than similar honeyeaters and lacks their pale face markings or yellowish wing-patches. The sexes are similar in plumage, being brown with a reddish wash. The bill is slender and sickle shaped, the eye is black and there is a darker patch around the eye. The legs and feet are brown. This species occurs in tropical northern Australia and further north to Papua New Guinea and the Moluccas, where it frequents lowland and monsoonal rainforests and similarly dense habitats, but also shows a preference for eucalypt woodland. It feeds primarily within the canopy on nectar, supplemented with invertebrates, but nestlings are fed largely on nectar. Breeding has been recorded in all months in Australia. The primary call is a repeated mournful whistle.

Peter Rowland

Torresian Imperial Pigeon *Ducula spilorrhoa*

This large pigeon is striking. It has predominantly white plumage, contrasted with black on the flight feathers and lower half of the tail, and some spotting on the thighs and lower ventral area. In Australia, it is found in coastal and subcoastal rainforests and mangroves of the north and north-east, from the Kimberley, Western Australia, to around Rockhampton, Queensland, but it is most numerous in the far north. Food consists

Angus McNab

of fruits, which are plucked from within the canopy area of trees. The birds must drink daily and descend in continuous streams to waterholes to drink late in the afternoon. The most familiar call is a deep *coo-hoo,* which can be heard from quite a distance.

Arnhem Long-eared Bat *Nyctophilus arnhemensis*

Anders Zimny

The fur of this bat is brown to reddish-brown above, darker on the bases of the hairs, and paler on the underside. The head is blunt. The species ranges through tropical northern Australia, including offshore islands, from Exmouth, Western Australia, through the northern Northern Territory, to far northwestern Queensland. It lives in rainforests, forests, open grassy woodland and mangroves. It roosts by day under loose bark or in dense foliage, emerging at dusk to forage slowly among dense vegetation mainly for insects, including beetles and termites, and some spiders. The species shares its range with the similar Pygmy Long-eared Bat *N. walkeri,* which has shorter ears and more contrast between the colour of the back and belly, and the larger Pallid Long-eared Bat *N. daedalus.*

Little Red Flying-fox *Pteropus scapulatus*

John Harris

The fur of this flying-fox is pale brown to rich reddish-brown, often becoming more greyish on the head, and occasionally with a yellowish patch on the neck and shoulders. The exposed skin is reddish-brown, and the wings are largely transparent in flight. The species occurs in a broad coastal and inland band (including several islands) from central Victoria, through New South Wales, Queensland, the Northern Territory, and Kimberley region, Western Australia, becoming more coastal in western Western Australia. It lives in various habitats, from semi-arid woodland to rainforests and paperbark swamps, feeding at night mainly on nectar and pollen, supplemented with fruits, sap and some insects. It roosts by day in large camps, often of several hundred thousand individuals, close to riparian zones such as rivers and creeks. Individuals roost in clusters very close together compared with other larger bats. It is generally nomadic, responding to food availability, and readily roosts with other fruit-bat species.

Northern Blossom-bat *Macroglossus minimus*

Australia's smallest fruit bat (<7cm), this species has pale reddish-brown fur, paler on the belly, with males having a pink 'V'-shaped gland on the chest. The snout is long and pointed, and the tail is short, with a small flap of skin from the base to the ankles. The bat occurs throughout tropical northern Australia, including offshore islands, from northwestern Western Australia, through the northern Northern Territory, to Cape York Peninsula, Queensland. It lives in wet monsoon forests and woodland, bamboo thickets and paperbark swamps, where it typically roosts during the day alone or in small groups within dense foliage. At night it feeds mainly on nectar and pollen, supplemented with some fruits, normally after landing, but can also feed while hovering.

Anders Zimny

Northern Giant Cave Gecko
Pseudothecadactylus lindneri

This is a large, cave-dwelling gecko. It is dark purplish-brown above, variably marked with indistinct yellowish to pale cream cross-bands on the body and blotches on the head. The head can be similar in colour to the body, or paler with darker bands, and has large ear openings. The tail is long, rounded and generally thick, with a specialized prehensile tip. The original tail is ringed with dark brown and yellowish-cream, but once lost it is uniformly brown. It feeds on insects and other invertebrates, and occasionally other geckos, and is also known to lick nectar from flowers. It inhabits sandstone escarpments in western Arnhem Land, Northern Territory, which support a range of rainforest assemblages. It is most active in the evening.

Angus McNab

319

Oenpelli Rock Python *Simalia oenpelliensis*

Scott Eipper

This large, slender snake was first described in 1977. Generally dark olive-brown, the upper surface is patterned with darker blotches, and the underparts are cream to yellow. Occurring in sandstone outcrops, it utilizes rocky crevices, tree hollows and caves. It can occur in dense vegetation (including monsoon vine forest), woodland, heathland and open rock surfaces in western Arnhem Land, and hunts both arboreally and terrestrially for medium to large mammals and birds. It can remain motionless for extended periods as it waits for prey to come within striking range. In the traditional Kunwinjku language, the species is called *Nawaran*. Populations of this elusive species are affected by altered fire regimes and changes in structure and extent of vegetation, which reduce the availability of prey species.

Shaded-litter Rainbow-skink *Carlia munda*

Angus McNab

This is a robust skink with highly variable colouration. It is brown to greyish-brown with light dashes and dark spots above, and has a narrow white stripe running from the snout to the top of the ear, and another from the bottom of the ear to the forelimb. Sexually active males have a greenish wash on the head, blue throat and orange-red sides. The underparts are whitish. The forelimbs have four digits and the hindlimbs five. The species is distributed through northern Australia, from the north-east Western Australia coast, through the Northern Territory, to northern and eastern Queensland, where it can be found in dry forests, woodland, rainforest margins, mangroves, shrubland and sandy grassland. It is terrestrial, and can be seen foraging among leaf and ground litter, feeding on small invertebrates, waving its tail.

Spotted Tree Monitor *Varanus scalaris*

This is a moderately robust, largely arboreal goanna, with a medium-length, cylindrical tail that has strongly keeled scales on the top and sides. It is generally dark grey, brown or blackish above, with large, dark-centred cream spots that form irregular transverse bands on the back and most of the tail, and numerous smaller creamish or yellowish spots and flecks. The remainder of the tail is blackish. The head normally has a blackish stripe from the back of the eye to above the ear. The belly is whitish. The species is distributed through northern Australia, from the Kimberley region, Western Australia, through the northern Northern Territory, to northern Queensland, where it is found in rainforests, forests and grassy woodland. It is arboreal, but hunts both on the ground and in trees for small lizards, frogs, invertebrates and nestling birds, seeking the safety of trees when disturbed and sheltering at night in tree-holes or under loose bark.

Angus McNab

Zigzag Velvet Gecko *Amalosia rhombifer*

This gecko is rich brown above, peppered with darker and paler brown speckles on the sides and limbs, and whitish below. The upper surface of the flattened body displays the broad 'zigzag' cream to brown band that gives the species its common name. The fingers and toes have distinctive pads and the third and fourth toes lack basal webbing in between. Largely arboreal in dry rainforests, woodland, rocky areas and urban areas, the species shelters by day under the loose bark of trees, within hollows, under leaf litter and in buildings. It occurs throughout northern Australia and with an outlying population in Alice Springs. The species is part of an unexplored species complex.

Angus McNab

321

Green Tree Frog *Litoria caerulea*

The colouration of this tree frog varies, although it is typically light to dark green, but can be brown or on rare occasions completely blue. Some individuals are a solid colour, while others show varying amounts of white flecks and blotches. The back is smooth, without bumps or protrusions. Found from New South Wales to Western Australia, the species occurs in a wide range of habitats, from rainforests and forests to grassland and deserts, as well as urban environments. It is mostly found around waterbodies, both natural and artificial, including roadside ditches and dams, as well as pools beside rivers, streams and creeks. It feeds on invertebrates and small vertebrates, including frogs, but has also been recorded eating small snakes, geckos and bats. The male's call is a deep, resonating *brawwk*.

Masked Frog *Litoria personata*

The colouration of this smooth-skinned frog is highly variable and can be plain, pale brown to grey, with or without bright yellow flanks, or mottled with faint blotching. A dark stripe extends from the snout, along the side to just above the front legs. The underparts are whitish. The species is restricted to the sandstone gorges and hills of the western Arnhem region, Northern Territory, where it occurs in seasonal creeks, springs and pools of rainwater in sandstone hills, but is also found among sedges and reeds along permanent water. It feeds on invertebrates. The male's call, a repeated *chirp*, sounding almost electrical in origin, is made while perched on rock faces.

Northern Territory Frog *Austrochaperina adelphe*

This tiny reddish to yellowish-brown frog often has darker longitudinal markings and numerous white flecks, and typically a dark stripe from the snout to past the shoulder. Some individuals have grey flanks. The underparts are white to cream. It is found in the Top End region of the Northern Territory, including offshore islands, occurring in swamps, monsoon forests and wet areas of open forests and feeding at night on invertebrates. The male's call, a short, repeated *beep*, similar to a warning from a smoke detector, is made from beneath leaf litter. The female lays about 12 eggs, which are guarded by the male until the small frogs hatch.

Angus McNab

Glasswing *Acraea andromacha*

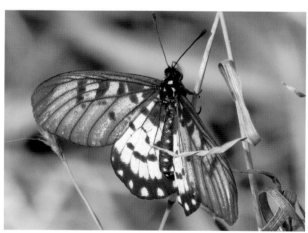

The forewings of this butterfly are translucent grey with some darker markings, while the hindwings are pale whitish with contrasting black veins and bands. The body is black with white markings, and the 'face' and legs are yellow. Caterpillars are orange with long, branched black projections over the body. The species is widespread across northern and eastern Australia, where it occurs in a variety of forested habitats, from rainforest margins to gardens. It utilizes native and introduced host plants in the passionflower (Passifloraceae) and violet (Violaceae) families. Adult males fly a couple metres from the ground in search of females, and may gather in numbers on hilltops, while females investigate possible host plants to lay eggs on.

John Tann (CC)

Kakadu National Park

This park lies at the junction of four Northern Territory bioregions: Arnhem Coastal, Darwin Coastal, Arnhem Plateau and Pine Creek. It is listed as a World Heritage Area with natural and/or cultural values of global significance, and is Australia's largest terrestrial national park, covering 20,000km². The national park was declared in three stages between 1979 and 1991. Kakadu includes the traditional lands of a number of Aboriginal clan groups, and the name Kakadu comes from an extinct local Aboriginal language, Gaagudju, which was spoken initially by the Gaagudju people and later by the Amurdak, Bininj, Giimiyu, Gundjeihmi and Umbugarla peoples. They have lived on this land for more than 65,000 years.

The habitat in the park is diverse, including coastal mangroves, rugged rocky sandstone escarpments, rainforests, open forests and woodland, and lowland wetlands. Depending on the availability of water the monsoon vine forest (rainforest) in Kakadu is either wet or dry, and ranges from tall (more than 30m) in the stone country to deciduous thickets in the coastal areas, which are often only 2–3m in height. The various habitats support about 281 species of bird, 77 mammals, 132 reptiles and 27 frogs.

Tourism Australia

Jim Jim Falls Walk

During the 'wet' season (November–April) huge amounts of water fall on the park, causing many of the watercourses to break their banks and form huge floodplains and turn trickling waterfalls into breathtaking cascades. The local Aboriginal people recognize six seasons: Gudjewg (December–March), Banggerreng (April), Yegge (May–mid-June), Wurrgeng (mid-June–mid-August), Gurrung (mid-August–mid-October) and Gunumeleng (mid-October–late December).

GPS Coordinates
-12.82145,131.96951 (Main entry)
-12.67100,132.81977 (Jabiru)

Getting There
From Darwin (250km) travel via the

Stuart Highway (35km) and Arnhem Highway. Darwin has an international airport that is serviced daily from all major Australian airports and Indonesia. It is also serviced via rail from Alice Springs and Adelaide. Car hire is available. Scenic flights also operate over the park.

Tracks & Trails
Mangarre Rainforest Walk (1.5km, loop) is a cluster of three short, easy loops through monsoon vine forest and along the East Alligator River (the first and shortest loop is wheelchair accessible). It is close to the Border Store, Cahills Crossing viewing platform and Merl camp ground. Make sure you observe all crocodile safety signs. Never enter or approach water where crocodiles are present.

Fees & Permits
Payment is required for entry to the park.

Facilities
A variety of accomodation styles is located in the park, including hotel style, camping and cabins. Numerous public toilets are found throughout Kakadu, including wheelchair-accessible toilets on Leichhardt Street and Tasman Crescent. Taps can be found at most camp grounds, but the water may not be suitable for drinking, so it is advisable to bring water with you.

Services Nearby
There are four main hubs in the park (Jabiru, South Alligator, Cooinda and Mary River Roadhouse), and each provides different levels of services. Jabiru is the largest, with fuel, supermarket, post office, bank, chemist, medical centre, restaurants, police and swimming pool. Other hubs have similar but less extensive services.

Nitmiluk National Park

Nitmiluk (Katherine Gorge) National Park covers an area of 2,950km². It is the traditional home of the Jawoyn people, and the name of the park translates as 'Cicada Place' in the Jawoyn language.

The climate in the region is tropical, with two distinct seasons: the 'dry' season (May–October) has an average monthly rainfall of 1–33mm, although up to 166mm has been recorded towards the end of the season. The 'wet' season (November–April) sees large amounts of rain falling on the region. The wettest month is January, with more than 265mm falling on average and a record high of 732mm.

The western section of the park surrounds a stretch of the Katherine River, and spectacular views of the river and surrounding area can be obtained from the walking trails and viewing platforms along the top of the gorge. The park contains patches of monsoon vine forest. It is mainly restricted to sandstone gorges, usually in areas protected from fire and associated with more permanent water.

Some 206 birds, 44 mammals, 78 reptiles and 25 frogs have been recorded in the park, as well as a huge number of invertebrates. About 1,400 plant species have been recorded, 19

Tourism Australia

Monsoon vine forest patches are mainly restricted to sandstone gorges near permanent water

of which are endemic to the park; 58 are not recorded in any other Northern Territory park.

Weeds such as the Gamba Grass *Andropogon gayanus* and Mission Grass *Pennisetum polystachion,* and feral animals, mainly the Domestic Cat, Cane Toad, Water Buffalo, Feral Pig, Feral Horse, donkey and cattle, pose a significant threat to the park's native fauna and flora.

GPS Coordinates
-13.25693, 130.84889

Getting There
The park is located 30km north-east of Katherine (four hours south of Darwin). Turn off the Stuart Highway and follow Giles Street and Gorge Road. Katherine

is on the Ghan train line and has its own airport.

Tracks & Trails
Jatbula Trail (60km, one way) is only for experienced and fit hikers. It is a reasonably difficult trail that takes 4–5 days to undertake. It starts at the Nitmiluk Visitor Information Centre and passes through monsoon vine forest at the Amphitheatre, 26km from Nitmiluk, on the way to Leliyn (Edith Falls). There is a large pool at the base of the falls and a shady picnic area at Leliyn. *Butterfly Gorge* via *Yambi Walk* (12km, return) is a shaded gorge, rich with colourful butterflies and lush rainforest. The shaded walk requires a moderate level of fitness. It starts at the Nitmiluk Visitor Information Centre and leads into the gorge. Seasonal swimming is permitted along the way, and the deeper water along the river is suitable for boating.

Fees & Permits
Fees or permits are not required to enjoy the park, but are required for camping, canoeing and fishing activities.

Facilities
The park is open 24 hours a day every day of the year, and the Nitmiluk Visitor Centre is open from 7.00 a.m. to 7.00 p.m. The park has camping, boating, swimming, cafe, picnic, barbecue, toilets, kiosk and restaurant facilities, as well as beautiful rock art, river cruises, scenic flights and luxury accommodation.

Services Nearby
Katherine is a large town with all essential services.

WESTERN AUSTRALIA

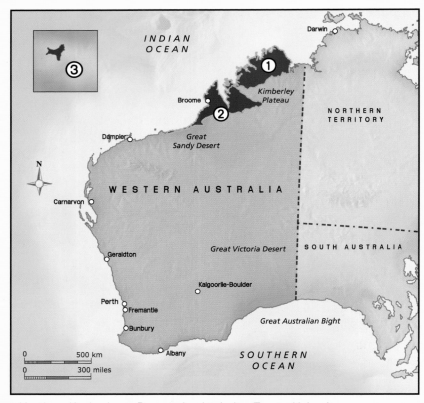

1. Northern Kimberley 2. Dampierland 3. Indian Tropical Islands

State Overview

Western Australia is Australia's largest state, covering an area of more than 2,500,000km², or nearly a third of Australia's entire land mass. Despite its large size, only a mere 70km² of rainforest has been recorded across the state. About 1,500 rainforest patches have been documented, which range from a few canopy trees that are struggling to hold on, to larger patches of more than 2km². The majority of the rainforests are scattered across two bioregions (Dampierland and Northern Kimberley) in the state's north. The southernmost extension of monsoon vine forest in Western Australia can be found in patches on coastal dunes near Broome.

Mitchell Plateau

Further into the Kimberley, some of the most identifiable and spectacular landscapes of Australia can be found, such as Purnululu (Warrumbungles) National Park, giant Boab trees growing alongside red dirt roads and amazingly picturesque waterfalls.

Due to the patchy nature of rainforest communities in the state, they were not recognized as being present until the 1970s. There are other areas outside the two bioregions featured here, which contain small patches of rainforest. Some of these rainforest patches can be found in Purnululu National Park, at El Questro Station and in protected gorges elsewhere.

From the southern coast to the tropics, the vastness of Western Australia covers wet forests in the south, to deserts, to monsoon plant communities in the far north. In fact, most of its eastern inland region is desert – more than 750,000km² of the state is occupied by the Great Victoria, Great Sandy, Gibson and Little Sandy Deserts alone. The Western Australia coastline is almost 13,000km in length (plus an additional 7,800km of island coastlines).

The state contains 26 IBRA bioregions and has eight of the country's 15 national biodiversity hotspots (the most of any state or territory), five of which occur in the south-west, while the South West Australian Floristic Region is one of the original 25 Global Biodiversity Hotspots.

Mining for iron ore, gold, diamonds and many other minerals, especially in the Pilbara region and eastern Kimberley, is big business in the state, employing more than 130,000 people in 2019.

Monsoon vine forest pockets

Northern Kimberley

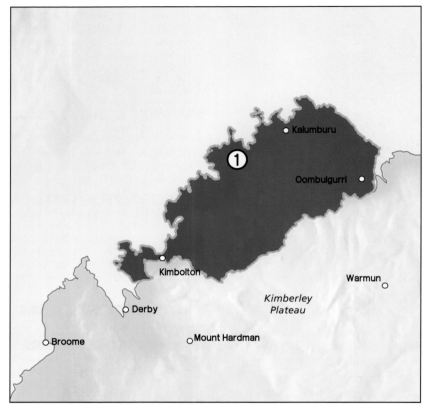

1. Mitchell River National Park

The Northern Kimberley bioregion is situated at the top of Western Australia, covering 84,200km² and containing amazing landscapes of rugged coastlines, dissected plateaus and spectacular gorges. The vegetation is characterized by tall, grassy savannah woodland with patches of rainforest in gorges and along watercourses. Nearly 3,000 plants, animals and fungi have been recorded, including approximately 230 birds, 60 mammals, 30 frogs, 145 reptiles and 350 insects. The bioregion has large numbers of invertebrates, with 90 per cent of earthworms and 48 per cent of camaenid land snails endemic to the region. About 15 per cent of the bioregion is conserved in 14 parks and reserves, three of which make up 98.5 per cent of the total area: Prince Regent Nature Reserve, and Drysdale River and Mitchell River National Parks. The remaining 85 per cent is either indigenous land or used for wide-scale cattle grazing.

Julie Sims

El Questro

The main population centre, Kalumburu, has average maximum temperatures of 30 °C across the year, while minimum temperatures drop to 14 °C in May–September. Kalumburu's yearly average rainfall is a little over 1,200mm, with nearly 90 per cent falling in December–March.

Prince Regent Nature Reserve, the largest reserve at around 6,350km^2, lies in the western area of the bioregion, with the Prince Regent River flowing through it. This reserve is mostly inaccessible to vehicles, making the rainforest patches out of reach.

The rainforests here are not the lush, evergreen, moist environments with mosses and ferns that you experience in the eastern states. In this part of Australia the larger rainforest plants are deciduous during the dry season to reduce water loss, when water availability is scarce.

The tourism industry is ever increasing here, with tourists taking the opportunity to visit during drier weather

Key Species

BIRDS

Arafura Shrikethrush, Bar-shouldered Dove, Brown Honeyeater, Green Oriole, Green-backed Gerygone, Kimberley Honeyeater, Large-billed Gerygone, Leaden Flycatcher, Orange-footed Scrubfowl, Pacific Emerald Dove, Pacific Koel, Rainbow Pitta, Rose-crowned Fruit-dove, Spangled Drongo, Torresian Imperial Pigeon, Varied Triller.

MAMMALS

Agile Wallaby, Golden-backed Tree-rat, Grassland Melomys, Hoary Wattled Bat, Kimberley Rock-rat, Northern Brown Bandicoot, Northern Leaf-nosed Bat, Rock Ring-tailed Possum, Scaly-tailed Possum.

REPTILES

Blotched Snake-eyed Skink, Bynoe's Gecko, Common Tree Snake, Fire-tailed Skink, Giant Slender Blue-tongue, Kimberley Rock Monitor, King Brown Snake, Northern Bar-lipped Skink, Ornate Snake-eyed Skink, Plain Ctenotus, Rough Brown Rainbow-skink, Rough-scaled Python, Tawny Snake-eyed Skink.

AMPHIBIANS

Copland's Rock Frog.

INVERTEBRATES

Bright-orange Darter, camaenid land snails, Chrome Awl, Common Crow (Oleander Butterfly), Green Tree Ant, Purple Oak-blue, Glasswing, Tailed Emperor, Two-brand Crow.

Peter Rowland

Nest of the Green Tree Ant

Arafura Shrikethrush *Colluricincla megarhyncha*

David Stowe

The Arafura Shrikethrush was separated from other Little Shrikethrush subspecies in 2018. It is quite different, being the largest of the species complex. Both sexes are dark grey-brown above, with a black rather than pinkish-brown bill, and grey-brown underparts with streaking, grading to a white mid-belly. The eyebrow is pale and the legs are grey. In Western Australia this species is largely confined to vine thickets, even small patches less than half a hectare in size, and occasionally waterside vegetation. It feeds mainly on insects, but will also eat other small invertebrates such as snails, from all levels of vine thickets to leaf litter on the ground. It is a loud and conspicuous rainforest bird throughout its range.

Bar-shouldered Dove *Geopelia humeralis*

Angus McNab

The Bar-shouldered Dove inhabits wetter forests and woodland, including vine thickets in gorges of the Kimberley, and utilizing vegetation along creeks and rivers. Its solid build, brown upperparts, with distinct black scalloping to each feather, bronze nape, blue-grey face and throat, and pale underparts, are distinctive. It occurs across northern and eastern Australia and is most often encountered singly or in small groups, usually feeding on seeding grasses and herbs, on the ground. When disturbed, it normally flies swiftly to a nearby tree, the flight lacking the undulating pattern of other similarly sized doves. The species is fairly sedentary, although some birds have been recorded ranging quite widely. The common call is a triple *coo* or *kook-a-wook*.

Brown Honeyeater *Lichmera indistincta*

Peter Rowland

This small, nondescript honeyeater is primarily brown with a long, downcurved bill. Adults have a small yellow triangular patch behind the eye. Their upperparts are dark olive-brown with yellowish-olive edges to the wing and tail feathers, forming a dull yellow patch in the folded wings. Males have a greyish crown, contrasting with an olive-brown nape and a black gape during breeding, otherwise yellow. Females have a shorter bill and yellow gape. The species is widespread in Western Australia from the south coast to the Kimberley, across to the central east coast of mainland Australia. It feeds on a variety of nectar sources and insects from the edges of the canopy to shrubs, and occasionally on the ground. It is a noisy bird with a range of calls; the breeding call, *sweet-sweet-quarty-quarty*, is sung from exposed branches. While not restricted to rainforest habitats, it is the most frequently found species across patches in the Kimberley.

Green Oriole *Oriolus flavocinctus*

In this species, the sexes are similar in appearance, being moss-green above and citrine below, and having a red eye and orange-yellow bill, but the female is more yellow and more heavily streaked. In Australia the Green Oriole is confined to north of the tropics, north of Mackay, Queensland, and west to around Broome, Western Australia. It seldom ventures far from water and can be seen perched high in rainforest trees. It is nomadic within its range, following the pattern of ripening fruits, which are harvested from the rainforest canopy. The call is a tuneful *yok yok yoddle*, which may be repeated continuously for more than 30 minutes. This species can be confused with the Olive-backed Oriole (p. 146) or the Australasian Figbird (p. 144).

Angus McNab

333

Leaden Flycatcher *Myiagra rubecula*

Peter Rowland

The male Leaden Flycatcher differs from other flycatchers in its leaden blue-grey upperparts and throat; females are duller and have a light orange throat and upper breast. The shape of the bill and graduation are important for distinguishing females from Broad-billed Flycatcher *M. ruficollis* females. The species is found in a variety of habitats, from open eucalypt forests and woodland, to coastal scrubs, vine thickets and mangroves. When not actively chasing flying insects in the canopy, it sits on a branch, rapidly quivering its tail up and down. Its noisy calls include a harsh *zzrip* and a whistled *zoowee zoowee*. It is one of the most frequently recorded bird species from rainforests in the Kimberley.

Varied Triller *Lalage leucomela*

Angus McNab

The male Varied Triller is predominantly glossy black above, with two white wing-bars, white edges to the flight feathers and white eyebrows. The underparts are grey-white with dark barring, a black rump with white mottling, and paler buff undertail. Females have grey-brown upperparts, mainly buff underparts with dusky barring, and undertail paler than in males. Although the species occurs throughout northern and eastern Australia and further north into Papua New Guinea, the Kimberley region has its own subspecies, *L. l. macrural,* which is largely confined to rainforest and dense riverine forests. The birds move through the rainforest canopy inconspicuously, foraging on a range of fruits, seeds, nectar and small invertebrates, and rarely coming to the ground. Of all the cuckoo-shrikes, this species builds the smallest nest and lays the largest egg in relation to its body size.

Golden-backed Tree-rat *Mesembriomys macrurus*

This beautiful mammal is generally greyish, heavily washed with dark yellowish-brown along the mid-dorsal area from crown to rump, and whitish below. The tail is long (about 150 per cent of the head–body length), greyish at the base and has a white-brushed tip. The species is distributed in northwestern Australia, from the northern Kimberley region, Western Australia (including several offshore islands), to the northern Northern Territory, although there are no recent records from the Northern Territory and it has disappeared from southerly parts of its former Western Australia range, including the Pilbara and southern Kimberley. It inhabits rainforests, eucalyptus woodland and rugged sandstone screes, and is crepuscular and nocturnal, feeding mostly in trees but also on the ground in less vegetated areas, mainly on fruits, leaves and invertebrates, including termites, but also on grasses. Individuals sleep in tree hollows and rocky crevices.

Anders Zimny

Grassland Melomys *Melomys burtoni*

This rodent varies in colour from dark grey to grey-brown and reddish-brown above, while being white, cream to grey below. The feet are dark grey to buff. It is the only small rodent in Western Australia with a mosaic scale pattern on a thin, grey-brown, almost hairless tail, and is sometimes referred to as the Mosaic-tailed Rat due to this characteristic. It is found in a variety of habitats, from grassland to woodland, while in Western Australia and the Northern Territory it is often locally abundant in monsoon forest, vine thickets and mangroves. This is a nocturnal species and is mostly active on the ground, while also being an adept climber. Its diet changes seasonally and consists of a range of plant material, from grass to seeds and berries, and also insects including grasshoppers.

Angus McNab

Hoary Wattled Bat *Chalinolobus nigrogriseus*

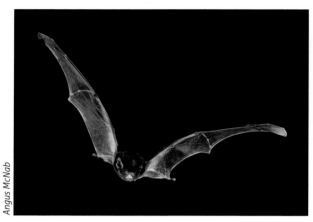

Angus McNab

The fur of this bat is greyish-black on the back and greyish-brown on the belly, with most individuals having white tips on each hair, giving a frosted (hoary) appearance, which is more pronounced in the west of its range. It is wide ranging in northern and eastern Australia (including offshore islands), from the southern Kimberley region, Western Australia, through the northern Northern Territory, and northern and eastern Queensland, to around Coffs Harbour, New South Wales. It is found in a variety of wooded habitats, including rainforests, vine thickets and sclerophyll forest, as well as coastal shrubland. It roosts by day in tree hollows, and less commonly in rock crevices, emerging at dusk to forage along watercourses and above the tree canopy for beetles, moths and other invertebrates. It has been recorded moving at speeds of 34km/h while foraging.

Kimberley Rock-rat *Zyzomys woodwardi*

Steve Reynolds

This rat is cinnamon-brown above, darker on the head, dispersed with dark brown hairs. It is pale below, with white tips to the hairs giving a more whitish appearance. The tail is short, moderately furred and swollen at the base. It is very fragile and often damaged or even broken during fighting. The species is endemic to higher rainfall areas of the Northern Kimberley bioregion, Western Australia, including several offshore islands, where it is found in rocky boulder outcrops and rock screes in a range of habitats, including rainforests, open woodland and pandanus thickets. It is nocturnal, feeding mainly on larger seeds of rainforest trees, supplemented with smaller grass seeds and fibrous plant material.

Rock Ring-tailed Possum *Petropseudes dahlii*

Joshua Bergmark

Rock Ring-tailed Possums have a stocky build, with short legs and a pointed muzzle. The fur is grey to reddish-grey above, and paler grey to greyish-white below. There is a black dorsal stripe from between the eyes to the middle of the back. The tail is one of the key identification features – it has thick, woolly fur at the base, tapering to near hairless by the mid-length. The species is found across the Northern Kimberley and into the Northern Territory. As its common name suggests, it inhabits rocky environments, usually associated with eucalypt woodland or vine thickets, and rests in rock dens by day. It lives in social groups of up to nine individuals. After dark, the mammals move as a group to forage on leaves, fruits and flowers in trees and scrubs away from the den.

Scaly-tailed Possum *Wyulda squamicaudata*

Steve Reynolds

This possum is grey flecked with brown, and has an indistinct darker stripe from the shoulders to the rump, and cream underparts. The tail is prehensile, with reddish-orange fur at the base, and scaled for the remainder of its length. The species occurs in the Kimberley region of northwestern Western Australia and the northern Northern Territory, into Queensland. It inhabits forests, woodland and vine thickets with areas of exposed sandstone boulders, sheltering by day in crevices in or underneath rocks, and emerging at night to feed mainly in trees on leaves, flowers, fruits and seeds. Females gives birth to a single offspring, which is carried in a pouch for about six months and fully weaned after a further two months.

Giant Slender Blue-tongue *Cyclodomorphus maximus*

Angus McNab

Another endemic species of the North Kimberley bioregion, the Giant Slender Blue-tongue is the largest species in its genus (230mm snout–vent). This large skink is bronze-brown to yellowish-brown in colour, with the hind-edge of the scales being pale yellow to cream, forming bands across the lower back and tail. The belly is cream or yellow. Juveniles are more prominently marked than adults. The species is found in a range of habitats, from escarpments to boulder-strewn areas with a variety of vegetation, from spinifex to dense vine thickets. It forages in dense, low vegetation for snails and other invertebrates, flowers and fruits. Females give birth to live young.

Kimberley Rock Monitor *Varanus glauerti*

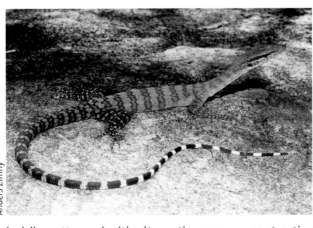

Anders Zimny

This medium-sized goanna grows to 0.8m in length. It is a slender monitor with a flattened head and body, and a long, thin tail (twice the head–body length). Its colour ranges from reddish-brown, through dark brown, to blackish, with transverse rows of large, lighter spots of light grey to olive across the back. The hindlegs have transverse rows of lighter spots. The tail is boldly patterned with alternating narrow, contrasting, black and white bands. The throat and belly are whitish. A rock-dwelling monitor, it is found in the gorges and escarpments of the Kimberley region, foraging for small vertebrates and invertebrates within dense vine thickets. Unlike other Australian lizards, monitors have forked tongues.

Rough Brown Rainbow-skink *Carlia johnstonei*

This skink is endemic to this Western Australia bioregion, and inhabits many large and small rainforest patches. It is a small skink (up to 10cm) with a dark reddish-brown back and darker black flecking, and darker sides with brown or white flecks. The lower surface is whitish to bluish-grey with the throat-scales edged black. Breeding males have rich reddish-brown flanks, and a black head and neck with sharp white flecks. The scales on the back have two keels. The species is found in leaf litter in tropical woodland, especially in dense vegetation, including rainforests, in gullies, gorges and well-vegetated rocky creek banks.

Anders Zimny

Rough-scaled Python *Morelia carinata*

This python is endemic to this Western Australia bioregion. It is pale grey to dark brown with a series of white, cream or pale yellow blotches that form irregular bands, becoming less so on the tail. A pair of temporal streaks usually extends from the eyes on to the neck. The underside is white. Each back scale has a blunt keel, giving the species its common name. Heat-sensitive pits are used for detecting prey, such as frogs, mammals and birds. The species is found from Mitchell River National Park to Hunter River, near Prince Frederick Harbour and also Bigge Island. It is restricted to remnant monsoon forest and vine thickets in protected ravines and sheltered gullies, in heavily dissected sandstone plateaus and scarps.

Steve Wilson

339

Mitchell River National Park

This park was gazetted in 2000. It covers 1,153km² on Ngauwudu (Mitchell Plateau), with the Mitchell River flowing through it. The greater northern portion of the park is in the Wunambal Gaambera people's exclusive possession native title and the Uunguu Indigenous Protected Area (IPA).

The journey to get to Ngauwudu and the park along the Gibb River Road, from either Derby or Wyndham, is an experience in itself. You pass many landscapes like those in tourist brochures or framed on gallery walls. Watch out for small patches of monsoon vine forest as you drive slowly along the usually corrugated dirt road (unless the grader has just been through).

The monsoon vine forest patches support a range of plants, including figs *Ficus* spp., the Lime Berry *Micromelum minutum*, Black Plum *Vitex acuminata*, Mango Bark *Canarium australianum* and Native Witch-hazel *Turraea pubescens*.

A stop in this patch of rainforest offers opportunities to see birds such as the Pacific Emerald Dove, Orange-footed Scrubfowl, Rainbow Pitta, Rose-crowned Fruit-dove and Torresian Imperial Pigeon. Other diurnal fauna includes Rough Brown Rainbow-skinks. A night walk to this patch may locate nocturnal mammals like the Golden-backed Tree-rat and Grassland Melomys searching for food. The endemic Rough-scaled Python may also be encountered looking for

Julie Sims

Mitchell Plateau

mammalian prey. This area has vast cultural significance to the Wunambal Gaambera people. The iconic Punamii-Uunpuu (Mitchell Falls) has significant Wunggurr values for them. Ngauwudu (Mitchell Plateau) is rich in the renowned Wanjina and Gwion art.

GPS Coordinates
-14.82086, 125.72088 (Punamii-unpuu Campground)

Getting There
From Derby take the Derby-Gibb River Road for 407km, to the Kalumburu turn-off. From Kununurra take the Victoria Highway towards Wyndham, then turn on to Gibb River-Wyndham Road travelling about 240km to the Kalumburu turn-off. From here, Drysdale River Station, roughly 60km north, is your last chance for fuel and supplies. About 100km north of

Drysdale River Station, turn on to the Mitchell Plateau Track (Port Warrender Road) and the camp ground is another 85km. Allow three days from Derby or two days from Kununurra, to the Punamii-unpuu camp ground (be prepared for a longer drive, especially if the road is corrugated, than GPS navigators may indicate).

Tracks & Trails
Punamii-unpuu/Mitchell Falls Walk (8.5km, 5 hours) takes you through a patch of rainforest between Bunjani (Little Mertens and Big Mertens Falls), while the views at the end of the walk are worth the extra effort.

Fees & Permits
A Ngauwudu Road Zone Uunguu Visitor Pass (UVP) is required to travel in Ngauwudu as you are on Wunambal Gaambera Country. UVPs and camping fees can be purchased from www.wunambalgaambera.org.au.

Facilities
Punamii-unpuu (Mitchell Falls camp ground) is the only camping area in the park. Toilets, fireplaces and picnic areas are scattered throughout. Drinking water should be treated. The park has a ranger office and information.

Services Nearby
Drysdale River Station (190km, four hours south on Gibb River-Kalumburu Road) is open during the dry season for fuel, supplies, and so on. Kalumburu (190km, four hours north on Gibb River-Kalumburu Road) has a number of accommodation options, a community store and fuel. Vehicle repairs and medical evacuations are very costly, so detailed planning and preparation are required before departing.

Dampierland

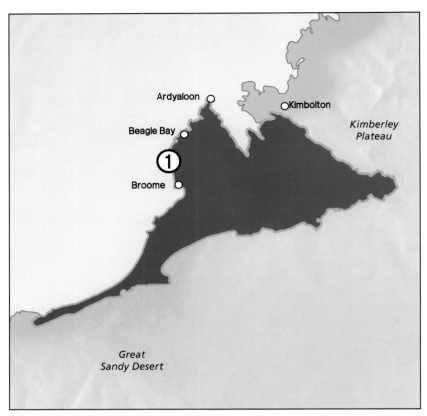

Ardyaloon

Kimbolton

Beagle Bay

Kimberley
Plateau

①

Broome

Great
Sandy Desert

1. Dampier Peninsula

The Dampierland bioregion covers an area of 83,608km^2 of the north-west coast, but only 1 per cent is protected in reserves. The bioregion stretches from the Dampier Peninsula, across to Derby, inland to Fitzroy Crossing, to the coast south of Broome and coastally towards Pardoo. There are 13 protected areas within the bioregion, including two offshore islands. About 60 per cent of the total protected area is in Coulomb Point Nature Reserve on the Dampier Peninsula. This bioregion is characterized by extensive plains, ranges and gorges. Nearly 75 per cent of the area is used for grazing.

Damian Kelly Photography

Walmadan –James Price Point

Key Species

BIRDS

Bar-shouldered Dove, Black-faced Cuckoo-shrike, Broad-billed Flycatcher, Brown Honeyeater, Brush Cuckoo, Channel-billed Cuckoo, Great Bowerbird, Leaden Flycatcher, Little Friarbird, Mangrove Golden Whistler, Oriental Dollarbird, Rainbow Bee-eater, Red-collared Lorikeet, Red-winged Parrot, Rose-crowned Fruit-dove, Yellow White-eye.

MAMMALS

Agile Wallaby, Arnhem Long-eared Bat, Black Flying-fox, Common Brush-tailed Possum (northern subspecies), Delicate Mouse, Dingo, Gould's Wattled Bat, Hoary Wattled Bat, Little Broad-nosed Bat, Little Red Flying-fox, Northern Blossom-bat.

REPTILES

Dampierland Slider, Horner's Dragon, Northern Bar-lipped Skink, Plain Ctenotus, Tawny Snake-eyed Skink, Western Two-toed Slider.

AMPHIBIANS

Green Tree Frog, Ornate Burrowing Frog.

INVERTEBRATES

Bright-orange Darter, Chrome Awl, Common Crow (Oleander Butterfly), Glasswing, Green Tree Ant, Pupasnails, Tailed Emperor.

The monsoon vine thickets of the peninsula are a threatened ecological community in Western Australia and the only Commonwealth-listed threatened ecological community in the Kimberley. While they make up only 0.05 per cent of land area, these patches contain 24 per cent of the flora found on the peninsula. The most southerly patches of vine thicket are on coastal dunes near Broome. Approximately 300 birds, 50 mammals, 150 reptiles, 20 frogs, 300 insects, 1,400 plants and 130 fungi have been recorded within the bioregion.

The largest town in the area, Broome, has an average rainfall of about 620mm, while the inland town of Fitzroy Crossing has 537mm; over half falls in January–February. The average daily temperature for both towns across the year is above 30 °C, except in June–July. Broome is world renowned for its pearls, which grow in the pristine waters of the area. The tourism industry triples Broome's population during the dry season, peaking in June–August.

As an aside, if travelling up the peninsula make sure to pop into the Beagle Bay community and check out the church, completed by monks in the early twentieth century.

Peter Rowland

Bower of a male Great Bowerbird

Great Bowerbird *Chlamydera nuchalis*

Angus McNab

This bowerbird is a dull fawn-coloured bird with darker mottling on the upperparts. The male's striking lilac crest, situated on the rear of neck, is revealed only during courtship and is reduced or absent in females. The species has a characteristic undulating flight pattern. It is distributed throughout northern Australia, north of the Tropic of Capricorn, where it inhabits rainforest, drier eucalypt forest and riverine woodland. The male constructs a large bower with two parallel, interwoven stick walls, decorated with a variety of objects, including bones and shells. Females are attracted to the bower by a series of calls, including mimicry of other birds. Mated females rear young by themselves. The species is wary, and its drab plumage makes it difficult to see among the foliage. It feeds on fruits, nectar, insects and seeds in rainforest and adjacent woodland.

Red-collared Lorikeet *Trichoglossus rubritorquis*

Peter Rowland

This large lorikeet is easily recognized by its striking blue head, purplish and orange shoulders, green lower back and wings, bright orange to yellow-orange breast, purplish-blue belly, yellowish-green undertail and bases of legs, and orange collar. The orange collar is the main characteristic that distinguishes it from the closely related Rainbow Lorikeet *T. haematodus*, which is pale green in colour. The two species do not naturally overlap in range, but escaped aviary birds of both species occur outside their native ranges. The Red-collared Lorikeet inhabits woodland, open forests and rainforests in northern Australia, west of the Gulf of Carpentaria. It is a noisy and conspicuous bird that feeds on nectar and pollen, some fruits and occasionally seeds.

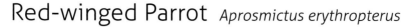

Red-winged Parrot *Aprosmictus erythropterus*

This parrot is a brilliant green, blue, black and red. Adult males are mostly bright green, with a black back, blue rump and bright red shoulder-patch, while females are green with a red wing edging. The bill is orange-red. The flight is buoyant with deep, powerful wing-beats. The species is found in small flocks, often travelling between areas of food, across northern and central eastern Australia. It feeds mostly in the canopy of trees and shrubs, on seeds, fruits, flowers and occasionally insects, in a range of habitats from rainforest and vine thickets in the tropical north, to open woodland and dry shrubland inland. Noisy in flight, its contact call is a metallic *crillic-crillic*.

Angus McNab

Agile Wallaby *Notamacropus agilis*

This wallaby is yellowish-brown above, with a pale buff stripe on the thigh and whitish underparts. Its snout is rounded with a whitish lower margin and a distinct dark border above. There is a short, dark brown, longitudinal stripe on the forehead (not always present). The species occurs in tropical northern Australia (including some offshore islands), from the Kimberley region, Western Australia, through the northern Northern Territory and coastal northern Queensland, to around Bundaberg. Also in Papua New Guinea. It is found in grassy habitats, including woodland and plains, riverine systems and coastal vine thickets, living in social groups, and grazing on grasses, fallen fruits and sedges. It is active mostly late in the afternoon and at night, and shelters during high temperatures in dense vegetation, sometimes in vine thickets. Movement between patches of vine thicket when food becomes available helps persistence of the thickets by dispersing seeds between patches.

Angus McNab

Delicate Mouse *Pseudomys delicatulus*

John Harris

This rodent is yellowish-brown or orange-brown to pale brownish-grey above with black guard hairs, and white or cream below (including the underside of the tail and lower parts of the muzzle). The nose and feet are pink; the top of the tail is pale brownish. It is the smallest native rodent, weighing only 6–15g. The species is found in tropical northern Australia (including offshore islands), from the northern Pilbara region, Western Australia, through the northern Northern Territory and northern Queensland, south to Fraser Island. It occurs in sparsely vegetated grassland, coastal sand dunes and vine thickets with softer soils. It sleeps by day in burrows, hollow logs or occasionally termite mounds, and forages at night on plant materials supplemented with insects.

Dingo *Canis familiaris*

Peter Rowland

The Dingo is typically sandy-yellow to red-brown above, occasionally darker brown to black. The underside is lighter tan or whitish. Hybrids with Domestic Dogs are very common, but cannot be accurately distinguished visually. Historically, the species occurred across mainland Australia, but is now restricted to northern Australia, north-west South Australia and areas along the east coast to the Gippsland region in Victoria. It inhabits a wide range of habitats and is active both day and night. It is an opportunistic hunter, normally hunting alone, but also forms small packs that work together to take down large prey. A variety of prey species is taken, including sheep and young cattle, which has led to Dingos being shot and poisoned by landowners. It also feeds on carrion.

Northern Bar-lipped Skink *Eremiascincus isolepis*

Angus McNab

This skink is pale brown to orange-brown above with numerous flecks of darker brown; the sides are more heavily speckled than the back. The belly is cream to white. The labial scales (lips) are edged with dark brown, giving a barred appearance, while the neck-sides have scattered white flecks. A moderate-sized skink, it measures to about 70mm from snout to vent. It has a fragmented distribution from northern Queensland to Exmouth Gulf, Western Australia, and occurs in a variety of habitats from vine thickets to dry woodland and coastal shrubland, and even suburban gardens. Given this, it is a characteristic fauna species of some vine thicket patches. Crepuscular in habit, it can be found sheltering under rocks, fallen timber, leaf litter and debris on the ground.

Green Tree Ant *Oecophylla smaragdina*

Peter Rowland

A mostly orange insect with a bright green abdomen, colonies have a single queen, which is larger than all workers (to 25mm) and greenish-brown. Major workers are larger than minor workers and have larger heads and jaws. The species is found throughout tropical northern Australia, from the western Kimberley, through the northern Northern Territory, to central eastern Queensland. It occurs in a range of open forests and woodland, where it forms nests in trees by joining leaves together and connecting them with silk produced by the larvae, which are squeezed gently by the adults to secrete and glue the silk to the leaves. A colony can have several nests in adjacent trees. The species feeds on the honeydew produced by scale insects, which are protected from predators by the major workers. It is aggressive when disturbed, biting with powerful jaws and spraying formic acid from the abdomen.

347

Dampier Peninsula

The rainforests in Dampierland are confined to the Dampier Peninsula, occurring between Broome and Ardyaloon (One Arm Point) at the top of Cape Leveque. Nearly all of the Dampier Peninsula has red clay sands called pindan, but vine thickets occur on the sandy soils of the leeward coastal dunes and swales. These vine thickets are the most southerly occurrences of rainforest in Western Australia.

There are 90 known patches of vine thicket covering nearly 29km² on the peninsula. As many as 151 native flora species have been recorded from these patches, including the Gubinge *Terminalia ferdinandiana,* Marool Plum *T. petiolaris,* Goonj *Celtis australiensis,* Jarnba *Exocarpus latifolia,* Banyan Fig *Ficus virens,* Mirda

Gyrocarpus americanus and Jigal *Bauhinia cunninghamii.* Climbers such as the Ngoorla *Capparis lasiantha* and Jinjalgurany *Abrus precatorius* are regularly found in vine-thicket patches throughout the peninsula, as are shrubs like the Gooralgar *Flueggea virosa* and Broad-winged Hop Bush *Dodonaea platyptera.*

Many fauna species found in these areas are not strictly rainforest species, but more commonly occur in adjacent areas, but there is a range of frugivores that are largely only found in these vine thickets, such as the Black Flying-fox, Channel-billed Cuckoo *Scythrops novaehollandiae* and Rose-crowned Fruit-dove.

The 1.9km² of monsoon vine thicket at Walmadan (James Price Point), along with other vine-thicket patches down

Tim Willing

Monsoon vine thickets at Quondong Point

the coast to Quondong Point, make up a significant proportion of the overall total of rainforest on the peninsula. These patches can be accessed by Manari Road, off the Cape Leveque Road.

Minyirr Coastal Park in Broome contains a 0.6km² patch of vine thicket, but this area is quite degraded with weeds, most likely due to its close proximity to urban areas, although management measures are trying to reverse this.

GPS Coordinates
-17.48730, 122.14546 (James Price Point)
-17.95255, 122.20943 (Minyirr Coastal Park)

Getting There
To access the vine thickets on the Dampier Peninsula, to the north of Broome, travel for 10km along Broome Road towards the Great Northern Highway (A1). Turn on to the Broome-Cape Leveque Road, which will take you all the way to Kooljamin (Cape Leveque) and Ardyaloon (One Arm Point), about 210km to the north. Allow half a day to travel the whole way, as much of the road is dirt and not suitable for two-wheel-drive vehicles. Works are underway to seal the remaining 90km of road between Manari Road and Beagle Bay. By plane, the Broome International Airport is considered the 'Gateway to the Kimberley', catering for both international and domestic flights.

Tracks & Trails
Minyirr Coastal Park can be accessed via Gubinge Road from the centre of Broome. There are a number of walks through this park that pass through vine thickets. *James Price Point (Walmadan)* is roughly 35km along the Manari Road. There is some interpretive signage and a short walk to the beach through the monsoon vine thickets.

Fees & Permits
There are no fees payable.

Facilities
As most of the patches of monsoon vine thicket are not in reserves there are no facilities.

Services Nearby
Broome has all of the services that would be expected in any large community. Fuel and some supplies are available at indigenous communities, such as Beagle Bay and Ardyaloon, although expect prices to be more expensive.

Indian Tropical Islands

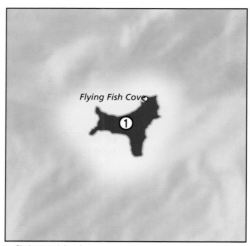

1. Christmas Island

The Indian Tropical Islands bioregion covers an area of 273.29km², of which 31.8 per cent (86.90km²) is held within protected areas. This bioregion is a recent addition to IBRA, along with the Pacific Subtropical Islands bioregion, Subantarctic Islands bioregion and Coral Sea bioregion. It contains Christmas Island, which is 136.64km² in size and has 85.41km² (62.51 per cent) of this protected, predominantly within the Christmas Island National Park. The bioregion also covers the Cocos (Keeling) Islands and Timor Sea Coral Islands. The tropical rainforests on the islands grow to an average of around 30m in height, but some taller stands (about 40m) can occur. The species composition is quite simple, mainly due to the remoteness of the islands, and incorporates several endemic species.

Angus McNab

View from Margaret Knoll, Christmas Island

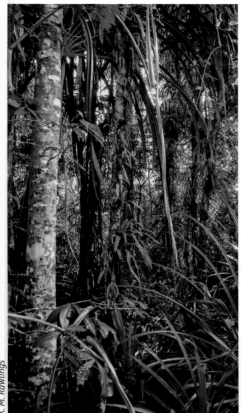

K. M. Rawlings

Christmas Island

Key Species

BIRDS

Abbott's Booby, Asian Emerald Dove, Brown Goshawk, Christmas Boobook, Christmas Island Frigatebird, Christmas Imperial Pigeon, Christmas Island Swiftlet, Christmas Island White-eye, Green Junglefowl, Island Thrush, Java Sparrow, Red Junglefowl.

MAMMALS

Christmas Island Flying-fox, Christmas Island Shrew (presumed extinct).

REPTILES

Blue-tailed Skink, Christmas Island Blind Snake, Christmas Island Whiptail-skink (extinct), Common Wolf Snake, Giant Gecko.

AMPHIBIANS

None.

INVERTEBRATES

Christmas Emperor, Christmas Island Red Crab, Christmas Island Stick Insect, Christmas Swallowtail, Robber Crab, Yellow Crazy Ant.

Due to the proximity of this bioregion to Java and Indonesia, migratory bird species that overshoot regularly end up on either Christmas Island or Cocos Keeling. It is therefore a mecca for birdwatchers trying to increase their bird lists and to see species not previously recorded in Australia. Christmas Island was, and may still be, home to Australia's only shrew species, the Christmas Island Shrew. It is also home to Australia's only introduced colubrid, the Common Wolf Snake, which played a large role in Australia's only known reptile extinction, that of the Christmas Island Forest Skink. It is very possible that the Christmas Island Blind Snake is also extinct, although so few individuals of this species have ever been found that it is unclear what its status is.

Angus McNab

Christmas Island Frigatebird

351

Christmas Boobook *Ninox natalis*

Angus McNab

Warm rufous-brown in colour, the Christmas Boobook is a small owl that inhabits the rainforests of Christmas Island. Its upperparts are dark brown and the underparts are heavily barred with rufous-brown and white. The underwings are heavily barred with grey; the legs are dull yellow. It is the bright, staring yellow eyes that are most striking. Relatively commonly heard across the island, the owl's call travels through the night from dusk until dawn. Hunting small invertebrates and geckos, these birds are often seen in pairs and will take advantage of street lights to take moths and other small winged insects. During the day, smaller forest birds will harass sleeping owls in attempts to move them on.

Christmas Imperial Pigeon *Ducula whartoni*

Angus McNab

Endemic to Christmas Island, this large, robust, dark purplish-blue-grey pigeon is commonly seen throughout the rainforest. Perching in the tops of trees, it appears black at a distance, often silhouetted as it sits on dead branches. However, it is subtly coloured with beautiful metallic greens through the wings. Certain body parts are colourful, the vent is rufous, the feet pinkish and the eyes bright yellow, though these are not always easily seen. Young birds are duller than adults, lacking the glossy sheen and yellow eye. It feeds on rainforest fruits, and it is common to see flocks of birds congregating in fruiting trees, in both the natural environment and gardens within the township.

Island Thrush *Turdus poliocephalus*

A subtly beautiful thrush, the Christmas Island subspecies *T. p. erythropleurus* has an olive-grey tail, upperparts, head, neck and throat, a yellow eye-ring, an orange bill and legs, rich rufous-orange flanks and a white belly. Extremely confiding, these birds hunt small invertebrates at your feet as you move along rainforest edges. Their diet also consists of seeds and fallen fruits, and may have once included endemic skinks. Breeding occurs throughout spring and summer, with nests built in trees. While some introduced species, such as the Giant Centipede *Scolapendra morsitans,* have become a prey resource, they are predominantly a threat; introduced cats predate on this predominantly ground-dwelling thrush.

Angus McNab

Christmas Island Flying-fox *Pteropus natalis*

Endemic to Christmas Island, this species' fur is mainly dark brown, but more blackish on the head and flecked with white (more so on the head and belly). It roosts during the day individually, in small groups or in large camps. It forages both day and night in a range of habitats and feeds mainly on fruits, supplemented with some flowers and leaves. More than 35 plant species have been recorded as food sources, and it may forage over 5km from its roost. The population has undergone a significant decline and possibly only about 1,500 individuals remain. By day it is common to see individuals flying from the Territory Day Park Lookout.

Angus McNab

Blue-tailed Skink *Cryptoblepharus egeriae*

Angus McNab

A small but beautifully patterned little skink, its body is dark brown with two almost golden stripes that run the length of the body, becoming blue as they merge into the tail. The flanks and neck-sides are heavily flecked with tan brown, and the underparts are cream coloured. Extremely quick and agile, these skinks once inhabited the rainforests of the island, but a multitude of introduced predators, including cats, chickens, Giant Centipedes and Common Wolf Snakes have removed the species from the wild. Now only living in captivity on Christmas Island, a captive-management programme has resulted in some individuals being released on to the Cocos (Keeling) Islands in attempts to help conserve the species.

Giant Gecko *Cyrtodactylus sadleiri*

Angus McNab

Not as big as the name 'giant' would suggest, the Giant Gecko grows to 80mm snout–vent length. The largest of the two native gecko species on the island, it is also the only extant native gecko, with the Christmas Island Gecko *Lepidodactylus listeri* now extinct in the wild. The larger size of the Giant Gecko may have played a role in its survival on the island, as only larger wolf snakes (a common predator) can eat it. The back of the lizard is varying shades of brown, with both dark and pale spots that form bars across the tail. The underparts are pale yellow. Highly agile and arboreal, these geckos cling to trees and limestone during the night as they wait for prey. During the day they hide in vegetation, epiphytes and rock crevices.

Christmas Island Red Crab *Gecarcoidea natalis*

The most famous migration undertaken by an animal in Australia is completed by this species. Moving from the rainforest to the shoreline for reproduction, this bright red crab lays its eggs in the limited shallow waters surrounding the island. The adults then move back into the forest en masse, although they are small in number compared with the huge, almost uncountable number of juveniles that move towards the forest after hatching. A predator to anything smaller than themselves, including their own species, the Christmas Island Red Crab is commonly seen scuttling through the forest. During migration the abundance of crabs causes much of the island to shut down and can be a significant inconvenience for anyone living on the island, as crabs emerge from every drainpipe and occupy every house.

Angus McNab

Robber Crab *Birgus latro*

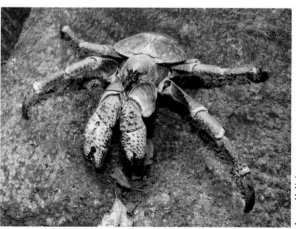

A very large and colourful crab, unlike anything else that occurs anywhere in Australia. Less commonly mentioned than the Christmas Island Red Crab (above) which is famous for its migration, the Robber Crab attains the size of a basketball. Living for more than 50 years and weighing up to 4kg, it is commonly seen walking around the island or climbing trees. It may be any number of colours, often reds, blues, oranges and purples. It is very inquisitive, investigating any changes in the forest, parked cars, new signs or freshly fallen trees, like the Arenga Palm *Arenga listeri*. When fallen or fruiting, the Arenga Palm attracts large numbers of crabs that tear the tree apart to eat its fleshy insides with their strong claws.

Angus McNab

Christmas Island National Park

Christmas Island is a small tropical island in the north of the Indian Ocean. It is closer to Indonesia (490km south-west of Jakarta) than Australia (about 2,000km to the south-east). It was first sighted on Christmas Day in 1643 by Captain William Mynors of the East India Company, hence its name. The island is popular with tourists for its annual crab migration, involving millions of Christmas Island Red Crabs (normally November or December), which is not to be missed. Enormous Robber Crabs are also found here. As is the case with many island environments, the local endemic fauna is extremely sensitive to introduced animals, the diseases they bring and habitat loss.

The accidental introduction of the highly invasive Yellow Crazy Ant to the island has reduced Christmas Island Red Crab numbers, which has, in turn, significantly altered the composition and diversity of the rainforest ecosystem. The Christmas Island Pipistrelle has dramatically declined in numbers, mainly due to habitat loss and the impact of introduced species, and is now presumed extinct. The explosion in Yellow Crazy Ant numbers has probably also accelerated this decline. Other introduced pests include the Black Rat, Common Wolf Snake, Domestic Cat and Giant Centipede.

The national park protects more

Angus McNab

Christmas Island National Park protects more than 62 per cent of the island's area and contains tropical rain

than 62 per cent of the island's area and contains tropical rainforest dominated by the Common Putat *Barringtonia racemosa* and Grand Devil's Claws *Pisonia grandis,* and containing the endemic Christmas Island Spleenwort *Asplenium listeri,* Screwpine *Pandanus elatus* and Lister's Palm *Arenga listeri.*

GPS Coordinates
-10.48560, 105.62621

Getting There
Serviced by air from from Perth (twice weekly), though for those coming from the east of Australia, flights do come via Jakarta (weekly) and can be les expensive than going via Perth.

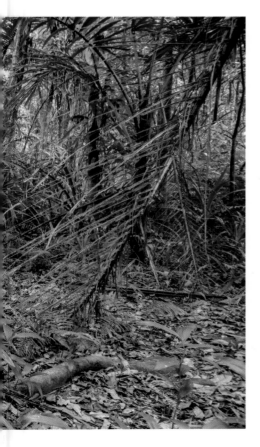

Tracks & Trails
There are limited walking trails (and some are not well signposted), so most exploring is via driving.
Anderson's Dale (1.5km, each way) is a moderately difficult walk and four-wheel-drive track that starts at Hugh's Dale Waterfall car park and passes through rainforest before ending at a stream. *West White Beach* (1.5km, each way) has two-wheel-drive access, but is a difficult walk with some steep sections passing through tall rainforest before descending down to the beach. *Winifred Beach* (550m, each way) has four-wheel-drive access and is a moderate rainforest walk that ends at the beach. *Dolly Beach* (1.8km, each way) has four-wheel-drive access, but is a moderate walk along a formed boardwalk, with sections of natural ground. It follows the shore through the rainforest to an isolated sandy beach. *Territory Day Nature Trail and Park Lookout* (1km, each way) is not well signposted and you can easily take a wrong turn. Christmas Island Flying-foxes roost here. *Margaret Knoll* is a nice lookout on the opposite side of the island.

Fees & Permits
No fees are payable.

Facilities
Punamii-unpuu (Mitchell Falls camp ground) is the only camping area in the park. Toilets, fireplaces and picnic areas are scattered throughout. Drinking water should be treated. The park has a ranger office and information.

Services Nearby
The island has supermarkets, limited car hire (which is essential to access the whole island), fuel, postal service, small hospital, chemist, restaurants, cafes, pubs, recreation centre and dive centre.

Further Information

Suggested Websites

Angus McNab Photography www.flickr.com/photos/angusmcnab
Atlas of Living Australia www.ala.org.au
Australia's Wildlife www.australiaswildlife.com
Australian Museum www.australianmuseum.net.au
Australian National Botanical Gardens www.anbg.gov.au/gardens
Australian Wildlife Conservancy www.australianwildlife.org
Birdlife Australia www.birdlife.org.au
Bureau of Meteorology www.bom.gov.au
Conservation Volunteers Australia www.cva.org.au
Destination NSW www.visitnsw.com
eBird www.ebird.org
Environs Kimberley www.environskimberley.org.au
Google Street Trekker in NSW National Parks www.nationalparks.nsw.gov.au/google trekker
KAPE Images www.kapeimages.com
Museum and Art Gallery of the Northern Territory www.magnt.net.au
Museums Victoria www.museumvictoria.com.au
Nature 4 You www.wildlifedemonstrations.com
NSW National Parks www.nationalparks.nsw.gov.au/app
NSW Office of Environment & Heritage www.environment.nsw.gov.au
Parks & Wildlife Service Tasmania www.parks.tas.gov.au
Parks Victoria www.parkweb.vic.gov.au
Pest Smart www.pestsmart.org.au/pest-animal-species
Queensland Government Department of Environment and Science www.parks.des.qld.gov.au
Queensland Museum www.qm.qld.gov.au
Tasmanian Museum and Art Gallery www.tmag.tas.gov.au
The National Aeronautics and Space Administration www.nasa.gov
Tourism & Events Queensland www.queensland.com
Tourism Australia www.australia.com
Tourism Cape York www.tourismcapeyork.com
Tourism NT www.tourismnt.com.au
Tourism Tasmania www.tourismtasmania.com.au
Tourism Western Australia www.westernaustralia.com
Visit Victoria www.visitvictoria.com
Wunambal Gaambera www.wunambalgaambera.org.au
Weeds Australia www.weeds.org.au
Wildlife Experiences www.wildlifeexperiences.com.au
Wildlife Tourism Australia www.wildlifetourism.org.au

Recommended Tour Operators & Agents

Alan's Wildlife Tours (N QLD) www.alanswildlifetours.com.au
Animal Tracks Safari (NT) www.animaltracks.com.au
Araucaria Ecotours (SE QLD & NE NSW) www.araucariaecotours.com
Australian Federation of Travel Agents (ALL) www.atas.com.au
Australian Walking Holidays (ALL) www.australianwalkingholidays.com.au
Autopia Tours (VIC) www.autopiatours.com.au
Bellbird Tours (ALL) www.bellbirdtours.com
Cassowary Tours (N QLD) www.cassowarytours.com.au
Daintree Boatman Nature Tours (N QLD) www.daintreerivertours.com.au
Daintree Rainforest Tours (N QLD) www.daintreerainforesttour.com.au

Daintree River Wild Watch (N QLD) www.daintreeriverwildwatch.com.au
Emu Trekkers (NSW) www.emutrekkers.org
Gondwana Guides (QLD) www.gondwanaguides.com.au
Inala Nature Tours (ALL) www.inalanaturetours.com.au
Kingfisher Park (N QLD) www.birdwatchers.com.au
Lockhart River Car Hire (N QLD) www.lockhartrivercarhire.com.au
Martin Cachard Birding (N Qld) www.martincachardbirding.com
Nitmiluk Tours (NT) www.nitmiluktours.com.au
NT Bird Specialist (NT) www.ntbirdspecialists.com.au
Peter Rowland Photographer and Writer (ALL) www.prpw.com.au
Rainforeststation Nature Park (QLD) www.rainforest.com.au
Rainforest Tours Australia (S QLD) www.rainforesttoursaustralia.com
Tasmanian Boat Charters (TAS) www.tasmanianboatcharters.com.au
Tasmanian Walking Company (TAS) www.taswalkingco.com.au
Tours Tasmania (TAS) www.tourtas.com.au
Trek Tours Australia (ALL) www.trektoursaustralia.com.au
Tropical Treks (SE QLD) www.tropicaltreks.com.au
Venture North (NT) www.venturenorth.com.au
Wait-a-While Rainforest Tours (N QLD) www.waitawhile.com.au
Wildlife Experiences (VIC & WA) www.wildlifeexperiences.com.au
Wildlife Tourism Australia (ALL) www.wildlifetourism.org.au
Wunambal Gaambera Aborignal Corporation (Kimberley) www.wunambalgaambera.org.au
Yellow Water Cruises (NT) www.yellowwatercruises.com

References

ABARES 2019, Forests of Australia (2018), Australian Bureau of Agricultural and Resource Economics and Sciences, Canberra.

Andrew, D. 2015. *The Complete Guide to Finding the Mammals of Australia.* CSIRO Publishing, Clayton South, Victoria.

Ansell, J., Evans, J., Adjumarllarl Rangers, Arafura Swamp Rangers, Djelk Rangers, Jawoyn Rangers, Mimal Rangers, Numbulwar Numburindi Rangers, Warddeken Rangers, Yirralka Rangers & Yugul Mangi Rangers. 2020. Contemporary Aboriginal savanna burning projects in Arnhem Land: a regional description and analysis of the fire management aspirations of traditional owners. *International Journal of Wildland Fire 2020,* 29, 371–385.

Anstis, M. 2017. *Tadpoles and Frogs of Australia.* New Holland Publishing, Sydney.

Australian Faunal Database. www.biodiversity.org.au/afd/home. Accessed 5/5/2020.

Australian Heritage Council. 2010. *West Kimberley Natural Heritage Assessment.* Department of Environment, Water, Heritage and the Arts, ACT.

Bishop, J. 2020. *Burnt Assets: The 2019–2020 Australian Bushfires.* WWF Australia, Sydney.

Black, S. J., Willing, T. & Dureau, D. M. 2010. *A Comprehensive Survey of the Flora, Extent and Condition of Vine Thickets on Coastal Sand Dunes of Dampier Peninsula, West Kimberley 2000–2002.* Unpublished Report. Broome Botanical Society (Inc), Broome.

Boles, W. & Edden, R. 1986. *Birds of the Australian Rainforest.* Reed Books, Frenchs Forest, NSW.

Clulow, S. & Swan, M. 2018. *A Complete Guide to the Frogs of Australia.* Australian Geographic, Sydney.

Cogger, H. G. 2018. *Reptiles and Amphibians of Australia (Updated Seventh Edition).* CSIRO Publishing, Clayton South, Victoria.

Commonwealth of Australia and each of its States and Territories. 2010. Australia's Strategy for the National Reserve System 2009–2030.

Department of Biodiversity, Conservation and Attractions. 2018. Interim recovery plan 2018–2023 for the monsoon vine thickets on the coastal sand dunes of Dampier Peninsula. *Interim Recovery Plan No. 383*. DBCA, Perth.

Department of Environment, Climate Change and Water NSW. 2010. *Border Ranges Rainforest Biodiversity Management Plan – NSW & Queensland*. Department of Environment, Climate Change and Water NSW, Sydney.

Department of Environment, Climate Change and Water NSW. 2011. *The Vertebrate Fauna of Royal & Heathcote National Parks and Garawarra State Conservation Area*. Department of Environment, Climate Change and Water NSW, Hurstville.

Department of Natural Resources, the Environment, Arts and Sport. 2020. Gove Peninsula and North-east Arnhem Coast – Site of Conservation Significance. www.territorystories.nt.gov.au/bitstream/handle/10070/254298/24_gove.pdf.

Department of Sustainability and Environment Vic. 2011. *A Field Guide to Rainforest Identification in Victoria*. Department of Sustainability and Environment, Melbourne.

Department of Sustainability, Environment, Water, Population and Communities. 2013. *Approved Conservation Advice for the Monsoon Vine Thickets on the Coastal Sand Dunes of Dampier Peninsula*. Department of Sustainability, Environment, Water, Population and Communities, ACT.

Department of the Environment, Water, Heritage and the Arts. 2009. *Littoral Rainforest and Coastal Vine Thickets of Eastern Australia*. Policy Statement 3.9.

Director of National Parks. 2014. Christmas Island National Park: Management Plan 2014–2024. www.environment.gov.au/resource/christmas-island-national-park-management-plan-2014–2024.

Director of National Parks. 2016. Kakadu National Park: Management Plan 2016–2026. www.environment.gov.au/topics/national-parks/parks-australia/publications.

Dutta, R., Das, J. & Aryall, A. 2016. Big data integration shows Australian bush-fire frequency is increasing significantly. *R Soc Open Sci*. 2016 Feb; 3(2): 150241.

Eipper, S. & Rowland, P. 2018. *A Naturalist's Guide to the Frogs of Australia*. John Beaufoy Publishing, Oxford.

Eipper, S. & Eipper T. 2019. *A Naturalist's Guide to the Snakes of Australia*. John Beaufoy Publishing, Oxford.

Fisher, J., Beames, L., Rangers, B. J., Rangers, N. N., Majer, J. D. & Heterick, B. E. 2014. Using ants to monitor changes within and surrounding the endangered monsoon vine thickets of the tropical Dampier Peninsula, north Western Australia. *Forest Ecology and Management* 318, 78–90. https://doi.org/10.1016/j.foreco.2014.01.010.

Flora of Australia. 2020. https://profiles.ala.org.au/opus/foa#/_=_ Accessed 5/5/2020.

Gill, F, Donsker, D. & Rasmussen, P. (eds). 2020. IOC World Bird List (v10.2). doi : 10.14344/IOC.ML.10.2. Accessed 5/5/2020.

Grose, M., Harris, R. & Lee, G. ACE CRC. 2012. Future climate projections for Tasmanian IBRA regions. A Report to the Independent Verification Group for the Tasmanian Forest Agreement.

Jackson, S. & Groves, C. 2015. *Taxonomy of Australian Mammals*. CSIRO Publishing, Clayton South, Victoria.

Keith, D. A. (ed.). 2017. *Australian Vegetation* (3rd edn). Cambridge University Press.

Kenneally, K. F. (2018). Kimberley tropical monsoon rainforests of Western Australia: perspectives on biological diversity. *Journal of the Botanical Research Institute of Texas* 12(1), 149–228.

Kooyman, R. M., Wilf, P., Barreda V. D., Carpenter, R. J., Jordan, G. J., Kale Sniderman, J. M., Allen, A., Brodribb, T. J., Darren, D., Field, T. S., Laffan, S. W., Lusk, C. H., Rossetto, M. & Weston, P. H. 2014. Paleo-Antarctic rainforest into the modern Old World tropics – the rich past and threatened future of the 'southern wet forest survivors'. *American Journal of Botany* vol. 101, Iss. 12.

Lenzen, M., Malik, A., Kenway, S., Daniels, P., Lam, K. L. & Geschke, A. 2019. Economic damage and spillovers from a tropical cyclone. *Nat. Hazards Earth Syst. Sci.* 19, 137–151.

Makinson, R. O. 2018. Myrtle Rust reviewed: the impacts of the invasive plant pathogen

Austropuccinia psidii on the Australian environment. Plant Biosecurity Cooperative Research Centre, Canberra.

McCormack, R. 2012. *A Guide to Australia's Spiny Freshwater Crayfish.* CSIRO Publishing, Clayton South, Victoria.

McGlashan, H., Coate, K., Gresham, J. & Hart, R. 2018. *The Natural World of the Kimberley.* Kimberley Society, Perth.

McKenzie, N. L., Johnstone, R. B. & Kendrick, P. G. 1991. *Kimberley Rainforests of Australia.* Surrey Beatty, Chipping Norton, NSW.

McNab, A. 2018. *The Guide to Tasmanian Wildlife.* Forty South Publishing, Lindisfarne, Tasmania.

Menkhorst, P. W. (ed.). 1995. *Mammals of Victoria.* Oxford University Press Australia.

Menkhorst, P., Rogers, D., Clarke, R., Davies, J., Marsack, P. & Franklin, K. 2017. *The Australian Bird Guide.* CSIRO Publishing, Clayton South, Victoria.

Monroe, H. M. Website – Australia: The Land Where Time Began (www.austhrutime.com). Accessed 17/3/20.

NASA. 2020. Climate Change – How Do We Know. Accessed 14/4/2020. https://climate.nasa.gov/evidence.

Nerem, R. S., Beckley, B. D., Fasullo, J. T., Hamlington, B. D., Masters, D. & Mitchum, G. T. 2018. Climate-change-driven accelerated sea-level rise detected in the altimeter era. PNAS. DOI: 10.1073/pnas.1717312115.

NSW National Parks and Wildlife Service. 1991. New England National Park: Plan of Management. Department of Environment and Climate Change (NSW).

NSW National Parks and Wildlife Service. 1997. Broadwater National Park Bundjalung National Park and Iluka Nature Reserve: Plan of Management. Department of Environment and Climate Change (NSW).

NSW National Parks and Wildlife Service. 1998. Budderoo National Park, Macquarie Pass National Park, Barren Grounds Nature Reserve and Robertson Nature Reserve: Plan of Management. Department of Environment and Climate Change (NSW).

NSW National Parks and Wildlife Service. 2001. Gibraltar Range Group of Parks (Incorporating Barool, Capoompeta, Gibraltar Range, Nymboida and Washpool National Parks and Nymboida and Washpool State Conservation Areas): Plan of Management. Department of Environment and Climate Change (NSW).

NSW National Parks and Wildlife Service. 2001. Blue Mountains National Park: Plan of Management. Department of Environment and Climate Change (NSW).

NSW National Parks and Wildlife Service. 2002. Myall Lakes National Park, Little Broughton Island and Stormpetrel Nature Reserves: Plan of Management. Department of Environment and Climate Change (NSW).

NSW National Parks and Wildlife Service. 2005. Oxley Wild Rivers National Park, Oxley Wild Rivers State Conservation Area, Cunnawarra National Park and Georges Creek Nature Reserve: Plan of Management. Department of Environment and Climate Change (NSW).

NSW National Parks and Wildlife Service. 2010. Barrington Tops National Park, Mount Royal National Park and Barrington Tops State Conservation Area: Plan of Management. Department of Environment and Climate Change (NSW).

NSW Office of Environment & Heritage. Website – *Rainforests* (www.environment.nsw.gov.au/threatenedSpeciesApp/VegFormation.aspx?formationName=Rainforests). Accessed 17/3/20.

Parks and Wildlife Commission of the Northern Territory. 2014. Nitmiluk National Park: Plan of Management. www.parksandwildlife.nt.gov.au/manage/plans/katherine.

Parks and Wildlife Commission of the Northern Territory. 2016. Litchfield National Park: Plan of Management. www.dtc.nt.gov.au.

Parks Victoria. 2019. Caring for Country – the Otways and You: Great Otway National Park and Otway Forest Park Management Plan. Department of Sustainability and Environment.

Quarterly Update of Australia's National Greenhouse Gas Inventory: June 2019,

Commonwealth of Australia 2019.

Robertson, P. & Coventry, A. J. 2019. *Reptiles of Victoria*. CSIRO Publishing, Collingwood, Victoria.

Rowland, P. 2008. *Bowerbirds*. CSIRO Publishing, Collingwood, Victoria.

Rowland, P. & Eipper, S. 2018. *A Naturalist's Guide to the Dangerous Creatures of Australia*. John Beaufoy Publishing, Oxford.

Rowland, P. & Farrell, C. 2017. *A Naturalist's Guide to the Reptiles of Australia*. John Beaufoy Publishing, Oxford.

Rowland, P. & Farrell, C. 2017. *A Naturalist's Guide to the Mammals of Australia*. John Beaufoy Publishing, Oxford.

Rowland, P. & Farrell, C. 2018. *Australia's Birdwatching Megaspots*. John Beaufoy Publishing, Oxford.

Rowland, P. & Whitlock, R. 2019. *A Naturalist's Guide to the Insects of Australia*. John Beaufoy Publishing, Oxford.

Rowland, P. & Whitlock, R. 2020. *A Naturalist's Guide to the Butterflies of Australia*. John Beaufoy Publishing, Oxford.

Russell-Smith, J. & Lee, A. H. 1992. Plant populations and monsoon rain forest in the Northern Territory, Australia. *Biotropica* vol. 24, No. 4: 471–487.

Sands, D. P. A. 2012. Review of Australian Phyllodes Imperialis Druce (Lepidoptera: Erebidae) with description of a new subspecies from subtropical Australia. *Australian Entomologist* 39 (4): 281–292.

Sheringham P., Richards P., Gilmour P., & Kemmerer E. 2016. A systematic flora survey, floristic classification and high-resolution vegetation map of Lord Howe Island. Lord Howe Island Board, Lord Howe Island, NSW.

Thorsell, J. & Sigaty, T. 1997. A global overview of Forest Protected Areas on the World Heritage List: A contribution to the Global Theme Study of World Heritage Natural Sites. Natural Heritage Programme, IUCN Gland, Switzerland in collaboration with the World Conservation Monitoring Centre.

Trembath, D. & Fearn, S. 2008. Body sizes, activity times, food habits and reproduction of brown tree snakes (*Boiga irregularis*) (Serpentes : Colubridae) from tropical north Queensland, Australia. *Australian Journal of Zoology* 56(3).

USGCRP. 2017. Climate Science Special Report: Fourth National Climate Assessment, Volume I (Wuebbles, D. J., Fahey, D. W., Hibbard K. A., Dokken D. J., Stewart B. C. & Maycock, T. K., eds). U.S. Global Change Research Program, Washington, DC, USA, 470 pp, doi: 10.7930/J0J964J6.

Vigilante, T., Ondei, S., Goonack, G., Williams, D., Young, P. & Bowman, D. M. J. S. 2017. Collaborative research on the ecology and management of the 'Wulo' monsoon rainforest in Wunambal Gaambera Country, North Kimberley, Australia. *Land* 2017, 6, 68: doi:10.3390/land6040068.

Webb, L. J. 1959. A physiognomic classification of Australian rainforests. *Journal of Ecology* 47: 551–570.

Wilkinson, I. & Priddel, D. 2011. Rodent eradication on Lord Howe Island: challenges posed by people, livestock and threatened endemics. pp. 508–514, in Veitch, C. R., Clout, M. N. & Towns, D. R. (eds). *Island Invasives: Eradication and Management*. IUCN, Gland, Switzerland.

Wilson, S. & Swan, G. 2021. *A Complete Guide to Reptiles of Australia* (6th edn). Reed New Holland, Sydney.

Woinarski, J. C. Z, Armstrong, M., Price, McCartney, M., Griffiths, A.D. & Fisher, A. 2004. The terrestrial vertebrate fauna of Litchfield National Park, Northern Territory: Monitoring over a 6-year period and response to fire history Wildlife Research, 2004, 31, 1–10. CSIRO Publishing Collingwood, Victoria.

WWF. 2018. Living Planet Report – 2018: Aiming Higher. Grooten, M. & Almond, R. E. A. (eds). WWF, Gland, Switzerland.

Zola, N. & Gott, B. 1992. *Koorie plants Koorie People, Traditional Aboriginal food, fibre and healing plants of Victoria*. Koorie Heritage Trust, Melbourne.

Appendix 1: Geological Time Scale

Geological Timeline				
(*million years ago)				
Era	**Period**	**Series/Epoch**	**mya***	**Overview**
Paleozoic	Silurian	Llandovery	443–416	• The earliest known terrestrial plants occurred. These were spore-producing plants.
		Wenlock		
		Ludlow		
		Pridoli		
	Devonian	Lower	416–359	• Fossil evidence of the emergence of insects and other arthropods. • Seed-bearing plants evolved.
		Middle		
		Upper		
	Carboniferous	Lower Mississipian	359–299	• The world's tectonic plates started to merge together (coalesce) to form the supercontinent called Pangea. • Australia's last major glaciation occurred during the late Carboniferous and early Permian.
		Middle Mississipian		
		Upper Mississipian		
		Lower Pensylvanian		
		Lower Pensylvanian		
		Lower Pensylvanian		
	Permian	Cisuralian	299–251	• Major sea level rises caused flooding to internal basins, including the Carnarvon and Sydney Basins. • Southern Conifers, Ginkgophytes and cone-bearing Cycadophytes (plants that did not need access to permanent water) became widespread.
		Guadalupian		
		Lopingian		
Mesozoic	Triassic	Lower	251–201	• Tasmania's highlands started to form.
		Middle		• The world's tectonic plates completed their coalescence. • Dinosaurs appeared. • Synapsids (mammal ancestors) survived mass extinction and developed.
		Upper		• Mammals became distinguishable from synapsids.
	Jurassic	Lower	201–145	• Widespread basaltic magmatic activity in the early to middle Jurassic signified a major thermal event.
		Middle		• The supercontinent of Pangea started to break up into Gondwana and Laurasia. • Conifer families (Podocarpaceae and Araucariaceae) became established.
		Upper		• The sea floor of the Atlantic and Indian Oceans started to spread and the rift valleys formed. • Continents started to split and form. • Rainforest lineages were widespread through Gondwana.

	Cretaceous	Early	145–66	• Africa/South America first to separate from Australasia/India/Antarctica. • Winter sea ice still formed around southeastern Australia. • The north-west of Australia was increasing in temperature. • Much of Australia was covered by forest containing conifers from the Podocarpaceae and Araucariaceae families; ancient elements of modern Australian rainforests. • Egg-laying mammals (monotremes) split from other mammals.
		Late		• Dinosaurs still roamed Australia. • Marine conditions began to disappear from central Australia. • Atmospheric carbon dioxide levels exceeded 1,000 parts per million (ppm) (possibly 1,500 ppm).
Cenozoic	Paleogene	Paleocene	66–23	• Dinosaurs became extinct. • Ratites (Emu, Ostrich, Moa and Rhea ancestors) evolved. • Gymnosperms dominated and Myrtaceae, Casuarinaceae and Nothofagaceae were in the minority. • Flowering plants (Angiosperms) were diverse.
		Eocene		• Cool temperate Nothofagus and rainforest possibly dominant over much of Antarctica. • Australia completed its split from Antarctica about 45–38mya (where Tasmania is located), allowing the Southern Ocean to form. • Australia carried its Austral paleo-Antarctic rainforest and warmed as it continued to travel north. • Humidity increased and Australia's rainfall was predicted to have been about 1,500–2,000mm per year. • Subtropical and tropical rainforests were widespread through Australia's south and western coasts, through to the north-west, and into parts of central Australia. • Eucalypts, banksias and grevilleas started to evolve. • Bats, birds and marsupials (bandicoots, dasyurids, numbats and thylacines) appeared.
		Oligocene		• Australia was no longer affected by the Antarctic's freezing temperatures, and the warming continent forced the retreat of the Paleo-Antarctic rainforest lineages to the few remaining wet areas.
				• Rainforest containing Nothofagaceae declined in Australia's north-west. • Main volcanic activity was occurring from the central coast of Queensland to central Victoria, and into Tasmania.

			• Mammals are not recorded in Australia between 55 and 25mya. • Kangaroos, koalas, possums and wombats appeared at the end of the Oligocene and early Miocene. • Hipposiderid, microchiropteran bats were diverse.
Neogene	Miocene	23–2.58	• Movement of some animal and plant species between Australia and Asia. • Rainforest dominated until the mid-Miocene, but as Australia dried out towards the end of the Miocene the vegetation changed to be mainly Myrtaceae, and possibly wet sclerophyll woodland. • Rainforest flora suffered a major decline throughout Australia by the end of the Miocene, and animal diversity also decreased markedly. • Fire became an integral part of the environment. • The ancient (possibly) Gondwanan mammal groups, the yalkaparidontians ('thingodontans') and yingabalanarids ('weirdodontans'), vanished along with the central Australian rainforests.
	Pliocene		• In the early Pliocene the Murray Basin had a period of high non-seasonal rainfall, which resulted in a brief resurgence of Nothofagus rainforest, but this gave way to wet sclerophyllous forest as the middle and late Pliocene entered a dry phase. • Rodents appeared. • Animal sizes started to increase (gigantism), and mammal megafauna roamed Australia until the Pleistocene, and included animals like *Procoptodon goliah* (a 200kg, 2m-tall kangaroo), *Zygomarturus trilobus* (a 500kg, 2.5m-long 'wombat-like' diprotodontid), *Thylacoleo carnifex* (a 160kg, 1.5m-long marsupial lion) and *Zaglossus hacketti* (a 30 kg, 1m-tall echidna).
Quaternary	Pleistocene	2.58–	• Atmospheric carbon dioxide levels dropped to just over 180 ppm. • Humans appeared. • Megafauna disappeared.
	Holocene		• Hipposiderid bat diversity declined in northern Australia (at least). • Dingoes first appeared.
	Anthropocene		(Not officially recognized.) • Atmospheric carbon dioxide levels at 4 ppm (March 2020)

Appendix 2: Australia's Most Significant Bushfires

Bushfire	Occurrence	Overview
Black Thursday	1851	This was the first documented of Australia's major bushfires, and it still remains as one of the country's most catastrophic fires. The Black Thursday blaze occurred on 6 February 1851 and ravaged a quarter of what is now the state of Victoria. The devastating blaze burnt 5 million hectares across the Portland, Plenty Ranges, Wimmera and Dandenong regions. Twelve people and more than 1 million sheep perished in it, and the heat of the fires pushed burning embers 32km out to sea.
Gippsland/Black Sunday	1925–1926	Victoria was once more devastated by bushfires in February–March 1926. These blazes destroyed more than 1,000 homes and killed 60 people, most of these in the Yarra Ranges town of Warburton.
Black Friday	1939	Victoria was again the location for the terrible fires of 13 January 1939, during which 71 people perished and 650 homes were lost. Some towns were lost entirely. Ash from the fires landed in New Zealand.
Western Australia	1961	From 20 January to mid-March 1961, the south-west of Western Australia saw a series of devastating fires that burnt through about 44,000ha of bushland around Dwellingup, Pemberton, Shannon River, the Augusta-Margaret River area and Kalamunda. The towns of Dwellingup and Karridale were largely destroyed, but there was no loss of human life; the small timber towns of Banksiadale, Holyoake, Marrinup and Nanga Brook were also destroyed.
Black Tuesday	1967	Tasmania's south-east was devastated by these huge fires, which advanced through the region, destroying 1,300 homes and 80 bridges as they advanced on 110 separate fronts, almost to the centre of Hobart. Sixty-two people perished, over 900 more were injured, and more than 62,000 farm animals died.
Blue Mountains and Illawarra	1968	Eastern New South Wales lost about 14 people, with around 70 more injured during the fires that burned over 1,000,000ha. More than 200 buildings were lost, including 38 in the Illawarra region, in the fires that burned for four weeks in November and December 1968.
New South Wales (& Queensland)	1974–1975	Although only three human lives were lost in these fires around Balranald, Cobar, Glendale and regions of the Lower Hunter of New South Wales, the fires damaged some 117 million hectares (15 per cent of Australia's land mass) and killed about 50,000 farm animals. There were also enormous crop losses and destruction of roads and infrastructure. Southern Queensland also suffered huge loss of land (7,300,000ha) in November 1974, but no human lives were lost.
Ash Wednesday	1983	Perhaps the most devastating fires of modern times, and 16 February 1983 will go down as their darkest day. About 180 fires burnt through 500,000ha of Victoria and South Australia, killing 75 people (47 in Victoria and 28 in South Australia), including 17 firefighters, and injuring a further 2,676. Beaconsfield, Victoria, was one of the worst affected towns. Upwards of 3,700 buildings were destroyed or damaged, and more than 340,000 sheep, 18,000 cattle and tens of thousands of native animals were killed.

New South Wales	1993–1994	More than 800 fires burned around Sydney and along a broad (100km) coastal strip of New South Wales, from around Grafton in the north to Batemans Bay in the south. About 800,000ha of largely unpopulated country burned, much of this national parks and nature reserves. Bundeena in the Royal National Park, Sydney, was isolated, and the remainder of Sydney was blanketed in thick smoke. More than 20,000 firefighters battled the blazes, mainly from 27 December 1993 to 16 January 1994. About 225 homes were lost, including 101 in the Como/Jannali region of Sydney.
New South Wales (& Queensland)	2002–2003	From 27 September 2002 to 24 Febraury 2003 (151 days), much of eastern New South Wales was affected by devastating fires that burnt almost 1,500,000ha. Three human lives were lost and over 400 significant injuries were reported. Queensland's Granite Belt region was also ravaged by fires that claimed the life of one person, a lady who was trapped in her home. Land totalling 28,500ha was burnt and 11 buildings were destroyed.
Great Divide Complex	2006	Although only one person lost their life during the fires that swept through central and eastern Victoria, more than 1,200,000ha of land was burned. The fires were ignited by a series of lightening strikes on 1 December 2006 and were finally brought under control on 7 February 2007. Fifty-one dwellings were lost and about 1,400 firefighters were injured in the huge firefighting effort. Melbourne's power supply was severely impacted during January 2007 when power lines were cut by the fires.
Black Saturday	2009	Over 400,000ha (including almost 100,000ha of national parkland) of eastern Victoria was destroyed in the estimated 400 fires of 2009, but 9 February (dubbed 'Black Saturday') became the day that would significantly change Australia's classification of bushfires via the Royal Commission that followed. More than 2,000 houses were destroyed, 173 people were killed (126 were inside homes, garages or bunkers and 11 in vehicles) and 3,500 structures were destroyed.
Yarloop, Western Australia	2016	On 7 January 2016, the town of Yarloop in Western Australia was devastated by an intense and unpredictable bushfire that ultimately burnt through 70,000 ha. In addition to the devastation caused at Yarloop, a number of towns were affected in the Harvey and Waroona areas, including Cookernup, Hamel, Harvey, Lake Clifton, Preston Beach, Waroona and Wagerup and Yarloop. A total of 162 houses were lost, 121 of them in Yarloop, two people died and over five more were injured. The township of Yarloop remained closed to the public for seven months.
Black Summer	2019–2020	Between 5 September 2019 (although fires had been burning in New South Wales since June 2019) and 9 March 2020, there were unprecedented bushfires across southeastern Australia, and an estimated 18,600,000ha were burnt. Almost 2,800 houses and more than 3,000 other buildings were destroyed. Thirty-four people are known to have died and an estimated 1 billion animals perished. Some endangered species may now be extinct, or become extinct, as a direct result.

Appendix 3: Major Australian Cyclones of This Century

Cyclone	Dates	Category	Overview
Ingrid	4–17 March 2005	5	Severe Tropical Cyclone Ingrid crossed the Australian coast in three states or territories, namely Queensland (just south of Lockhart River, Category 4; Northern Territory, islands off the Arnhem Land coast, Category 5; Croker Island and the Coburg Peninsula, Category 4; and the Tiwi Islands, Category 3) and Western Australia (Kimberley coast, Category 4). It was an intense cyclone that caused heavy rainfall (for example 445mm in 24 hours at Emma Gorge in the Kimberley) and large sea swells. Although no human deaths or serious injuries were reported in Australia, several people drowned in a boat capsize in Papua New Guinea.
Larry	17–20 March 2006	3	The eye of Cyclone Larry crossed the tropical north Queensland coast near Innisfail and remained at hurricane-force intensity as it moved over the Atherton Tablelands. No human lives were lost and no serious injuries were reported, but significant damage to about 10,000 homes, rail and road infrastructure, native forests and crops was reported, totalling upwards of AUS $500 million.
Monica	17–25 April 2006	5	Cyclone Monica made landfall 40km south of Lockhart River, Queensland, in a remote part of Cape York Peninsula, although Monica crossed Cape York Peninsula at a remote location, avoiding Lockhart River and Coen. Up to 70 per cent of the region's trees were damaged by the wind gusts of 109km/h, which intensified to 130km/h as Monica passed Cape Wessel and hit maximum speeds of 148km/h at Maningrida, about 120km to the north-east of Nhulunbuy.
George	27 February–8 March 2007	5	George was the most destructive cyclone to affect Port Hedland since Cyclone Joan in 1975. It was at its maximum intensity when it crossed the coast 50km north-east of Port Hedland with wind gusts of about 275km/h. Winds decreased rapidly as the system moved inland, but large amounts of rain fell in the northern Kimberley and Northern Territory. Three human fatalities and numerous injuries were recorded, and only minor property damage was sustained.
Yasi	31 January–3 February 2011	5	Yasi made landfall near Mission Beach in Queensland's Wet Tropics as a category 5 cyclone. It is one of the most powerful cyclones recorded in Queensland since Cyclone Mahina in Princess Charlotte Bay (1899), which killed more than 300 people, and the unnamed cyclone that hit Innisfail in March 1918, killing up to 100 people. Yasi recorded wind gusts of up to 285km/h. The highest rainfalls were recorded at South Mission Beach (471mm), Hawkins Creek (464mm) and Zattas (407mm). A storm-tide surge of 5m was recorded at Cardwell. Despite its intensity Yasi only caused one human fatality, a 23-year-old man who suffocated from generator exhaust fumes while sheltering from the cyclone in his shed. Yasi caused AU $3.5 billion in damages when 30 per cent of the houses in Tully and 75 per cent of the region's banana crop were destroyed.

Marcia	18–20 February 2015	5	Cyclone Marcia crossed the Queensland coast somewhere near Shoalwater Bay (north of Yeppoon) with about 15km of the surrounding area exposed to the full impacts of the winds. The township of Byfield sustained major damage and Yeppoon received significant damage. The area of Shoalwater Bay had a large number of trees uprooted and large-scale beach erosion. Townshend Island experienced almost complete defoliation of its trees, and the coastline of Pearl Bay had extensive tree defoliation as well as significant soil erosion.
Olwyn	8 March–13 March 2015	3	This was perhaps the most significant tropical cyclone to affect the Western Australia coastal area between Exmouth and Shark Bay in decades. Heavy rainfall affected the western Pilbara and western Gascoyne districts and localized flooding was recorded, closing roads throughout the area. The cyclone also caused moderate damage to homes and infrastructure, as well as significant damage to plantations.
Debbie	25–28 March 2017	4	This cyclone made landfall near Airlie Beach, Queensland. It was a slow-moving (6km/h) cyclone with wind gusts of up to 263km/h. The island resorts of Daydream and Hamilton in the Whitsundays suffered devastating damage, as did the townships of Airlie Beach, Bowen, Collinsville and Proserpine. After the cyclone had passed, the effects of the torrential rainfall (up to 986mm over a 48-hour period) on the Burnett, Condamine, Fitzroy, Logan and Tweed Rivers caused devastating floods and mass evacuations. More than 63,000 emergency calls were made and over 50,000 insurance claims lodged. The estimated cost to industries, particularly farming, mining and tourism, was in excess of AUD $2.2 billion.
Trevor	23–27 March 2019	5	With maximum wind gusts of 250km/h at its peak, Tropical Cyclone Trevor made landfall just south of Lockhart River on the Cape York Peninsula, Queensland. After weakening slightly, it intensified when crossing the coast between Port McArthur and the Northern Territory/Queensland border. Trevor caused large-scale damage to Iron Range National Park and the township of Lockhart River. Damage was less noticeable in Borroloola and Robinson River. The cyclone caused heavy rainfall and flooding, with more than 300mm recorded in a 24-hour period in Lockhart River. Other parts of Queensland and parts of the Northern Territory also received significant rainfall and flooding, with several drought affected areas receiving their most rain in several years.

Appendix 4: Significant Invasive Species In Australia

Common Name	Scientific Name	Overview
Black Rat	*Rattus rattus*	Introduced, most likely with the arrival of Europeans in the eighteenth century. Usually found around human habitation, with strongholds around cities but also found well away from human settlement. Origin thought to be the Middle East. Feeds on animals including insects, mice, birds, eggs and lizards, and is a major cause of ecosystem damage.
Brown Rat	*Rattus norvegicus*	Introduced, most likely with the arrival of Europeans in the eighteenth century. Usually found around ports and human habitation, with strongholds around cities. Origin is thought to be the Caspian region of eastern Europe.
Cane Toad	*Rhinella marina*	Widely distributed around the world, the Cane Toad was released at Gordonvale, Queensland, in 1935 to control pests of sugar cane, and has since become a major pest.
Common Wolf Snake	*Lycodon capucinus*	One of the most invasive snake species globally, in Australia it only occurs on Christmas Island, where it has contributed significantly to the decline and possible extinction (in the wild) of at least four reptile species.
Dog	*Canis familiaris*	Predation by dogs can have a major impact on remnant populations of endangered animal species, which are seemingly more vulnerable to predation than larger populations.
Domestic Cat	*Felis catus*	The number of feral cats in Australia has been conservatively estimated at around 4 million, with each cat killing up to an estimated 30 animals every day. Cats have become established in every habitat throughout the continent.
Dromedary Camel	*Camelus dromedarius*	Camels were first imported into Australia in 1840 as a form of transport and for exploration in Australia's arid areas. By 2008 more than 1 million feral camels were estimated to occur in Queensland, New South Wales, the Northern Territory, South Australia and Western Australia. They cause damage to vegetation through foraging and trampling, and suppress the ability of native plants to recover from environmental disturbances. They also trample wetlands and compete with native fauna for food and water.
Eastern Gambusia/ Mosquitofish	*Gambusia holbrooki*	This species was introduced in the 1920s as a biological control for mosquitos and, consequently, mosquito-borne diseases. It is now known to be no more effective at eliminating mosquitos than native fish, and has become a major pest. It preys on the eggs and tadpoles of native frogs.
European Rabbit	*Oryctolagus cuniculus*	Domesticated rabbits were first introduced into Australia in 1788, and the first feral populations were recorded in Tasmania in 1827. They have since spread to most parts of Australia, with the exception of the majority of the tropical north. The species grazes on young seedlings and grasses, as well as the roots of larger plants. It competes with native animals for food and shelter, and causes significant losses of vegetation and soil erosion.
European Red Fox	*Vulpes vulpes*	Along with the Domestic Cat, this species has had an enormous impact on native mammals and other animals, with an estimated 400 different vertebrate species being hunted as part of their collective diets.
Feral deer	Cervidae	Deer were first introduced into Australia in the nineteenth century, as a source of food and hunting for European settlers. Six species of deer are recorded: Chital *Axis axis*, Fallow *Dama*

		dama, Hog *Axis porcinus*, Red *Cervus elaphus*, Rusa *C. timorensis* and Sambar *C. unicolor*. Deer compete with native mammals, such as kangaroos and wallabies, for food, break saplings, assist the spread of weeds into new areas and cause erosion of riverbanks and the degradation of water quality in waterways.
Feral Goat	*Capra hircus*	Goats arrived in Australia in 1788 with the First Fleet. They were brought as a source of meat and milk. The species has since established itself as a feral pest over almost a third of Australia. It is most common in the east and west, as well as Tasmania, but is less successful at populating areas where dingoes and wild dogs are present. The animals consume a broad range of plants, and graze on all plant parts. They compete with native animals for food, water and shelter, and cause significant vegetation losses and soil erosion.
Feral Horse	*Equus caballus*	Found mainly in open habitats, such as open woodland and grassland, this species is responsible for significant damage to fragile ecosystems. It needs to drink at least every few days and has been noted digging in dry creek beds to obtain water.
Feral Pig	*Sus scrofa*	This species is widespread in Australia's east and north, and has isolated populations in Victoria, Tasmania and Western Australia, as well as islands such as Kangaroo Island in South Australia. It arrived with the first European settlers. The pigs dig up soil and forest litter, and consume a range of native plants and animals (beetles, centipedes, birds, small mammals, frogs, lizards, snakes and turtles are all potential prey). There is also some evidence that they spread the damaging root rot fungus *Armillaria luteobubalina*.
House Mouse	*Mus musculus*	The House Mouse was introduced, most likely from the Mediterranean. It is found in most habitats throughout Australia, often in close association with humans. Its adaptability has allowed it to thrive.
Red-eared Slider Turtle	*Trachemys scripta* (ssp. *elegans*)	Listed as one of the world's top 100 worst invasive species and a severe ecological threat to Australia, this species is regularly intercepted at Australian ports (almost half of these in New South Wales), but populations have been recorded in the wild in New South Wales – Goodwood Island, Yamba (now eradicated); Queensland – Brisbane, Caboolture, Cairns, Hervey Bay and Townsville; Northern Territory – across Arnhem Land; Western Australia – Christmas Island and Cocos (Keeling) Island, and it has been intercepted at Fremantle Port.
Flora & Fungi		
Asparagus Fern	*Asparagus scandens*	This damaging weed is native to southern Africa. It is widespread throughout Australia and invades a range of habitats, including cool temperate rainforest, mainly in areas of disturbance.
Balloon Vine	*Cardiospermum grandiforum*	This long-lived vine is native to Africa, the tropical Americas and the West Indies, and is widespread in northern New South Wales and southeastern Queensland. Sprawling masses of the vine smother native vegetation and prevent plants from receiving enough sunlight for photosynthesis.
Blackberry	*Rubus* spp.	This scrambling, shrub-like groundcover plant is native to Europe. It has spread throughout Australia, with the possible exception of the Northern Territory. Blackberry can form extensive dense thickets that out-compete most other plants, and can also provide food and shelter for pest animal species.
Black-eyed Susan	*Thunbergia alata*	The Black-eyed Susan is a vigorous, perennial vine native to parts of Africa and India. It has become a pest species of eastern New South Wales and Queensland, where it smothers native vegetation.

Blue Billygoat Weed	*Ageratum conyzoides* (ssp. *conyzoides*)	This short (<1m), upright herb is native to Central America, Mexico and the Caribbean. In Australia it grows in disturbed areas and along waterways, where it displaces native plants, and reduces both faunal and floral biodiversity.
Blue Thunbergia	*Thunbergia grandiflora*	This long-lived and vigorous climbing plant is a native of India and parts of China. It infests riparian areas, roadsides, forest margins and disturbed areas of forests and woodland in tropical and subtropical parts of Australia. It is a significant environmental weed and can severely defoliate rainforests within just one or two decades.
Cabomba	*Cabomba* spp.	There are five species of this aggressive aquatic plant in Australia, but *Cabomba carolina* is the only species known to be naturalized. It is native to North and South America, and was introduced into Australia as an aquarium plant. It can form dense underwater canopies that displace native plants and animals and reduce water quality.
Camphor Laurel	*Cinnamomum camphora*	This highly invasive south-east Asian evergreen tree invades disturbed areas of forests, including rainforest, but is not a weed of healthy environments. It has a tendency to form single-species communities, excluding native vegetation. The ripe fruit is eaten by native birds, which then spread the seeds.
Cape Ivy	*Delairea odorata*	This sprawling weed is native to Africa. In Australia it is highly invasive and suppresses the growth of native vegetation by smothering the ground and climbing into and across the canopy.
Cat's Claw Creeper	*Macfadyena unguis-cati*	This aggressive climber is a native of tropical America. It was once a popular garden plant, but has become a weed of national importance. It has the ability to completely smother native vegetation, including mature trees.
Chinese Elm	*Ulmus parvifolia*	A large (10–30m tall) deciduous tree with spreading foliage and smooth greyish bark, this is a weed of riparian areas (like waterways and riverbanks), roadsides, rainforest margins, woodland, parkland and disturbed areas. It occurs in coastal and near-coastal areas of central and southeastern Queensland and northeastern New South Wales.
Chytrid Fungus	*Batrachochytrium dendrobatidis*	This fungus causes mass mortalities in frog populations (chytridiomycosis). The infection is spread through waterborne zoospores that infect the skin of its host, causing erosion, ulceration and sloughing of the skin, and a host can become terminally ill after just 10 days following exposure. Chytridiomycosis has devastated the world's frog populations, especially where they are already under threat from other environmental and anthropogenic pressures.
Harungana	*Harungana madagascariensis*	Native to Africa, Madagascar and Mauritius, this tree is a common weed in rainforests of Far North Queensland, and can form large stands that exclude native plants and destroy wildlife habitat.
Hymenachne	*Hymenachne amplexicaulis*	This perennial grass is native to South America. It was originally imported into Australia as food for cattle, but quickly spread, and now occurs from northeastern New South Wales to northern Queensland and into the northern Northern Territory. It invades wetlands, riverbanks and irrigation areas, and reduces water quality and degrades the habitat of native fauna and flora.
Lantana	*Lantana camara*	This tangled, scrubby weed is largely restricted to disturbed areas, including recreation areas and along the edges of roadways. Lantana has been recorded in a number of vegetation communities, including the fringes of rainforest.
Large-leaved Privet	*Ligustrum lucidum*	This serious environmental weed is a native of southern China. It can form dense infestations that threaten the

		native biodiversity. It readily invades subtropical and coastal rainforests, rainforest margins, and warm temperate and dry rainforest.
Madeira Vine	*Anredera cordifolia*	A vigorous climber native to South America, this species can alter entire ecosystems. It is an invasive weed in Australia that blankets and smothers shrubs, trees and entire forests. The weight of the masses of vines can cause the native vegetation to collapse.
Miconia	*Miconia calvescens*	This native South American tree species is an aggressive invader of Australian rainforests. It thrives in moist, shaded habitats and can form dense thickets.
Mistflower	*Ageratina riparia*	Native to Central and South America, this weed was introduced into Australia as a garden plant in the 1870s. It has spread through disturbed areas of native bushland and along river systems in subtropical Australia, where it competes with the native vegetation.
Moth Vine	*Araujia sericifera*	This invasive, fast-growing vine is native to South America. It smothers native vegetation and is poisonous to animals.
Myrtle Rust	*Austropuccinia psidii*	This disease is caused by the fungus native to South America. It threatens trees and shrubs in the Myrtaceae family and can cause defoliation, deformed leaves, reproductive failure, stunted growth and plant death. About 350 native species have proved susceptible to the fungus. It was first detected in Australia on the New South Wales central coast in 2010, and has since spread to far north Queensland, Victoria, Tasmania and the Northern Territory. Myrtle rust spores are easily spread by native animals and contaminated objects, such as clothing, hair, skin and machinery.
Myrtle Wilt	*Chalara australis*	This fungal pathogen causes Myrtle Wilt, a fatal disease that affects the rainforest tree Myrtle Beech *Nothofagus cunninghamii*. The fungus is believed to be naturally occurring at low levels, but can reach epidemic levels. Soil disturbance is thought to increase the risk of it spreading.
Passionflowers or Passion Vines	*Passiflora* spp.	Most passionflower species are native to the Americas. They aggressively spread along the margins and within native vegetation, and severely impact local flora and fauna. Many species are poisonous.
Orange Pore Fungus	*Favolaschia calocera*	This fungus is native to Madagascar, China and Thailand. It has become widespread throughout Australia (closely associated with the timber industry) and has the potential to displace native fungi.
Pond Apple	*Annona glabra*	This small tree is native to the Americas and parts of Africa. It has become an invasive weed in wetter tropical and subtropical parts of Australia, and occurs along waterways, in mangrove communities, in rainforests and rainforest margins, and along roadways. It is an aggressive plant that forms dense thickets, altering ecosystems and destroying habitats.
Singapore Daisy	*Sphagneticola trilobata*	This aggressive groundcover plant is native to tropical parts of America. In Australia it spreads rapidly in disturbed areas, and outcompetes the native vegetation.
Small-leaved Privet	*Ligustrum sinensis*	This once popular hedge plant is native to eastern Asia. Its seeds are spread over long distances by birds, and this allows it too establish itself in native bushland, particularly in riparian areas and moist gullies.
Thickhead	*Crassocephalum crepidioides*	A herbaceous plant native to parts of Africa, this is a weed of disturbed areas in Australia and also invades forest margins. It is easily spread via the wind and through the attachment of seeds to clothing and animals.

Acknowledgements

This book aims to provide the published knowledge acquired by researchers who have studied the wildlife and rainforests of Australia over the years and deliver it in a simplified format for the general natural history reader. Their patience and dedication to the scientific world, during countless hours of research and field study, is gratefully acknowledged. Peter, Angus and John (the authors) thank all of these men and women; their work has been treated with respect.

A book such as this that covers a huge range of sites in Australia involves massive amounts of survey and travel time, which would not be possible without the support of family and friends. The authors thank all those who have made this possible. Peter Rowland makes special mention to his wife (Kate), who encouraged him to embark on the many trips needed to study the sites described in the book (and the many others that were not included). Not only did she accompany him on some of the more exciting ones, but she unselfishly endured his numerous and often extended absences. He also thanks his parents (Keith and Pat) for support and encouragement over many years, and his children (Tom, Meg and Georgia) for keeping him young at heart. Angus McNab thanks his mum (Heather) for providing somewhere to live in the few weeks he was home during the writing of the book. Similarly, he must thank Hayley Atkins and James Corrighan for providing a place to live in Laos during the Covid-19 lock-down, where the book was completed. John Harris extends a heartfelt thanks to his wife Kathy, who accompanied him on many field trips to various rainforest locations, helping to take notes and photos and assisting with research, reviews and chores as deadlines approached. He also thanks his late parents (Wally and Ethel) for nurturing his childhood passion for nature, his children (Emily and Zoe) for indulging him on the many field trips to the bush during 'dad and daughter time', his mentors Dr Graeme Ambrose, Wallie Coles and Helen O'Donnell and lifelong friend Fred Bohner, who first introduced him to the spectacular beauty of rainforests and their diversity of wildlife in far north Queensland.

We are deeply indebted to the many contributors of images used in the book, including Tim Bawden, Joshua Bergmark, Steve Bittinger, Ian 'Bushrat' Bool, Rohan Cleave, Jono Dashper, Destination NSW, Bernard DuPont, Scott Eipper, Chris Farrell, Ryan Francis, Brian Gratwicke, Mark Gillow, Lachlan Hall, Alan Henderson (Minibeast Wildlife), Kathryn Himbeck, Donald Hobern, Jean and Fred Hort, Conrad Hoskin, Aaron Jenkin (Aquatica), Patrick Kavanagh, Owen Lishmund, Stephen Mahony, Peter Morris (sydneyheads.com), Charlie Price, Wayne Quilliam (Aboriginal.photography), K. M. Rawlings, Steve Reynolds, R. Bruce Richardson, Thomas Rowland, Akash Samuel, Aniket Sardana, Michael Schmid, Julie Sims, Kate Stevenson, David Stowe, Michael Swan, John Tann, Tom Tarrant, Jason Thompson, Bruce Thomson, Tourism Australia, Beverley Van Praagh, Peter Vaughan, Tom Vigilante (WGAC), Dave Watts, Alan Wiggington, Tim Willing and Anders Zimny.

The authors also thank the peer reviewers: Georgia Badgery, Louise Beames, Walter Boles, Renee Chamberlin, Elliot Connor, Mark Cowan, Scott Eipper, Peter Homan, John Nielson, Kate Stevenson, Terry Tweedie, Beverley Van Praagh, Peter Vaughan, Tom Vigilante and Jude Westrup. Your assistance in ensuring that the content is technically correct and as current as possible has been invaluable.

Special thanks go to Thomas Rowland, who assisted with image corrections, layout designs and the provision of maps throughout the book.

Lastly and by no means least, we thank the publishers, in particular John Beaufoy and Rosemary Wilkinson, for the opportunity to produce this book, Krystyna Mayer for her thoroughness in reviewing and editing the text, and Sally Bird of Calidris Literary Agency for her professionalism and assistance through the entire process.

Index